Palgrave Studies in Oral History

'A premier publisher of oral history.' - CHOICE

The world's leading English-language oral history book series, *Palgrave Studies in Oral History* brings together engaging work from scholars, activists, and other practitioners. Books in the series are aimed at a broad community of readers; they employ edited oral history interviews to explore a wide variety of topics and themes in all areas of history, placing first-person accounts in broad historical context and engaging issues of historical memory and narrative construction. Fresh approaches to the use and analysis of oral history, as well as to the organization of text, are a particular strength of the series, as are projects that use oral accounts to illuminate human rights issues. Submissions are welcomed for projects from any geographical region, as well as cross-cultural and comparative work.

Youwei Xu • Y. Yvon Wang

Everyday Lives in China's Cold War Military-Industrial Complex

Voices from the Shanghai Small Third Front, 1964–1988

palgrave
macmillan

Youwei Xu
Department of History
Shanghai University
Shanghai, China

Y. Yvon Wang
Department of History
University of Toronto
Toronto, ON, Canada

ISSN 2731-5673 ISSN 2731-5681 (electronic)
Palgrave Studies in Oral History
ISBN 978-3-030-99687-1 ISBN 978-3-030-99688-8 (eBook)
https://doi.org/10.1007/978-3-030-99688-8

This Palgrave Macmillan imprint is published by the registered company Springer Nature Switzerland AG.
The registered company address is: Gewerbestrasse 11, 6330 Cham, Switzerland

Units, Measures, Currency, Ages, and Names

li: a Chinese mile, approximately 1/3 of an imperial mile or 500 meters. For simplicity, we have rendered all references to *li* into imperial miles.

jin: a Chinese pound or catty, approximately 1.3 pounds avoirdupois or 604 grams. For simplicity, we have rendered all references to *jin* into imperial pounds and ounces.

yuan: the official currency of the People's Republic of China; also known as renminbi. We have rendered colloquialism like *kuai* [块] and *mao* [毛], or one-tenth of a yuan, as "bucks" in the text.

mu: a Chinese unit of land measurement, equal to about 666 square meters or 1/6 of an acre. For simplicity, we have rendered all references to *mu* into acres.

Ages: by traditional counting, newborns were one *sui* [岁] at birth and gained another sui every Lunar New Year. Thus, someone who is 15 *sui* could be as young as 13 years old. People since 1949 use both methods of accounting ages, though the international age system, where an infant is one *sui* on their first birthday, is the official one. For simplicity, we render all translated ages as "years old."

Note that we have translated the names of the factories to better convey their political connotations; place names and personal names are directly transliterated from Chinese.

Acknowledgments

We wish to thank just some of the many colleagues, students, and interview subjects who have made this project possible. Without them, these stories would never have appeared in print in English for a broader audience.

We have included a list of all those whose words are included in this book at the back of the volume along with short biographies, but we wish here to express first our sincere gratitude to each of them. In addition, we thank the many others who offered their time and memories over the course of the Small Third Front projects led by Xu, but who were not included here.

Warm thanks are also owed to every one of the assistants who took part in the arduous work of collecting and transcribing interviews in the field in Anhui, Shanghai, and elsewhere, including Chen Jiajun [陈嘉俊], Chen Yingying [陈颖莹], Chen Yuan [陈元], Gao Menglin [高梦琳], Hu Jing [胡静], Li Ting [李婷], Li Yun [李云], Lu Haoxuan [陆昊玄], Qian Haomin [钱皓旻], Qiu Wenling [邱文玲], Shen Jiawen [沈佳文], Wang Qike [王其科], Wang Ting [王婷], Wu Jing [吴静], Wu Xiaomin [邬晓敏], Xuan Haixia [宣海霞], Yu Xiaosi [俞晓思], Zhang Yiwei [张亦唯], Zhou Shengqi [周升起], Zhu Haozhong [朱昊中], Zhu Lin [朱琳] and Zhu Jiawen [祝佳文].

Colleagues, friends, and family offered tremendous support by reading drafts and giving encouragement along the way. Among them, we are particularly indebted to Covell Meyskens, Gina Anne Tam, Fei-ling Wang, and Max Srinivasan for their comments.

Finally, we deeply appreciate the professionalism and patience with which our editors and the team at Palgrave Macmillan have guided this project through the publication process.

Youwei Xu
Y. Yvon Wang

Contents

List of Figures

Translator's Introduction

A Brief History of Shanghai's Small Third Front

In the mid-1960s, from the perspective of the ruling cadres of the Chinese Communist Party (CCP) in Beijing, Cold War tensions were at a breaking point. Not only did the People's Republic of China (PRC) continue to regard the United States and other capitalist nations as enemies, but also, following the Sino–Soviet split in 1960, the USSR under the leadership of Nikita Khruschev had likewise become a dangerous rival.[1] Meanwhile, the nation was still recovering from the catastrophic economic damage and loss of life incurred during the Great Leap Forward campaigns.[2] High-level policymakers like Liu Shaoqi, Li Fushun, and Deng Xiaoping saw restoring small-scale commerce and standard of living as preeminent, but by the spring of 1964, the Party's supreme leader, Mao Zedong, was growing increasingly anxious about China's enemies abroad—and rivalries for his own power from within.[3]

[1] Except where noted, background information about the Third Front and Small Third Front in this Introduction comes from Xu Youwei's "Overview of the Small Third Front" in Zhonggong Anhui shengwei dangshi yanjiushi ed., *Shanghai xiao sanxian jianshe zai Anhui koushu shilu* (A true oral record of the Shanghai Small Third Front project in Anhui), Beijing: Zhonggong dangshi chubanshe, 2018, 1–10.

[2] For more on the Great Leap campaign and attendant crises, see the Further Reading list following this Introduction.

[3] Covell Meyskens, *Mao's Third Front: The Militarization of Cold War China*. Cambridge: Cambridge University Press, 2020, 4–9; Ch. 1.

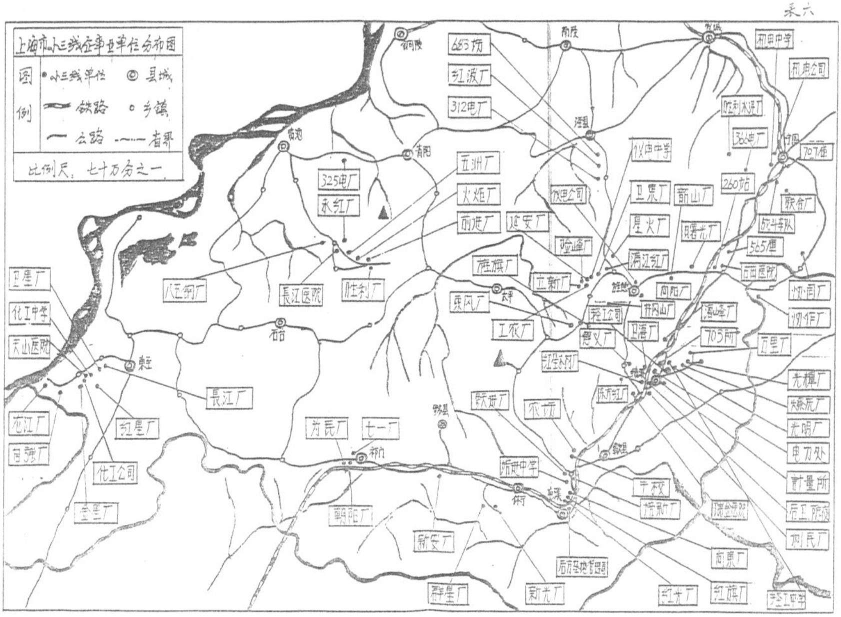

Image 1 B&W map of Small Third Front operations in Southern Anhui, provided by Xue Zhiming

In the face of these perceived threats, Mao pushed other members of Party Central as well as the Central Military Commission of the People's Liberation Army (PLA) and the PRC State Council to relocate strategic industries, primarily those making military supplies and weapons, from more densely settled areas of the nation into remote, rural areas. This nationwide program was known as the "Third Front" (*sanxian*), referring to less developed, generally poorer areas deep in hilly or otherwise inhospitable surroundings, as opposed to the "First Front" (the major cities of the eastern seaboard, up to Manchuria and down to the Pearl River Delta) and the "Second Front" (smaller cities further inland from the coast).

There was also a distinction between the "Big Third Front" (*da sanxian*)—located in the distant provinces of the Northwest and Southwest, like Qinghai, Sichuan, Guizhou, and Yunnan—and the "Small Third Front" (*xiao sanxian*), which referred to areas in the rugged, remote parts of core provinces like Shanxi, Anhui, and Hebei. Central government authorities oversaw factory relocations to the "Big Third Front," while municipal and provincial leadership on the First and Second Fronts managed moves to its "Small" counterpart.

It might seem preposterous to uproot tens of thousands of workers and hundreds of key industrial centers to the hinterlands. But, as Covell Meyskens argues, the Third Front initiative must be understood in a broader context of post-WWII geopolitics. The Soviet Union and United States were also devoting massive resources to defensive preparations and offensive armaments while drilling citizens in a militaristic view of international relations, following what Meyskens calls "the excessive rationality of the global Cold War."[4] For Mao and other high Party officials, their days of fighting guerilla battles against Nationalist rivals and invading Japanese troops set the model for building up "base areas" in remote regions of the country. Extensive discussions about the relocations began in 1964 among the CCP's top leaders in Beijing, even as they clashed over the future direction of the nation. Some, like Liu Shaoqi, were concerned about a return to technically shoddy and economically damaging Great Leap-style industrialization campaigns. Mao, meanwhile, increasingly linked external dangers to "revisionism" within the Party, a foreshadowing of his toppling of Liu and others whom he saw as rivals for supremacy just a few years later.[5]

The Gulf of Tonkin incident in August 1964, which led the United States to intensify its military campaigns against North Vietnam—an ally of Beijing—further sharpened Party leaders' concerns. They now feared imminent atomic war with both the Americans and the Soviet Union.[6] Unlike the more decentralized Great Leap, Party leadership charted a course for the Third Front that was much more standardized from the top down.[7] Commissions to oversee the Third Front in different regions, provinces, cities, and counties were set up to manage the transfer of urban workers and industrial enterprises, all under Beijing's oversight.[8] After all, though the local governments of the hinterlands were to coordinate in the building efforts, the Third Front was supposed to be the entire nation's best hope against an all-out invasion.

[4] Meyskens 2020, 226.

[5] Meyskens 2020, 59.

[6] See a brief account of Mao's role in pushing for the Third Front in Barry Naughton, "The Third Front: Defense Industrialization in the Chinese Interior." *China Quarterly* 115 (1988), 351–388. 352–356.

[7] Meyskens 2020, 66, 125–130.

[8] Meyskens 2020, 84–88.

On March 8, 1965, Party Central approved plans for the Small Third Front.[9] That year, 14 "rear front" (*houfang*) areas were selected. Shanghai and the larger East China Region were to relocate their key military-industrial enterprises to the hills on the borders of Zhejiang, Jiangsu, Jiangxi, and Anhui. Shanghai's leaders also decided to form a rear front specifically for the city in the mountainous southern portion of Anhui and set up a special administrative bureaucracy to oversee it.

Shanghai's was the most expansive of the PRC's Small Third Front projects; at its peak, it had on its registers 54,000 workers, 17,000 family members, and 81 work units from an array of military-industrial infrastructure to supporting institutions like schools, trucking companies, and hospitals.[10] In total, more than 354,900 Shanghai residents were sent to work on Third Front projects across the nation, so the city's own Small Third Front represented a considerable portion of the total numbers sent to toil in these remote, secretive locales. The Anhui portion was the centerpiece of Shanghai's relocation efforts. The city's "rear base" there would come to occupy an area about 250 kilometers east to west and 200 kilometers north to south, officially dedicated as "a multi-function manufacturing base for anti-aircraft and anti-tank weaponry."[11] Between March 1966 and 1971, over 60 work units—42 entire factories, mills, and plants plus auxiliary operations like schools, transportation teams, and hospitals—were moved from Shanghai and its suburbs to Anhui. By the time the Shanghai "rear front" office was shut down in September 1991, 14 more work units had been completed in the province. Following Mao's directives to build "against the mountains, hidden, and dispersed," thousands of city folk and rural villagers laid roads and constructed, brick by brick, state-of-the-art steel mills, chemical plants, electronics assemblies, and instrumentation factories in difficult terrain, often working by hand. Production of weaponry began as early as June 1966, including rocket-propelled grenades, anti-aircraft guns, and hand grenades. Like its other Third Front counterparts, Shanghai's Small Third Front was very much

[9] Meyskens 2020, 129.

[10] Shanghai Municipal Archives B246-1-106-9, "Situation and major issues regarding the Shanghai rear-front development project and our comments," March 1967, cited in Chen Xi, "Sanxian chang yu nongcun de hudong guanxi—yi Shanghai xiao sanxian jianshe wei zhongxin" (Interactions between the Third Front Factories and Rural Society: The Case of Shanghai's Small Third Front). *Ershiyi shiji* 171 (2019), 64–79, 65–66.

[11] Shanghai Municipal Archives B246-1-106-9, cited in Chen 2019, 65.

envisioned as part of a fearsome nationwide network of military power both extensive enough to resist a major enemy incursion and dispersed enough to withstand concentrated attack by nuclear armaments.

The Cultural Revolution, which was officially launched in the summer of 1966, disrupted the buildup of the Third Front considerably. The secrecy of the Third Front helped work unit leaders resist Red Guard incursions.[12] But armed violence nonetheless broke out at various points in the Third Front's nascent projects, with fighting among workers, officials' suicides, and tense standoffs between factory leadership and restive rebels; tens of thousands of Shanghainese workers from their remote postings to their hometowns and had to be forced to return, according to historian Chen Donglin.[13] The Party Center reasserted control by the summer of 1968, as concerns mounted over political disarray as well as over the Soviet Union taking advantage of the situation to invade.[14] Construction on many of the larger industrial projects in the hinterlands resumed in force by 1969, and Shanghai's Small Third Front boomed into the early 1970s. Another seismic geopolitical shift was coming, however: the beginning of diplomatic relations between the PRC and the United States in 1972.

As Beijing progressively built economic and diplomatic connections with the United States, the Cold War rationale for the Small Third Front began to fall away. After Mao's death in 1976 and the political downfall of the Cultural Revolution's chief boosters, Shanghai's Small Third Front began to shift away from weapons and military goods to civilian products. Even the secrecy surrounding these factories started to lift: the leading national Party newspaper, the *People's Daily*, mentioned the Third Front openly in 1978 for the first time.[15] The transition was not smooth. A new national budget that drastically decreased military spending in 1980 left many rear front factories financially struggling, with a steep decline in government orders for weapons and as yet low demand for consumer goods. Of the 17 plants producing military items, five were shut down in 1981; nine of the remaining 12 were redirected to making consumer

[12] Meyskens 2020, 143.

[13] Meyskens 2020, 143–147. Chen Donglin, "Sanxian jianshe," in Chen Donglin ed., *Zhongguo gongchandang yu sanxian*. Beijing: Zhonggong dangshi chubanshe, 2015, 188, 190.

[14] Meyskens 2020, 148–151.

[15] Meyskens 2020, 1.

goods. More broadly, some Big Third Front projects, such as the Jiaozuo-Liuzhou Railroad through central and southern China, had just begun to function as intended many years after they were begun due to construction delays and many needed repairs on hasty work.[16]

By August 1984, central authorities decided to terminate the Small Third Front program. The 250 Small Third Front enterprises under the jurisdiction of 28 provinces, cities, and autonomous regions through the PRC had employed 280,000 workers; over two decades, 33 billion renminbi (RMB) had been invested by the government in these operations, with an official net profit of 11 billion RMB. Building the Big and Small Third Fronts between 1964 and 1980 had taken up almost 40% of the PRC's total capital construction budget.[17]

In an attempt to retain at least some productivity from the factories, Party leaders decreed that administrators in places like Shanghai should negotiate with their counterparts in Small Third Front areas to transfer these former military-industrial complexes to local, civilian control. April 1985 marked the start of lengthy discussions between Shanghainese and Anhui officials. The transfer process officially began in October 1986, and all 80 enterprises of Shanghai's Small Third Front had been handed over to local authorities by April 1988. The only Shanghai Small Third Front factory in Zhejiang province soon followed suit.

Over 54,400 registered employees and their 17,000 family members had to be accounted for. Those who had been Shanghai residents were moved back to the city in batches out of concern for social stability. The official policy was that the local peasants who had been given work in the factories after their land had been requisitioned and "personnel who were unsuited to enter big cities" would be given new work by local authorities.

The Third Front: Assessments, Outcomes, and Narratives

Despite the Small Third Front's enormous impact over decades on the lives of tens of thousands and its influence on inland economies in otherwise rural, impoverished, agriculture-centered areas, there is relatively little scholarly work on the program. This situation has been due in part to

[16] Meyskens 2020, 206–208.

[17] Covell Meyskens, "Third Front Railroads and Industrial Modernity in Late Maoist China." *Twentieth-Century China* 40:3 (2015), 238–260; 238.

the high secrecy of the Third Front project as a whole. Local gazetteers, published collections of documents, and published personal memoirs formed the source base of early studies, which tended to focus on top-down policy and official processes rather than any specific region or group of individuals involved in the Third Front. By the mid-1980s, as projects ended or were dramatically transformed, Chinese discourse began to discuss the Front's massive costs and complex effects. The conclusion drawn at that point, as in most accounts since, was that the Third Front was extremely inefficient and had "a negative impact on China's economic development that was certainly more far-reaching than the disruptions of the Cultural Revolution."[18]

More recently, however, new attention has been paid to the Third Front, drawing on simultaneously more local and personal experiences and more global comparisons to complicate negative assessments of its impact. Covell Meyskens' work on railroad-building and the global Cold War dimensions of the Third Front, for example, argues that, though there were numerous problems and inefficiencies, the Third Front was not necessarily a failure in the eyes of PRC leadership. Their aim, as Meyskens notes, was to secure industries vital to the regime's continued survival, *not* to boost economic growth or productivity.[19] Nor, as Chen Xi argues, was the primary goal to industrialize the more remote areas of the nation; resources and support given directly or indirectly to local residents were more an effort to buy their cooperation than a sustained or principal aim of the Third Front.[20] In the arduous and frequently dangerous process of implementing the Third Front, individual relocated workers and local residents were moreover inculcated with a rhetoric of hard work and sacrifice by the state, a rhetoric that Meyskens has found to remain meaningful among former workers well into the twenty-first century.[21] Materially, the Third Front did help bring new possibilities and productivity to China's inland areas, not just in military-industrial necessities like coal and natural gas, but also in infrastructure helpful to everyday people like quicker postal service, more reliable train lines, and paved roads, as well as consumer goods like television sets.[22] Finally, the Third Front's "paternalist approach

[18] Barry Naughton, "The Third Front: Defence Industrialization in the Chinese Interior." *The China Quarterly* 115 (1988), 351–386; 351.

[19] Meyskens 2015, 258–259.

[20] Chen 2019, 64–79, 76–77.

[21] Meyskens 2015, 245–248; 2020, 191–194.

[22] Meyskens 2015, 258; 2020, 210–226.

to national development" can still be seen in contemporary PRC initiatives like the Belt Road Initiative launched in 2013.[23]

Examining such a massive project as the Third Front from a local and individual perspective sheds a new light on how Mao-era policies translated, with many ironies, complexities, and unintended outcomes, into daily experience. Taking a ground-up view also reveals how Chinese people have made sense of the larger forces around them during decades known for dramatic, indeed violent, political and social change, and how present-day phenomena in PRC society are rooted in the legacies of years past.

In the last 15 years, there has been a surge in output and public discussions about the Third Front, including the Small Third Front, from China-based scholars.[24] Edited volumes of primary documents on the Third Front like government directives, enterprise archives, and newspaper articles have appeared, enabling more grounded research into myriad geographically and temporally specific dimensions of the program.[25] Documentaries, online communities, and scholarly organizations have

[23] Meyskens 2020, 236.

[24] For example, Wu Xiaolin, *Mou Takutou jidai no kougyouka senryaku: sansen kensetsu no seiji keizaigaku* (Industrialization strategy of the Mao Zedong era: the political economy of the Third Front), Tokyo: Ochanomizu shoubou, 2002; Chen Donglin, *Sanxian jianshe—beizhan shiqi de xibu kaifa* (Constructing the Third Front: western development during the period of wartime readiness), Beijing: Zhonggong zhongyang dangxiao chubanshe, 2003; Li Caihua, *Sanxian jianshe yanjiu* (A study of Third Front construction), Changchun: Jilin daxue chubanshe, 2004; Xu Youwei and Wu Jing, "Weiji yu yingdui: Shanghai xiao sanxian qingnian zhigong de hunyin shenghuo—yi Bawu Gangchang wei zhongxin de kaocha" (Risk and accommodation: the marital lives of young workers on the Shanghai Small Third Front—a case study centered on the Eight-Five Steelworks), *Junshi lishi yanjiu* 4 (2014), 34–43; Zhang Xiuli, "Wannan Shanghai xiao sanxian zhigong de minsheng wenti yanjiu" (A study of livelihood issues among workers on the Shanghai Small Third Front in southern Anhui), *Anhui shixue* 6 (2014), 145–53; Xu Youwei and Chen Donglin eds., *Xiao sanxian jianshe yanjiu luncong* (Collected research essays on the Small Third Front project) vols. 1–2, Shanghai: Shanghai daxue chubanshe, 2015, 2016; Cui Yi'nan and Zhao Yang, "Qianru yu huzhu: sanxian jianshe zhong gongnong guanxi de weiguan shenshi" (Insertion and symbiosis: a micro-analysis of peasant-worker relations in the Third Front project), *Hua'nan nongye daxue xuebao (shehui kexue ban)* 1(2016), 134–40.

[25] See a contextualized review of scholarly, community, and individual output about the Third Front in Xu Youwei, "Exploring New Frontiers in Contemporary Chinese History Studies: A Case Study of Third Front Construction," *Social Sciences in China* 41:2 (2020), 164–182.

sprung up, even as former Third Front workers and their descendants continue to publish their own experiences.[26]

Since 2009, Xu Youwei, Professor at Shanghai University, has led historical projects with strong governmental funding support to research and preserve memories of the Shanghai Small Third Front. Teams of interviewers have conducted many hours of oral history research among factory workers and their family members, employees in auxiliary enterprises like transportation teams and hospitals, cadres within the factories and in neighboring communities, and villagers living alongside relocated plants. In the eyes of some individuals, too, the Small Third Front was far from a waste of resources; instead, they see China's post-Mao economic transformations as stemming directly from the heavy investments of the state as part of the Third Front campaign. Many also remember the Small Third Front with great fondness, especially the material benefits in place in these factory towns once they were fully operational, such as weekly movie showings, high-quality medical care, and the plentiful, varied food sold cheaply in factory canteens.

At the same time, recollections show that great numbers of men and women faced significant physical danger, social friction, emotional distress, political persecution, and material privation as a result of the Third Front project. We also see that individuals rarely had the ability to contravene the decisions made by often opaque bureaucratic hierarchies. These decisions could determine everything from whether one worked on the front lines of a steel forgery or a quiet office, whom one married, whether and when one had a second child, to whether one could continue to live in one's family home and till the land long farmed by one's ancestors.[27]

Xu and others' publications have transformed the formerly little-known area of Third Front studies in Chinese. Our collaboration in this volume grows out of a realization that many of the oral histories that the recent generation of Third Front scholars have relied on are compelling in their own right for students and researchers working in comparative fields who would otherwise be unable to access these rich materials in their original language.

[26] Xu 2020, 167–169.

[27] Meyskens 2020, 167–199 describes some of the contradictions between proud or even happy memories and recollections of privation, fear, and frustration.

About This Collection

We have thus set out in this collection to capture some of the breadth of experience documented in the Small Third Front factories relocated from Shanghai. There were four geographic destinations for these factories: rural Anhui, rural Jiangsu, rural Zhejiang, and rural Jiangxi. Due to the geographic concentration of work units in Anhui, most of the accounts will be from Small Third Front locales in the rugged hills of the southern part of that province. Readers will find first-person narratives, most of them from oral history interviews and a few from written documents, by a range of men and women from the 1960s through the 1980s. We have arranged these accounts by theme. Topics addressed include how narrators came to be employed by the Small Third Front; their experiences of the early years of building up the factories and settling in; the intersection of military and political affairs with day-to-day experience; details about quotidian life, including housing, food, healthcare, and entertainment; gender in the workplace; sexual, romantic, and family relations; appraisals of relationships between Shanghainese workers and local peasants; and praise, complaints, and critiques about their lives on the Small Third Front. Of course, some accounts will contain elements of other themes, reflecting the complexity of experiences on the Small Third Front.

The Small Third Front was not just a top-down political campaign. It was a way of life. Many spent decades of their lives in these remote areas of China. In fact, I spent my first six years of life among extended family in a Small Third Front factory complex set up by Anhui province. The factory had once produced military-grade weapons in Anhui's Dabie Mountains; it relocated to the suburbs of Hefei, the provincial capital, in the late 1980s. A 2021 poem by my grandfather, who was an office head in this provincial Small Third Front factory, includes lines like these about the move out of the hinterlands:

> The two sides contracted at the Nanyue Mountain Villa;
> Huaihai Factory would be transferred without compensation.
> Twenty-two years of military manufacturing,
> now left for posterity to judge.
> Third Front transfers were the national strategy,
> courage was needed to plan for the greater good.
> We took photos at Nanyue as a commemoration,
> we left the old factories and built the new.

Unlike official accounts from the Party-state or the relatively unusual experiences of exceptional people, such as those who immigrated outside the PRC as students and later wrote bestselling memoirs about the era, stories like the ones gathered in this book allow us to come into more intimate contact with the textures of daily life in socialist China. In what did people find pleasure? How did they deal with setbacks, losses, and difficult relationships? The stories recounted below are often humorous, poignant, and deeply personal, and I have translated with an eye to preserving the colloquial, first-person flavor as much as possible.

At the same time, first-hand testimony, as any other historical source, is produced by individuals embedded in contexts with specific political, cultural, and social norms. Most people selected to work in the Third Front defense industries had to pass stringent political loyalty tests, and all the people included in our collection were interviewed in the PRC by fellow PRC nationals (or wrote their textual reminiscences down in the PRC for fellow citizens), so it may not be surprising that there are almost no voices of strong, consistent, complete critique against the Third Front, Mao, the Chinese Communist Party's leadership, or the state generally. Even hints of interpersonal tension are scattered; many paint a halcyon image of local farmers bonding with Shanghainese workers, camaraderie among the workers and between workers and cadres, and, aside from the initial years of hardship during the relocation process, living conditions that were far more comfortable than those of rural people in the surrounding areas. But the absence of overt, sustained criticism makes the points at which narrators allude to tensions, crises, alternative readings of the circumstances, and counter-currents that do not fit in with official narratives all the more notable and interesting.

Through these sometimes self-contradictory accounts, readers can better understand how the CCP regime maintained—and continues to maintain—its authority beyond violent campaigns, how the People's Republic's present economic clout in a global market economy has built on foundations from the seemingly autarkic high socialist era, how the transnational logic of the Cold War structured daily life in the PRC, and how memories of the time of Mao's supremacy continue to impact Chinese society in the twenty-first century.

To help students and teachers more readily use this text in the classroom, I have included brief translator's notes and suggested questions for discussion at the beginning of each thematic chapter. A few broad questions or project/essay prompts are also included at the end of this introduction. Further explanatory translator's notes, indicated with "TN" and brackets, are included in the text. Passages from individual accounts have been arranged by the last name of their narrators within each chapter. Up to 12 keywords and phrases are provided at the beginning of each narrative to help readers gain a broad sense of the contents. At the end of each chapter, I have provided related further English-language readings. In some chapters, I have included other useful resources for teachers and students, as relevant. Short descriptions of each respondent appear with their names throughout the text, and more detailed biographies can be found in alphabetical order in the Appendix, along with a brief Glossary of common Chinese terms as they have been rendered in the text.

Please note that several narratives contain allusions to and descriptions of self-harm, sexual assault, and violence that may be disturbing; further warnings are included before them. In a few cases, names mentioned by our narrators have been altered to protect individuals' privacy; these alterations are noted where they occur.

Suggestions for Discussion, Debate, and Classroom Projects Using All or Part of the Book

1. Roleplay (A): Ask students to imagine conversations on a particular subject between two or three different narrators whose testimonies appear in one or more chapters.
2. Roleplay (B): Ask students to compile questions they would want to ask if they were the interviewers. Then ask them to imagine how a given narrator or set of narrators might answer their questions.
3. Roleplay (C): Ask students to draw lots for a particular "role" and have them write a diary or narrative of their own as a Small Third Fronter, based on research and the narratives presented here.
4. Contextualization (A): Ask students to compare and contrast the contexts that narrators describe on the Small Third Front to contexts with which they are more familiar, either through their studies or through their lived experiences.
5. Contextualization (B): Ask students to design a virtual "museum exhibit," lecture with visuals, or documentary video or audio presentation about the Shanghai Small Third Front based on the narratives below; different target audiences for these projects should change how students present the material.

Y. Yvon Wang

Further Reading

Overviews of PRC History

Timothy Cheek, ed., *Mao Zedong and China's Revolutions: A Brief History with Documents*. New York: Palgrave, 2002.
Rebecca Karl, *Mao Zedong and China in the Twentieth-Century World: A Concise History*. Durham, NC: Duke University Press, 2010.
William C. Kirby ed., *The People's Republic at Sixty: An International Assessment*. Cambridge, MA: Harvard University Press, 2011.
Julia Lovell, *Maoism: A Global History*. New York: Knopf, 2019.
Roderick MacFarquhar ed., *The Politics of China: The Eras of Mao and Deng*. 2nd Edition. Cambridge: Cambridge University Press, 1997.
Maurice Meisner, *Mao's China and After: A History of the People's Republic*. New York: The Free Press, 1999.
Andrew Walder, *China under Mao: A Revolution Derailed*. Cambridge, MA: Harvard University Press, 2015.
Felix Wemheuer, *A Social History of Maoist China: Conflict and Change, 1949–1976*. Cambridge: Cambridge University Press, 2019.

Overviews of the Great Leap Forward

Jasper Becker, *Hungry Ghosts: Mao's Secret Famine*. New York: Holt, 1998.
Alfred L. Chan, *Mao's Crusade: Politics and Policy Implementation in China's Great Leap Forward*. Oxford: Oxford University Press, 2001.
Frank Dikötter, *Mao's Great Famine: The History of China's Most Devastating Catastrophe, 1958–62*. London: Bloomsbury, 2010.
Roderick MacFarquhar, *The Origins of the Cultural Revolution*, Vol. 2: *The Great Leap Forward 1958–1960*. New York: Columbia University Press, 1983.
Kimberley Ens Manning and Felix Wemheuer eds., *Eating Bitterness: New Perspectives on China's Great Leap Forward and Famine*. Vancouver: University of British Columbia Press, 2011.
Ralph Thaxton, *Catastrophe and Contention in Rural China: Mao's Great Leap Forward Famine and the Origins of Righteous Resistance in Da Fo Village*. Cambridge: Cambridge University Press, 2008.
Yang Jisheng, *Tombstone: The Great Chinese Famine, 1958–1962*. Edward Friedman, Stacy Mosher, and Jian Guo eds., Stacy Mosher and Jian Guo trans. New York: Farrar, Straus and Giroux, 2012.

Overviews of the Cultural Revolution

Paul Clark, *The Chinese Cultural Revolution: A History.* Cambridge: Cambridge University Press, 2008.

Woei Lien Chong ed., *China's Great Proletarian Cultural Revolution: Master Narratives and Post-Mao Counternarratives.* Lanham, MD: Rowman and Littlefield, 2002.

Frank Dikötter, *The Cultural Revolution: A People's History, 1962–1976.* New York: Bloomsbury, 2016.

Joseph Esherick, Paul Pickowicz, and Andrew Walder eds., *The Chinese Cultural Revolution as History.* Stanford: Stanford University Press, 2006.

Daniel Leese, *Mao Cult: Rhetoric and Ritual in the Cultural Revolution.* Cambridge: Cambridge University Press, 2011.

Roderick MacFarquhar, *The Origins of the Cultural Revolution, Vol. 3: The Coming of the Cataclysm 1961–1966.* New York: Columbia University Press, 1997.

Roderick MacFarquhar and Michael Schoenhals eds., *Mao's Last Revolution.* Cambridge, MA: Harvard University Press, 2006.

Frederick C. Teiwes and Warren Sun, *The End of the Maoist Era: Chinese Politics during the Twilight of the Cultural Revolution, 1972–1976.* Armonk, NY: M. E. Sharpe, 2007.

Yiching Wu, *The Cultural Revolution at the Margins: Chinese Socialism in Crisis.* Cambridge, MA: Harvard University Press, 2014.

Yang Jisheng, *The World Turned Upside Down: A History of the Chinese Cultural Revolution.* Stacy Mosher and Jian Guo trans. and eds. New York: Farrar, Straus and Giroux, 2021.

Overviews of the Third Front

Lorenz Lüthi, "The Vietnam War and China's Third-Line Defense Planning before the Cultural Revolution, 1964–1966." *Journal of Cold War Studies* 10 (2008): 26–51.

Covell Meyskens, "Third Front Railroads and Industrial Modernity in Late Maoist China." *Twentieth-Century China* 40:3 (2015), 238–260.

Covell Meyskens, *Mao's Third Front: The Militarization of Cold War China.* Cambridge: Cambridge University Press, 2020.

Barry Naughton, "The Third Front: Defence Industrialization in the Chinese Interior." *The China Quarterly* 115 (1988), 351–386.

Barry Naughton, "Industrial Policy during the Cultural Revolution: Military Preparation, Decentralization, and the Leaps Forward," in William A. Joseph, Christine P.W. Wong, and David Zweig eds., *New Perspectives on the Cultural Revolution.* Cambridge, MA: Harvard University Press, 1991. 153–182.

Other Materials and Resources

Chen Jiagang's photography series *The Great Third Front* (2008); selections available at http://photographyofchina.com/blog-ch/chen-jiagang-sanxian and http://works.ccsph.com/detail_2734.html

Stefan Landsberger, comp., Chinese Propaganda Posters; featuring images from the 1920s to the contemporary PRC as well as a multimedia bibliography (1997–), at https://chineseposters.net/index.php; 250 reproductions in Marien van der Heijden, Stefan R. Landsberger, Kuiyi Shen, *Chinese Posters: The IISH-Landsberger Collections*. München: Prestel, 2009.

Covell Meyskens, comp., Everyday Life in Maoist China; multimedia artifacts from the 1930s–80s (2016–), at https://everydaylifeinmaoistchina.org/

Paul G. Pickowicz, William A. Joseph, and Stephen MacKinnon, Committee of Concerned Asian Scholars Friendship Delegations Collection; photographs from 1971 and 1972, at https://library.ucsd.edu/dc/collection/bb5737145r

PRC History Group web site including online journal, primary documents, research notes, book reviews, and links to online resources and collections (2014–), http://prchistory.org/

Michael Schoenhals ed., *China's Cultural Revolution, 1966–1969:* Not *a Dinner Party*. Armonk, NY: M.E. Sharpe, 1996, a collection of primary sources.

Memoirs and Autobiographies

Guanlong Cao, *The Attic: Memoir of a Chinese Landlord's Son*. Guanlong Cao and Nancy Moskin trans. Berkeley: University of California Press, 1996.

Jung Chang, *Wild Swans: Three Daughters of China*. New York: Simon and Schuster, 2003.

Nien Cheng, *Life and Death in Shanghai*. New York: Grove Press, 1986.

Ji Xianlin, *The Cowshed: Memories of the Chinese Cultural Revolution*. Chenxin Jiang trans. New York: New York Review Books, 2016.

Yang Jiang, *A Cadre School Life: Six Chapters*. Geremie Barmé trans. Hong Kong: Joint Publishing Company, 1982.

Ning Wang, *Banished to the Great Northern Wilderness: Political Exile and Re-education in Mao's China*. Vancouver: UBC Press, 2017.

Rae Yang, *Spider Eaters: A Memoir*. Fifteenth Anniversary Edition. Berkeley: University of California Press, 2013.

CHAPTER 1

An Official Account of the Small Third Front in Guichi, Anhui

Translator's Note

This account is from a local government official, Yu Shunsheng, in Niutou Township, Guichi District, Chizhou, Anhui. Yu sums up the background of, and official line on, the Shanghainese "Small Third Front" factories based in what was then Guichi County, in southern Anhui Province. The Yangtze River forms the northwestern border of Guichi; toward the south, the county rapidly rises into rugged, hilly country, where the Small Third Front factories and their personnel were settled. Beyond the southeastern borders of the county loom two of the most famous peaks in China, Huangshan and Jiuhuashan. Even in 2019, a satellite image reveals two-lane county highways snaking around large parts of the area that are still dominated by lush, unsettled ridges and valleys.

We present Yu's recounting for readers to have an official benchmark for the subsequent narratives from people on the Third Front and farmers who lived in adjacent communities. Yu's story is largely positive and celebratory, even as it notes the economic and logistical difficulties of the Small Third Front industries and the personal challenges of the people who staffed them, and the lives that were lost setting up the factories.

Some of the narratives that follow will recapitulate Yu's narrative arc, while others contradict or complicate it. For example, Yu's rhetoric of heroic hardship among the initial group of workers and cadres sent into

Y. Xu, Y. Y. Wang, *Everyday Lives in China's Cold War Military-Industrial Complex*, Palgrave Studies in Oral History,
https://doi.org/10.1007/978-3-030-99688-8_1

the hilly, rural region to build factories and living spaces for themselves is one part of his account that is frequently repeated by Small Third Front people. Those who actually participated in the early setup of the factories do display a sense of pride, passion, and even nostalgia in their material self-sacrifice and physical risk. At the same time, they also express more complex feelings about the inefficiencies and dangers of building the factories by hand. It is therefore suggested that students return to Yu's narrative as a reminder of the official line on the Small Third Front as they read some of the other accounts in this book.

Questions for Discussion

1. What does Yu identify as the main problems faced by the Small Third Front factories in Guichi? What does he see as their main accomplishments? How does he talk about each (using statistics, anecdotes, personal recollection, or other methods)?
2. What changes in the larger political and social landscape between the late 1960s and late 1980s were reflected on the Small Third Front, according to Yu?
3. How does Yu characterize the reaction of local villagers to the Small Third Front? How does he characterize the reactions of workers assigned to these factories? Do you think all of the villagers and workers would fully agree with Yu's portrayals?

* * *

余顺生 Yu Shunsheng, male, Anhui native, township-level cadre in Guichi County.

The Shanghai "Small Third Front" was established in the mountainous areas of southern Anhui and western Zhejiang against the tense international backdrop of the 1960s according to the strategic planning of Party Central, the State Council, the Central Military Commission, and Chairman Mao to improve battle readiness and reinforce national defense. They were to be rear-guard industrial bases for mainly producing conventional military weapons. In the Guichi area, there were a total of 12 factories and accompanying support enterprises mainly around the production of 57-mm anti-aircraft guns. Of these, the Forever Red Mechanical Plant, the Five Continents Electrical Plant, the Torch Mechanical Plant, the

Image 1.1 Aerial photograph of the Victory Machinery Factory site in southern Anhui, 2010s, by Rao Yi

Forward Mechanical Plant, and the Victory Mechanical Plant were called the five gun factories (Image 1.1). The Eight-Five Steelworks was set up for steel needs (Image 1.2) and the 325 electrical plant was set up for electricity needs. Five other units were set up as support: the Changjiang Hospital, two driving teams at the Number 683 Driving Team, the Number 703 Power Plant, the Number 707 Materials Warehouse, and the Number 260 Telephone Communications Group.

There were four phases in the total of 20 years from the establishment of the Small Third Front in Guichi in 1969 until the restructuring was completed in 1988.

...

1.

In mid-February 1966, the Shanghai Municipal Committee and the Municipal People's Committee approved the establishment of a Rear Front Leadership Group in Tunxi, Anhui, and lifted the curtains on the establishment of the Anhui-based Shanghai Small Third Front. In December 1969, the Shanghai Municipal Revolutionary Committee

Image 1.2 Aerial photograph of the Eight-Five Steelworks site in Meijie Township, southern Anhui, 2010s, by Rao Yi

approved the formation of the 507th Project Headquarters (or the 507 HQ) to oversee the Small Third Front in Guichi. The first phase of the Shanghai Small Third Front construction—the basic infrastructural construction phase—in Guichi lasted from 1969 to 1971. There were three steps: selecting locations, requisitioning land, and building the factories. The project was, overall, carried out per the strategic requirements of "against the mountains, hidden, and dispersed." The first step was to pick locations, mainly the locations of the five gun factories and the Eight-Five Steelworks. The primary considerations were to be "close to the mountains, near the water, set up a big base." The leadership of the Nanjing Garrison and military cadres trekked into the mountains together to pick locations; teams included Shanghai-based leaders and technical and engineering staff in the areas of electricity, communications, hydraulics, water supply and drainage, mechatronics, construction, bridges, and tunnels, as well as personnel from the financial and staple and non-staple food sectors.

The factory sites were over 30 kilometers from the county seat. First we found the highest peaks, then we looked for sources of water, to see if they would be sufficient for production and living use, then we checked to see if the terrain were covert. The cars for the selection team would reach the foot of the mountains; if there wasn't a road then you'd have to climb on foot. If there were a road, it'd be a dirt road built up with mud and dirt and rocks: narrow, uneven, with a lot of turns. A jeep turning and turning in those hills, sometimes you'd round a turn and then you'd run right into a car coming the other way. Traffic accidents were common.

Via the field surveys, the five gun factories (Forever Red Mechanical Plant, Five Continents Electronics Plant, Torch Mechanical Plant, Forward Mechanical Plant, and Victory Mechanical Plant) were set up in Meijie Township's Liujie Village and Heping Village, and Tangxi Township's Cao Village and Bai'an Village (Forward and Victory were both in Bai'an). The Eight-Five Steelworks was selected to be set up in Panqiao Village in Meijie Township.

After determining the locations, next came getting the land. Mainly it was Shanghainese negotiating with the local communes and [production] brigades, then reporting that up to the county revolutionary committee, then after confirmation the county revolutionary committee reporting to the provincial revolutionary committee; after approval, then we could use that land. Mostly we picked a good spot and just started working and caught up with the paperwork afterward. Whatever spot the Shanghainese chose, they'd be provided with it. The land requisition was almost without compensation.

Building the factories was especially difficult. In those hidden deep mountains, without roads, we had to open the hillsides to build roads, build bridges over bodies of water, level the ground. Because there weren't any mechanical tools, we counted on manpower to dynamite the hillsides, then to break up the larger rocks and use the smaller stones to make the road. Often it'd be one truck up ahead filled with people, and the truck behind full of bamboo [for construction girders], lumber, shovels, and such tools. The trucks would drive among all this dust and dirt to a spot, put down the tools and materials, and begin to work.

To move as fast as possible, they'd be blasting the hillside over here, and pebbles would still be flying over the top of the hill, and then over there they'd begin to build the factories. It was a time filled with risk. At the time, staple foods couldn't be fully supplied, so often [workers] relied on porridge and sweet potatoes or plain buns with pickles to fill their bellies. Because there weren't dormitories, the workers borrowed space in local villagers' homes or in temporary sheds or the [production] brigade headquarters, using thatch and grass as mattresses. Nighttimes, not only were there mosquitoes and bugs stinging them, there were at times also poisonous snakes, centipedes, geckos, and mice that pestered them. Though the difficulties were many, everyone's passions ran high and they devoted all their energy to the construction of the factories.

By the end of 1971, the Small Third Front factories (except the 325 electricity plant) were all basically set up. Then they entered the second phase, which was their *raison d'être*: the production of military-industrial goods. This phase was approximately from 1972 to 1978, and it was the glorious pinnacle of the Small Third Front. Guichi mainly saw four of the gun factories and the Eight-Five Steelworks producing anti-aircraft gun parts separately, with the fifth gun factory assembling the parts. These guns were exclusively anti-aircraft weapons and could be combined with several at once as a battery, with fire directed by radar. Testing happened on the seaside of Fengxian near Shanghai. During that time, they also produced a few Eight-Five anti-tank guns that were testing right in a local valley. The Forever Red Mechanical Plant mainly produced the aiming mechanisms for the anti-aircraft guns; this was precision machinery.

The Five Continents Electronics Plant mainly produced the necessary electronics components for the guns, making J-03-022 electrical motors and 40 kw and 65 kw motors also. The Torch Mechanical Plant mainly made the barrels of the guns and the Forward Mechanical Plant mainly made the gun mounts. The Eight-Five Steelworks was called a steel mill, but it was actually a complementary factory making blanks for the military industries. One workshop specialized in making gun barrels, including for the 57-mm anti-aircraft guns. The Victory Mechanical Plant was the main assembly plant for the 57-mm guns. Of the 683 driving team, one carried military supplies for the entire rearguard area—taking the parts from each plant to the Victory Plant for assembly, then delivering the finished guns out.

According to a witness of the time, when they were transporting the finished guns, each gun was covered with olive-green sailcloth and the military trucks came one after another in a line too long to see the front or end of, for a really impressive sight. All the local villagers would exclaim in amazement. At first, shipping the 57-mm guns out would only happen at night. There'd be this rumbling on the roads for the whole night and locals would have no idea what was happening. They'd hear the sounds but not see a thing. But then later on they'd also ship them in the daytime.

Each factory's production assignments were passed down through the ranks. They'd make just as many items as were ordered. All of the products were received securely. In reality, the products of each factory, and where they got shipped, all of it was a military secret. Each factory had a military representative sent by the Shanghai Garrison to each factory and work unit. They represented the recipient to test and accept [the guns]. Whenever the factory had some issue, they'd actively seek out the military representative and ask them to help make a decision. They were usually graduates of universities or military academies, sent to the factories to strictly oversee the products. Quality control was up to them; if they didn't sign off on it, the product couldn't leave the plant.

At first the power for each of the Small Third Front [work units] was provided by the province of Anhui. They provided about 5000 kilowatt-hours. Then it became difficult to provide this electricity, so the Shanghai side began to plan the 325 plant, which comprised two 25,000-kilowatt generator groups, located in Zhongpu Village, Dunshang Township, Guichi County. They broke ground on construction in August 1970. From site selection to beginning to generate power for the grid only took less than two years, really something of a miracle. The two generator groups went online in May 1972 and March 1974, respectively.

The Changjiang Hospital was a complementary unit for the Shanghai Rear-guard Small Third Front and began construction in 1969 and began trial operations in the latter half of 1970. The hospital occupied five acres of land. At its peak in 1972–1973, the medical staff was up to between 200 and 300 people. Internal medicine, surgery, gynecology, pediatrics, Chinese traditional medicine, orthopedics, physiotherapy, contagious disease, among others, for 13 departments in all. There were 150 beds, an ultrasound machine, gastroscopy, X-rays, and other medical equipment—all the hardware and software along the lines of a properly set-up full hospital. It oversaw the medical work of the Guichi area, including the Eight-Five works, the Forever Red Mechanical Plant and the other factories. Because the Small Third Front factories were all far from urban centers and deep in mountainous areas, industrial production did not have the accompanying provisions [for workers]. In order to preserve independent production and development, an autonomous system had to be pursued, so warehousing, the telephone communications group, the concessionary shops in each factory, schools for the workers' children, medical clinics in each factory and other such units were all successively established.

Deng Xiaoping once said, "China won't fight a war for twenty years." Most of the national defense industry was transferred into civilian products. In this period, active development of civilian production was undertaken in line with the "Army and People Unite, Nurture the Army on the Basis of the People" plan. From 1979 to July 1984 was the third stage, the hybrid stage in which military goods were turning over into civilian goods. In this period, each of the Small Third Front factories fell upon especially hard times. In 1980, the state decreased national defense spending and the production goals for military-industrial products sharply declined. Each of the Small Third Front factories turned to manufacturing civilian goods.

The Forever Red Mechanical Plant turned to producing hydraulic supports for the DZ-type coal mining machines; Five Continents to freon-resistant motors and fractional horse-power motors; Torch to single-phase electricity meters, mainly 2.5 A and 5 A meters; Forward to conveyor belts, freight elevators, and cotton blenders; Victory to 90-mm plastic extruders and machinery for plastic film and plastic bag production. The civilian goods made by these five factories were all typical market commodities without much competitive advantage, plus all the raw materials had to be shipped in from Shanghai to the various mountainous areas of Guichi and the products shipped back to Shanghai for sale. The expense of transportation was massive and raised the production costs, and high production costs triggered high retail prices. In a market economy, there was no way for these goods to get sold.

When the Eight-Five Steelworks was a military-industrial enterprise, they were using an electric furnace and [the steel] was special-grade steel. Then, after they turned to civilian goods, they made civilian-use ordinary steel. For that, they could just use a coal furnace to lower production costs. Electric furnaces were used to produce alloys and high-grade steel. Using an electric furnace to make ordinary steel caused the production costs to rise significantly, and the problem of the huge transport costs was still there. These six factories making military goods for a planned economy in a deep mountain had been all right, mainly in two ways: one was that the military-industrial goods were of good quality and sold well, so overall they could make a little profit. Another way was that when the quota for the military goods was relayed down, the products would be bought by the state at 5% markup no matter what the costs had been, because they didn't calculate costs for military supplies and the state picked up the tab. But with civilian goods, they were going the market economy route, and competitive pricing as well as good quality were the name of the game. Because the Small Third Front factories were deep in the mountains, sales would necessarily be challenging. More and more problems were surfacing. The six enterprises were losing money across the board. Their employees' commitment grew shaky, and the production cycle became unsustainable. Restructuring and handing over control became a historical inevitability.

The 325 electricity plant's situation was also different from the six factories just mentioned. Because it generated and sold power, its production and sales levels were always among the best among peer enterprises. Its power supply coal consumption levels were at the top national levels for equipment of the same class. In 1985, it generated about 400 million kilowatt-hours or so, and also earned a certain amount of profit. Though the 325 plant later experienced many obstacles, basically it remained productive. Now they do biomass generation and their economic and social efficacy are still fairly good.

In the early phase of building up the Small Third Front, the people who went there all had to undergo a political investigation to determine your class background, your family situation and your overseas relationships and so forth. Politically, you had to be dependable; you all had to be the crème de la crème. At the stage when the Small Third Front factories transferred from making military supplies to civilian goods, the people who had set up the factories couldn't feed their aged parents or find themselves wives. The common situation of the Small Third Front [by the conversion to civilian goods] was that the costs of production were especially high, market information was hard to come by, sales were extremely difficult, and the life of the production-line workers was harsh. All sorts of issues were blatantly obvious and the need for restructuring was urgent.

The fourth phase of the Shanghai Small Third Front was from 1985 to 1988, the restructuring and transfer of management phase. In the first month of 1985, Shanghai and Anhui province signed the *Agreement Regarding the Restructuring and Management Transfer of Shanghai's Small Third Front in Southern Anhui between the Shanghai People's Government and the Anhui Provincial People's Government* and reported it to the State Council. That same April, the State Council approved the agreement. In May, the Guichi County Committee first secretary Jiang Zongliang and county head Gu Guolai took the reins themselves and formed a transfer work leadership group with the deputy county head Qian Rangyou as group leader and the chair of the county Political Consultative Conference, Xu Huaikun, as consultant. Over 100 cadres, workers, and technical staff were selected to form this working group, and moved into the various units of the Small Third Front to begin the transfer work.

The overall principle of the transfer was that all fixed assets would be given without compensation to Guichi County. The Shanghainese workers in each unit would, according to their individual wishes, mainly be withdrawn and settled in Shanghai. On the first day of 1986, the 325 electricity plant was handed over and renamed the Guichi Electricity Plant.

The five machine factories were handed over in the second batch, and the Eight-Five Steelworks was last. Of these, the 325 and the Eight-Five were handed over while production continued, while the five machine factories closed during the handover. By January 1988, the transfer of the seven factories and the five auxiliary units was complete. Overall, the handover process between Shanghai and Guichi was fairly smooth. After the handover and refurbishing, the production value of the original Small Third Front enterprises reached over 21 million yuan and tax revenues of 6.3 million yuan, employing over 1200 people.

2.

The process of setting up the Shanghai Small Third Front in Guichi was one of going from the two sides being strangers to gradually harmonizing and understanding each other well. The people of Guichi made huge contributions to, and had enormous effects on, the establishment of the Small Third Front. In terms of land provision, based on the needs of the Shanghai side, when they picked a place—no matter whether it was fields in the mountains, barren hillsides, or good farmland, the Guichi side provided all of their best spots unconditionally and wholly without much compensation. They also helped coordinate large amounts of surveying work. Then later, building roads and expanding the factories required continuing land requisitions, demolitions, and moving [people], and the compensation standards were also very low. The Shanghai Small Third Front requisitioned ___ acres [TN: redacted in original] of land in Guichi. When the farmers had less land, that meant less production capacity. In those very difficult years, it was even harder to subsist. Though later some farmers went into the factories to do some hard physical labor jobs, their pay, relative to the Shanghainese, wasn't very high either. And most farmers had to rely on themselves to produce and find their own living.

In terms of basic infrastructure, when setting up the [Front] first began, the county Party committee and county government organized more than 5000 farmers to work on building [the factories], blasting the hillsides, leveling the ground, digging ditches, building roads and bridges, making dams, drilling deep wells, setting up high-voltage power lines, constructing the factory buildings, and such—the dirtiest, the hardest, the most tiring work, most of which was undertaken by local folks. There was no mechanical equipment, the working conditions were brutal, and they used farm implements and the most basic techniques, carrying things on their shoulders and in their hands, moving things on wooden wheelbarrows, figuring out where to stay and what to eat on the hillsides.

Some peasants, while using these primitive techniques to blast the hillsides, accidentally injured their arms and legs, and some even paid with their lives. In the provision of grain and cooking oil, the local grain stations mainly took care of the rice and vegetable oil for each of the Small Third Front factories, and some was shipped in from elsewhere. The local Chikou rice processing plant and the county vegetable oil plant also supplied a portion. Each factory and each worker's household used ration tickets to buy [these staples]. But during holidays and when work was busy in the factories, the grain stations delivered grain and oil directly to the factories to make it more convenient to buy and to save the workers' time.

In terms of daily living, when the Shanghainese first arrived in the mountains, quite a few of them stayed and boarded with the local population, typically staying with them for two or three years, up to four in some cases. The locals not only provided bamboo, sand and rocks, wood, farm tools, and other such basic supplies for the construction process, and also supplied the day-to-day living of the Shanghainese by providing, for example, pork, eggs, sweet potatoes, vegetables, and large quantities of other non-grain foodstuffs. The locals helped manage the various problems that the Shanghainese met when working in the mountains, like when the Shanghainese got stung by centipedes or bitten by lizards and poisonous snakes, the local villagers would rush to dig up medicinal herbs and help put them on the wounds and prevent the poisons from spreading, facilitating the next step of treatment. The county Party committee and the county government set up a special organization in order to resolve problems in areas such as human resources, materials, transport, and land use. You might say that without the total support and enormous sacrifices of the Guichi County Committee and the government as well as the local populace, the Small Third Front in Guichi would have been almost impossible to set up.

3.

The Small Third Front factories and the auxiliary units were all located in the rugged mountains and deep woods. The setup, development, and completion objectively brought huge impacts to each dimension of Guichi; they prompted the all-around improvement of the economy, society, and all areas in Guichi. In terms of transportation and shipping, there had been no real roads in Miejie or Tangxi. They were located in the mountains and difficult to travel to. The builders of the Small Third Front factories opened the mountains and cut the roads. When they came across water, they built bridges. At the same time as they put into place the basic transportation infrastructure, they also fundamentally improved the transportation situation of the mountainous areas and made travel more convenient, expanded interactions with other areas, and facilitated the flow of locally produced goods.

In terms of the provision of power and running water—at the time, the Guichi mountains had no electricity, and typically people used dim kerosene lamps for lighting at nighttime. After dusk, every mountain village would be jet black. The building of the 325 power plant and the generation of a power network completely changed the mountains' lack of electricity and propelled the improvement of cultural entertainment, industrial and agricultural production, and the residents' daily life for the masses of the mountainous areas. Back then the Meijie area, deep in the mountains, got lit up bright as day as crowds bustled; a large range of activities were on offer, and things were exciting and energetic. They called it "Small Shanghai."

Before the Shanghai Small Third Front got here, the local villagers were drinking spring water from the mountain gullies. This spring water was heavily alkaline and wasn't suitable for long-term consumption. There were also blood flukes in some of the streams. The Small Third Front enterprises brought running water to the homes of peasants near the factories and provided convenient water for daily life and agricultural production, improving the hygienic conditions of the village too.

In terms of farm production, because of the Small Third Front factories' arrival, local products that used to be valueless like dried bamboo shoots, wild greens, "wood ear" mushrooms, peanuts, and eggs all could be sold for money. During the agricultural busy season, not only did the Small Third Front factories form teams to help farmers with their work—like threshing, making hay, building paths through the fields, taking the rice seedlings into the fields before planting, installing water pumps, and the like. They also provided, as much as possible, material support: helping farmers buy bicycles, sewing machines, tractors, pumps, and other things considered rare at the time.

In these close daily interactions, the locals imitated the Shanghainese in clothing and accessories, everyday behavior, tastes in food and drink, and language and writing, among other areas. At the time, you could use ration tickets to buy candy, biscuits, soap, cigarettes, and such in the concessionary shops in each factory, items rare even in the county seat of Guichi.

In terms of education and culture, whether in human resources or educational principles, the elementary and secondary schools set up in the Small Third Front factories were fairly progressive. These schools also recruited among local students, and the children were exposed to relatively state-of-the-art educations for the time, serving as a model for education throughout Guichi. Each factory regularly held various cultural and entertainment activities, showing movies once or twice a week. Televisions entered the farmers' fields of vision. At the same time as these cultural elements brought visual impact to the locals, they also gradually affected their cultural attainments, opening their eyes, and increasing their knowledge.

In terms of medicine and hygiene, the Small Third Front enterprise units set up the Changjiang Hospital in Meijie, and each factory had its corresponding clinic. The quality of medical treatment and technical expertise in these facilities were far superior to the local hospitals of Guichi. Plus, they served the local population with affordable prices. This not only elevated the level of medical treatment in Guichi but also improved the difficulties faced by locals in receiving medical care. Those with major, serious illnesses were able to get timely resuscitation and treatment.

In terms of economic development, only because there was a 325 electricity plant was it possible to have the "major electricity plant" project approved. Because there were a batch of key talents trained at the 325 plant, the planning and setup of the "major electricity plant" was smooth and successful. After the five mechanical factories were transferred, all the related enterprises in Guichi enacted direct-matching transfers—prioritizing the use of received equipment and producing goods to suit consumer demands. Though they later experienced bankruptcies and personnel restructuring, the existing technology, human talent, experience, and sales [of these transferred factories] always affected business development in Guichi. For instance, the Baiying Corporation, which is now headquartered in the Guichi District Provincial High-Tech Innovation Industrial Area, is a major enterprise of Guichi City; about half of its production equipment was received from the Shanghai Small Third Front enterprises. The material and immaterial resources left by the Eight-Five Steelworks are still impacting the economic developments in Guichi today. Some of the [Small Third Front] factory buildings have been used by a succession of businesses invited in by local administrators. The Guihang Special Steels Company in Qianjiang Industrial Park, which puts out three million tons of special-grade steel a year, for example, has used the Eight-Five Steelworks and the eliminated production capacity of some smaller steel mills in the area.

The effects of reinforcing national defense and social stability during the establishment of the Shanghai Small Third Front may be only memories today, but no matter back then or now, [these factories] have had an enormous influence on Guichi. Many Shanghainese who worked on the Small Third Front still frequently return to the place where they used to work to reminisce today. Through contacts and socializing, they haven't forgotten their old friends and have made new ones. Guichi and Shanghai, with the Small Third Front as foundation, have continued to develop new channels of interaction, perpetuate the growth of emotional exchange, and promote the development of both places.

CHAPTER 2

Going to the Small Third Front

Translator's Note

The following accounts show how people of various backgrounds came to work and live on the Small Third Front. From the 1960s to the 1980s, quotas and assignments issued from Party officials dictated many aspects of life, from which students received further schooling to which graduates got a coveted work position. Working in a Small Third Front factory or an auxiliary enterprise was no exception.

Notice from the testimonies below that it was not always easy for someone to get assigned to a Small Third Front factory, whether they came from the city or the local countryside. For many, these assignments were highly desirable for their political prestige and economic security. Moreover, after supply systems grew more robust after the initial years of setting up the factories via difficult physical labor, Small Third Front employees enjoyed state-sponsored privileged access to everything from technical training and special foods to weekly movies. Initially, service at the Third Front was off limits for those plagued by "bad class backgrounds" or other political stains due to their previous actions and affiliations or those of their family members. Likewise barred from transfer were those who struggled with physical limitations like chronic illness, those who "had reason to be dissatisfied" with the regime, and those with "serious" criminal records. For those chosen, refusing to go to an assignment

Y. Xu, Y. Y. Wang, *Everyday Lives in China's Cold War Military-Industrial Complex*, Palgrave Studies in Oral History,
https://doi.org/10.1007/978-3-030-99688-8_2

could mean losing Party membership or the privilege of being assigned to a state-owned enterprise at all. Soon, though, concerns about the shifting of too many experienced and politically reliable workers away from the First Front led to a softening of selection policies for physical ability and political background.[1] As narratives from those of "bad" background show, some of them at least initially saw the Small Third Front as a place of exile.

Even those who report having been enthusiastic about going to the Small Third Front remember having to make difficult choices. Some married in—taking a leap into the unknown professionally and personally in answering the personals ads put out by factory administrators worried about unmarried male workers' discontent, a theme that reappears in the chapter on marriage, sexuality, and families below. But keeping family members geographically close to one another, whether spouses or parents and children, was not typically a priority in work assignments, especially in the politically heated earlier days of the Small Third Front. Thus, several of our respondents talk about leaving siblings, spouses, children, and elderly parents behind to take up their posts in the rugged countryside. To gain employment in the factories and auxiliary enterprises, locals might have had to rely on family and friends' social connections or give up their farmlands to government requisition, often for trivial financial compensation or even none at all.[2]

Questions for Discussion

1. How do people recall their own attitudes as they joined the Small Third Front? Do they seem to have changed these attitudes in the intervening years?
2. Do you think that the backgrounds of the respondents have influenced their attitudes toward joining the Third Front, whether at the time or today? (Hint: think about the alternatives open to them at the time.)

* * *

[1] Meyskens (2020), 89–95, 104–121, 167–172.
[2] Chen (2019), 73.

丁秀玉 Ding Xiuyu, female, technician at a Small Third Front steelworks who later rose to cadre positions in Small Third Front Party organs, including head of the Birth Planning office.

Keywords: camaraderie, family, manual labor, nostalgia, political training, sent-down youth, work assignments

Well, that time in history is really worth remembering. That time, till now, I still think it was giving our most beautiful youth, our most valuable years to this mountain gully. But I have no complaints or regrets. I feel like it was worth it. When I went, I was only 22; it was December 23, 1969. We were the No. 10 Light Industry Company. Light industry, all young people [...] all the students from the factories [...] were assigned there. Yes, assigned. The requirements for going to the Small Third Front were very high. Our generation all got sent down to the countryside, you know. Going there [to the Small Third Front] was among the best, because it was a military factory, requiring the best people and resources. So we were randomly chosen, among the students. The family history had to be clear [and good]. Then those with various kinds of family difficulties, like if they were the oldest kid, they'd be taken care of [by being assigned to the Small Third Front]. Or if all the siblings of the family were away.

Me, I had an older brother and an older sister. He was outside [Shanghai] and my sister had already married. My younger brother, class of '69, would definitely be assigned outside [Shanghai], so they took care of me [and had me go to the Small Third Front]. Yes, because it was closer, because it was a factory, for sure I'd enter a factory. [...] I first arrived in Huizhou, Jixi: Hu Jintao's hometown. [...] We were several tens of kilometers outside Jixi, another mountain gully. That factory I went to was called The East is Red Materials Factory. Our company was made up of six schools [from these factories]: the second plant of the No. 3 Steelworks, the Shanghai Metallurgy Factory, the silicon steel plate factory, and the Xingfu Steel Factory, and me from the copper factory of the Metals Corporation, and another factory I forget. Anyway, six schools, divided into three platoons for one company. I was in the Third Platoon, and they even asked me to be deputy platoon leader. Me, so small, having me be platoon leader. When we first got there we lived in grass huts and slept on bamboo beds. Ten girls and 13 boys went from our school, 23 total. There were several hundred students at our school, and only 23 could go. They [the other students] all really envied us.

So it was a military industrial work unit first of all, then secondly it wasn't far, in Anhui, thirdly our household registrations didn't get moved over there. Because of not moving our registrations, we all felt like it was a temporary thing, for training, and we'd come back. So everyone was very happy. We rode a bus for a day on December 23 to get there. We were organized into a company, military style, and led by the military propaganda team, then the workers' propaganda team from school followed us, with the commissar and the company captain overseeing us. [...] We followed the Shanghai 208 Construction Team and the 8th Squad of the No. 2 City Infrastructure Company. Yes, this was training-through-labor. We moved bricks, lumber, and pushed handcarts with the workers of the 208 Engineer Team, that's what we did. Because construction sites would always have bricks to be moved and needed carts to move the scrap lumber, especially in the winter, in the snow, we'd also have to work.

Of course life was really hard, but we were young then, so we didn't mind. We ate at the company cafeteria. Back then we weren't allowed to cook for ourselves or go home. Especially at the Lunar New Year, not being allowed to go home. If you went home you'd have to write a [self] criticism; you'd be a deserter. They monitored you really closely. At the Lunar New Year, we wanted to go home, especially some girls; we all cried together. They'd often have meetings too then, and if your labor performance wasn't good during that period, then you couldn't become an official worker, you couldn't enter the factory. That was the training-through-labor.

When I went, the No. 4 Workshop wasn't in production yet. The real production at the Eight-Five Steelworks was in the later years. The scale of the factory was there, but the equipment wasn't complete yet, so we couldn't get straight to work. So a portion of us students went to the Shanghai No. 5 Steelworks to intern. So glad they were, to come back to Shanghai. When so many people were sent to the factory, they had to be split into different types of work. In the factory, female comrades would do the cranes ... because we were producing steel tubing.

[Other female comrades] did logistics work. I got a very good assignment. ... I was assigned to the physics lab and got to wear a blue [lab] coat. I was assigned to the physics lab of the No. 4 Workshop. Then I was sent to Shanghai for an internship for six months. That was my first time back in Shanghai from December 23, '69 to about November of '70. When our work types were assigned, a minority of people stayed in the No. 4 Workshop. There was nothing to do, just goof off. Most people went back to Shanghai to intern, and the interning people were really happy. With a monthly ticket, living with the parents, riding the public transit, it was really nice. At that time four people from the No. 4 Workshop went to intern in Shanghai. I was one of them.

There were four girls in all. One left a real deep impression on me. She was a student at the Shanghai No. 2 Industrial University, in physics. Even now she still often keeps in touch with me. She was two years older than us. Because she was a physics major university student, of course she'd be doing this job. Another girl was a deputy captain from another company, and others really admired her too. I thought I knew how to operate a crane, because I kind of liked operating a crane, and I quite wanted to be assigned to the crane group, but I never thought I'd be assigned to the physics lab. Then in May '71, I returned to Anhui. When I got back, the factory was still not up to size and couldn't operate normally. So the steel-making workshop was still not in production, and the factory was basically still in the building stages. I guess they were doing the Cleansing the Class Ranks Movement, or the One-Strike Movement [TN: the Cleansing the Class Ranks Movement of 1968, or the One Strike-Three Anti movement of 1970], I forget.

At that time, they took me and Wang Wenqing—you know her? [...] We two lived in the same dorm. Haha, our friendship was an old one. We were living in the same dorm, then we got picked to go do research work, an office job. One of the deputy [Party] secretaries in our workshop, and an old worker, a man, plus us, four people doing research work. What research? Materials for the movement, for the "beating-smashing-looting elements" [TN: the official term for people seen as disturbing social order] during the Cultural Revolution. Me and Wang Wenqing were partnered up. Then we went back to Shanghai, very happily, and got our monthly [bus] tickets again. We'd often go out with the old worker. Back then we two would go to the police station, to other people's work units, researching. Nowadays this happens too. I already forget if it was the Cleansing or the One Strike, Three Antis, but it was that time. We kept at it until '72, nearly a year. We were almost done around May '72.

There were no rules [from above about when we could go (back) to Anhui]. Yes, there were no rules. Anyway, we were young then, very naive. In May '72, our Eight-Five Steelworks was going to do a bunch of Marxism and Leninism study courses. Me, I was in the first batch of students. Our workshop leadership was pretty nurturing to me. Yes, so they picked me to participate in the Marxism and Leninism study course, held in the factory administrative offices. After my internship [in Shanghai] I came back to do the [political] movements, then after the movements ended I joined the study course. They held the course for about one month. The admin offices held it, and each workshop formed a class. I was in the first group of students. After the study, I should have gone back [to the workshop], but they kept me as a staff member. I was a staff worker for the Marxism and Leninism study course. I'd contact people, help them organize things, do stuff like that. This study course was co-organized by our Organization and Propaganda Departments from our Eight-Five Steelworks. I was basically "on loan" from the No. 4 Workshop to the Organization Department to help them with work.

I was really very lucky. So I have no complaints or regrets about this phase of history; I felt like it was really worth it. The classes were held until '73, in all for a year, and they pretty much wrapped up. In '73, the new factory needed personnel, cadres—at that point the proportion of young people was very high in the Steelworks. All these schools—not just our company; there were ten in all. I was in just one of them. At that point they moved me from the No. 4 Workshop to the study course. Originally I was in the rosters under 4, on leave, then they formally transferred me to the factory administration. In reality my time in No. 4 Workshop was really brief; I did virtually nothing, then I was transferred to the factory administration as the deputy department head for the Propaganda Department. Originally we were called the Propaganda Team, what's now the Propaganda Department. I was deputy department chief, a mid-ranking cadre among the 5000-plus people.

* * *

伏如山 Fu Rushan, male, worker at a fuse explosive factory.

Keywords: living conditions, homesickness, manual labor, rural vs. urban, sent-down youth, work assignments

[TN: The below translation comes from a written recollection penned by Fu.]

In 1968, our cohort of technical school students who should've stayed in Shanghai faced work assignments. The situation of the time and the assignment plans were that most of us would leave the city, 76% to go to the Second Command Center in Jiangxi and the Central No. 1 Light Industries department. Twenty-four percent would stay in town—those with illnesses or who were only children. [...] I made the mental preparations to leave, but I was worried that my mother would be sad, because my departure would bring her pain. But what could we do? The entire society was emphasizing "going up to the mountains and down to the countryside." If we could get assigned to factories and mines, we were among the lucky ones.

...Our fates, due to the turns of history, brought us catastrophe and determined our destinies—an unavoidable and terrifying path. On August 13, 1968, I finally received my assignment notification, to the Second Command Center in Jiangxi. To tell the truth, though I knew I had to leave Shanghai, but because it wasn't too far away and was a military factory, and was in the South, I was relatively calm about it and my family wasn't overly upset. Anyway, in a respectable family of workers, what good would being upset about it do? In the flood of tens of millions being "sent down," they also gained perspective on what counted as good fortune.

The day after I got the notice, I reported to the Ruijin Apartments on Huaihai Road. That's when I found out our factory was actually a military factory built by the Shanghai Electronic Tools Factory. Though everyone at the reception tried to make everything sound great, we knew it wasn't great, but what could we actually do? We students were too naive. We thought that it'd be okay as long as we had diplomas. We thought that the world worked so simply. Maybe these reception staff knew from the start about how we thought and were tricking us childish students to just get us to Jiangxi and complete their mission.

Later on we found out that we were part of the Shanghai factory's quota because they couldn't get any of their staff workers to go to Jiangxi ... but if we were part of the Shanghai factory's quota, why wouldn't they make us official workers? At the same time, they asked us to leave Shanghai just a week after we reported in. And they wouldn't give us any stipend at all [for the move]. But official workers at the Shanghai Electronic Tools Factory typically got up to several months between the assignment notification and also some assistance funds. Wasn't this flat-out deception? Luckily one of us, Wang Dabao, fought for a month's wages for everyone, or else we really would have been cheated by the factory.

Now that I had to leave my parents and cosmopolitan Shanghai in just a single week, my mother shed tears every day and my heart was filled with pain. I couldn't understand why the world would be so unfair and why we had to take up tasks other people were unwilling to do. The week passed too quickly. I didn't have a chance to have a good chat with my classmates or have a nice round of fun in Shanghai before I found myself on an express train, the number 57 from Shanghai to Nanchang, leaving the

Shanghai I'd lived in for 21 years together with 11 male comrades and five female ones. I was only 21! A lot of people were at the station bidding their farewells that day. We took a photo at the plaza in front of the station. Everyone was reluctant to say goodbye and the entire north plaza was roiling with crowds of people. Who wouldn't want to be assigned to Shanghai? But for things that were impossible, we could only throw away our impossible ideas and let our fates arrange our paths for us. Yes, we were really too young, and which mother or father wasn't heartsore? Which family wasn't sad? The train began to pull out and sounds of crying filled the train and the station. I saw the resentment and discontent behind those tears.

...Where the factory was, exactly, nobody knew. We stayed two days in the Jiangxi Hotel in Nanchang. The hot city was intolerable—a real furnace that wouldn't let you sleep soundly. No one had the spirit to go check out the town. The girls were even more anxious; they'd ruminate all day and cry, and then move from tears to more ruminating, as though that could offer some relief. We couldn't wait to get to the factory; in Shanghai, the reception staff said the factory was near Nanchang. So why were we in a hotel? Then the dawn of the third morning, a big truck took us on a five-hour drive in mountains we'd never seen before. It was the first time I'd been on such a long drive, plus it was in the back of a truck. I really hated it. Why did they set up the factory in this crappy place? We all cursed the whole way...

After five hours of bumping and thumping, we finally saw a poor hamlet. Mud houses whose front doors opened onto the mountains were the only habitation. You had to walk up to a half hour to get a meal, and there weren't even streetlamps. You saw snakes all over the place. A lot of the girls cried in fear. There wasn't running water then either; you had to go to the river to get it yourself. There were so many unimaginable difficulties in everyday living, nothing like what the Shanghai factory leadership bragged about to us.

I shared a room with Yu Baoxin and Jiang Wenda. The factory hadn't begun official operations yet, so work was relaxed and easy. Plus the factory only had 300 or 400 people at that point, so the canteen's food wasn't bad. There was only a totally ramshackle little People's Commune town near the factory—Huanggang Township of the Huanggang Commune, Yifeng County, Jiangxi. The farmers here were all very poor. Some lived in deep mountains and virgin forests and had never even seen a car, much less something like a cultural life. If they could see a movie or

Image 2.1 B &W photograph of Wang Qinglong as a young man in Jingde County, Anhui, 1969. (Collection of Wang Qinglong)

a decent opera, that was an amazing thing. I looked at the houses on mountaintops and couldn't understand how they lived. If we hadn't come here, I wouldn't have ever known that there were forgotten corners like this in China (Image 2.1).

* * *

傅锡林 Fu Xilin, female, secondary school teacher at a Small Third Front steel mill.

Keywords: critique, Cultural Revolution, frustrations, higher education, intellectuals, marriage, work assignments

My husband got assigned in '62 to the Shanghai Copper Factory, but after we got married, we couldn't get transferred to the same place. I was actually supposed to be the class of '65. You should know about this history. I was at the Tianjin Normal University; I'm from Tianjn. We couldn't live together after we got married and we were really upset and anxious. He went first to Support the Interior, so then I followed him. [...] Of course, there were more Shanghainese and fewer from outside.

[Her husband chimes in:] Seventy to eighty percent of the technical personnel at our factory went to Support the Interior. Why? Well, the government had a policy that if you went to Support the Interior, you could bring family members. If you didn't, you were very passive. Your household registration was controlled by the government, and your work could be transferred to the city but not your registration. If the work unit wouldn't let you go, you also couldn't get transferred here. So there was no other way.

[Fu:] We were really helpless then. Yes, [we got married first and then came to the Eight-Five Steelworks]. It was all like that. You had to be spouses to be brought over! Unmarried people couldn't. Yep, we got married in Tianjin—but he's from Shandong. He had relatives in Tianjin and went to school there, you know. It wasn't very early—we got married in '68. He was already 30, I was 28, 29. I was born in '42. You really can barely stand to talk about the Cultural Revolution times. Nothing special about [being a college grad]! My daddy came out of Peking University. I was unlucky. I matriculated in '61, and I should've been the class of '65.

I was in the history department at the Normal University. When I was a junior, our department and school got restructured. We had two arts and social science classes then, about 50-odd people in all. [...] So, after the restructuring, our teachers and leaders were pretty worried, which makes sense even now. Because we were juniors, and then there was also a sophomore group, but they still needed three years to get things done—they were going to do away with the department! So they got really anxious. We had three departments [being restructured], geography, history, and biology. Geography and biology didn't have a close department [to be transferred into], so [the students] all got transferred to Hebei University. Only us in the history department could be handled closer to home. The Chinese, foreign language, and political education departments were all okay. But they were also going to drop us down a class year. How many teachers did you even have, back then? How could you just do this! The students in my class were relatively older, too.

And then when the Cultural Revolution rebellion started, they went through our dossiers; this I blame them for. I'd put myself down for the Chinese department then. Typically, people got turned away from the foreign languages department, because that wasn't a very good specialization. A few of the Overseas Chinese students wanted to go into the foreign languages department and learn Russian, but no luck. So I put myself down for Chinese because I didn't like political education. They did a pledge drive, because [they needed] a lot of people in political education, you know! They opened up a class and got a bunch of people to go into it. I got moved into political education. Actually, I was history and political education. Then I spent a year studying and we all got dropped down a class year during the Cultural Revolution and became the class of '66. The Cultural Revolution just happened to be June '66 and we graduated in July; we were supposed to start getting wages in '67. But then we got stuck there, and in the end I only left school in '68. Just look at all that time I wasted.

[...] Actually, our political education class was under 40 or so people, and we got assigned all over the country. At first I got assigned to the Hydroelectric School out in Wenchuan [Sichuan], and I thought it was pretty fun. I didn't know, but that's where the big earthquake [of 2008] happened. In order to get [re-] assigned, I married him in '68. He was in Shanghai at the time; he said that Sichuan was the Big Third Front, and he worried that if we got sent there we wouldn't be able to transfer out. So then I changed over to Handan, Hebei. Back then you had to negotiate [a change] with the University—I hadn't left yet! So I traded places with a girl in my class. Then this girl reneged, but I wouldn't change back. So then she traded with a boy in our class, and he ended up going [to Sichuan]. After that we lost touch, so I don't know what happened with him in the '08 earthquake. Anyway, he never came back. I stayed three years at the Handan No. 6 Secondary School, because we couldn't get transferred to the same place after we got married. Then we went to Support the Interior. He went in December '70, and I went in February '71.

When I got there in February, I was there but my files weren't, and my affiliations weren't. There weren't schools on the Third Front yet, then. Then, when Teacher Yu [and other colleagues] went over, they even got sent down to the workshops. I had no place to live when I got there, so I rented a room in a villager's house. [...] Yep! Nothing to do all day, just waiting at home. My school [in Handan] also wouldn't let me go [until 1971], so I had to finish that semester. Then I went to Tianjin for a visit and came with him out here. That was February. Folks were all renting spaces in villagers' homes back then.

[…] After I got to the factory, I waited for the school to open in the propaganda department. […] Four or five people, like Yu Cuiying and them, they were put in the workshops. Then two went to the primary school; Yu Cuiying went to the secondary school. I kept waiting. Then they started building the school in July, then a lot [of teachers] came and they didn't need to be put in the workshops. We all sat around the propaganda department waiting. We were all women. Our secondary school was separate from the primary school. At first the secondary school had only four teachers, one of which was a man. […] Then afterward it was still mostly women. A lot of them came from Shanghai Normal University.

* * *

顾国籁 Gu Guolai, male, Anhui native. Technician who rose to administrative leadership roles in Anhui.

Keywords: Cultural Revolution, higher education, intellectuals, Reform and Opening, work assignments

At the time I was a "Stinking Number Nine" [TN: Cultural Revolution epithet for an intellectual or highly educated student], you know, we all got assigned as a batch. [Class of] '69. [I was] an urban planning [major]. The point of our education was to become mayor's assistants. […] In '75 we were all Worker, Peasant, Soldier University students. [After graduation], yes, [we were dispatched] to "facing toward the borders," "facing toward the workers and peasants," "facing toward the grassroots," something—[Interviewer interjects, "The Four Facings Toward"]. Yes. At the time I was assigned to be a worker. I was a "Stinking Number Nine," and you were all assigned as a whole, nationwide. I was down there [as a worker] for a lot of years.

Basically when the Gang of Four was smashed, slowly in '76 the policy became more supportive, slowly I became a technician, assistant engineer, engineer, then senior engineer, then administrator, then deputy department head, deputy bureau head; by '83, '84, when Deng Xiaoping promulgated "Reform and Opening," my luck was pretty good, I went from the deputy bureau head of the Bureau of Construction straight to county head. […] The Guichi County Bureau of Construction, yes. […] I became county head at 36, for three years. […] I started in '84 […] until '87.

Then when Guichi County was made administratively to be under Anqing, I was transferred to the Anqing administrative office to be the Economic Committee head, then when the Anqing Area merged with Anqing City, afterward, I was the Transportation Committee head, in '90 I was deputy bureau head, then in '93 I was transferred back [to Guichi].

* * *

季美华 Ji Meihua, female, kindergarten teacher at a Small Third Front steelworks.

Keywords: Cultural Revolution, living conditions, manual labor, post-Mao, travel and transportation, work assignments

I went to the Small Third Front at first for, how do they say, "training-through-labor." I graduated in '68. The training-through-labor was in Huizhou to assist in the urban construction company. Then I was assigned to the Eight-Five Steelworks. When I first went there it was really run down, just terrible. When I started [...] I'd move some bricks, paint the walls [...] it was really, really hard, but at the time because I was so small and skinny, they looked after me and I got to just work in the dining hall. And I requested to leave, to do harder work. People were pretty progressive [TN: politically correct] in their thinking back then. [...] The training-through-labor was for a year and a half. Then I was assigned to a factory [...] directly to the Eight-Five Steelworks.

[...] At first heading out [to Shanghai for teacher training] was very hard, because you had to take a boat, steerage class, it was a pain. Yes, you had to wait for the boat, and eat two meals on there. It was a pain. In the 70s, I guess after the Gang of Four collapsed, it [got a little better]. Most people in the factory didn't take the boat, but the buses instead. Early on, the buses would take over ten hours, at least seven or eight, because there weren't any highways.

I never saw an accident, but my colleagues have. Yes, [there were times that, because it was a ten-odd hour trip, you were driving the mountain roads at night]. Such hard times have passed, and when I try to remember them, they're not so bad. Yeah, I was young then; I thought it was really interesting.

* * *

吕建昌 Lü Jianchang, male, Small Third Front pharmacist at the Ruijin Hospital.

Keywords: Cultural Revolution, frustrations, higher education, intellectuals, medicine, work assignments

I was a pretty good student in secondary school, so my homeroom teacher wanted me to keep studying. At the time there were two options for more studying, either technical school or hygiene and medicine. I figured all boys got sent to technical school and thought I'd be assigned to a factory for it, but the notice came to go to work directly at the Rear Base Ruijin Hospital. I was really surprised. When the batch of us (all graduates of 1972) reported to the hospital, they decided to put us into medical training. We boys had two kinds of tracks, oral health and dentistry or pharmacy. Girls were all nursing. We didn't have the right to choose; it was all up to the teachers. So I got put in pharmacy.

The training conditions at the Rear Base Ruijin Hospital were pretty poor, then, so we got there and they sent us back to the Shanghai No. 2 Hospital's school of hygiene for a year's basic pharmacy courses. That year we took classes with their regular students. [...] The full name was "Hygiene School Attached to the Shanghai No. 2 Hospital," where Xinhua Hospital is today. [...] After one year's basic theoretical training, we went to intern back on the Rear Base. A lot of us in pharmacy were chemistry students, especially organic chem. When studying we were all so ambitious, resolving to develop cancer-fighting drugs. But then we went back to that hospital, took a look around; that was what we had to work with—no way to come up with cancer-fighting drugs there. So we gave up.

* * *

潘雅珍 Pan Yazhen, female, worked as laboratory technician and in the mechanical department workers' union at a Small Third Front steel mill.

Keywords: children, Cultural Revolution, family, frustrations, marriage, political problems, political training, veterans, work assignments

I went to the Eight-Five Steelworks because my husband used to be a military instructor [...] from 1970, well, their training base turned into a foreign-troop training station and they started training large numbers of Africans. So, well, they called him back. Another thing, I had family in Hong Kong. During the Cultural Revolution, I joined the party just in '65, and I was working at the propaganda department of the central offices for the [...] Shanghai No. 5 Steelworks. [...] Then [my husband] changed jobs, but he wasn't from Shanghai. He's from Jiangsu. So we had no other choice. One of our deputy Party secretaries helped me arrange the office to recommend me for the Small Third Front. At first, they put me in the technical office doing that work, doing metallographic engineering. Then when the Cultural Revolution started, I'd just joined the Party, so I think they wanted us to "exercise ourselves in the great movement of the revolution," so the work team had me taken out to do the movement, and then I became the target of struggle sessions. Then I didn't go back to the steelworks, but it was all full of rebel factions; it was a total mess. So I didn't participate in that.

Then when I did go back, the "Support the Left" faction thought I didn't have a strong enough [political] viewpoint. Of course I did, but I didn't join in the earlier activities, so I didn't have any grudges or benefactors. So they sent me to do study classes. After that they put me in the head office in the propaganda department. Actually, I don't like doing political work. Because I have family outside [the PRC], it was a pretty sensitive thing at the time and if some question came up, I'd get my family in hot water. So I preferred my specialty, metallography.

[…] Well, then because we married in '68, after I came back [to the factory] they had me leading study classes. My husband was a military representative there to "Support the Left." He came into our factory. At first, we were strangers. Then their leader, their commanding officer, introduced us and we were married. When they were doing the political investigation, they [allowed it] because I was a Party member, and two, well, they knew about my work performance. But I wasn't supposed to have been able to marry a soldier, because my family background was bad, and I had family abroad. I wasn't clean. Then my husband was re-deployed. He wasn't from Shanghai so he couldn't stay.

Then there was a policy that if your family were in the city you could stay. But by '68 we already had two kids. Then our deputy Party secretary suggested we go "support the interior," and then you could bring your spouse. So [my husband] went in '70, then I went. He was a League branch secretary or something at first, because he was only 30 then. Then he was the commander of the armed militia company. At the time the people at the [No. 5 Steelworks] thought it was really something of me to go to the propaganda department, too; they thought I'd gone there for love into those backwoods, sacrificing living in greater Shanghai.

I had three siblings—actually four, but one died of illness. Not much my mom could do about it at the time. Because I went to the Small Third Front, the "sent down" quota was canceled. Because I'd gone to a non-Shanghai factory or mine, that got canceled. So my younger brother stayed in Shanghai. [...] Mainly, me, it's not that I wanted to go, it was that my husband had to go. The Party committee secretary came up with this idea to have us fill the Eight-Five Steelworks quota, but with me also transferring my registration over there to go with him.

* * *

王金忠 Wang Jinzhong, male, Anhui native and farmer who worked in a Small Third Front chemical factory.

Keywords: family, nepotism, pay and benefits, politically correct, rural vs. urban, veterans, work assignments

Like when we first began constructing this factory, the folks here didn't know what this factory was for. Back then, because they were coming from the military district, a lot of PLA, the Military Representatives, had come here already, in uniform and looking fierce. The folks looked at them and felt afraid. They didn't know why they were building this factory, so when the factory came to take eminent domain over our land, and take in a few locals ... in '72, they tried to take in us locals. The batch of people who were to be taken in were afraid to go.

[...] Because they were afraid that if they were taken in, they'd have to go to war. They were afraid that if there were fighting, then the people who were taken in would be transferred away. Some families only had one son and didn't want to let him go, because there was no telling if maybe he'd leave with the Shanghainese. The parents couldn't think around it, they couldn't bear it. But then by '75 things were different. Everyone fell over one another to get into the factory ... at that point, the factory set limits on hiring locals as workers.

[They limited the hiring by] giving the quotas for hiring workers locally to the local government, then the local government would release the quotas and take in some people. The lives of the people who entered the factory in '72, their social circles, were totally different from the folks who didn't go into the factory. Their salaries were very low when they entered the factory, but folks then had no money. Even if the people who went into the factory were making 30 bucks [a month], that meant a buck a day. That was something that folks didn't have. They'd practically kill themselves for a buck 30 in shared profits.

So when the factory was hiring locally in '75, everyone was scrambling to get in, but it was hard; they couldn't get in. In '75, the people who got into the Red Star Factory were in several categories. One was those with family difficulties, with kids ... another were people who were "pioneering," particularly "pioneering" [TN: politically activist]. Another kind were those with pretty solid credentials locally, like military children, production cadres' children; these people could get in. Not many local people got into the Red Star Factory. We had a total of nine get in, from our village.

[...] Well, as for me, [I got into the Factory] because my father was the work brigade chief in the village. That I was able to get in, I can only say there were two reasons. One was because he was a village cadre who'd been at it for a long time, and another was that he had won the trust of his superiors through his work style and management. They felt like "we can arrange for one of your family's kids to go into the factory." At that time, in this village, other people, like fathers and sons, the village committee, these people had views on this, and criticisms, because they also wanted to have their kids go in, and people in the factory wanted to introduce friendly people into the ranks, but they were not able to. But after I got in, there was a man named Tang, who was the township committee secretary in Hezhen Commune—that was what Xiangyu was called at the time—he got along very well with my father. He thought that my father did after all have a son, so he said he could make arrangements, and he was able to arrange me getting in. At the time, Hezhen Commune also had a Party Secretary, surnamed Fang; he didn't agree with this, but it didn't matter; this Party Secretary's words didn't matter. I entered the factory on November 20, 1975.

* * *

王美玉 Wang Meiyu, female, chair of the Shanghai Rear Base Management Bureau workers' union.

Keywords: nostalgia, Party members, pay and benefits, politically correct

The "Supporting the Interior" was after the natural disaster, the three years of difficulty [TN: referring to the Great Leap Forward and subsequent famine], were over. Us in the Instrumentation and Electronics Company started around '67, '68. I went in when I was 27. The requirements were very high at the time. If you were to go, they checked you back three generations. Normal people couldn't go. These three generations had to be of good political background, good thought; all the people going in were Party members. Back then you could tell at a glance who was and who wasn't a Party member. How? Party members at that time would always be volunteering to do things and pick up other people's slack. Giving a small example: a typical small group leader giving out movie tickets would always keep the worst one for themselves but give the good ones to others. [...] If you had any connection to ... [TN: elided in the interview transcript], even if you longed to go, they wouldn't let you. You had to be absolutely loyal to the Communist Party.

This kind of loyalty wasn't the lip service loyalty of today, but loyalty that came through in action. Some of our Party members and cadre today can't compare to those days of ours. In our thinking, becoming a Party member was a very hard thing. Even after you joined the Party, you still felt a distance between yourself and the Party. [...] In case Shanghai had to fight a war, Shanghainese workers moving [out there]—Shanghai is the lifeline of the Party Center and industry couldn't stop, so [the staff] had to undergo strict selection. [...] When we were motivating people [to go], we promised a few things that wouldn't change: living standards wouldn't change, salaries wouldn't change, household registrations and affiliations would still be Shanghainese. After you got there, we'd guarantee your living with staple foods, and tickets for grain and meat rations; all of that would be supplied by Shanghai.

* * *

伍先权 Wu Xianquan, male, Anhui native and veteran. Worked in Small Third Front factories as a worker and driver.

Keywords: politically correct, rural vs. urban, veterans, work assignments

I was brought in in 1975, locally; we were brought in because the Small Third Front took our land for use. At that time we were veterans; veterans had priority. Xu Guangfu, who I just mentioned, he was a discharged veteran too. The factory used our land, and we were veterans, so veterans had priority.

Back then we were discharged veterans, so politically we didn't need to be checked. I don't have a lot of education, just primary school. My spouse, she got in first. She got in because her land got used. The Third Front Factory used our village lands and then gave our village a few spots [to work in the factory], and she was one of them. Telling you true, no one wanted to go; no one knew what the factory would be like, so nobody wanted to go, they'd rather stay in the village working. Going in the factory, they sent someone to come do thought work. Some people didn't want to go in, and some wanted to go in but didn't realize they could. My spouse used to be the women's team leader in a production team, and was relatively advanced [politically], so then we started working at this Third Front Self-Strengthening Factory.

* * *

许汝钟 Xu Ruzhong, male, deputy head and chief engineer of a Small Third Front steelworks.

Keywords: children, conflicts, critique, Cultural Revolution, family, frustrations, political problems, work assignments

I graduated from the Beijing Steel and Iron Institute with a technical high school degree in 1957 and was assigned to Shanghai, where I began at the No. 7 Steelworks [...] in 1961 I was sent to the No. 5 Steelworks and before 1970 I was doing technical work there. I went to the Eight-Five Steelworks on the Small Third Front in 1970. [...] At the time the No. 5 Steelworks had too many "Support the Interior" projects, like one steel mill in Jiangyou, Sichuan, and the Xinyu Steelworks in Jiangxi. Our Small Third Front was the Anhui-based Eight-Five Steelworks.

My fate was arranged by the Party. The first batch were the best of the best; all the ones they sent to the Big Third Front were from workers' families. They wanted good political backgrounds. I didn't have one so I couldn't get a spot there. I joined the Party in 1959 and was Party branch secretary plus in the technical department at the No. 5, so during the CultRev [TN: the Cultural Revolution, or *Wenhua dageming*, is often abbreviated colloquially as *Wen'ge*; "CultRev" is used throughout this book to convey the shortened form] we were the targets of struggle sessions. After being struggled, they had us doing the "Grand Alliance" [TN: a directive from Party Central in 1968 urging the cessation of armed factional conflicts]. With the Grand Alliance, we were basically set free again. But after we were liberated, those old rebels were still in power. The technical department didn't want to make use of us oldsters so they sent me to the Small Third Front. I was basically cast aside by the rebel faction. I was definitely upset about this. I thought, well you No. 5 Steelworks technical crew don't think much of me, you don't want me, I'll go where I can show off my talents. Plus, just before this two cadres hadn't gone to the Small Third Front for this or that reason so they really wanted people.

The leadership had a chat with me and I didn't talk back. I said sure, and I didn't tell my family either. My wife complained that I hadn't talked it over with her. My kid wasn't three years old yet then, too little [to take along], so my wife raised our kid herself after I left. Because we were concerned about the kid's education, we didn't want to bring the family over. We were afraid that if we went to the mountains, our kid's studies would be badly affected.

* * *

徐小英 Xu Xiaoying, female, cadre, teacher, and office administrator at a Small Third Front steel mill.

Keywords: camaraderie, Cultural Revolution, family, manual labor, men vs. women, nostalgia, politically correct, post-Mao, sent-down youth, work assignments, work schedules

Back then, I was at a vocational secondary school, class of '68. Then I happened to be in a batch—I graduated junior high in '64, got into a four-year vocational high school until '68, and we should have been all assigned [to jobs] in Shanghai, but then among the secondary students there was a sea of "red" [TN: political enthusiasm] that appeared; we got made "red" by them, a whole sea. After that, I was the oldest in my family; back then [we were] two class of '68, one '69, one '70 in our household. Inside of three months, three of us left. I was taken care of, me, as the oldest.

Going to Anhui was taking care of me. If your [class] background was good at the time, "good people can best forge the best weapons"; all the people who went to the Third Front were like that. My little sister was class of '69, [and got sent to] a military-industrial farm, then I went to Anhui, my little brother was sent down to the [rural] brigades in Nanhui, our ancestral place. After two years of being sent down, he joined the military.

We did training-through-labor [when we went in]. Training-through-labor until August. Then before I'd finished, the Shanghai No. 5 Steelworks was building a steel mill, and organizing a [Youth] League [Branch]; I was chosen and told to go do the training with them, then go with a bunch of hiring people from the No. 5 Steelworks to go to various work units in Shanghai to hire workers. After we'd done half the hiring, then they were organizing a League [Branch] in the mountains, they called me in, so I was organizing a League [Branch]. I was in the Infrastructure Department, then when they were organizing the ranks, then the Mechanical Department's League Branch was founded; I was in the first class of League Committee members in the plant, the equivalent of Wang Wenqing, all the female comrades in the plant, there were three female comrades who entered the Party in the first place. Wang Wenqing was one of them, I was one, and Shi Zhiding's wife. Mm, just us three. The first female comrades to enter the Party.

At that time we really gave it our all, we didn't pay attention to anything else at all. Training-through-labor was supposed to be one year, then it was ended before it was a full year. Then I entered the plant. At the time we were just building the Eight-Five Steelworks. The company I was in was building the plant's main offices and two workshops. The workshops were the forges. At the time we really put it all into our work. We took the middle shift in the middle of the night; you started at 10 p.m., all by yourself, you ran into the mountain gully. Mm, just all by yourself, and no one else. Because female comrades were few at the time.

[...] Then when I got recognized as a "Study the Selected Works of Chairman Mao" Activist, then I put my name in at one of the mobilization meetings, just kitty corner across. I said, "Mr. Wu, I want to go to the Eight-Five Steelworks too."

At the time my thinking was really naive. That was the education I had gotten. Yes, [I felt like I was helping out Chairman Mao]. Plus at the time they'd say "dig deep tunnels, store grain widely, don't seek hegemony." As though if the Third Front construction didn't proceed well [Mao] wouldn't be able to sleep. Plus, now many positive elements of propaganda out there, we could also accept it. Plus, what I sometimes hear what they now say about positive energy, this sort of thing was all easy to accept. In reality, I was already assigned to the Shanghai No. 5 Steelworks, I didn't even have to put my name in, plus each workshop [head] said I was someone who needed training. So I casually chatted with the planning and construction group, then I mentioned it to the people in the No. 6 Workshop. Basically, I entered the Shanghai No. 5 Steelworks' Workshop No. 6 on November 16, 1968, then January '71 I went there [to Anhui]; basically I stayed at the No. 5 Shanghai Steelworks for two years.

Now when I think about it, it's kind of hilarious, but at the time when I was leaving I even bought a pocket edition, a highlights of *Chairman Mao's Selected Works*, and gave it to the cooks in the cafeteria; they all came to see me off. [...] there weren't many young girls like us who had purely gone to Support the Interior. There were relatively more if [you counted] the women who were brought along when the man went [to Anhui], and these women weren't necessarily from Shanghai. Yangzhou, or Zhengjiang, mostly, and another group were technical secondary school grads from the class of '68. Tech school kids, well, at that time, they'd have graduated by

’71 or ’72, right, so then there were the “Four Facings”; some of them went to Gansu, Heilongjiang, and Guizhou. Going to Anhui was relatively nearby. And some university grads, that type of female comrade was relatively more common. So then at the time our thinking was, there was no choice: if they asked you to go, you went.

* * *

杨秀珍 Yang Xiuzhen, female, worker and cadre for a Small Third Front steelworks.

Keywords: family, manual labor, nepotism, Party members, poverty, sent-down youth, work assignments

When I went in, honestly at the time the policy had become more humane. My older brother had gone to the Victory Factory on the Small Third Front. [...] Not cement, but machinery. The Victory Machinery Factory, the farthest [in the mountains]. Like this, here’s Guichi, we’re at the Eight-Five Steelworks, then next came the Torch Factory, then the Forward Factory, and then the Victory Factory, the farthest inside. When they came out they had to pass by us here. That mountain in there, if they went over that they’d be in another county seat town. Why humane? Because it took into account the workers’ children. At the time, you know, a lot of workers’ children and family members had gotten sent down [to the countryside], you know, “a sea of red” and all that. If you were a sibling or a child, you could get hired in closer [to your relative] when you got sent down.

So, me, I’d gone down before ’68. But I’d just gone down as myself. Back then [we were] really very enthusiastic. After that call for students and educated youth to go to the villages, that came down at the end of the year for us, and then before the next Lunar New Year, we were the first batch who went down. Because my parents—well, in ’54 they’d gone to Support the Great Northwest, so our household was from outside [Shanghai]. My older sister graduated from the Customs Academy and she got assigned to Zhuhai in Guangdong. The third kid in our family was my older brother. At first he was at the No. 3 Machine Tool Factory. Actually, then he was an apprentice—he was three years older than me and he was a factory apprentice, so they arranged for me to Support the Interior. And he went to Anhui. At the time I was already in Jiangsu; our hometown was near Tai’an, Jiangsu, so I was sent down there. But with the [family] policy, I could have one of my siblings in a factory be my lead person. If their sibling was a worker, or if their sibling was much older, and had gotten sent down, those of us who'd already been sent down or who were getting ready to be sent down were called together to be sent somewhere closer.

[…] I was already in Tai County, [Jiangsu]. […] So I got to come back from Jiangsu. That was '71; I'd gone [to Jiangsu] in late '68. Then I went out to Guichi in '71, I think June. When I was sent down to [Jiangsu], oh, it was just like being a peasant farmer, in the countryside. It wasn't a farm or anything. They sent you to a production team, a brigade, a team, all the way to the production team. It was pretty tough in that place then, too. It was hard living then, and sometimes you'd not even have a meal to eat.

After I got to Guichi, thanks to my uncle, I went to the most remote, interior part, Bamboo Gulch, to the village. There was a Shimen production brigade, so we got sent down there. Well, it's a mountainous area, so the several of us were in that production brigade, all of us with siblings who were workers at the Victory Factory. We were the Victory Factory squad. So they had a lumber processing plant, an integrated factory. But we also had to climb the hills, chop firewood, go up and plant the fields. Those hills there have terraced fields, you know, and we planted rice there. [No, we didn't go do training-through-labor and practice pouring cement with master workers,] those folks were actually from technical and vocational middle schools, they didn't actually get sent down [to the villages]. Yes, they were a bit later than me, but they never went to [live in] the villages (Image 2.2).

When they started building [those factories], they needed land, right? […] So you took people's land and you were supposed to hire the locals as workers. There was a policy then where both sides would discuss and negotiate a deal. […] So how did I end up in the factory? Well, it was pretty strict back then. Only the children of workers could go directly into the factories, but I'd reached the public hiring period. Back then, if you had gotten sent down but you were a bit better behaved, like—have you heard this from the others? You could get transferred "up," you'd have a chance to transfer up. […] You could become a worker or leave to go to school. Yep, [we thought it was very good to become a worker.] It was like this, then—there were a few who left the commune to go study in Shanghai. But [I] just wanted to become a worker. So this quota came down to the commune and the commune handed down the quotas to the work brigades. So I was there in that commune, plus I had this connection—my brother was at the Victory Factory, so I got in when they were

Image 2.2 Woman doing "May Seventh" labor training standing in a Dawn Light Factory field, 1972

hiring. But I didn't go to the Victory Factory. I went to—in our batch, some went to Victory, some went to the docks. So basically, I started [at the docks] in May '72, the 507 Docks.

[…] These docks were actually built up by the Shanghai Harbor Authority. Some older workers at the Authority, including their leadership, and some veterans [came out]. Of course, some of the veterans also complained [about this]. [...] My post as League branch secretary wasn't assigned. So when we went in, our team was for the docks but they didn't have any young people there. Our team really became the backbone of the 507 Docks, our one team. And I remember back then, the organization—like League organization and Party organization, you had to have 'em. At the time, well, [I was promoted] to temporary League leadership probably because I performed relatively well. And then temporary leadership turned into temporary League branch secretary work, until I entered the Party. I went in '72 and joined the Party at the end of '74, then I got promoted to deputy Party branch secretary. Of course, this had a historical context, too. At the time they emphasized cadre teams [of diverse generations]. They took the cultivation of young people seriously. But it was pretty hard to join the Party back then. All those people on the docks and only two of us entered the Party.

* * *

袁彩霞 Yuan Caixia, female, Anhui native who married into a Small Third Front factory.

Keywords: conflicts, education, family, frustrations, manual labor, marriage, political problems, rural vs. urban, work assignments

I was born in Guoyang County, [Anhui], in the Huaibei [TN: the area north of the Huai River in Anhui, Jiangsu, and Henan provinces, known as an impoverished region]. When I was little we were extremely poor. We didn't have a bed; we slept on stacks of earthen bricks. Because I worshipped things from Shanghai, I used my first month's salary to buy a Shanghai-made bedsheet, and soap holders—I also liked Shanghai-made soap holders, my bicycle seat just had to be from Shanghai or else, and same for the towels I used. I saw the "sent-down youths" from Shanghai in our neighborhood walking tall, like they were kings!

[...] My family "class background" was bad, so if I wanted to marry a soldier, I'd have no chance. I'm pretty ambitious, so I decided to try the university entrance exams. I took it, took it again, and got older and older. I had a girlfriend who was worried about me being an old maid. Her older brother Ma Pinjun was the military representative for the Shanghai Steep Cliffs Small Third Front Factory, and came from the same village. One time he came home for a visit and my girlfriend told him, "Caixia hasn't married yet, if you know someone nice in your factory, link her up with him." So Ma ended up being the one to introduce me to my husband.

With someone else playing matchmaker I wouldn't really trust them, but Ma Pinjun had a lot of respect in the village and a lot of status; he for sure wouldn't trick me. So I went along with him to southern Anhui and went to the Steep Cliff Factory. Ma is my matchmaker and I'm grateful to him. These days, every year I go home for a visit, I always buy him a carton of cigarettes as a gift. [TN: Yuan's marriage certificate shows that she was 28 at the time of her wedding.]

My daddy was pretty understanding about my marriage, but my ma didn't have a lot of education and said, "You little brat, why do you have to be so high-and-mighty? Don't you have rice to eat at home? Why do you have to run off all that far off?" My salary [as an English teacher] at the time was 15 or 18 yuan a month, and I didn't spend much of it, I was mostly saving it up myself. I thought, this is my own decision, you don't want to give me any [wedding] money, I'll just use my own savings, I'll take the train to meet my partner. If it works out, it works out, and if it doesn't, whatever. My teacher said to me during a party, "eat a chicken wing, you're about to fly." My former colleagues saw me and were all so envious. My classmates and girlfriends all thought it was so wonderful to go to Shanghai. I also thought so. A girl from the village going to Shanghai! I felt constantly like I was in a dream.

The Steep Cliff Factory made microscopes and telescopes. These military factories on the Small Third Front had more men than women and some older men couldn't find wives. Shanghai women didn't want to go into the deep mountains either. So [the men] made some noise at the Shanghai Labor Bureau. The Bureau said, you can look all over the nation, even if they're from the countryside, that's fine. With these benefits, women could join the factory; their rations entitlements would be transferred to the factory. I got in because of this policy. Once I was on the Small Third Front, I gave that teacher position to my younger sister.

[…] I went to change my *hukou* registration after I got a marriage certificate in my hometown. After picking it up, the factory's human resources department would go to my county seat's grain station to change my *hukou*. When I was back home, the county people asked, "How did your rural *hukou* go to Shanghai? Can we go too?" They were really envious of me. They thought, how did this little girl from the village get to Shanghai? I grew up in the suburbs of the county seat town, and though my registration was in a Small Third Front factory in Anhui, the factory belonged to Shanghai. This was such good luck. I'd dreamed of going to Shanghai and there I really was!

[…] When I first arrived at the factory I didn't have a job. They arranged for me to go clean the bathrooms. I'd been a teacher back home and now I was sweeping toilets—I was so depressed. In fact, I even helped workers review Classical Chinese and gave extra classes for them while I was pregnant, twice a week. I did this for a few months and got several hundred yuan out of it. But this is because they saw I was a high school graduate; it was just temporary. But my main task was cleaning bathrooms. Me and several other girls who were pretty close with me, also from the countryside with similar backgrounds, all of us were cleaning bathrooms. We went into this big collective and people looked down on us, plus we were all from villages. They looked at us with kind of condescending gazes. We felt so terrible, we'd sweep and cry. Then two of them got jobs in the workshops, but my husband was pretty straight-and-narrow; he didn't have much of a special connection with the HR department. Those two might've had some sort of background, so they went to do janitorial work in the workshops, which sounded a bit better than what I was doing.

* * *

张燕芳 Zhang Yanfang, female, teacher turned production statistics and logistics cadre at a steel mill.

Keywords: conflicts, critique, Cultural Revolution, family, frustrations, marriage, political problems, violence, work assignments

I [went to the Small Third Front] because I was forced to move by the Cultural Revolution. I originally graduated from the No. 1 Normal School. Yes, to be a teacher. From No. 1, [I] came out to teach Russian … to work with East China Normal [University] to do education reform. At the time there were no foreign languages in elementary school, right? The early 60s. In the end I taught Russian for two years, then the Sino-Soviet split happened; they had a fight. After the fight they didn't teach Russian anymore. So I ended up going to do training and got transferred to Fuxing Middle School. I taught politics and was a homeroom teacher.

Then at that time—before I got to Fuxing—the Cultural Revolution began. I had a very hard time in the Cultural Revolution. I had a sign hung [around my neck]—a blackboard bigger than this [Zhang gestures], hung using steel wire. No, no, no relation to my specialty [in Russian]. They said I was a "Royalist." We were all young at the time and everybody quite wanted to be "progressive," organizationally […] in reality, we suffered a lot. What good was it all for? How hard it was! Entering the Party, being sent down to the countryside, doing the Four Cleanups [Movement]. Back then it was really […] This Cultural Revolution, you all have no way of understanding it, only people like us […] Like me, I'm 70 this year, I really had my fill of bitterness…

Spirits, well, I'm pretty good. Anyone who sees me would say I'm in good spirits. Later on, well, teachers struggled teachers, but students actually didn't struggle me. Teachers struggled teachers, then would hold struggle sessions. Our Party branch secretary would be in front; I would follow him. After the signs were hung—I had it all done to me. Being kicked with a "bang" by somebody, I got it all. Then I got angry, I stopped being a teacher. By chance my husband was at the Shanghai No. 5 Steelworks. Mm, so I followed my husband to the Shanghai No. 5 Steelworks, then to Support the Interior; I went to the Small Third Front, that's how I went. Eh, yep yep. Because of the Cultural Revolution, well, I would never be a teacher again [laughs].

[…] Yes, I was at the Logistics Department ever after. […] Logistics, I worked there until '82, when my ma passed. I had my ma and pa in Shanghai, and my son, three in all. […] I had my son in '70. When I left [for Anhui] he was only a little over one year old. I had him in Shanghai. No no no, I had the kid then—then left with my husband [for Anhui].

* * *

赵惠瑛 Zhao Huiying, female, worker and kindergarten teacher at a Small Third Front steelworks.

Keywords: family, homesickness, living conditions, manual labor, work assignments

At the time my older brother had gone to Xinjiang and my younger brother had gone to Jilin, and they sort of took care of me by letting me go to the factory. So, I went to the Small Third Front.

[…] I didn't directly go to the kindergarten. The kindergarten hadn't opened yet then. There weren't any houses or buildings there when I got there. It was really hard when we first got there. We all lived in open-air shelters. I was working in the factory, working in a factory workshop, workshop No. 1; it was the steel foundry inside and the electric supply outside. I was an electrician. When they needed power for the steel, I'd open up the power supply. I did that for about five, six years! I went in '70. At first when we got there we had these broken roads, and we built the houses! We were all doing such things.

[...] So little by little the factory buildings, the office buildings were built up. At the time we were all living in open-air huts ... multi-level. When it snowed heavily outside the snowflakes would drift in the cracks of the hut. We lived in this kind of place. It was really tough, but people at the time thought it was pretty okay. People at the time were very simple, very innocent. When it was Lunar New Year and we had to go back [to Anhui], we'd all cry together, and we'd be all right again after having a good cry.

* * *

朱岳林 Zhu Yuelin and 王燕珍 Wang Yanzhen, husband and wife. Zhu was a cadre at a Small Third Front steelworks and eventually for the entire Rear Base; Wang was a worker at the steel mill who eventually rose to an office job.

Keywords: Cultural Revolution, children, family, living conditions, marriage, medical issues, work assignments

Zhu: I went with my wife [to the Third Front]. Why, you say? Because at the time I was at the May Seventh cadre school [TN: where cadres around the country were "sent down" for manual labor to the countryside during the Cultural Revolution]; they were deploying the May Seventh cadre schools. I originally worked at the provincial liaison office in Shanghai. When I was in the cadre school, they put out the "Four Facings Toward." The cadres in the cadre school also had to do the "Four Facings Toward." We cadres had to go to places like Meishan, Heilongjiang.

At the time [my wife's] health wasn't great. Her health was always poor. I thought, if I left alone, she'd be left with two kids, and it'd be hard. ... She was at the Shanghai No. 5 Steelworks, heh heh. The Shanghai No. 5 Steelworks was just planning to construct the Eight-Five Steelworks, a Small Third Front factory. [...] So the two of us talked it over, and thought, if that was how it was, rather than having just me leave alone, we might as well go together, so we decided to go together to the Eight-Five Steelworks. But she wasn't in good health, and the factory knew it, so she stayed behind at first at the Eight-Five Steelworks Shanghai operations office.

[...] So we were saying, this process. So we decided to go to the Eight-Five Steelworks in Anhui, in '70 [...] in the fourth quarter of '69, we decided. After deciding, I went to Anhui around the Lunar New Year, before the New Year. I went first to Anhui. ... I spent Lunar New Year there, Lunar New Year in '70. She was working at the Shanghai operations office, working, I left alone first.

Wang: Well, as for me, at this time, when he left I hadn't been transferred, I hadn't left yet, I had to take care of the kids and I wasn't in great health. When they were planning [the Eight-Five Steelworks] they needed people in Shanghai, so I was like the eyes of the plant among these people in Shanghai, I was overseeing everything, doing a bit of everything everywhere. Information, personnel movements, telephone contact and so forth, I oversaw it all.

[...] Zhu: We later brought the kids.

Wang: We brought them later. At first it wasn't good for them, at first, because...

Zhu: The conditions there were bad.

Further Reading

On the PRC's "Class Background" System

Aminda Smith, *Thought Reform and China's Dangerous Classes: Reeducation, Resistance, and the People*. Lanham, MD: Rowman & Littlefield, 2013.

Jeremy Brown and Matthew D. Johnson eds., *Maoism at the Grassroots: Everyday life in China's Era of High Socialism*. Cambridge, MA: Harvard University Press, 2015. Part I. Crimes, labels, and punishment, 19–128.

Brian DeMare, *Land Wars: The Story of China's Agrarian Revolution*. Stanford: Stanford University Press, 2019, Ch. 3.

Michael Schoenhals, "Demonising Discourse in Mao Zedong's China: People vs. Non People," *Totalitarian Movements and Political Religions* 8: 3–4 (2007), 465–482.

Tsai, Wen-hui, *Class Struggle and Deviant Labeling in Mao's China: Becoming Enemies of the People*. Lewiston, NY: Edwin Mellen Press, 2001.

Covell Meyskens, *Mao's Third Front: The Militarization of Cold War China*. Cambridge: Cambridge University Press, 2020.

On the "Sending Down" and Exile of Urban Dwellers

Thomas P. Bernstein, *Up to the Mountains and Down to the Villages: The Transfer of Youth from Urban to Rural China*. New Haven: Yale University Press, 1977.

Michel Bonnin, *The Lost Generation: The Rustication of China's Educated Youth (1968–1980)*, Hong Kong: Chinese University of Hong Kong Press, 2013.

Alexander Casella, "The Nanniwan May 7th Cadre School," *The China Quarterly* 53 (1973), 153–157.

Sing-Nan Fen, "The May 7 Cadre Schools in the People's Republic of China: 1968–1976." *Administration & Society* 18:1(1986), 29–43.

Emily Honig and Xiaojian Zhao, *Across the Great Divide: The Sent-down Youth Movement in Mao's China, 1968–1980*. Cambridge: Cambridge University Press, 2019.

Yihong Pan, *Tempered in the Revolutionary Furnace: China's Youth in the Rustication Movement*. Lanham, MD: Lexington Books, 2003.

Helena K. Rene, *China's Sent-Down Generation: Public Administration and the Legacies of Mao's Rustication Program*. Washington, DC: Georgetown University Press, 2013.

CHAPTER 3

On the Job

Translator's Note

Work—either in the production of military-industrial goods or in auxiliary and support roles in and around the factories—was the raison d'être of the Small Third Front. Working in a state-owned enterprise like the Small Third Front factories was a coveted position, but the work itself was often, according to almost all the narrators below, brutally difficult and demanding. From physicians and logistics staff to steel workers and drivers, hours could be long and tasks arduous, both physically and emotionally. Holidays and days off were scanty, and pay, though set to the Shanghai urban standard and therefore much higher than what rural people in neighboring villages could hope for, was modest, with few raises over the years. Factories had unions, but these were run by Party members and were more about dealing with workers' quotidian conflicts and human resource issues than about negotiating on workers' behalf for improved working conditions or remuneration; in any case, the "management" in this case was the Party-state itself. Workers' outcomes—from raises to plum job assignments to the other aspects of life dictated by work units, like living quarters or extra visitation leaves—depended heavily on idiosyncratic relationships with the various cadres and leaders, what

Y. Xu, Y. Y. Wang, *Everyday Lives in China's Cold War Military-Industrial Complex*, Palgrave Studies in Oral History,
https://doi.org/10.1007/978-3-030-99688-8_3

some scholars characterize as client-patron relationships that were almost familial in nature.[1]

In fact, withstanding harsh working conditions, being separated for long periods from kin and friends, and even risking physical injuries on the job were publicized as signs of good citizenship and political loyalty. Metaphors and figures of war and victory that drew on the CCP's early days as underground agents and guerillas, as well as the PRC's Cold War conflicts, lent discussions of ideal workers in all roles a militaristic flavor that was especially strong given the Small Third Front's status as a national defense secret. Work also seamlessly meshed into the relational and everyday lives of our narrators, most of whom entered the Small Third Front as very young people; they were defined in their workplaces by their duties and roles, and the workplace also shaped their social, familial, and emotional lives.

Questions for Discussion

1. How do narrators remember their work lives on the Small Third Front? What are the commonalities and differences, and what do you think causes these divergences in recollections?
2. Are there aspects of any of the accounts that surprise you? What about elements that are the least surprising to you, either in substance or in how the narrators recount them?

* * *

丁秀玉 Ding Xiuyu, female, technician at a steel mill, later rose to cadre positions in Small Third Front Party organs, including head of the Birth Planning office.

Keywords: camaraderie, children, conflicts, education, food, living conditions, manual labor, men vs. women, nostalgia, pay and benefits, work schedules

[In] '71 [I went in and began doing production statistics work]. In '72 [...] early '73, I guess, [I stopped]. Then, they transferred me to the factory administration offices. Overseeing [workers'] daily life. Oh, I was

[1] Walder (1988).

so delighted...our workers wanted to bring their families. At that time we all had family housing inside [the factory compound]. I was a family member, right? Even though the little guy didn't make it in—my son was in Shanghai. My husband and I got in. Bringing family members—some had the old and the young together. About 6000 people in total. These 6000 people were like a mini-society. Our Party secretary, our factory head, they were like the heads of this giant household. Births, deaths, illnesses, aging, they had to oversee it all. Today it's like, you—who had a baby? The logistics people had to pay special attention [to them]. At this point they switched me into logistics. The two older comrades in logistics, they—Party members and cadres at that time, I have to say—you can't understand. They're nothing like cadres today. Nothing at all. [Interviewer remarks that many people, if not all, have said the same.] Yes. Oh, yes. Our number one—there were three of us in our [logistics cadres group], I counted as the rookie kid, so the day-to-day miscellaneous things all were my responsibility. Yes, at the factory admin offices. At that time we were called the logistics group.

Yes, logistics. But we had to oversee every bit of daily life, eating and voiding and all, for over 6000 people in the entire factory. Under our department there was the medical clinic, equivalent to a hospital, bigger than even the local hospital now. Commissary, all the cafeterias, the nursery, the little vegetable market, we oversaw all of it. No, the nursery didn't belong to the Education department, but to us. Starting with kindergarten, it belongs to the school. Yes, yes, [the nursery was still logistics]. We had a higher collective. The higher collective specifically oversaw them. Oh [...] our logistics [department] was pretty big. There were the vegetable market workers [...] specifically there were about...in my time, when the labor and compensation officer went to visit his family, I even helped him do [his work]; there had to be about over 300 people. Yes, a lot.

[...] Day and night—especially after I transferred to logistics, I was busy day and night. Because there was just no free time. Sometimes the pastries in the cafeteria in the mornings were no good and the masses would take a lot of umbrage, and I'd have to follow up with the canteen people—meaning, I'd say to them, you all got to do something novel once in a while, make some fried dough sticks, right? Make some open-top steamed dumplings, make something [new]. So sometimes if you didn't go yourself, they'd say, "Why, you—" because the early shift was very tough. If you had that shift, you were up from 2 a.m. Other folks would come buy breakfast at six or seven, and this breakfast wasn't just for the workers. Family members would also be buying it, and you had to prepare a lot. So I'd have to go follow the shifts myself. Then at night, too—you know?

So I always felt like I seemed not to have any energy to carry on anything romantic, or very fun. None! I just felt very tired. Then say the beer came in from Shanghai. Beer used always to be in square frames—right, you've seen it, in thermoses. You won't go carry it? No, you've got to play the packing plant worker. When the pork came, half-chest after half-chest of pork, you'd go together to move it. Cutlassfish, [frozen] block after block, 40 pounds per block, the trucks coming in and there's not enough labor power [to move them]; I also had to [pitch in].

People back then weren't like how they are now. Now everyone's real careful with their bodies, but back then it was like putting your life on the line, everyone…so if you ask Wang Wenqing, Ding Xiuyu, someone as short and small as Ding, they'd do [this work] too. Really. Like Yang Xiuzhen, she'd really work it. She'd work—I did everyday goods, she was really [moving] raw [industrial] materials; how tough that was! So sometimes people would work so they were hardly like people. Really hard. So Yang Xiuzhen, I really respect her. She worked harder than [people] in the workshops, because her stuff was tough, dirty, heavy.

Yes, we oversaw this too in logistics. So we would go buy produce and put it in our little vegetable market. Our special market was all stocked by us. […] 100% perfect doesn't exist. There's no way to please every single person either. But I felt like life was very fulfilling. Anyway, you wouldn't even be given time to sit down. [Working still made me] pretty happy. Because everyone—interpersonally, the relationships were really good. Like our Party secretary still has good relations with us now. Yes, [Chen] Suosuo. Even now we get along well with him. Why? Because there [in Anhui] he truly cared for the comrades a lot, speaking fairly. "Look out for yourself." You know?

[…] [Working in the Logistics Department] was very odds-and-ends. Work stress, I guess I'd say, was pretty high. Why? Because all these people had to eat, had to be clothed, had to [have things to] use, right? Yeah, if there were conflicts anywhere, you had to rush over like a firefighter. Your non-staple food supply—the foods in storage you had to carefully mind. How much fish? How much meat? At all times you had to supply information to our boss. Our boss was really good.

[…] Leaders back then, with ordinary folks, with people like us—theoretically we'd count as mid-level cadres, right? But the bosses didn't have a front. They really cared—not just caring about us mid-level cadres, no, but including [people] under [us]. I remember in the No. 3 Workshop there was a worker, really a nuisance. He was always late to work, not putting in effort, one of those. There's always those, right? At the time, you know, they'd often scold him in the workshop, always trying to help him and whatnot. Anyway, he didn't have a very good reputation. Even those of us at the admin offices heard about him, right? But his parents had passed on, and there was only a younger brother in Shanghai. His brother got sick or had something happen, I can't remember. But Chen Suosuo wouldn't look at you differently because you were off the pace. No. He'd help when he was supposed to help, and take care of him, had him go work at the Shanghai office. This kind of comrade was really good.

All these things for logistics, the people with most potential under us were the team captains. In reality the core leadership was just us three, but under us were the team captains for each team. The head of the dining team, also from Shandong, people called him Little Shandong, also a retired cadre, also passed away now. These comrades were really good. There were lots [of people] under the dining team. Finance, including the produce buyers, the little vegetable market, and such. That was the dimension covering what was served in the restaurants. Another was—now what was it called—they specially oversaw stationery and office supplies, and the commissary store and such. And a team of drivers, separate. And refrigeration. The machine maintenance group, lots of equipment; if the [dough] mixer broke down or whatnot, they'd have to go fix it. And sometimes the trucks needed fixing too.

[...] "Though the sparrow is small, it has a full set of organs." It was like a whole little society, you had to mind all of it. Yes, the team heads would oversee [these specific tasks]. But if they encountered some issue, they'd come to you to sort it out. What issues? Anything; you'd have to show up. You couldn't possibly sit in the office every day. You had to check on every team. So I'm very practiced at riding a bike. That was all hilly roads there, ahh, charging down[hill], charging over there, whatnot. Wherever there was something going on. No, I don't think [anything left a deep impression, no especially thorny problems], I just feel like it was very odds-and-ends. And nonstop, anyway.

At that time, you got one day a week [of break], one day's time. Just Sunday. No two-day weekends back then. Two-day weekends were later on. Why do you think the Eight-Five Steelworks people all have such good relationships, up till now? Because 24 hours [a day], except the time you shut your eyes and stayed at home [to sleep], you were together.

Right, don't you think? So everyone was really empathetic. You get me, and I get you too. Usually if there were a meeting you did have to go [for things like March 8th International Women's Day activities], but not all the time. Typically this kind of [event] would be put on by the workers' union.

As for ourselves, well, for instance Women's Day, the admin offices would give some money and we'd also put in some money and buy something for the women, something to reward them. So we were away from Shanghai—the biggest difference between working in the workshop and in logistics was that I could contact Shanghai very conveniently [in logistics]. Back in the production workshop there was nothing to say. I was just 24 hours, going to work or being at home, right? Then there was family housing. But in logistics, if I wanted something, people said to me, "Can you help out?"; one word and I'd right away write up a note, I'd chip in some of my own money toward the money for the driver and ask [the driver] to help bring a little something. Yes, [it was convenient], very convenient, contact was very quick. Because there was me in logistics here, and another setup in Shanghai, to ensure this material provisioning. I couldn't possibly have one truck carry everything. There was a transfer point in Shanghai. Just in the Shanghai No. 5 Steelworks office building, down[stairs], there was a room, just for the use of Eight-Five Steelworks logistics.

Yes, everyone working together, very happily, right? Not always so seriously, "You're the office head, you can't be talked to." If you work together, then everything can be really easily discussed. So I got used [to that]. In Shanghai, well, what was my work? Even though I was still deputy secretary, then it was restructured. Then I was still deputy chief in the outpost office, but I still oversaw logistics, our logistics. At that time [in the steelworks] there weren't secretaries or chiefs; at that time it was just—secretary, deputy secretary. I was deputy and our number one was the secretary. Not the Party committee, just the Logistics Department. Our work unit at the time was overseen by the Party General Branch, then it belonged to a branch—the mid-levels below [the plant] belonged to the Party branch. Because our Eight-Five Steelworks was set up by the Party General Branch. [The entire factory had one] Party committee, with Party branches below it.

Then after coming to Shanghai, well, I sat at the offices of the Shanghai outpost office. You go to load a shipment of cigarettes, I'd also go load with them. When they packed beer in Shanghai, they'd be from the No. 1

Food Store—back then beer was all rationed, you know. How much would you want per person? Sometimes they'd go directly to the beer plant here to pack [shipments], then put them in the warehouse after packing. We had a special warehouse, an intermediary warehouse, that is to say, a truck leaves the plant, comes to your intermediary warehouse at the outpost office to [get] the [materials]. Often, I mean, I'd even go to the plant admin offices. I was still [overseeing] how many truckloads of stuff was in the warehouse and what we needed to load. Sometimes, [things] like meat and such had to be directly pulled [to the factory], right? Typically we could be an intermediary here. Sometimes, for example, if the warehouse couldn't fit [things], we'd have to ask people to borrow their freezers. Everything had to be moved by someone! That's what I worked on.

[...] After I went back [to Anhui], my boss at the July 21st University [TN: Cultural Revolution-era part-time programs set up by factories based on a July 1968 comment by Mao Zedong], the Party Secretary—I was deputy—he came to talk to me, saying that the university wasn't going to be able to continue. It was really hard to have a factory-run university. I'd definitely be leaving there, and he asked me where I'd like to go. I said I really liked being a teacher and wanted to be an elementary school teacher. The Secretary said, well, you probably can't be a teacher; you have to have a title. I said, what title. He said, you can be Party Branch Secretary. I had no way around it. The leadership had arranged it. Originally we were one Branch with the elementary and middle schools and kindergarten, one united set. Then they felt like the elementary and middle schools and kindergarten should be separated out, because the middle school was at Ershibakai while the elementary school was in Xihua, really far away. So they requested a separation and basically a lot of people went to the middle school and the elementary school was short-handed.

So I got transferred to the elementary school as Party Branch Secretary. Yes, including the kindergarten, yes. In total two elementary schools, one at Ershibakai, closer to there, and another at Xihua, but that was a bigger school, plus a kindergarten. I went on January 1, '80. [...] Being Party secretary in a school was really a kind of formality. The school was the responsibility of the principal; in my mind, anyway, it was the principal who was boss. The branch secretary at most would hold some meetings, relay some situational reports. On June 1st [Children's Day], you go give a speech. No big deal. During faculty meetings, you go talk to them. You can't resolve real issues. For example, if a teacher says they have problems and need to go back to Shanghai, I can't help them, because the principal had already assigned courses to them and I can't change those arrangements. So, I thought that this secretary job wasn't so much fun. In these years I was secretary, we got a raise once. At that time, raises were tiered [by performance], so that burden fell on my shoulders.

* * *

葛鼎学 Ge Dingxue, male, worker at a Small Third Front steelworks.

Keywords: frustrations, living conditions, manual labor, medical issues, work assignments, work schedules

When we first arrived, the [Eight-Five Steelworks] arranged for me to go do blacksmithing in the forging workshop. Our nation was preparing for war back then, and the components on the 57 mm anti-aircraft guns were hammered out by us by hand. This was an integrated process; we used forging presses and pneumatic hammers to hammer those parts into shape. I did that for I guess five or six years.

They say there are three kinds of hard lots in the world: poling a boat, beating metal, and grinding tofu. I guess I got one of them. In the factory workshop, they had the exhaust fans blowing right on us from behind and in front of us was the steel that'd just come out of the hot furnace that we had to beat into shape. In front it was burning hot, in the back it was very cold, and most people got bad backs out of that. It wasn't long before I got switched to the storeroom because they needed a serious, careful person. Back then I'd been my class president and the group leader for youth group.

Life then was really boring, living there in the mountains. Eight hours' work, like me in the forge, I'd go in in the morning and in the afternoon, but after I finished there was nothing else to do. We lived in the dormitories and ate there too. When it was quiet on the job we'd also sneak back to our bedrooms (Image 3.1).

* * *

顾国籁 Gu Guolai, male, Anhui native. Technician who rose to administrative leadership roles in Anhui.

Keywords: food, frustrations, living conditions, manual labor, marriage, pay and benefits, work assignments

Back then, well, I didn't mind [the difficulties of life]. Lemme tell you, not long after I began the job, the work unit barely had anybody in it, and I cooked lunch by myself. Yes, the peasants helped cook. The difficulties,

Image 3.1 Color photograph of worker ID pass from the Dawn Light Factory, 1970s–1980s

well, I won't talk about it. Because it was physical labor, I had to upgrade my food. I'd be clearing stone, then come back for lunch and still not feel full after a meal of red-braised pork, haha. I'd eat a pound of rice, a pound of braised pork, and still be hungry.

[...] At first my salary was 42.50, the national standard, for Category 4 or Category 5 areas. [...] I'd use it up, going back and forth to Shanghai visiting the family! [I married] very late, '75. My wife was a worker at the time, in the Tongyong Machine Factory, yes, just in Guichi County. It used to be in Qingfengling, but not anymore. Back then, because she'd studied wireless electronics, she was put at the radio station. In the radio station it was too quiet, nothing to do; she oversaw the storage. Then she felt it to be really boring, so she requested to become a worker.

* * *

胡善莉 Hu Shanli, female, Anhui native hired into a chemical factory as a concessionary worker.

Keywords: living conditions, work assignments, work schedules

At that time the factory commissary store needed someone, so they took one look at my file and moved me [out from the training farm]. [...] I worked at the Weixin Factory commissary store [selling things] the whole time; I never worked on the factory floor [...] until the Shanghainese left. I went into the factory in '75 and worked until '86. Then when the factory was handed over to local administration, there was no work for me anymore.

[...] I was the stocker and the sales clerk! When I first went to the store, those older Shanghai workers would say, "Hey, this little girl is good!" They all knew that before I went to the factory I'd run a little shop for a few years by myself. ...There were several people, taking turns. There was a day shift from 7 a.m. When the shop opened to 8:30. Then at midday, the workers got off at 11:30 am, we'd open at 11, keep it open until 1:30 pm or so. The workers who had early shift would get off at 4:30 pm, so we opened again at 4, and do it until 7 p.m. This way the shop was open three times a day.

* * *

季美华 Ji Meihua, female, kindergarten teacher at a Small Third Front steel mill.

Keywords: camaraderie, education, living conditions, nostalgia, work assignments, work schedules

The atmosphere was very good, not like now, with these gift-giving customs, and no teachers would be demanding this or that. Being a kindergarten teacher was most objective. You were making an honest bowl of rice. Elementary school, middle school, high school teachers, you'd be looking at your promotion rate [onto further schooling]. The kids in kindergarten, you can't really lecture them; there's no promotion rate to speak of. You were a teacher based on your own goodwill. I'm sure there were irresponsible ones, but they'd be going against their consciences. You had to have a loving heart. When you see a kid being naughty and causing trouble, you would also have to reprimand him, but then after a time you'd talk sensibly with them. Sometimes [they'd cry]. The naughty ones didn't cry; the naughtier the less likely to cry. My Mandarin is pretty standardized; it's probably because I was a teacher. When I was teaching back then I'd have to prepare the lesson first and pronounce it up to standard. [Class prep] wasn't a big deal.

[...] I could prep for class right in the classroom. When the kids were napping I'd prep. They'd nap from noon until two or three pm; all this time I could be preparing in my office; I didn't have to do it at home. We were four or five to an office. After they finished construction there were more offices. The atmosphere [in the offices] was good; we were really lighthearted. Very few rivalries and conflicts.

[...] Some kids would arrive early. Each class had an early group of children whose parents were on the early shift too. There were more kids in Shanghai, 30 to 40 kids in each class. [On the Small Third Front] there were only 20-some kids. Commuting was tough, but the work was the same though there were more children. Teaching work is all about the same. It was just a longer time on the road. No changes in the curriculum in Shanghai. Yes, I was still leading my old classes, telling stories and such.

* * *

吕建昌Lü Jianchang, male, Small Third Front pharmacist at the Ruijin Hospital.

Keywords: finances, living conditions, medicine, political training, poverty, rural vs. urban, work assignments, work schedules

I worked first at the pharmacy department in the hospital. There was an outpatient pharmacy and an inpatient one, a sterile compounding room and an ordinary one (we called it the "drug factory"), several divisions in all. I worked in all of these. For example, handing over prescriptions for outpatients, going to check the expenses and supplies in storage, et cetera. Some of the medicines we'd made ourselves in our compounding rooms. Like some prepared Chinese medicines, some drinkable medicines, some creams and pastes, we could make all of these ourselves because the compounding rooms were well equipped. Inpatient pharmacy was exclusively for people staying in the hospital. It was in the sickroom area, and you started work at 8 a.m. and at 8:30 [the previous shift] ended. After that, doctors would do their rounds and by 10 a.m. the nurses would have the prescriptions all ready to go and give us the scripts to have us fill them and send them out. The sterile compounding room often made glucose saline, because there was a lot of demand for it and it'd be impossible to only ship it from Shanghai, so we had to make it ourselves. Now we'd talk about it entrepreneurially, because you could sell that, but at the time we didn't have this financial sense. Everybody ate from the same big pot; your salary was 36 yuan and so was mine; we didn't think about this at all.

In late 1974 me and a colleague from the pharmacy (a friend from secondary school who'd come to Ruijin with me) were transferred to the political work department of the hospital. The hospital wanted to develop but lacked staff so they moved us up as "special cultivation targets." There was the organization and propaganda teams in this department, just like the organization bureaus and propaganda bureaus today with a Party committee. But apart from training and evaluating cadres, the organization team also included HR work for the work unit; the propaganda team mostly oversaw political study and day-to-day propaganda. During the CultRev, there was a lot of political study, a real ton. Every week you had two political study sessions, and also "daily read-alouds" and all that. Every day there was a task; you had to find texts and write them up. One was to follow directives from above, another was to also use your own brains to organize people to study.

[…] In order not to "separate ourselves from the masses," there were rules then that we cadres had to go do labor every Thursday. Labor at the hospital was things like planting watermelons, gathering herbs, doing gardening work, digging a fishpond. Our traditional Chinese medicine pharmacy had an old wizard; he knew that Anhui had a lot of Cherokee roses and wormwood and you could go gather it; basically he knew all about the herbal medicines in Anhui, so pretty much every week we'd go gather herbs. Because our political work department leadership would go, our head honcho Old Cui and his second-in-command Zhang Guifang would go, so the setup was pretty nice. First the driving team would get us a car, and we'd eat out for lunch.

[…] According to Chairman Mao's June 26 Directive [of 1965], every year we'd organize a healthcare team to go to the nearby villages. Actually, it was really basic, just a few doctors pulled from internal medicine, orthopedics, gynecology, and pediatrics and sent to local towns or villages to do a circuit. But really, this was a pretty good practice. They'd see you were a fancy big city doctor and would let you treat a lot of their problems, plus these treatments were basically free. We'd give them some medicine without asking for money. This was covered by the hospital budget because the finances of the hospital then were all covered by the government; whatever you needed was allotted from above.

The Ruijin Hospital was often in the red back then. We often had to go ask debtors for payment; we called it "debt collection," jokingly. Every year as we neared the Lunar New Year, we'd organize a team in the hospital to go to the nearby villages, the farthest to Tunxi. Our hospitals also served local patients, and when they came to see us, they didn't have deposits or anything. They came and we treated them. If they had to stay overnight, then there'd be a lot of costs in the sickroom. If you couldn't pay, you'd just put it on credit. In theory, if you hadn't cleared the bill, you couldn't leave, because you had to go through the whole exit procedure (like how graduating students had to get stamps from each department). If you still had money outstanding, you wouldn't get the stamp and you couldn't leave the hospital gates. But if the hospital didn't let them go, they'd sneak off. They'd even abandon their bags and effects and leave secretly. But when they registered they had their names and addresses, so we'd go search for them with that information. Typically, we could find them, but the patient wouldn't be able to pay. They were very poor.

Aside from having logistical staff go ask for repayment, the hospital would also get some healthcare workers and administrative staff to go. I've been on these trips—after I'd gotten transferred to administration—and I went with a colleague who worked at the hospital's little commissary store. We went to a patient in She County to collect on his debts. Transportation wasn't very convenient there. You had to ship things in and out by boat. But stuff was very cheap. Some people say that the "Peach-Blossom Spring" that Tao Yuanming wrote about was there [TN: reference to the tale of a hidden utopia from the early fifth century CE]. Of course, that was just a legend, but anyway, getting in and out of there was really tough, that was real. After the patient stayed at our hospital, though his illness was under control, he hadn't fully recovered, and that was when he fled back home. After he ran away, he ended up dying. He owed a ton of money.

There were quite a few of these cases back then: we'd go looking for a patient with fees outstanding, we'd ask "Is so-and-so here"? They'd say yes. "Did they stay at the hospital?" They'd say yes. We'd ask if they owed such-and-such amount of money, and they'd also admit that too, but they just wouldn't be able to pay it back. And we'd even go first to their People's Communes and have [cadres] from the Commune go down to the village with us. This was very standardized. We'd send an introduction letter to the commune saying who we were looking for and how much they owed. One year, I remember I went with a commune secretary. We were driven to the commune headquarters and then walked to a village together. After we found [the patient's] house, we saw that this person was poor beyond belief. His house truly had not a stick of furniture, just one broken bedframe and one broken stove and the four bare walls.

At the time, we had rules that whenever we went out, the hospital would cover only very few expenses. You could go eat with the locals. He couldn't give us much to eat, just a few mouthfuls of watery gruel and a few bites of pickles. He was so poor that I was embarrassed to drink too much of his gruel, so I stayed hungry, just like him. I told the people with me, forget it, forget it, because there was no way we were getting paid. Even if we waited there in his house, even if we stayed overnight with him.

He was very polite and said he truly could not pay us. We reported these things all to the hospital once we returned. The hospital had no way to deal with it either. Ever year they had to request a bunch of debts to be forgiven by the higher-ups, just like a bank with bad loans. Every year our hospital had to get rid of a lot of bad loans, all of them owed by patients. The government would pay for these back then, because hospitals were fully state-funded back then.

Our rules meant we were open to folks from Small Third Front factories too. How'd they come to see us? They had weekly shuttles, because the factories had their own clinics, like a school hospital. Small issues could be cleared up there, but with serious or urgent illness they'd have a special car drive to us, because the distances between factories and work units were very big. Two hours was considered pretty close, driving all over these windy mountain roads. If it was an urgent case then we'd immediately go into resuscitation without talking about fees or whatever, because if it's from a factory there wouldn't be much of an issue. It was all [through] labor insurance; they wouldn't leave it unpaid.

[…] Some local patients came from towns and cities. Our hospital did really well, locally, because our treatments were high quality. The county-level hospitals around us could definitely not compete with us, and even the regional Huangshan hospital couldn't, so their leading cadres often came to us to get treated. The municipal committee secretary, the Revolutionary Committee head, would come to us if they got sick and stay in our inpatient rooms. One deputy provincial governor for Anhui also stayed with us. The local leadership was very cordial to us and strongly supported our work. Whatever we needed, they'd provide as much as they could.

* * *

邱云德 Qiu Yunde, male, pharmacist and Rear Base medical cadre.

Keywords: communications, Cultural Revolution, family, medical issues, medicine, politically correct, rural vs. urban, travel and transportation, work assignments, work schedules

The Rear Base Health and Hygiene Team (RBHH for short) was set up in 1969, not long after the Shanghai Small Third Front was set up. Staff were mainly drawn from the Shanghai No. 2 Hospital (today's Jiaotong University Hospital) and from the municipal Department of Health. […] Another team member was a doctor from the Shanghai Occupational

Disease Hospital who looked after the day-to-day medical work. The team [...] mostly was responsible for inspecting and operationalizing the basic buildup of the four Rear Base hospitals, the staff and equipment for operations, and acquiring the medical equipment and so forth.

The hospitals included, first, the Ruijin Hospital built by the East is Red Hospital (today's Ruijin Hospital) back in Shanghai affiliated with the No. 2 Hospital, with 200 beds. It served the Rear Base headquarters, Jixi, She County, Xiuning, Yi County, Qimen, and other areas including 32 Small Third Front enterprises. Second, there was the Gutian Hospital, with 150 beds, set up by the Worker-Peasant-Soldier Hospital (later renamed the No. 3 People's Hospital, and today's Renji Hospital) affiliated with the No. 2 Hospital. Gutian served Ningguo, Quande, and the Ling'an region in Zhejiang, a total of 29 Small Third Front enterprises. Third was the Changjiang Hospital set up by the Number One People's Hospital under the city Department of Health, also 150 beds, overseeing Guichi and environs, including the Eight-Five Steelworks and nine other major factories. Fourth was Tianshan Hospital under Changning District, with 100 beds, that oversaw eight work units in the Dongzhi area. [...] When we arrived in June 1970, Ruijin, Gutian, and Changjiang were already fully designed and had begun laying foundations.

[...] Ruijin Hospital was built in a mountain gulch called "Toad Pit" in Xiong's Road Village six kilometers away from the Jixi county town, relatively close to the RBHH headquarters; the other three were rather far away. Gutian was in a valley in the Hule area of Ningguo County, about 45 kilometers away. Changjiang was in the mountains of Meijie in Guichi County, even further—you had to pass through Quande, Jing, Nanling, Qingyang counties to get there from Jixi, about 250 kilometers. The Tianshan Hospital was going to be built in Dongzhi County near the Jiangxi border to serve seven work units, and you had to travel through She, Tunxi, Xiuning, Yi, Qimen, Shitai counties to get there, also about 200 kilometers' distance. If we were taking our own car to inspect these hospitals, it would take us about ten days. Half that time was spent on uneven, winding, narrow mountain roads that were rarely paved and were filled with potholes; it was very difficult going.

Apart from using small vehicles to travel directly to the hospitals, the RBHH typically used an old-fashioned hand-cranked telephone to communicate with them. Because the communications technology was so backward, it was extremely difficult and time-consuming to make a call.

Either you couldn't get the call out, or if you did, you wouldn't be able to make out what they were saying on the line. The other person's voice would be as faint as a mosquito's buzzing and you had to shout and yell to be able to hear each other. Sometimes you had to squat under your desk for a little quiet to hear them. This situation didn't improve until after the Rear Base communications network was completed in 1971.

Taking the car to various medical work units was also very challenging. From the RBHH headquarters to Changjiang Hospital in Guichi it was a whole day's ride with lunch in Nanling or Qingyang county. Restaurants in the county town had simple offerings, with mashed taro balls on the side. Once you got to the hospital and figured out the situation, it was impossible to get back the same day, so you stayed in a bed that the construction crew were using (in a local farmer's home), or in a shabby little hostel in a nearby country town lit with oil lamps where you'd often be bitten by the bedbugs on the bed boards and you'd never get a good night's rest. Cars weren't in good shape then, either. Our main transport was an old-fashioned "Roma" off-road vehicle, plus the roads were awful, so it constantly broke down en route. Good thing our drivers (from the Shanghai Emergency Rescue Brigade) had a lot of experience. We basically never had any major traffic incidents.

[...] In June 1970, just on the eve of the anniversary of Chairman Mao putting out his June 26 Directive to "place the priority of medical work into the villages" [in 1965], with our planned hospitals not yet complete, the Shanghai Ruijin Hospital organized a group of about 20 medical and nursing staff to go into the mountains ahead of time. Beginning on June 26, 1970, they set up a temporary clinic in the hospital staff dormitories that'd just been completed to offer healthcare services to the Small Third Front workers and local people (Image 3.2).

[...] Not long after the Ruijin Hospital began its temporary clinic, one farmer from She County suffered a serious accident when setting alight some explosives to blast a hillside for stones. He was blinded in one eye and covered in blood; the situation was critical. They heard that the Shanghai doctors had set up in Jixi so they rushed the patient to the dormitory clinic. The medical staff saw this gravely wounded patient with hardly an intact inch of skin on him and mobilized without hesitating. They did their very best to use the basic equipment and medicines to clean his head, torso, and limbs, operate on him, and care for him closely. There was no sickroom so they put him on a temporary sickbed in the dorm, resuscitating him and nursing him round the clock and through the night.

Image 3.2 A Small Third Front medic team walking into Lixin Village, Ningguo County, in the 1970s, collection of Gu Mingyue

This patient could not recover his vision in that one wounded eye, but he managed to heal. From that point, the dedication and skill of Shanghai doctors in tending to the injured and ill spread throughout the southern Anhui mountains. They kept up that temporary clinic until the hospital was officially open.

[...] The hospital equipment and care had to be first class; we had to be "small but complete"—not large scale, but with every specialty represented. The Shanghai-based hospitals truly put in a lot of support in human resources and material goods. Many accomplished medical staff were transferred into the mountains. Apart from the standard specialties like internal medicine, orthopedics, gynecology, pediatrics, ENT and optometrists, and traditional Chinese medicine, we even had neurosurgeons, cardiologists, and burn specialists.

[...] In 1971, three of the four hospitals (except Tianshan) opened for patients. Because the doctors were skilled and ethical, they not only quickly gained the trust of Shanghai Small Third Front workers but also the warm reception of local cadres and masses, especially peasant farmers. Their fame spread through southern Anhui, and patients from neighboring Zhejiang, Jiangxi, and the northern shore of the Yangtze River, like Anqing and elsewhere, also came to seek treatment.

As the number of patients gradually grew, the originally planned spaces for the hospitals became insufficient so we had to expand. By 1975, the Ruijin Hospital was up to nearly 250 beds and Gutian and Changjiang Hospitals were also over 150 each. Though work was very busy, in order to build good relations with the locals, if any of the people's hospitals in the counties where the hospitals were located requested help, they would get it. The RBHH even arranged for their medical staff to get extra training. Late nights, if a farmer fell acutely sick or a woman were in difficult labor, our doctors would immediately go out to fight these nighttime battles, running over single-track paths in the hills to treat these folks at home. When serious car accidents caused cranial fractures and broken limbs, our orthopedic surgeons and brain surgeons would go out to resuscitate the victims, often to great praise. Meanwhile, the pharmacists and traditional Chinese medicine herbologists as well as some doctors would go collecting herbal medicines on the hillsides along with hospital leadership almost weekly. They compounded these into stringy stonecrop syrup, liver-protecting syrup, and other herbal medicines. This saved the hospital on expenses and also helped patients.

[...] Because it was the CultRev era, under the influence of extreme "left" thinking, industrial and military propaganda team leadership were posted at the Shanghai-sponsored hospitals, and emphasis was put on the remolding of intellectuals. Thus, there was a lack of material care and help for staff who had family challenges—like those doctors and nurses who had sickly parents but no one to look after them, or those who had young kids without caregivers. This caused some staff to have trouble concentrating on their work and to go about unhappily with sad faces in the Rear Base hospitals. This caused a lot of pressure for the hospital leadership. They tried to make some arrangements, for example sending staff with serious illness (like cancer) back to Shanghai for treatment and care and arranging for those with family difficulties to be posted back in Shanghai at the offices for "Supporting the Interior" there so they could look after their kin.

[...] One brain surgeon at the Changjiang Hospital said that he had a young child at home and his in-laws who lived with the kid were over 70, and his father-in-law moreover had dementia and had to be fed at mealtimes. After we found out about this, the RBHH cadres took time to visit his family while going back to Shanghai to report to the Department of Health and discovered this to be the real situation: his family was truly struggling. And this surgeon's workload on the Rear Base wasn't very large; he performed more surgeries at the No. 1 People's Hospital [in Shanghai] in a week than he did in a year on the Rear Base. So the RBHH wrote a report on this and suggested the Department of Health allow this surgeon and a neurosurgeon to return to Shanghai with the understanding that they'd continue to be assigned to the Rear Base. If there were a patient for them, they were to immediately return the same day to the Rear Base. This flexibility allowed these two doctors' families to be cared for but also didn't impact the stability of the staffing and even added to the resources of the Shanghai hospitals while enabling Rear Base patients to be looked after.

* * *

史志定 Shi Zhiding, male, Communist Youth League cadre at a steel mill.

Keywords: environment, food, frustrations, manual labor, politically correct, rural vs. urban, travel, work assignments, work schedules

During our training labor on the construction sites in Anhui, we got only 16 yuan a month in pay. Once we were formally in the factory, we were paid according to the Wuhu Shipyard's standards. At the time, you got 36 yuan in Shanghai; we got 33.

The first day there was really pathetic. At the time all the roads were just uneven wet mud, no asphalt of course. The trucks were all old-fashioned tractor-trailers. Our luggage was put on top and passengers got in the bus to ride into the mountains. Packing that luggage in the middle of the night, we could hardly knot the rope well. There wasn't space in the truck cab, so we'd lie on top of the truck, holding onto the ropes. The truck was packed very, very full, totally over load capacity, and with the terrible rocking and bumping, pieces of luggage constantly fell off. Whenever one fell I'd yell for the driver to stop. It took a very long time to reach our destination with this start-and-stop progress. [...]

At the time, students were the main workforce, and managed to accomplish much alongside the workers of the Shanghai No. 2 Construction Company. We really exulted the "Daqing Spirit" [TN: a petroleum-industry city in Northeastern China that became a national exemplar] and assembled the Eight-Five Steelworks with truly shocking speed. ...The rules were strict then. Our 202 Construction Team was also the Shanghai No. 2 Construction Company's second team. There was also the 201, 204, 207 teams, and so forth.

Every day I joined in the cement work and other tasks; there were only five or six master-workers in each team and ten-odd assigned students. The male students usually had one wheelbarrow per person, filled very, very full, sprinting along very steep mountain paths. Back then all of us could really eat. Every meal I'd eat 22 ounces [of grain] and still have some room in my belly, and for every couple ounces I'd also get a yam pancake. I'd buy all of this myself from the canteen. The days were hot and we'd work during the nights, typically working 9 to ten hours a day, so you could say we were really exerting ourselves and burning a lot of it off.

Working all night long, working so much that you could barely walk at the end. Like us in the cement team, we had these tall work boots on; we'd drag them into the dormitories and fall straight down to sleep, maybe washing our faces first. We slept on reed mats on bamboo bedframes, in reed-mat huts, ten-odd huts linked together. If there'd been a spark of fire it'd all have been burned to a cinder in five or ten minutes. In fact, there was once a fire; one of the students at one of the chemical plants wanted to clean off a used paint can from the construction site so he could put stuff in it. He couldn't clean it well, so he decided to light a fire in it, but then as soon as it caught light, boom, the fire was leaping to the hut's roof, taking out the entire temporary dormitory in about 15 minutes.

In Southern Anhui they'd also get floods every year. When those came, we'd use aluminum pails and the bigger wash basins to bring steamed buns for our workers. When we first went in, we'd blast mountainsides to lay down roads where there were no roads and build up factory buildings and residential areas where there was nothing.

Back then the [recruited local] farmers weren't able to beat us on the job. With our cement wheelbarrows, one of us students were as fast as two farmers. We students were working like our lives depended on it. There was talk that only those who performed best would be allowed into the factory, and also pretty intense influence from propaganda, like "beating the imperialists and revisionists with speed and efficiency," to get the Small Third Front running before war could break out. So we were really working for dear life, never mind the hours or the difficulty. So it ended up taking us only five months to make our first batch of steel. They even praised us in 1970 in *Red Flag* [TN: the leading Party publication] saying we were the factory that was fastest set up and most worthy of emulation in the whole 507 Headquarters and the 812 Headquarters in the national defense industry system.

* * *

王文青 Wang Wenqing, female, worker and propaganda cadre at a Small Third Front steel mill.

Keywords: camaraderie, frustrations, Party members, pay and benefits, rural vs. urban, work schedules

[…] Our Party Committee Secretary Chen Suosuo was really very good. It used to be that leaders got 4.3 yuan for bonuses and workers got 5.4, workers actually higher than cadres. Yeah, we just called him Mr. Chen; my daughter used to call him grandpa when she saw him; they were just really close. Plus, when it was time for lunch, Chen Suosuo's office was really simple, very casual; it wasn't that distant, not like [with cadres] now.

In the past, at night, we always had to have Party meetings, and I'd bring my daughter to them, to the auditorium, for the meeting. They always held them, at least three a week, Mondays Wednesdays Fridays or Tuesdays Thursdays Saturdays. One neighbor was real nice and took my daughter to his home and after we finished the meeting we could go pick her up. […]

[Interviewer asks about differences in work between Anhui and Shanghai.] Possibly back then our thinking wasn't so complex. Back then it was all right. It was in Shanghai that things were more anxious. It was relatively relaxed [in Anhui]. Of course everyone took work seriously, but—this—in Shanghai there were lots of tests, grade promotion evaluations, and such, you know, there were more at the No. 5 Steelworks.

[…] I don't think there were [people who made a fuss about pay] either. Sometimes there were conflicts with raises, but not to the point of leaving [me] a really deep impression. There weren't any really huge things. Two percent or 5% increases in salary; there were always [people] who weren't comfortable about it in their hearts. There was a ratio for this; every time there'd be a ratio. Like one person in our radio broadcast room did get upset over a pay raise, so we did some of our [persuasion] work [with them] and it was okay. Mm, everyone went together [to talk to them], and I was the deputy chair at the time. We just talked to them together and it was all right. I don't think there were any really intense incidents.

* * *

许春华 Xu Chunhua, male, Anhui native and worker at a Small Third Front steelworks.

Keywords: conflicts, food, nostalgia, pay and benefits, work assignments, work schedules

I went to the Eight-Five Steelworks because when they were building the factory, they requisitioned land and were hiring local workers. So that's how I got in. I remember it clearly; it was May 16, 1972. Workers were a wide range of ages at the time in there, from 20-somethings up to some experienced veteran masters who were 50-something. I was 25 when I went in and I was in the No. 4 Workshop, where they rolled steel tubing. The tubing on cannons, the steam pipes on the steel furnaces, that was all made by our workshop. We had the most people, over 300 workers, in three shifts of eight hours each.

There was a set of matching rules and regulations from the factory. You were strictly forbidden from being late or leaving early or nodding off while on shift. All of that would earn you criticism. The first time they found out you'd get a warning, the second time would be a severe criticism, and the third time would be punishments and withholding pay. Sometimes they'd have a short meeting before the shift started in the mornings and that was mainly for the shift captain to remind us about safety, announce workload, and give job assignments. Sometimes when finishing in the evening there'd be another shift meeting, mainly for reporting on progress and work conditions.

After I got into the factory, I got 28 bucks a month in pay during the six-month trial period. Then my salary was adjusted to 33 bucks. I ate and slept at home but had a meal at the factory every day. If I got the graveyard shift there'd be another 30 cents for extra food. Every month I'd probably have to work overtime four or five times. You got a rest day once a week, and usually I spent it at home doing chores, not much in the way of fun activities. When there was a major work task, we'd have overtime even on Sunday.

Whenever they gave us overtime, they also gave us a compensatory leave permission slip, and when it wasn't so busy, we could cash in those slips for leaves. Because I had a lot of household chores and had to look after my kid, when I had to do a night shift the night before, I'd be out of it the next day. I'd be walking that mile or so to the steelworks and people there would see me and laugh, "Hey Little Xu, you're napping while you walk." When I got off shift, I'd pull some grass for feeding the pigs on the way home. Our workshop Secretary Zhong saw me and teased me, "Little Xu's always trying to make a buck, eh." I got pretty embarrassed.

The tubing we rolled in our workshop had to go through layers and layers of inspections. There was real-name documentation for which small teams had made which pieces and the factory had a special inspection team, all of them very experienced workers, who'd take electric lights to the tubes. The tubing couldn't have any friction marks, any hairline marks; they strictly maintained the quality control and anything that didn't pass was sent back to us to be remade. If the tubing your small team had helped to roll passed inspection, that was a very proud moment.

At the Lunar New Year and on holidays, the steelworks would have some benefits for us too, like giving us some fruit, fish, or duck. On Lunar New Year, the factory head and Party secretary would go to greet us in each of the workshops, hold a tea-and-chat, and give us chocolates. There'd be two or three days of vacation for the Lunar New Year and for National Day. If we had to do overtime on a holiday, there'd be three days' pay for one day's work. I still remember our workshop head well. He was a really excellent Shanghainese man; he never bullied the newcomers. No matter who you were, he treated you like a comrade. When you ran into issues you didn't understand he'd patiently educate you. I remember once I actually got in a bit of a fight with someone over some little thing, and our workshop head—Wu Guanglong—had a talk with me, telling me to not fight with them and to go to him directly if I had things to say. I still remember that like it was yesterday.

* * *

许汝钟 Xu Ruzhong, male, deputy head and chief engineer of a Small Third Front steelworks.

Keywords: conflicts, finances, pay and benefits, weapons, work assignments, work schedules

The Eight-Five Steelworks was the largest in the Rear Base; we'd say we had up to 10,000 [workers]. By name, we were a steel mill, but actually we made unfinished components for the military. After I arrived, the factory had me put in charge of the setup of the technical side. From the start our goal was to ensure the production of the first batch of steel on May 1, 1970. [...] At first, I worked at the Shanghai [planning] offices for a period. A couple of weeks before the first batch of steel, I went into the mountains. We thought very carefully and picked out some key technical staff. I named some of the technicians who were the best, most familiar to me, and most experienced in actual operations from the Shanghai No. 5 Steelworks. It didn't matter if these people wanted to go or not; they had no choice even if they didn't want to go. If they were named, they had to go. After they were named, the factory did thought work to get them to go. All sorts of production equipment were shipped in bit by bit from Shanghai. [...]

We had eight workshops in total. The No. 1 Workshop was steelmaking and casting, including precision forging using wooden molds; No. 2 was forging, including using molds and without, plus afterward a barrel processing section (but the rifling inside the barrels was done by the Victory Factory). The forging workshop later turned to making civilian-use steel wires, like the wires they use in sewing machines. The No. 3 Workshop was for steel rolling, mainly bar rolling. No. 4 made steel tubing with the 76 mm piercing machine; the seamless tubing made after drawing were all alloys. The No. 5 was transport and was responsible for vehicular transport inside the factory. The Rear Base also had driving teams; the 683 Driving Team worked with us to transport [products] out, but internally we took care of things. Guichi had two docks, the old one from before and the new one we built after arriving. To save on costs, the storage and transport of our raw materials all went via our own dock. The short-distance connections here were all via our own vehicles, which saved a little money. If we had the 683 Driving Team do it, we'd have to spend a bit more.

The No. 6 Workshop was the chemical and physical inspection room. When our steel left the premises, it had to go with a quality assurance document. The No. 7 Workshop was casting—aluminum casting, copper casting, die casting—all producing unfinished component parts for the military. Another thing was being responsible for the repairs and maintenance of the whole steelworks. Usually, all small and medium repairs were done by us. We'd only call outside help for major repairs that we couldn't handle. They also oversaw the power, water, and electricity needs for the whole factory. The No. 8 Workshop specialized in producing gas with four gas producers. We made industrial gas because the forging and rolling needed heating and steelmaking needed gas to heat the auxiliary materials, too. Plus, we needed the gas for the ladle and the annealing furnace.

[…] The quality of our products was pretty good, because the people sent by the Shanghai No. 5 Steelworks were pretty good. We'd first go through the steelmaking room and then proceed step by step with forging next, because you'd have steel ingots that you had to make into things. […] The No. 2 Workshop had three-ton hammers to pound the ingots into bars and other forged products. The miscellaneous unfinished parts for the 57 mm anti-aircraft guns came to over 400 components: parts made with sand casting, aluminum casting, precision casting, copper casting, die casting, and forged parts, we had to produce all of it. We had five factories behind us in our area, behind Meijie [Town]; we produced the unfinished parts and they produced the guns, Victory and Forward and the others. We'd hand over our forged and cast parts to them and they'd finish and assemble them. […]

The relatively heavy demand on our steel tubing was for the combustion chamber of the New 40 grenade launchers [TN: so called because they were 40mm in caliber], where you put the explosives. The New 40s were also called "third grade rockets." We made silicon mangalloy tubes and shipped them to the Cooperation Factory in Lin'an, Zhejiang. They'd assemble the New 40s and give them to the troops for attacking tanks and bunkers. The Eight-Five Steelworks took two years and some to fulfill the requisitions set by the nation and Shanghai's investment, what was said to be a 50 million RMB investment. What you got for 50 million yuan back then you couldn't build up for 50 billion today. The No. 5 Steelworks in Shanghai also gave us some equipment parts for free. The Eight-Five Steelworks had an office in Shanghai with a few buyers specializing in equipment parts and they bought metallurgical equipment from all over the country.

The proportion of military goods was very small, but we had to complete our assignments. The steel rolling workshop supposedly could turn out 100,000 tons of steel products but the steelmaking room could only make about 30,000 tons or so. There wasn't enough steel; there was a very small electric furnace that made ten tons per batch and a small electric furnace for forging parts. Excess molten steel we just forged into ingots, cast into parts, and sold off. The casting workshop kept the factory fed and running. When we didn't have enough steel billet, we'd go ask for more from the Shanghai Metallurgy Bureau. Then they also had difficulties.

Apart from transferring allocations to us at controlled prices, they told us to go figure out a way to buy more. We went to buy more in Hubei—in Daye and Huangshi—and we also bought some through the Shanghai Municipal Steel Company to even out our civilian production.

* * *

应长荣 Ying Changrong, male, driver then cadre in a factory transport department.

Keywords: camaraderie, conflicts, manual labor, nostalgia, politically correct, travel and transportation, work assignments, work schedules

After returning from our field training in early 1971, the organization arranged for me to learn to drive. This was a job that a lot of young people dreamed of getting, but for me it was kind of a disappointment. My dream was to become a bench worker in a workshop, learning to work the lathe and to plane, mill, grind, and trim metal. But you didn't get to pick and choose your job in those years. The organization wanted me to do a job, so I was going to do it well.

Coincidentally, they had me assigned to learn to drive the "Little Roma" off-road car. Jeeps [TN: it is common to call all off-road vehicles "Jeeps" in Chinese] were rare back then; only county-level cadres could ride in them. From the get-go I fell in love with the car. These "Little Romas" were Romanian products [TN: an Auto Romania, or ARO, widely exported throughout the world from the late 1950s through the early twenty-first century]. They had a four-cylinder gasoline engine and were highly reliable off-road cars with all-wheel drive and a powerful motor. They could seat, per regulation, up to eight including the driver. Each Rear Base factory had one of these Jeeps. There were also Beijing Jeeps and Shanghai Jeeps. Of them all, Shanghai ones were the worst quality; they kept breaking down. "Little Roma" accompanied me through my apprenticeship and trained my driving skills as well as my mechanic abilities. I have the deepest feelings for it. Though the car is long since junked, to this day I still have a few of the carry-along tools from the "Little Roma" as mementos (Image 3.3).

The master driver who taught me was named Cai, middling height and a real good guy, really open and warm to people. I heard that he'd been driving for a boss since before Liberation. He drove and could also fix up cars: an all-around, old-fashioned driver. I was tickled pink; I'd ply him with questions all day long, "Master Cai, what about this" and "Master

Image 3.3 Color photograph of Jinggangshan Factory representatives posing with an off-road vehicle and their ground artillery radar equipment, 1970s

Cai, what about that." I almost wanted to learn all of his skills at once. Quickly I learned the various structures and parts of the "Little Roma" inside and out and we two took care of the year-end vehicle maintenance and repairs ourselves. They hadn't assigned vehicle mechanics to us yet, so these full inspections and repair jobs were great training.

In that half-year I not only had to study the on-paper knowledge like mechanical basics, operating procedures, and traffic rules, but I also had to actually drive the car. I mainly self-studied the written stuff. During the day I'd be out in the car with Master Cai and didn't have time to read up, so I'd take the time at night. After three months I took a first test on the written material and then took the course test. The course test had reversing into the garage, parallel parking, road U-turns, hill parking, and course navigation plus other items. Then we moved outside the course. Everyone had to take the test maybe four or five times before they could think about getting out on the road, and some even took the tests nearly ten times. After you got on the road you were still on trial basis for another half a year. Only if you didn't have any accidents could you get the official driver's license.

In late spring and early summer, I'd been studying for five months, so I went with Master Cai in a "July First" brand truck [TN: July 1 is celebrated as the founding day of the CCP] to Shanghai to transport some raw materials for the factory and to also do my road test. The factory rule was that an empty truck could have five passengers but absolutely no more. Originally, we were to leave at 6 a.m. in the morning, but unexpectedly a worker's family member also wanted to tag along to go back to Shanghai. After they climbed aboard they totally refused to budge, much less get off again. After breaking our backs to convince them, our truck finally pulled away from the factory at 10 a.m. Li Xiaoshen, Shen Meijun, Niu Jia'ni and two other young workers were on board as passengers. In the morning, their busy movements, chattering voices, and anxious faces as they tried to persuade that family member to quickly get off the truck, coupled with that person's motionless, silent, statue-like face, made for a scene that stuck deeply in my memory.

[...] After six months' trial on the road, I got my official driver's license on January 31, 1972, and I did fairly well the whole way through. That ended my apprentice days. In everyday work, I strove to be diligent and continue improving my professional skills and mechanical abilities while strengthening my theoretical knowledge and studies. I drove several hundred thousand kilometers while on the Small Third Front in southern Anhui and had zero accidents, earning many awards for driving safety and excellence from the Rear Base.

The driving team shouldered two responsibilities: for production transport and for living needs. Production transport mainly meant shipping completed products to Shanghai and delivering to various factories in the city, where they'd be transferred to clientele across the nation, as well as shipping back raw materials already purchased in Shanghai for the Huangshan offices. Another task was to provide vehicles for various work units in the Rear Base, like periodically carrying construction materials and so forth.

For living needs, our job was mainly as follows: transport workers and their family members to Cai's Bridge where they could take the "Shanghai direct" bus, go buy fresh produce early every morning to supply workers and their families for their daily meals, to help purchase and transport non-staple foods and goods on an as-needed basis, to drive the regularly scheduled buses to Shanghai that ran during the winter and summer holidays to bring kids to the factory for vacation and to take workers and families home to Shanghai for the Lunar New Year, drive regularly scheduled medical transports that took workers and family members to the Gutian Hospital set up just for the Small Third Front at Hule (54 kilometers away) and the Ruijin Hospital in Xionglu (57 kilometers away). We also took urgent care cases when summoned.

For all of the above, a department would have to fill out an application and submit it to the dispatch office and have them coordinate the arrangements for a vehicle. So, every morning the dispatch office doorway was teeming like a marketplace with roaring engines and human chatter. Some were applying to get a vehicle, others were there to find out where vehicles were headed to catch a ride. In those mountains, apart from starting up your own two legs and tough-soled pair of feet, the best option was on four wheels. Bicycles were scary unless you were extremely technically good, because it was so easy to have accidents. Every early morning, we left with the morning fog over our heads and came home late at night with the stars like a cloak around our shoulders. That was definitely us, the drivers—we were some of the most hardworking staff in the Third Front factories.

At the time, the Rear Base 812 Project Command Center's projects around Deshanli—the—were all basically completed, but not the Steep Cliff factory. They'd picked the highest-elevation and most precarious location in the area for Steep Cliff, hence the name. The Shanghai Optical Instrumentation Factory sponsored Steep Cliff and they mostly produced high-precision optical equipment urgently needed for national defense. Their security was especially high as one of the major accessory factories of the Rear Base Third Front's "Project 507." Due to the intended location, the construction process was extremely difficult and there was also a lot to do, so progress was slowest. In particular, the road that led to the factory site was intersected by Copperstone Hill. Going around the hill took time, effort, and wasn't safe. Bulldozing this monster impeding the road and clearing the way to the factory was a pressing task. For this, the company organized various factories to assemble "shock teams" for a "final battle" with Copperstone Hill.

Our factory also enthusiastically responded, sending a "shock troop" of ten-odd people. They raised up the "not afraid of bitterness, not afraid of death" revolutionary spirit and began to dig into the hill from both sides at the same time, even holding a competition between teams. That increased the efficiency of the project. They battled hard for 60 days on the site. With the July sun blazing overhead and daytime temperatures soaring to 42 degrees centigrade, everyone worked mornings and evenings, avoiding the midday high temperatures.

In those days, with a lack of machinery, basically it was all manpower—loads carried on shoulders or dragged by hand, so it was especially tough work. Master Li Xun who led [our factory] team came from construction and was extremely good at his job. He led everyone to work hard, cleverly, and well. Master Xu Huimin, who'd been a railroad construction trooper, was like a big brother to us, always taking care of us as he led us to work safely. Male comrades rushed ahead to claim the dangerous and heavy tasks. After a day, they'd wash up, eat, and directly collapse onto their beds in their dorms. After the women comrades got back, they'd fight over helping to wash up the men's dirty clothes and socks. Everyone cared for and looked after one another and for two months it was like that every day. Weekends, I took them back to the factory in "Little Roma" and felt pretty worked up to see them all so darkened by the sun and skinny. Every time I picked them up they'd be extra happy to see me, too. On the way back to the factory, everyone would describe with laughter the interesting things while they were battling it out with Copperstone Hill. This revolutionary optimism still touches me and I remember it well today. Later, this "shock war" would be unforgettable for all of us when we talked about it.

Whenever a factory vehicle left for Shanghai, the workers' grapevine would be working overtime. Especially when we were taking products back to Shanghai. On loading day, the truck would be parked in front of the 408 finished product warehouse and everyone would come out beside it bright and early. After the crates were loaded, everybody would scramble to stuff their packages, hand luggage, rice sacks, and everything onto the truck. Inside were just things like peanuts, mung beans, sesame seeds, eggs, and other farm products that they'd ask the driver to take to the factory office in Shanghai for their relatives in Shanghai to go pick up. After everything was loaded up and the oilcloth was tied down, you'd have this jam-packed big truck. Once they even crushed the helper springs on a four-ton Liberation-brand truck with the weight.

In those days of the planned economy, all of these things were rationed in Shanghai and were rare goodies, too. Fetching some for Mom and Dad to relieve some homesickness, that was reasonable and understandable. We drivers were all happy to help. We even helped take stuff to people's homes and chatted with our colleagues' elders about how things were in the factory, reassuring them that all was well. On the return trip, if we brought a package or mail or something, that'd be a surprise for our colleagues. Sometimes when the truck passed Si'an or Xiaofeng townships in Zhejiang, we could also get a few little bamboo chairs and hang them behind the truck cab to take back to Shanghai. Those were the most popular things. Enjoying the evening cool with a new, finely made little bamboo chair or lounge in your doorway, that would definitely bring a lot of envious gazes. The advantage of us drivers was that we could go back to Shanghai often, check up on our parents, and could also deliver a little warmth and care on behalf of the workers and their families who were so far from the city. You know, ordinary workers only had one family visit holiday a year, but drivers could do the roundtrip five or six times a year.

Let me tell you a real story that happened in the factory. There was a young lady who'd recently started at the factory in one workshop. She was desperately homesick and she'd used up her visitation days, and she had no excuse for more time off, so what did she do? She just up and left without saying a word! Instead of taking the "Shanghai direct" bus, she took a local bus bound for Wuhu and transferred her way toward Shanghai. "The girl's gone!" Her workshop head was frantic. It was a huge deal! How would they explain this to the girl's parents? After reporting to the factory leadership and checking with the gate patrol, if she left at that hour it must have been to catch the Wuhu bus. We chased her down in the "Little Roma" all the way to near Nanling (about 80 kilometers from the factory) before we were able to stop that bus. A-ha, there she was sitting on the bus, refusing to budge for the life of her until there was a direct administrative order. Then we were able to half-cajole, half-trick her into going back with us to the factory. At the time the organizational discipline was extremely strict.

* * *

张燕芳 Zhang Yanfang, female, teacher turned production statistics and logistics cadre at a steel mill.

Keywords: camaraderie, manual labor, nostalgia, politically correct, work assignments, work schedules

Yes, [I was in] production statistics, but we often had to "Battle the High Temperatures" and go down below [to the work floor]. We did everything. Above the hammer, putting the steel grades on, that was several hundred degrees, you know. The just-forged steel was coming down and the steel was still blood-red. Even in June, and for three months afterward, we'd go down to "Battle the High Temperatures" and still had to do our own tasks well. We'd go do the three shifts alongside the workers.

For example, these steel bars, one by one, one chromium 18 nickel nine titanium [TN: a steel grade corresponding to ASTM A276-96, the industry standard for stainless steel bars and other shapes], this stainless steel, you have to pound the grade number on there; [this type] can only be used to make knives and tools, that type can only be used for making brushed steel; each kind varied and you couldn't mix them up. Every piece had to have its grade stamped on it. How many degrees—that temperature was several hundred degrees. I had to stamp even though I was a production statistician. [...] Normally I was really idle. I'd do the production statistics, just "Battling the High Temperatures" during those three months; you had to go down there. Yeah, that's how we did it.

At that time I was pretty happy about it. The workers were really nice. I realized, you know, going from school to the factory, that workers were really decent and simple. They'd see you coming down from the office and really take care of you. But between us, we couldn't make it like I should be taken care of, either. I had to fight to work [alongside the others]. I'd drive the steel delivery cart. An 18-inch spindle, over three tons, burning it till it was blood-red from the annealing furnace, from the reheating furnace. Otherwise you couldn't forge the steel. [They'd] bring it onto that cart, and I'd sit by the side driving it. That steel spindle was bigger than this entire countertop. It was three-dimensional. "Boom," and I'd drive it over. If it wasn't enough, you had to use that stirring rod. I couldn't manage it; the workers would come do it. Oh yes, but it was really fun.

Production statistics was like, for example, in a workshop, how much material came in per month? After the materials came in, how much finished product did I have to send out? In the process of making the finished product, in the process of production, which billet was at which stage? For example, if the forging were complete and we had 230 carbon steel, or small carbon steel, then, after getting to that, you had to anneal it—people who do metallurgy know this. Large pieces of steel need annealing; if you don't then it's really brittle. [...] And there's the pickling; for example if your surface isn't good, you need to pass it through the acid and clean it up before you can process it further.

So I'd say, this month, how much material came in, where's that material in the production process, for example if it's in the forging stage, what kind of standard was coming out, how many tons of that standard, how much material was left. And the things that had been forged at a standard, have they reached downstream processing—downstream processing had a polishing stage. That kind of grinder, I don't know if you've seen it before—a grinder, this big [gestures]. Two workers and a machine to polish the [steel's] surface, *shaaa*—very dangerous. At first when I went there, because I was a teacher—yeah, [originally a desk job], I was very afraid. But then after looking a while I got used to it and didn't mind. Plus workers treat people very well. They're very honest and true.

Because after some time [on the job], everyone knows if you are deliberately causing grief for people or if you really had no choice. So sometimes I feel like I was very happy during this period, even though there'd be conflicts between people about this and that. So, when I transferred into logistics from the factory, others didn't think much of me. What do you know, you're here pretending to be a leader. Right? Yes, there was that, too. Yes, [I heard] it all. These were no big deal.

[...] After all, I counted on my efforts and my abilities; I did as best as my abilities allowed; I didn't slack off; I did as much as I could. I couldn't be good in everything, right? That's not possible. As for what you want to say [about me], I can't do anything about it. Some things, there will always be conflict. And if two of you have some conflict, you can go talk them down, you can go mediate the conflict, but in the end there's always one party satisfied and one party not. What can you do? Right? I'd explain [myself] all day and night? Meaningless.

* * *

赵惠瑛 Zhao Huiying, female, worker and kindergarten teacher at a Small Third Front steelworks

Keywords: education, nostalgia, sent-down youth, work assignments

Training, well! I've always been a quick study, plus I like this job, because my first goal after graduation was to go into early childhood education. So, when I met an old middle school classmate in there, she said "Hey, your dreams have become reality," I said "Yes!" Somehow, I got arranged to do my favorite work...I'm really enthusiastic, and really quick, so after half a year I was all in the Party Committee and such, and the Shanghai Bureau of Education and such were all recommending me, saying that I was very good toward the kids and toward administration, all quite good, so I was promoted relatively quick!

So then, I began as assistant kindergarten principal, then when our principal was transferred to the Education Department, I became principal! All the way until the Eight-Five Steelworks retreated [back to Shanghai]. I was stationed until the end, until I'd seen off all the teachers, then I came back; that's how it was. I was in the final batch [to leave].

No, [I didn't announce my goals after middle school then take an exam to go to teachers' school]. At the time, kindergarten teachers were an automatic promotion unit, no testing. But I really liked it. At the time I had pretty good grades. You had to fill out [a goals form for further assignment]. You'd give it a go yourself. If you scored higher on the tests than other people they might take you. In that process I'd definitely not have been admitted. Our entire Putuo District—I was in Putuo—only took eight people. It was really very few, really rare, so then I wasn't admitted. Then I went to a technical school, then after that I was sent down, and then I went to Anhui.

Further Reading

Joel Andreas, *Disenfranchised: The Rise and Fall of Industrial Citizenship in China* New York: Oxford University Press, 2019.

Chao Chen, *Toleration: Group Governance in a Chinese Third Front Enterprise.* Basingstoke: Palgrave Macmillan, 2018.

Mark W. Frazier, *The Making of the Chinese Industrial Workplace: State, Revolution, and Labor Management.* Cambridge: Cambridge University Press, 2002.

Deborah A. Kaple, *Dream of a Red Factory: The Legacy of High Stalinism in China.* New York: Oxford University Press, 1994.

Hou Li, *Building for Oil: Daqing and the Formation of the Chinese Socialist State.* Cambridge, MA: Harvard University Press, 2018.

Li, Huaiyin, "Worker Performance in State-Owned Factories in Maoist China." *Modern China* 42:4 (2016), 377–414.

Xiaobo Lu and Elizabeth J. Perry, *Danwei: The Changing Chinese Workplace in Historical and Comparative Perspective.* Armonk: M.E. Sharpe, 1997.

Andrew G. Walder, *Communist Neo-Traditionalism: Work and Authority in Chinese Industry.* Berkeley: University of California Press, 1988.

CHAPTER 4

Material Life and Healthcare

Translator's Note

In this section, we showcase the range of material objects in people's everyday lives on the Small Third Front and experiences surrounding them, from the perspectives of both city workers who went to these remote outposts and rural people who lived in surrounding communities. We also highlight recollections about healthcare, where the resources of the Small Third Front's state-owned enterprises intersected with the physical bodies and life-and-death emotions of workers, their families, and their neighbors in the countryside.

Despite the material challenges of the first years of the Small Third Front, most of our respondents recall a dramatic contrast between the variety and quality of goods and quality of medical care available to workers and affiliates of the Small Third Front and what villagers in neighboring areas could access. Small Third Fronters brought electricity, running water, automobiles, and greater quantities and qualities of cigarettes and food delicacies to isolated communities; their arrival brought highly trained doctors, surgeons, and nursing staff. The material story of the Small Third Front demonstrates that the gap between life in the PRC's cities and countryside, very much observable today, was even starker in the 1960s through the 1980s. Even for the relatively better-off workers, though, foodstuffs (as opposed to the newest consumer gadgets) are among the outstanding memories, suggesting the material lack to which most had become accustomed.

Y. Xu, Y. Y. Wang, *Everyday Lives in China's Cold War Military-Industrial Complex*, Palgrave Studies in Oral History,
https://doi.org/10.1007/978-3-030-99688-8_4

Another dimension in several respondents' recollections is the perception that material life has changed for the worse since their Small Third Front days, though most observers would regard the nationwide rationing system of these years as full of privation compared to the teeming Chinese marketplaces of the twenty-first century. Echoing the official account of the Anhui Small Third Front provided at the outset of this book, people remember inexpensive, high-quality goods, highly professional medical care, well-regulated distribution channels, and even relatively mild interpersonal conflicts over coveted goods.

On the one hand, such testimonies confirm the degree to which the PRC's leadership used agricultural production as the basis for modern industrialization and military preparedness, providing for the workers of the Third Front defense manufactories (following initial hardship during surveying and construction) at the expense of farmers across the nation.[1] On the other, it is clear that even something as apparently objective as the types and quantity of food and clothing, and the outcomes of medical treatments, are experienced in idiosyncratic ways, both in the life of an individual and against the backdrop of an era. Moreover, regional and inter-community divides in material life could be enormous within the PRC, despite its promise of socialist equity. Even as residents of rural Anhui were amazed by electric lights, some of their fellow citizens could enjoy commodities like watches, razor blades, lighters, and pens trafficked from Hong Kong and Macao.[2]

Questions for Discussion

1. What do the respondents remember as the best aspects of material life, including healthcare, on the Small Third Front? What do they remember as the worst?
2. How do villagers in communities neighboring the Small Third Front remember the material goods of the Front? Do their recollections differ from those of workers who had moved from the city?

[1] See, for example, Brown (2012), as well as material on "Shanghainese vs. Locals" later in this book.

[2] Philip Thai, *China's War on Smuggling: Law, Economic Life, and the Making of the Modern State, 1842–1965*. New York: Columbia University Press, 2018, Ch. 7.

3. Given that the public discourse of the Mao years celebrated workers, soldiers, and peasants as the backbone of the nation, what do you make of the contrasts and similarities between the material lives and expectations of rural farmers and urban workers in the following accounts?

* * *

卞建华 Bian Jianhua, female, driver for the Rear Base militia headquarters.

Keywords: food, living conditions, manual labor, nostalgia, rural vs. urban

Really it was like an independent country there. The Rear Base had all its parts, from food on up, everything, and everything was very good, including the provisioning. Some was shipped over from Shanghai; some was supplied locally. Vegetables were largely supplied locally, those couldn't be shipped from Shanghai. Meat and such, things that could be supplied non-locally, came from Shanghai.

Now thinking back on it, we stayed a lot of years in the Rear Base. The food and living conditions here were really great. These days young Shanghai boys getting married can't afford housing, but getting married back then, everyone got a little apartment to live in. We brought our own furniture. Wood was plentiful, you could go buy some good stuff. When we were leaving, I'm not too sure, but waste was pretty bad. I heard people say that if you gave your housing to a local they'd ask for money from you.

* * *

储瑛娣 Chu Yingdi, female, Party cadre at a precision optics factory.

Keywords: environment, food, living conditions, medical issues, medicine

In the mountains it was pretty hard to see a doctor for an illness. When our workers had an urgent problem, it took over an hour to get to the Hule Hospital. Once a worker went to catch a big old black carp. Someone said that it was good for the eyes to eat fish gallbladder, but black carp gallbladder was poisonous. He ate it and got poisoned. He couldn't go to the Rear Base hospital, you know, so we had to take him by car overnight to Shanghai. Thankfully we made it in time, or else his life would've been in danger.

Another young man had a stomach hemorrhage and fell unconscious. It was snowing heavily, and we couldn't drive him anywhere. So we had no choice but to go on the PA in the middle of the night and call for someone with AB type blood to come forward as a donor. He was really lucky too; it so happened there was a medic team sent out from the Shanghai Contagious Diseases Hospital to investigate lung flukes and were staying in our factory. These doctors saved this worker.

There was this very tough disease caused by lung flukes locally. Because Shanghainese like eating crabs, they'd go off into the little ditches by the lake to catch them. They'd catch them and marinate them in some liquor to make "drunken crabs" [TN: that is, raw crabs anesthetized by the alcohol] and eat them just like that. Eating them without killing the parasites meant that these flukes would eat one little hole after the other in your lungs, each small as a grain of rice. The Shanghai medic team conducted some experiments on dogs they were keeping as test subjects; when they dissected the dogs, they found them all like this. Even inside the bones, these [flukes] were crawling like ants.

Then they found the source of the problem and they sent blood samples to the Union Medical College in Beijing. They diagnosed it as lung flukes and went to buy some imported medicines from Japan that treated them. After that everyone was too scared to eat the crabs from the little streams. Frogs, amphibians, armadillos, they caught these and ate them all. Shanghainese love to eat, but then they got sick from their eating. Several people ate [the crabs] and felt bone pain. This medic team [...] diagnosed them [...] it was said that this disease was very rare in China, but these workers were saved.

* * *

丁秀玉 Ding Xiuyu, female, technician at a Small Third Front steelworks who later rose to cadre positions in Small Third Front Party organs, including head of the Birth Planning office.

Keywords: food, living conditions, poverty, travel and transportation, work assignments

[We did training-through-labor] for eight months. Yes, and then we entered the Eight-Five Steelworks. [...] From '69 December 23 through July '70, I was working [in training], then our company was taken away by truck, driven an entire day from Huizhou, to the The East is Red Materials Factory—in a mountain gully. This material factory was a heavy industrial plant built under the Shanghai No. 7 Radio factory, to make parts. Then one hot day in July '70 they transferred us from Huizhou to Chizhou, that is, Guichi. [...] we worked there for a month, also training-through-labor, also working alongside a construction team.

After a month of working like this, in August, they took us to what is now the Eight-Five Steelworks, the administrative offices. I was originally assigned to Workshop No. 4, the 04 Workshop...at that point we were living in the offices, in grass huts, it was really very hard. [The huts] leaked rain. Especially the winters, they were very bitter. We were young then. When we had nothing to eat, if we got sick sometimes and wanted some noodles, there was no way to cook them. There wasn't a gas stove, or a [wood-fired] stove. So we had the idea to take the bundles of noodles we'd brought from Shanghai and stick them into our hot water thermoses, then go fill them with boiling water. After a night, the noodles would be all gummed together. We'd eat this, then take some spicy pork sauce from Shanghai, and mix it in and eat it. Yes, the noodles were all broken. We'd eat this and feel like it was a real upgrade.

We did have a cafeteria, but we couldn't eat our fill, because there weren't any dishes. Sometimes the cafeteria would only have one dish of greens and two ounces of rice [a person], so there was no way you'd be full. Sometimes when sleeping in on Sunday, and you got up late, the cafeteria would be closed, so we could only eat noodles. We tried to improve our diet...the vegetables in the cafeteria had no oil in them. Young folks like us, we could eat it. The situation was basically like that. Some people would bring some stuff from Shanghai; people who were better-off would bring some nicer things. Worse-off people would bring worse things. Like me, my family wasn't well-off, so I brought some little square cakes, 48 cents a pound. There was no filling, just a wheat flour cake. I'd buy two pounds of cakes, 96 cents, bring it over, and eat a bit when I got hungry. There was also cooked wheat flour. Just slightly stir-fried wheat flour. Better-off people could put some sugar in it, and the worse-off would just mix it with some boiling water and eat it. That's how we survived then. But we were young then, and we didn't think it too tough.

* * *

顾国籁 Gu Guolai, male, Anhui native, technician who rose to administrative leadership roles in Anhui.

Keywords: food, frustrations, living conditions, movies, rural vs. urban, travel and transportation

[…] At the time farm produce in our Guichi here was extremely cheap. When I first began working, it was one buck for four pounds of peanuts, one buck for four pounds of crab, 10 cents for three eggs. When they [the Shanghainese] came over, there was a run on these items, but on the other hand, this helped improve the income of local farmers. At the time, four pounds of crab for one buck! A big carp, a black carp, was three or four pounds for one buck, you know. Because their [Shanghainese workers'] lives were also pretty dull, you know, aside from working in the daytime, then you'd drink at night. Drinking, well, you'd buy local eggs, chickens, fish and while away the extracurricular time, of course. The extracurricular time there was very boring. Maybe you'd show a movie once or twice a week, and then nothing much else. You could only come back [to Shanghai] once a year to visit the family, once or twice.

* * *

胡善莉 Hu Shanli, female, Anhui native hired into a chemical factory as a concessionary worker.

Keywords: camaraderie, consumer goods, food, living conditions, rural vs. urban, travel and transportation

The goods [in the concessionary store] were all from Shanghai, all shipped from Shanghai. Even the table salt came from Shanghai. The Shanghainese didn't eat the local stuff. If they did, they'd eat the local white rice, pork, and fish. For fish, they all wanted to eat the largehead hairtail fish [TN: cutlassfish] from Shanghai. If local folks wanted to buy things, like matches and such, we'd have them use cards or coupons. Every week the factory would send two big trucks, you know, to get more stock from Shanghai. There were lots of products! Knit things, wool, snack foods, and daily goods. There were four display cases for the daily goods; we had oil, salt, vinegar, soy sauce. The factory residential area had some family members who cooked for themselves, so we had those things. We also had toothpaste and toothbrushes, towels and wool and things, and also some undershirts and such, but we didn't carry too much of those. The store mostly sold daily goods […] all from Shanghai (Image 4.1).

The quality was very good! Some [local] people tried to buy things directly from me, but the factory policy was not to sell to outsiders.

Image 4.1 The Yan'an Factory's commissary shop, 1980s?

Otherwise the factory would lose out. They shipped it over and didn't add a single cent of markup. You needed cards to buy things at the time, so some locals would look for Shanghai people, and the Shanghai people would buy for them.

"Day-use cards," [they were called]. When they came once to buy something, we'd register it once, and sell in limited quantities. For example, your matchsticks. In Shanghai they were two bucks a box, and after shipping to the Dongzhi commissary, we'd still sell at two bucks a box. The soy sauce was 35 cents; we'd still sell at 35 cents, not a penny extra! [Not even the transport costs!], not a cent! Because that was to serve the factory and the government didn't let you arbitrarily add [to the price]. Not like now. Back then things were very done by the book. The government didn't let you and those Shanghai workers were of very good character! They treated people well! The manager of our commissary was an old Party member, surnamed Lu, Lu Dexian, a pretty good person.

Some locals got familiar with the Shanghai workers and used that connection to buy [things], especially white sugar, Big Qianmen Gate and Pegasus cigarettes; these the locals liked a lot. They didn't have them locally! They only had cigarettes like Two Cats, 19 cents a pack, Brightness, or Big Iron Bridge; all of these were local cigarettes. 'Course the Shanghai stuff was better quality! Like our toothpaste, the toothpaste that came from Shanghai, the quality was different from the local stuff. It was definitely better! It was very obvious! Shanghai goods were just different. Even a box of matches, the quality from Shanghai was absolutely better than the local stuff. Like, the local matches, a lot of them wouldn't shed a spark. But the Shanghai ones, take one and "pshh," you'd have a flame. Back then we didn't use natural gas to cook like these days. We all had to use wood fires then; we were all using matches.

I did get to know a lot of people working in the commissary, but I maintained my principles. If local folks wanted to come, oh, come and buy our things, we had to see what it was they wanted. If it were really like cigarettes and such, these things you bought with ration coupons, we couldn't just sell them those willy-nilly because we had to keep accounts of those every month. When Shanghainese workers came with their ration tickets, we couldn't be out of cigarettes! They used coupons for cigarettes and [we'd write down] one pack, two packs. We couldn't sell too many of those. Every month was pre-planned. Labor brand cigarettes didn't need coupons, so we could sell an extra one or two packs.

Local folks usually wanted to buy matches, you know, theirs weren't as good as ours. We tried to control the buying as much as possible, because the factory also told us, if locals came, we shouldn't let them leave empty-handed, you know, so you can sell them some [matchbooks], two or three, but don't give them too many. And they also liked Shanghainese soap and laundry powder, because these were very good. We could also sell them a bit of these. And some people used their connections with the Shanghai workers to come buy stuff. The workers all had cards. You'd make a note in your notebook, you'd control how much you sold. Every week, two big trucks would come and go [to Shanghai for goods].

Like, the beer they shipped from Shanghai, back then locally they didn't have beer. Once I went home and took my daddy two bottles. My daddy said, "oh, they have such nice tasting beer. Hmm, it's tasty, but it kind of tastes like water used to rinse rice, eh? Kind of rotten tasting?" You know. Yeah, so I told him, "that's good stuff!" The Shanghai workers had even kept it cold. But my daddy was still not used to it and told me to not bring any more next time. Then later I gave a bottle of beer to another relative. He said straight up, "this stuff is nasty, yuck!"

[…] The canteen food back then was pretty good, too. Lots of variety every meal. Pork buns, scallion buns, plain steamed bread. The flour in those buns were so incredibly white. It was called fortified flour. Every

Sunday when I went home, I wouldn't bring anything else, I'd just take some buns home with me. So tasty, those buns, and nicely risen too.

* * *

桂胜莲 Gui Shenglian, female, Anhui native and worker at a Small Third Front steel mill.

Keywords: food, living conditions, pay and benefits, rural vs. urban, work schedule

When I first entered the factory, I was in the No. 4 Workshop at the Eight-Five Steelworks. I was pulling steel tubing. My kid was pretty young at the time, plus I wasn't in great health, so they moved me to the main cafeteria to work. Then I worked the rest of the time at the Eight-Five Steelworks main office cafeteria. Cafeteria workers had several shifts, about 50 or 60 of us total. At the very beginning, the cafeteria rules were really strict. It was all "big-pot cooking" at the time. We were in there doing miscellaneous things, steaming the rice and stuff. Back then when the workers came to eat in the cafeteria they didn't have to bring bowls. They all used the enamel basins in the cafeteria. Then the cafeteria gradually began using basins less and less.

The rice steamers in the cafeteria were all in divided squares. One square of steamed rice was four ounces. Once it was cooked, you didn't even have to weigh it. It used to be that it was pretty hard to sell the rice in our cafeteria. I think the rice was 16 cents. When the ol' Shanghais bought rice back then, they'd ask for change even if it were half a cent. So it wasn't easy keeping accounts when we were selling the rice. Like, some people who could read had it a little better. But we couldn't read, so making change was pretty hard. Then after doing it for a long time, it got easier.

At the time, fish was 12 cents, a big cut of pork (a very big piece) was 12 cents, then a plate of vegetables. The ol' Shanghais always cut real big pieces of pork. The dishes all had different prices. All sorts of dishes were put in little plates. It used to be all the dishes would be set up with little plates. Each window would have a table and you'd put the plates on there. This way it was easier for the workers to dine. The rules were real good back then. The workers all lined up [for rice and dishes] by themselves. Nobody cut the line. At the time the cafeteria had five or six windows for picking up rice and dishes. There were a lot of workers. It was a big cafeteria, you know, the main cafeteria.

At first when the Shanghainese came down it was really hard. There was rice and dishes in the cafeteria, but workers only got that little bit of salary every month. At first when we went into the mill we all got only 28 bucks a month. After being in the steelworks for six months, we were made official employees, but even after being made official, we'd only get 33 bucks a month. How many years did I get 33 bucks? The salary never went up, it was just always 33 yuan.

The Shanghainese who started working in the mill with us, their salary and benefits were all the same. Some had come just after they graduated junior high. Workers ate at the cafeteria using ration tickets for rice and dishes. The salaries were so low then, who could possibly bear to eat good dishes? The amount the workers saved after a month was totally dependent on how much each person could scrimp and save. Lots of people couldn't bear to eat the good stuff. It was real tough! Those masters and aunties who came from Shanghai also saved up. Their salaries when they first came was also just over 30 bucks a month. Some still had family in Shanghai; some had problems at home and had to send money back to support them in Shanghai. Think about it, nobody had an easy time back then. Like, if you ate at the canteen, every meal was only 15 cents, but who'd spare all that? Even we who worked in the canteen, we brought in our own dishes; we didn't want to pay for dishes at the canteen. If the Shanghainese had some guests come over, they'd go get some good stuff from the canteen. Otherwise, they bought some vegetables and things and cooked themselves. They really followed the rules. The ones who worked at the canteen never took food from there. They were very rule-abiding.

At the time, us working in the factory, we were all very enthusiastic. We often had night shifts. If we fell asleep and woke up seeing other people having cut a whole basket of vegetables or something, we'd be all anxious and hurry to get things done. Night shifts, we often began our shift at 1:30 in the morning, then work until past eight a.m. the next day and go home. In the night, well, we'd fix the food for the morning, then make pastries. When they were first building the factory, there weren't many dough-mixing machines. Dough was all made by hand. So the master cooks in the factory would use their hands—dough-making isn't easy. Back then, there were two big old [gestures with hands] bowls. After the flour was mixed and kneaded and left to rise, it'd be put aside while we cut vegetables on the side. The master cooks would then begin making plain and stuffed buns and other pastries and we'd also help alongside. Later on, the Eight-Five Steelworks bought their own dough machine and it was easier on people. You wouldn't know, but hand-mixing dough back then, it was several hundred pounds at a time. How did people take that? Our cafeteria was big, you know, most of the workers would come buy pastries at ours.

* * *

胡进 Hu Jin, female, cadre at a Small Third Front-associated farm, then transferred to a transport department.

Keywords: conflicts, food, living conditions, movies, nostalgia, pay and benefits

[Back then me and my husband] usually ate at the cafeteria. [It's not that we didn't have time,] it's that we didn't even have a gas stove; we had to use a kerosene stove, it was really inconvenient. The cafeteria was very good. After I came back from Jilin, my first meal, I went crazy buying side dishes, they were so very cheap. In Manchuria there weren't really vegetables, always radishes, Napa cabbage, and taro, and then also always eating mixed grains. After I came and saw the stir-fried tripe and green vegetables in the cafeteria, I'd not eaten dishes like this for so long. And every Saturday they had wonton skins and wonton filling for sale; you can make your own wontons. And they had upgrades too. During the Lunar New Year and holidays, the food was pretty good.

[...] No, [we didn't feel very tired working or doing housework and such there], it wasn't a big deal. Yes, [with the kid there it was different]. Every Saturday was like a holiday. The auditorium in the factory showed movies. [Indicates photo.] This was taken in front of the auditorium. We were all dolled up to go see the movies. We looked forward to watching the movies every Saturday. Yes, every week. Saturday and Sunday, they played the same film.

[...] One time our factory was giving out [flavored popsicles], one a person. One old worker, a retired cadre, he'd given me his bicycle seat when mine broke. I installed it and it was pretty comfortable when I rode it. That time there were some popsicles left over so we of course, well, tried to help out the workers with little kids. He had a grandson. But one person in our finance department had a lot of kids so I gave [some extra popsicles] to him, and the [old man] got insanely angry. When I got off work, he'd taken off my bike seat and I couldn't leave, [laughs]. But then I explained things to him: the other person had three kids, and they were all little, after all; you have a son and a daughter who got popsicles and can save them for him [the grandson]. Then he wore a long face for more than a week, and I have a thick skin too, so after a week I went to talk with him again and it was fine.

* * *

徐小英 Xu Xiaoying, female, cadre, teacher, and office administrator at a Small Third Front steel mill.

Keywords: camaraderie, conflicts, food, living conditions, nepotism, nostalgia, travel and transportation

In the mountains, this batch of us in the [dormitory] building, it seemed like everyone's relationships were pretty harmonious. Mm, sometimes [if a kid needed taken care of, a neighbor would go help look after them]. [...] Sometimes I'd do some laundry, do some chores. Next door was an office. Two neighbors helped me watch my son. At the time, in the [dormitory] building, everyone's relationships were, really pretty harmonious, pretty good.

So, our secretaries and such, our archival secretaries, sometimes they'd buy some groceries, [our boss,] he'd say come, come, everybody, come to this very large conference room in our main offices, everyone would gather at one table, hang out together, it was pretty nice. No, not really any things like that [conflicts with people when doing their dossiers, or female comrades with their own issues]. Usually, me and other people, I'd not really get upset with them. In the school, there was some [conflict around me being a] supervisor, what do I mean? Because when I went over from the factory offices, the head seemed to treat me pretty well and gave me a promotion. Mm, he put me in a key position, being this deputy head of teaching affairs, I guess a pretty important post.

Other people had been teachers for years and years and didn't get to be [this role], so [they] thought I seemed like the pet of the secretary, there was a bit of that. Mm, they'd talk about me behind my back. Yep, yep, they seemed to think I was the pet of some boss, but actually the superiors, if you want to say that the bosses gave you influence, that had to depend on you working for it yourself. Because you—like me in the infrastructure department, the commissary store next to our department got a big truckload of very nice-looking bowls they'd brought over. Our boss was very strict; other people could go buy them if they wanted, but we weren't allowed to go out to buy them. You had to lead by example. It was a collective dorm. At the time, for example, one dorm [room] had four bunks that would sleep eight people. The infrastructure department had seven female comrades, right, so I let them pick first and then I went to pick. I couldn't—you know. He [my boss] had me be like this. Have them settle things, then I would sleep where no one else wanted to. Like that.

Especially me in the factory offices, for example other people, if we were buying groceries, wanted something we'd have to go buy it in Guichi, especially shrimp, fish, and such. Our factory offices would receive a truck every day from the docks; when staff came from Shanghai to the Guichi docks they'd always [ride] our factory office shuttle.

Mm, we all had natural gas in our homes. Yep, we had a natural gas workshop, and the natural gas workshop had through pipes installed to everyone's homes. At the time our gas bill was about one yuan a month, one yuan or 80 cents. No, [other factories didn't have natural gas], the other factories didn't have a natural gas workshop, just us the Eight-Five Steelworks. Later on we were like this [previously, coal stoves], every home had natural gas; you could use it as you liked. If you had to cook something, the fixed price was one yuan or 80 cents a month. It was all right living there. Living there, and living on, you got used to it. But my son said later, of the several places [I've lived] I thought Anhui was best. Mm, [and close to Shanghai, so pretty convenient].

* * *

王文青 Wang Wenqing, female. Worker and propaganda cadre at a Small Third Front steel mill.

Keywords: children, environment, family, food, frustrations, living conditions, marriage, nostalgia

[...] At the time the Small Third Front had to provide food, clothing, shelter, and transport for its workers. Even now everyone still remembers the lifestyle then fondly. Look at today's metro Shanghai—of course, [by] getting to this step, we're all very happy; being holed up in the mountains isn't good either. Back then development didn't happen that quickly, so those leaders [came to Anhui] and said the birds were calling and the flowers were sweet, and well, we also thought the air was really good, but, well, after you stayed a long time, you felt bored. Plus, you thought about the kids and such, many kids weren't brought there, lots of them were put with their grandmas and grandpas, or their aunties and such, living under someone else's roof.

Image 4.2 Two porcelain teacups issued to workers at the July 1st Medical Equipment Factory, 1970s?

A lot of our food and such was shipped in from the outside. If we were eating crabs everyone ate crabs together, if we had pears everyone had them together. One or two truckloads came in and then everyone would split them or buy them. Yep, apart from not sleeping together on the same beds, [we did everything together], so the folks from Eight-Five are really close (Image 4.2).

I married my husband at the end of '78. Just in Shanghai. When we married he was still in the military, then he moved to the Jing'an District Militia. Mm, [we were apart], so then in '80, I had my daughter on March 8th, then at the end of the year he transferred to...yes, at the time we were married we were apart. We married in late '78; in '79 I [got pregnant with] my daughter, then kept running to and fro while pregnant, all the way to Anhui. In Shanghai people loaned their flats for us to stay in, like that. Yeah, afterward they assigned us a flat [in Anhui, in the family dorms]. Yeah, they assigned us housing [only after he was formally transferred]. Then my in-laws helped take care [of the kid] for a while, then we put her in the [factory] nursery and kindergarten. I think that back then it wasn't like now [in terms of being tiring], like for my daughter. Now there's two old people, her mother-in-law helps take care [of the my grandchild], and maybe her [my daughter's] job is tougher than ours before.

[...] At the time we were renting housing [in Baoshan]. It was still before [we got assigned housing]. When we got back in '87 there wasn't housing. We moved in '90 or '91. They were still building [the housing] at the time. When we came back we all rented places.

* * *

徐新东 Xu Xindong, male. Anhui native, secretary to a cadre at the end of the Small Third Front.

Keywords: consumer goods, food, living conditions, movies, nostalgia, rural vs. urban, travel and transportation

Back then, there weren't movies in the towns, so some people specially went over to the Small Third Front factory to watch movies. The Small Third Front factory had a movie theater in it, a library and such, and almost all the little daily goods and things. The [quality of things from Shanghai was much better than locally], for sure. Just speaking of a simple cigarette, the best cigarettes then were Big Qianmen Gate, Pegasus, and if you wanted to buy them, you had to go to the Third Front factory commissary to buy them. In the towns, locally, you couldn't find them for sale. Cigarettes, soap, white sugar, and candy, they were all very hard to find.

[Yes,] in the 1970s and 80s, [folks in Meijie hadn't seen cars, but when the Small Third Front came, cars ran all over the roads]. The mountains had no cars at all before. When the Small Third Front came, mountain folks' thinking was made livelier, and their cultural lives too. We didn't use to be able to watch movies, but in the Third Front factory we saw them all the time.

* * *

王金忠 Wang Jinzhong, male, Anhui native and farmer who worked in a Small Third Front chemical factory.

Keywords: consumer goods, electrification, environment, food, living conditions, movies, nostalgia, rural vs. urban, travel and transportation, water and irrigation

Shanghai people's clothes and look were very simple, very plain. Some younger people, their clothes were a little improved, the woman workers might wear skirts, do a little lipstick, but nothing else. When it came to eating and drinking, back then food and drink were great, and very cheap. Compared to today, money back then was harder to earn, but worth more. Back then, 30 cents was worth more than three bucks today. You could get red-braised pork for 25 cents, a hefty portion, and the Shanghainese would cook it well. By contrast, ordinary local folks would never have meat to eat at home, no way!

Then after '78, things got better a little, the factory cafeteria—the 'internal' cafeteria, they provided the workers' meals. The nearby folks had no dishes, so they would let the folks buy some too. The factory cafeteria didn't use to let folks in, they couldn't have any. Then the factory cafeteria's breakfast food, like buns, spring onion rolls, stuffed rolls, fried dough sticks, and some other ones I don't know the names of, lots of varieties, stuff that folks hadn't even seen before. Shanghai people were very open, too, so then the local folks got to eat these things. Though those Shanghai workers weren't so highly paid, they were generous. Some folks, they got acquainted, they would let the folks buy a bit extra to take home to eat. They knew that our lives were tough, they felt bad for us, so they'd let us buy some pork buns, some sweet rice cake from the cafeteria, they'd let the folks eat some.

[…] It used to be very hard to even get to Xiangyu town. It was all small roads. Before the Small Third Front came, many folks here had never been to town, not even Xiangyu town. They never went out. After the Small Third Front came, then they'd go out, but still very few people went to Xiangyu town. If we were going there, we'd take the factory truck. Some drivers would let you hitch a ride, but some drivers would say no and not take you. You ask him when he's leaving and he wouldn't answer you, then you couldn't ride with him. Young people were different: oh, you're driving off? Well, I'll just climb on. Some drivers had okay attitudes; they wouldn't drag you off. But some younger drivers, they had more violent tempers, they'd pull you right off the truck, and if you weren't lucky, they might even hit you, then you couldn't hitch a ride. The older drivers were all right.

[…] At first this road, they built it real narrow, and it was just dirt. As soon as the roadbed was done, we saw the Shanghai people driving in. From far off you heard the rumbling sounds, and folks here, everyone was happy. The Shanghai people were coming, cars were coming. Back then folks here for sure had never seen a car. If they had, it was really rare. In Xiangyu town then there were only a few cars, you might see one only every few days or even a couple months there, much less us in the mountains here. Back then, the roads from Xiangyu to Dongzhi were all very narrow, then the roads from Xiangyu up here were even narrower little mountain tracks. Only people with good driving skills could drive in here. We're all high ridges here, uphills and downhills, the roads were always uneven, and back then we were in a sea of virgin forest, to wrap arms around a tree you needed several people. These great big trees to the sky, you couldn't see the sun, [...] you couldn't see the sky.

When the Shanghainese came, they opened the roads from Xiangyu to us here. It all used to be just forest, wolves, leopards, tigers, tons and tons of them. The pigs and chickens the folks kept at home would often be taken by wolves and tigers. Then the Shanghainese developed it, opened the factory, and the animals disappeared. There was a lot of blasting. Back then it was just the blaster rumbling all day long, blasting the animals far away.

[...] Before the Shanghainese came, we all used kerosene lamps at home [...] and drank stream water from the gulches. When the Shanghainese first came, they also drank that water. The factory's running water system was opened only in '72.

[They didn't install running water for us,] because, well, I say that the village is together with the factory, but there's also some distance. At the very least, for a village to install running water, that was a whole engineering project, so they couldn't possibly install that for you. If you wanted tap water, you could go to their place and get some, and if the fields needed tap water to prevent drought, they'd install some pipes in the fields. Back then, the Yangtze River water hadn't come in yet, so they also used the mountain gulch water. They used a pump to get water from a stream to provide for the cafeteria. When the factory began producing officially, then they needed a lot of water, they brought in Yangtze River water for the production workshops. They needed several dozen tons of water a day, you know.

[In terms of electricity,] they began with a 38 horsepower... generator, including the homes of folks nearby here, all began getting electricity and stopped lighting oil lamps. The time for using electricity was before nine at night. At 9:45, they'd have a signal. How, you ask? They'd make the electric lights flash three times, telling you to go to sleep. The folks used the factory electricity too, so when the lights blinked three times at 9:45, then you were supposed to go to bed.

[If you didn't go to sleep,] their electricity would stop anyway. The factory's electricity stopped, and so did the ordinary folks'. Because the generator got shut off all at once, then it'd start again at 6 a.m. The next morning. When the factory got power, we would too. Then […] they had high-voltage electricity, they were generating a lot of power, so the factory went to folks' homes and hooked up electric wires. When we needed power, we'd go into the factory to look for him—the electrician they arranged to help us get electricity. We got electricity and back then power didn't cost any money. Now people like us in our 50s, we still remember the favors that the Shanghainese did for us. People over 70, they can't remember, when they get old their brains get confused. The younger ones are used to living a life with electricity, they don't care. But our generation's different, we feel very blessed!

[…] On Monday and Friday the commissary store would be open and us folks would all run over there to buy things. […] We'd all run to the little store to see if the door was open; if it was, then we could go shopping. Back then we could get Pegasus and Big Qianmen Gate brand cigarettes from Shanghai, and the cheapest Honored Gentleman cigarettes for ordinary folks, eight cents a pack, I think the Pegasus was 20 cents. Some older [Shanghainese], they were a little better-off, the ones who got along better with folks, they'd give Big Qianmen Gate to folks to smoke. Then more cigarettes got to circulating and the Shanghainese couldn't control it, because we country folks like cigarettes, and the supply was tight.

It used to be that you needed [ration] tickets to buy anything, then the commissary store found out that folks had gotten their hands on a lot of the cigarettes, causing the supply for workers to buy to fall short, so the workers complained. Then they set a rule to ration. People who wanted these brands were issued tickets. The limit per month for Big Qianmen Gate was five packs and one carton for Pegasus, and there was a high-end Phoenix one. By '73, '74, I heard that cigarettes were scarce in Shanghai, but they weren't here. We could all smoke Big Qianmen Gate and Phoenix. Phoenix was real popular here. If someone were smoking a Phoenix somewhere, all the folks around could smell the fragrance. Once my father smoked a Phoenix in a bus and the other passengers were all looking around trying to figure out who was smoking such a nice-smelling cigarette, but they couldn't figure it out. Other folks around here couldn't get this cigarette, but we could.

* * *

杨爱玉 Yang Aiyu, female. Interviewed together with her husband, 张要华 Zhang Yaohua. Anhui natives and villagers near the Small Third Front Longjiang Water Plant in Xiangyu Township, Dongzhi County.

Keywords: camaraderie, conflicts, consumer goods, electrification, environment, entertainment, food, living conditions, medical issues, movies, nostalgia, rural vs. urban, pay and benefits, water and irrigation

[TN: Please note that this narrative contains references to self-harm that may be disturbing.]

Yang: Forty years ago, the factory had a walk-in freezer. We here in the villages had never seen that before. In my house we'd use a thermos and get some of that ice water and carry it back home. That was 40 years ago. I'm 50 now, and usually [back then] village folks couldn't get iced water, but we could. When the ol' Shanghais saw us kiddos bringing our thermoses, they'd all help us get some [ice water]. And when the factory showed movies and such, for outsiders you had to buy a ticket. But really, how were we kids going to come up with money to buy a ticket? So we'd stay in this little corner until they finished selling tickets, and then the people there would let us go in to watch. And then—at first it was movies, but then the water plant got a big TV, and we hadn't ever watched TV out here back then either.

Zhang: In '72, they shipped in that TV. We couldn't believe our eyes. How could any of us buy a TV for home back then, right? We couldn't imagine. So culturally, they really brought great enjoyment for us folks. We grew up with them! But the Shanghainese, some of them looked down on us villagers. So when watching movies, sometimes our young guys got into fights with them. Those were really some knock-down drag-out fights! And when that happened, the factory leaders would have to sort it all out. But we folks were just like that, nothing complicated.

[…] Yang: Look at my hand here, look at this finger here, look. If this were just in the village back then, they'd call me disabled. What happened was, I was chopping firewood on a hill and when I chopped, my finger fell right off. I was just twelve. I had a lot of siblings at home and my mama wasn't that bothered. She told me to just come back by myself. And then my daddy, he was doing some small jobs around the water plant, so I went to go looking for him. Then my daddy took me to an old doctor from Shanghai and he used this thing like a sponge to wrap my hand up, and then a stick to splint it, and kept at it until my hand was better. He didn't charge us a cent. He was a doctor at the water plant clinic; all of them in the plant were ol' Shanghais, even the doctors. They fixed my hand up and didn't charge us anything. My own granny felt bad and brought that doctor more than a dozen eggs, but he didn't take 'em.

If I'd gone to our village clinic for sure this hand would be mangled. But my finger'd fallen off and I don't know what medicine he used, he just said, this is a good medicine, don't worry, you won't be disabled. And I remember that the skin on my finger was all rolled up, but anyway he just put that spongy thing on there, it sucked onto the wound and the blood melted away. After a while my hand was fixed. Thank goodness for that ol' Shanghai! [...] I remember there was also an old granny, I don't know if she's still around—her name was Tan. We called her Granny Tan. She gave me a pair of black sandals, oh, I was over the moon, I was so happy. She was Shanghainese, yeah, she was a worker back then in the plant.

Zhang: They also brought us beer, you know, otherwise we wouldn't know what the heck beer was. And Pegasus cigarettes, and Forever cigarettes, all of 'em 13 cents a pack. Anyway, we folks would go to buy these, and they'd also sell to us, they'd sell to us outsiders and take care of folks. [...] Yang: The toilet paper they used, 19 cents a pack, that quality was sure great. In our minds, from when they came out here to when they left, that's all in our minds. So if a thing comes out from Shanghai, we just feel in our minds like that thing is definitely reliable. Because the Shanghainese lived here and their technology was just good, so their stuff is high quality.

[...] Zhang: All the workers they hired to help build the plant and the docks were from outside [Shanghai], like from Tongling, Zongyang [TN: in southern Anhui], and also from near here. Building [techniques] were backward then; it was all by hand, at most with a wheelbarrow or cart to move dirt from the hills. Sometimes if you pulled a cart for a day they'd give you eight bucks. That was a real high wage for the time. Sometimes local folks would do small jobs for the plant and get three bucks a day. It was really high—apprentice workers in factories only got 18 bucks a month back then. So doing small jobs and getting three bucks a day, we thought it was crazy high back then.

[...] The factory at the time was giving us tap water, but some families didn't want to install a tap. It was free but some folks didn't want it. [Sighs.] Folks had some backward thinking then, very backward. When did they start putting tap water in? Not till '78, when the main staff were beginning to leave [for Shanghai]. Why didn't they [locals] want to put in tap water? One reason is that the factory asked each of us to pay a little money, each household. The big money they covered, but you know, at the time, some families would need to buy a pair of tennis shoes on credit. Thirty cents for a day's pay, you save for a year, husband and wife, but then there was no Birth Planning so at the least you'd have three or four little ones at home. So that's to say, if you had a piece of pipe put in and a tap, that was ten bucks, but you really couldn't spare the ten bucks. You understand what I'm saying? It's not that folks didn't want taps, it's that they were too poor to pay. Back in the 70s, you couldn't spare that ten bucks.

[...] Yang: When we were little kids, we saw the Shanghainese wearing rayon clothes. Some folks, especially the older ones, they'd say, "How could you wear that?" They all said those were see-through. As younger people, we saw the Shanghainese wearing them and also wanted to follow along and wear 'em. I remember my first nylon blouse; it was a granny from Old Qiu's family who brought it from Shanghai. Like, later on, when we went out, we dressed more fashionably, more fashionably than people from other villages. Like it used to be that we didn't wear bras in these villages. Then when the Shanghainese came, we understood, and we ran off to the commissary stores they opened to buy them. You couldn't buy them in the village. All the girls nearby started wearing them. For sure, when our girls near here went out, they always seemed fancier than other people.

[...] I think a lot of local folks owe our lives to the Shanghainese. A woman near us, I think had a fight with someone at home and took an overdose of sleeping pills. The Shanghainese had good medicine, good doctors all of them, and saved her. If it weren't for them, she'd be a goner. I remember that lady had taken all those pills and they carried her to the factory clinic. They saw they had no way to help her so they took her by car right away to the Tianshan Hospital. Of course we villagers didn't have cars then. The Shanghainese took their car directly to bring her to the hospital to save her. They didn't take a cent of money. I'm telling you, no lie.

Zhang: And in '72, we were teenagers, we could see them bringing beer from Shanghai. We drank it back then and thought it was "pig trough water." How could people drink this stuff? But we saw them drinking it and we slowly started drinking it, too. We started drinking beer 20 years before other ordinary farm folks. Back then the Shanghainese ate white rice, short-grained rice; we'd all eat the paddy rice we planted in the countryside. They had a nice living standard. Every day they had steamed rice and about two ounces of meat, with lean and with fat, pretty tasty when you cooked it. They definitely had a higher standard of living than we village folks.

[...] Yang: I remember when I was a little kid, I used to pick the wild greens they call kalimeris and sometimes we'd go to the pond and get some snails. I'd often go peddle these to the Shanghainese, five cents for a pound and a quarter. Sometimes I was nice to them and didn't ask for money. So that Auntie Tan, she gave me a pair of sandals, the plastic kind, you didn't see them at all in the village. I was so happy then, so sometimes when I got some snails I'd give them to her for free. She knew that my father smoked, so she gave me cigarettes, a kind with a seagull drawn on them. I remember they were nine cents a pack back then. She gave those cigarettes to me and right away we got to know her.

If I went to go visit her at home, she'd take some sour plums, put them in water, and add some rock candy and give us that to drink. We'd be so happy. You know, we didn't even have tea for drinking in the village then. But we could get some sour plum drinks. I have this very strong recollection, when we were really little, we'd take a little thermos—the thermoses then all had bamboo woven on the outsides, still—we'd run to the factory freezer to get a bottle of ice water. Nobody had refrigerators back then. In the summers in villages then, you'd never see ice water. But the factory had it so I'd get a bottle, bring it home, keep it covered with a towel to keep it cool. If my granny hadn't passed she'd be over 100 by now. I remember she loved drinking that ice water. Who could get ice water in the summer? We were so happy then!

[…] Zhang: When the military factory really started production, older outsiders they didn't let in, but us kids would still go hang out in there all day and got familiar with the factory. The guards at the gates, we still remember them. The guy named Li, we called him Uncle Li; the one named Wang was Uncle Wang. We went every day to play near the factory, and when the mister in the gatehouse saw us, he'd call to us, "hey kiddos!" A bunch of us together, we'd run in to get grass for the pigs [at home], and we'd go pick up some [used wooden] templates to use in our cooking fires. When it came to movies at night, of course our parents would never give us money to get tickets, so we kids would wait until they finished selling tickets and the movie had been playing a while. Then the mister in the gatehouse would say to us, "run on in there, kiddos!" They wouldn't take our money, because we were all from nearby.

* * *

张渭德 Zhang Weide, male. Anhui native, cadre in Guichi County during the Small Third Front.

Keywords: education, environment, medicine, nostalgia, rural vs. urban, travel and transportation, water and irrigation

One should say this: the Small Third Front set up in mountainous areas and gave a big economic boost to our economic development in Guichi, especially the mountainous zones. It used to be that the lowlands were better-off than the highlands in Guichi, like the Wusha area, that's flat-land; the overall economy was pretty good. But in the hills, transportation was pretty difficult, and the education and cultural life of the mountains was all a bit worse [...] but after the Shanghai Small Third Front set up in Meijie, that situation changed.

First, they fixed up the roads. A road we've got here, the Qishi Road, was built by "shock troops" after the Shanghai Small Third Front came. There used to be no road at all. That road from Qishan to Shimen'gao was built for the needs of the Small Third Front. At the time, they organized militia from all over the Chizhou area to build it "shock troop" style. They activated the old Anqing area, the old Chizhou area; in the 60s, it was the old Chizhou area that sent militia. Just in Guichi County, they organized 6000 people—6000 militia members as "shock troops" to go in and build the road. So, they opened that road in a very short amount of time, so the Small Third Front's path into the mountains was clear. There used to be no road. No road, no electricity.

Water, well, the Meijie village near the factory, every home, all the folks there, got tap water. How'd you ever have tap water in the mountains, before! Back then, even in our Guichi town, tap water was only just put in. Another thing was medical care. After the Shanghai Changjiang Hospital set up in there, not only around these our Guichi parts, but people all around us, were impacted. Back then, so many people from Nanjing, you know, and Zongyang [County], all came to get treated at the Changjiang Hospital. They had the best facilities, the best doctors. A lot of the doctors had been abroad, you know (Images 4.3 and 4.4).

Not only did the county hospital not compare [to Changjiang Hospital], but even the Anqing District Hospital couldn't match it, you know. The old district hospital was no good, either. The Changjiang Hospital was really famous in our county. Also, the impact on education was very big too. The Small Third Front factory in Guichi did a few schools, secondary and elementary, matching sets. And when the Shanghainese came to the mountains, apart from stimulating the economy for local folks, what other economic help did they give, you ask? Things that weren't worth anything before became valuable. It used to be that nobody wanted the baby

Image 4.3 Color photograph of the gates of the Changjiang Hospital, 2017, by Ma Ping

bamboo shoots on the mountains, but when the Shanghainese came, when the shoots came out, they were worth money, and pumpkin seeds and whatnot became worth money, and your taro, your peanuts, things like that too. This really made the economy in the mountains much more alive.

* * *

章亚光 Zhang Yaguang, male. Anhui native of a village neighboring a Small Third Front factory, later a local historian and lawyer.

Keywords: conflicts, consumer goods, manual labor, politically correct, rural vs. urban, pay and benefits

[TN: The below translation comes from a written recollection penned by Zhang in August and September 2012.]

[…] Jixi was a closed-off small mountain county and Jixi people's lifestyles were relatively conservative, or even backward-looking if you want

Image 4.4 Color photograph of buildings in the Changjiang Hospital compound, 2017, by Ma Ping

to put it that way. After Liberation, Mao Zedong promoted the "Big and Communal" [People's Communes], the political campaigns came hard and fast, the [political] "wrangling" was non-stop, and people's lives were extremely difficult, with no spiritual or cultural lives to speak of. And then we were also in the CultRev period, we were heavily critiquing capitalist thought and mightily cutting off the remaining "tails" of capitalism. In my old hometown—the Yingzhou production brigade's Forever Red production team—they saw the value of their work points drop and drop. Eventually it became that ten work points could only buy you a pack of Eastern Sea cigarettes, at a price of 28 cents. Most peasant farmers' lives were really and truly bitter beyond words. The 20-plus enterprises and work units transferred to Jixi from Shanghai and the over 10,000 workers and their family members and children improved the people of Jixi's incomes and impacted and enriched the people's cultural lives.

Jixi had to build over 20 Small Third Front work units all at once, which was a huge amount of construction. The No. 4 Construction Company they transferred from Shanghai was definitely insufficient, so many communes and brigades within the county organized construction teams and joined the building of the Small Third Front. Demand for casual laborers (Jixi people called them "rough workers") was even bigger. A big batch of farmers used agricultural downtime or "snuck" onto the construction sites to do various jobs to earn some cash. Unemployed people among town residents also joined in. Also, the volume of items the Third Front needed to transport was big. They used their vehicles, but nearby farmers rushed to work on loading and unloading, which was also quite a bit of income. [...] Though county, commune, and brigade cadres took up quite a few spots in the hiring quotas [in the early 1970s], when this [local] group of labor power entered the factory, their daily pay was much, much more than the price of a pack of Eastern Sea cigarettes.

* * *

张燕芳 Zhang Yanfang, female, teacher turned production statistics and logistics cadre at a steel mill.

Keywords: conflicts, consumer goods, critique, family, food, frustration, nepotism, political problems, travel and transportation

[...] Where did that money [budgeted for the logistics department] go? So, I mean, this kind of old comrade, really you couldn't find someone [good] like him these days if you carried a floodlight to search. I mean, living here, all these people had to have food, clothing, things, right? It was all ration tickets back then. These skimpy meat tickets, cigarette tickets, whatever, none of it was enough. For example, if you wanted to [help your workers] eat fish, or meat, aside from what was supplied from the Shanghai area, you could also go [find] it yourself. If you do that, you gotta go make good with the local vegetable companies, seafood companies, subsidiary food companies, and the commander of the army region and such. At this time there wasn't such a thing as using public funds to dine out; there was nowhere to get reimbursed, he had to do it himself. So in the end, he didn't have [any] money. Every time, "Little Zhang, I'm going on a business trip." Going on business trips was going to get supplies for poultry and fish and meat, other food. So our factory had the best provisions of any of the whole 50-some Rear Base factories.

Did the others tell you? The best food. It was all our old comrade. Nothing for his own home, nothing for himself. His old lady—Dacron at the time—I don't know if you know what that is? You should go home and ask your grandma. Dacron at the time needed special coupons. It was really hard to get. This type had just been released. His old lady had a Dacron Sun Yat-sen suit [TN: also known as the "Mao suit"] made for him in Shanghai. That meant money and special coupons. He said, "Little Zhang, I'm going on a business trip. I'm out of cash, lend me a little." I said, why are you borrowing money, you're going on public business [so you can use public funds]. But he refused; he'd sooner die than do that [use public money]. He said, "you're young, you have kids and elders at home. I'm okay, it's just my old lady and me."

He had me sell the Dacron Sun Yat-sen suit that his old lady brought, sell it to somebody else; he gave up the special coupons to bring back the cash. Every time before salaries were released, before he left, he'd say, "whoever I owe money to, you help me pay that off." In the end he had no real money at all. He was like this, wholeheartedly throwing himself into his work. Our work unit could eat so well; the credit to this old comrade was really—people all know of him now. He looked really fierce and mean. When I first got there to report to him, I was afraid of him too. But he was actually so kind. He was so good to folks. [...] His face was really fierce. His surname was Chi, the *chi* of "being tardy" [TN: *chidao*], everyone called him "Tiger" Chi. Really.

[...] In the 80s, later on, when my parents had passed, I went back to Shanghai. Not the work unit in Shanghai but the office. There was one in Shanghai. Why? Well, like, all these groceries [...] the local Anhui-made things, actually the materials were really good, but the craftsmanship, the technology, wasn't up to par. The same soy sauce, our soy sauce, really, in a big tank, we put it ourselves in a stainless steel tank, and brought it over there from Shanghai. Shanghainese weren't used to the local soy sauce. The local soy sauce was sour. The fermentation technology wasn't any good. Like, cigarettes, candy, things at the commissary, cotton shirts and pants, soap and toilet paper and such, all of it was brought over from Shanghai. And beer. I accompanied the trucks [to go to Shanghai, pick up the goods, and bring them back to Anhui]. I didn't go every week. This wasn't my duty, my work. But sometimes, if there wasn't anyone to accompany the trucks, and I happened to want to come to Shanghai to see our little guy, then I'd come along. This wasn't all the time. It was a pretty, pretty rare opportunity.

We had a driving group—we in logistics had a special driving group that used the trucks. This was all managed [from above]. Yes, we in logistics took care of our own drivers. There was a refrigerated truck for your meats and such; if it were hot, the meat would [otherwise] get defrosted, but inside, it wouldn't go bad. We shipped cutlassfish. So every year, to and fro with beer, and if there were something else that came onto the market, we'd also eat that. We ate real well in [the factory]. Like, if we were going to have hairy crab, our trucks would go out and load up on hairy crab. It was all our boss's hard work. He had all these connections outside [the factory], because he used to be in the military. Previous subordinates—he used to be a company commander, his former subordinates are now all more titled than he is. He goes down there and says, "I need such and such," and people would give it to him. Sometimes we'd also ship some steel materials out [to trade for food], because back then our steel was really worth something outside [the factory].

[…] If I talk about it I might laugh. At that time inside [in Anhui] there was a Party Rectification. Why would I laugh when I talk about Party Rectification? I'm very thick-skinned; I'm not afraid of heaven nor earth. You tell me to do personnel work I'm anxious, but you talk about me being too tough, I'm not afraid. That's how I am. About '82 I left [Anhui]. '86, Party Rectification. So my Party affiliations were all inside [in Anhui], so they requested that I go back in, to do the Rectification. It killed me; what was I going to do about [my family in] Shanghai? One old man [my father] and one kid, what would I do? I'd already bought a refrigerator by this point. At that time there were very few fridges out there. Nothing for it, I bought a fridge. I—a week, I was going to be a whole week in [Anhui]. One week's stuff, all the cans, I laid them out nicely, for my daddy, like this. My husband was over there, in Anhui. Yes, he [came back] later than I did. Much later.

It was really hard [working in Shanghai]. Lemme tell you, I'd crawl [out of bed] before the sky was light in the mornings and then everything in the house would have to be done properly, breakfast, lunch, and dinner. So my son, well, he could cook rice from the time he was in primary school; he'd hang a key around his neck. Even before I got home, he'd have cooked the rice for me. Well, then a rush—the bus to Wusong then, there weren't the elevated highways yet; the #51 [bus] would rock and rock and rock for over an hour; after all that rocking there I'd have to go to work. After work, back then it was still a bit more flexible; if there weren't other things at 3 or 4 pm, then I could go home, it was all right. Then rock and rock and rock back home. Grocery shopping, cleaning the food, and cooking, it was all me.

* * *

赵惠瑛 Zhao Huiying, female, worker and kindergarten teacher at a Small Third Front steelworks.

Keywords: camaraderie, conflicts, family, medical issues, nostalgia

[Interviewer: I'd heard from Teacher Ji that among the first batch (of teachers), there was some reason to give blood, so she went along with the truck to go (donate).] We often had things like this over there, because people there were really good and earnest, not like now; blood donations require a lot of motivational work. Yeah, [you'd just drink a packet of milk that they gave you afterward and be done]!

People were really simple and good back then. Like our Zhang Aiping. Her husband was in Shanghai at the time at the No. 5 Shanghai Steelworks. So, every year they'd do family visits. We had several on our end who were single, men, with wives in Shanghai, so they were going [to Anhui] to visit and such. Once on the way there was a car accident—not a full wreck; their car bumped the one ahead of them on the way, but the truck ahead was [carrying] acid or something, some kind of chemical, and splashed them all. The news got to our kindergarten and everyone was real worried. [Zhang] was even more nervous, in a real panic.

Then me and our hygiene teacher, the two of us kept her company, saying not to fret, comforting her, because we didn't know exactly what had happened. We heard they were burned, that it was chemicals, that the crash was really bad. So even now Zhang Aiping and I have a good relationship. Her husband says, "Teacher Zhao, this I won't forget till the day I die, you basically gave us a huge hand back then." Me, I'm just okay as a problem solver. When this happened I thought first about what to do. I said, quick, Dongmei, run to the commissary to buy two sets of cotton shirts and long johns, their clothes are burned, the clothes are no good, [with these underthings] they can at least get changed. Then I went with [Aiping] in the car, I don't remember what we took to get there. We left our Guichi and were in Anqing or somewhere, then finally we found this group of people. [The husband] and her son, the two were burned into a mess after all, but fortunately only the surface skin.

When we went, they'd just covered him up with some blankets in the hospital, and all his clothes had been burned off, so we took the clothes we'd bought and hurried to get him changed and cleaned up, then I came back to Shanghai and kept them company. No problem at all, mentally. Now they're doing well. Because of this—because many women [in Anhui] had their men in Shanghai, and because I was principal, I'd specially look after them, these wives living alone. I'd often call them to my house to visit, have a meal, so everyone was very harmonious. Me, I'm usually pretty unstinting and fast in doing things, too, so if there were really bad things going on I would be pretty tough when I was giving criticism. Basically they all knew this. But if you had any difficulties, I'd definitely try my best to think of ways to help you. So, in this process, everyone in recollection would say, Teacher Zhao, you're really a good person, it was like making friends, and now like being old sisters.

* * *

汪福琪 Wang Fuqi, male, Anhui native and county-level cadre in Jixi. Helped oversee transfer of Small Third Front to local control.

Keywords: consumer goods, food, living conditions, nostalgia, rural vs. urban

[The workers' residence buildings] of the time were all [built] to national standards. The height of each floor, 2.8 meters, that was all standardized. One hundred million [yuan] was invested. Up to 10,000 Shanghainese people worked for the Small Third Front factories in Jixi.

[…] So many people came from Shanghai then, so the supply of grain and the supply of vegetables [had to be worked out]. Before, there was no regular vegetable market in the county town. After they all came, they produced, well, folks—the farmers—would take their vegetables to the county seat to sell. At first it was on a small scale, still without a proper market, just selling a little along the streets, especially Sundays; the workers from the Third Front factory would come to town to buy some things, so that shaped a market. But the major supplies of produce and meat they still bought from elsewhere, because Jixi couldn't provide enough variety. So that stimulated exchange here. On the local folks' side, it was like this. The Third Front factories, they had some supply problems. For example, white sugar and cigarettes used ration coupons back then; even now they're rationed by tickets. Some Shanghainese would take these things to trade with the local …. They'd take the ration tickets to the farmers to trade for some eggs, trade for an old hen, for meat, have some furniture made. So this way this folk exchange was worked out.

[…] Then in terms of exchanges in daily life, that was also very notable. The Shanghainese were pretty choosy in what they wore, their clothing was pretty nice. Back in the day around our parts here, they wore synthetic material, the quality kind, polyester. Yes, really good [stuff]. They had these polyester shirts; especially some female workers would wear these polyester blouses. We folks around here saw that and thought it was really high-end, so they'd exchange those things with us—the fabric and style of clothes.

The most classic thing I remember was the pants that the Shanghainese wore at the time with really narrow legs, as narrow as six or seven inches, real long, very long, dragging down [the leg], then some very fashionable shoes. Around here, we wore wide-leg pants. Their fashions really affected local people. Yes, many people began to imitate how the Shanghainese dressed. Many young people, most of them had been hired [into the factories] as workers. Men and women. They were hired to Shanghai. Then when they came back they dressed like the Shanghainese. Everyone thought it was great. Then everybody started dressing like this. So, this way, there was this clothing and accessory interchange among locals and the Shanghainese, and there was quite a lot of that, too.

* * *

Further Reading

On Medicine and Healthcare

C. C. Chen, *Medicine in Rural China: A Personal Account*. Berkeley: University of California Press, 1989.

Deborah Davis, "Chinese Social Welfare: Policies and Outcomes." "The People's Republic of China after 40 Years" special issue. *China Quarterly* 119 (1989), 577–97.

Xiaoping Fang, *Barefoot Doctors and Western Medicine in China*. Rochester, NY: University of Rochester Press, 2012.

Judith Farquhar, "Market Magic: Getting Rich and Getting Personal in Medicine after Mao." *American Ethnologist* 23:2 (1996), 239–57.

Miriam Gross, *Farewell to the God of Plague: Chairman Mao's Campaign to Deworm China*. Berkeley: University of California Press, 2016.

On Material Life

Robert Ash, "Squeezing the peasants: Grain extraction, food consumption, and rural living standards in Mao's China." *The China Quarterly* 188 (2006), 959–998.

Lein-Lein Chen and John Devereux, "The iron rice bowl: Chinese living standards 1952–1978." *Comparative Economic Studies* 59:3 (2017), 261–310.

Jacob Eyferth, *Eating Rice from Bamboo Roots: The Social History of a Community of Handicraft Papermakers in Rural Sichuan, 1920–2000*. Cambridge, MA: Harvard University Asia Center, 2009.

Jie Li, *Shanghai Homes: Palimpsests of Private Life*. New York: Columbia University Press, 2014.

Hanchao Lu, "Bourgeois Comfort under Proletarian Dictatorship: Home Life of Chinese Capitalists before the Cultural Revolution." *Journal of Social History* 52:1 (2018), 74–100.

Alfreda Murck ed., *Mao's Golden Mangoes and the Cultural Revolution*. Zürich: Scheidegger & Spiess, 2013.

Jeffrey Pilcher, Yu Wang, and Yuebin Jackson Guo, "'Beer With Chinese Characteristics': Marketing Beer Under Mao." *Revista de administração de emprêsas* 58:3 (2018), 303–315.

Melissa Schrift, *Biography of a Chairman Mao Badge: The Creation and Mass Consumption of a Personality Cult*. New Brunswick, NJ: Rutgers University Press, 2001.

Dorothy J. Solinger, *Chinese Business Under Socialism: The Politics of Domestic Commerce, 1949–1980*. Berkeley: University of California Press, 1984.

CHAPTER 5

Education, Media, and Culture

Translator's Note

Education and culture were key auxiliaries to the Small Third Front's industrial campaign, once the factories were built, staffed, and running. The following lengthy recollections attest to how kindergartens and schools for the children of factory employees were run, and how people—most of them women, many of them the spouses of male workers in the Third Front factories, some of them without much formal training in childcare or education—came to take up positions in these fields. Staffing kindergartens and schools was urgent because they permitted workers to move their families to the Front, reducing worker complaints at having their families separated. Factory-provided childcare and schooling also greatly eased the daily lives of working parents, as all adults, regardless of gender, on the Small Third Front were expected to work full-time in some capacity.

The following accounts also highlight the visceral craving that both urban Small Third Fronters and their neighbors in isolated villages felt for movies, music, recreational sports, books, and other forms of entertainment and culture that are often taken for granted in wealthy, developed parts of the world today. Just as relatively high-quality food, clothing, medicines, and other material goods were brought across great distances into the backwaters of rural China for Small Third Front employees and

Y. Xu, Y. Y. Wang, *Everyday Lives in China's Cold War Military-Industrial Complex*, Palgrave Studies in Oral History,
https://doi.org/10.1007/978-3-030-99688-8_5

their families, so too were urban educational standards and pedagogical practices as well as urban cultural goods like newly released films and musical pieces brought into the countryside. There, people jockeyed, sometimes fiercely, for access to such items, so hard to come by in much of the PRC's rural hinterlands.

Enthusiasm for movies, libraries, and schools might seem at odds with the prevalent political suspicion toward formal education and cultural goods in the 1960s and 1970s. Even before the CCP's victory in 1949, Party leadership had sought to purify the cultural landscape along politically correct lines. In 1942, for example, Mao Zedong explicitly demanded that writers and artists in Yan'an, the remote wartime Communist headquarters, use their craft to serve the Party's political aims. Campaigns were mounted nationwide to purge politically and aesthetically suspect materials in the 1950s and 1960s and replace them with approved items. Highly educated people, including teachers, professors, and students, experienced heightening scrutiny of their political loyalties. Historians view the "Anti-Rightist Campaign" beginning in 1957 that targeted intellectuals and experts as a turning point toward suspicion of the educated and creative classes. The Cultural Revolution's intense early years marked a violent escalation of efforts to control cultural products and producers. Items containing associations with the pre-1949 past, the world beyond China, anything erotic or "individualistic," and featuring political leaders who had fallen from grace were confiscated by Red Guards and destroyed by individuals afraid of being caught with them.

Just as our respondents in other sections demonstrate sometimes complex feelings in looking back on their time on the Small Third Front, so too do educators and cultural workers evince mixed views of their work on the Small Third Front in retrospect. Some see the organization and quality of teaching and of cultural products as very high and superior to those they witnessed subsequently; others reveal challenges and obstacles they feel were impossible to overcome in the Small Third Front milieu.

Questions for Discussion

1. What kinds of cultural goods, according to the people interviewed, were most in demand on the Small Third Front? Why do you think these were so popular?
2. How did educational and cultural workers on the Small Third Front see themselves vis-à-vis those in both their neighboring rural com-

munities and their urban counterparts? What were some of the particular challenges or conflicts identified by our respondents that they might not have had to face in an urban setting?

3. Why do you think many of the closely politically vetted workers in Small Third Front factories and their rural neighbors were so eager for cultural goods, despite the political risks? Do their accounts fit with the standard view of the Cultural Revolution years as a culturally and educationally barren era?

* * *

卞建华 *Bian Jianhua, female, driver for the Rear Base militia headquarters.*

Keywords: conflicts, entertainment, living conditions, movies, nostalgia, performing arts, rural vs. urban

There was sometimes fighting over movies. The movie halls were all made of bamboo back then. We were an industrial area, then under our jurisdiction there was a movie-screening team. At certain times they'd come to you, all prearranged, on such a date in such a month. After coming to you, they'd build the bamboo shed, and use a piece of cloth for the screen, then they'd start the show. Showing, well, you can imagine it, big chairs and small, adults and kids. Then there'd be arguments. Some couldn't see and would yell about it and such.

Tunxi was a little better. In Tunxi they'd show movies indoors, a special building. There'd be an auditorium and people maintaining order. [Outdoor squares and such wouldn't have people overseeing them.] If someone came to show [movies], if you were standing on a hillside, you could watch too; if you could see that far, you could feel free to watch. Back then life was very dull. We were a little better in 683, because we had cars. Sometimes we'd have the Shanghai Song and Dance Troupe to come perform in the Rear Base. We'd have to build a stage. Seeing Shanghai people coming was like having guests come over; it was really exciting. But people who couldn't see wouldn't be so happy. That kind of thing would happen. This kind of thing would happen anywhere.

* * *

傅锡林 Fu Xilin, female, secondary school teacher at a Small Third Front steel mill.

Keywords: conflicts, critique, Cultural Revolution, education, frustrations, living conditions, work schedule

[At first] there were very few male teachers, I think! When the "worker-peasant-soldier" students came in [TN: those who attended universities in the late Cultural Revolution, who had been admitted on the basis of their class backgrounds], then there were more. Two men [at first], that's about right. One was Zheng Yuzhi, one was Zhang Jiandong, our principal.

[…] I was leading the second year junior high schoolers, yes, until the end. […] No, no, I didn't do all their classes. I taught math. I studied history; when I was first teaching at the Handan No. 6 Secondary School, I thought, based on my Tianjin understanding, that this school must be pretty highly ranked. Actually, Handan had only five secondary schools and the sixth one was recently converted over from an agricultural tech school. There were a lot of specialized teachers. But you know, it was the start of the Cultural Revolution! There were ten teachers who were being "remodeled" as "cow demons and snake spirits" [TN: epithet for various enemies and villains during the Cultural Revolution]. When I went to that school, there were 26 teachers. Then ten cadres got "sent down" to us [to fill in the vacancies]. What did that mean? Well, weren't there loads of cadres who got "sent down" to the villages? These ten people were the crème de la crème of the city committee. Their political backgrounds were spotless, and everything else too, so they got sent to the secondary school.

But ten of them showed up: one was an accountant, two were technical cadres. Okay, well those technical cadres could teach a little physics and chemistry. But the seven others were all leading cadres. When you went and asked these leading cadres what they could do? Well, they could only teach Chinese, others could only do politics. When I got to that school, I was doing politics. There weren't history classes anymore, so you did politics. So that's how you end up changing your specialty. You know, the Cultural Revolution was really warped. […] Big batches [of normal school graduates] were sent outside [the city], because they didn't keep you in big cities! When I got there [to Handan], they asked if I could change my specialty. I said, okay, I'll change it! I'll teach math! So I started doing math. I taught math for six years in Handan, and when I got over here [to Anhui] I still didn't have [history to teach]! I kept teaching math.

Mm-hmm, I taught math for ten years. Imagine: when I got to the X functions, I was really out of my depth, because I'd been in the liberal arts class all the way through my last year of senior high, and I'd only studied

[math] for a few months at that Peiguang Secondary School! After I got back they said I had been very diligent and such, but it was really because I was forced to do it and had no other options. But I was still able to teach it; I managed. Then in '77, things changed and we were teaching history [again]. They only started history classes back up in '77, not only [Chinese] history but also Shanghai local history. Even a lot of Shanghainese people couldn't lead [that class]. You Shanghainese are kind of dumb [laughs]—so I taught [history] for a year or two. When I first started, I began with modern [Chinese] history. Just me by myself teaching, then later they hired another person.

Later on we came back to Shanghai for training and study—we had a connection with Huangpu District, you know! When we were doing the training, a teacher from Guangming Middle School named Liu Zhongkui, he was a pretty great teacher. He taught world history, and when I was chatting with him and asking him questions, I told him that I was doing all the [history] courses at my school. Because we had history classes for second and third year junior high school and first year of senior high, right? Well, they were supposed to get ancient [Chinese] history, modern [Chinese] history, and world history, right? For doing it faster, I was trying to teach them all, and I was really anxious doing this. I'd never been such a great student, and I'd left all of this cold during the Cultural Revolution, so I was really out of my depth! But I was also very anxious!

Then I did that for a year or two, like I was telling that teacher; I had three courses, ancient, modern, and world. That teacher said, you're going to kill yourself! How can you possibly handle all that?! I couldn't; my kid was born in '76, I had her only when I was 36. So I had this little baby, no one to take care of us, and I was running all these classes. [... A neighbor who also taught] said Shanghainese slept really late, and I looked at our lights—just us three with our lights on when everyone else had turned theirs off, because we had to prep class! We had to really put our all into it! Nothing for it, we had to rush it!

[...] Tiring, yes, tiring. A bad thing about how our classes worked then was—they weren't like after I'd retired and continued to teach, where I saw ten-odd classes of students only once a week for one lecture, so I only had to prep that one lecture. Not like [back then] with three or two [different course preps] and you had to prep at least four lectures [a week] [...] like me, so unfamiliar [with the content], I kept having to go back and forth. At first when I was teaching four classes at once, doing modern [Chinese] history, it was only when I got to the fourth lecture that I'd get into it.

[…] We were really pretty exhausted back then, but we got through it. Then I pushed off one of the courses. The leadership found me a younger teacher [to take it over]. […] She was a music teacher, a junior "worker-peasant-soldier" student—she hadn't gone to university, she was a vocational school grad. She taught music. But she thought teaching music was no way forward, so she wanted to lead a course. Nothing for it back then [if you taught something outside your specialty]. Like with us in the arts, you could get by—just study up on your own! Yep, as long as you could give a lecture, you were okay. I've only seen two people who couldn't lecture. It was really just these things, you got familiar with them, you made them your own, and then you regurgitate it, that was fine. All you had to do was to understand and digest it.

[…] Let me tell you […] why didn't our school have a good reputation? It was all because our rates of student promotion just didn't go up, they just stayed stuck. The factory blamed us from dawn till dusk about it; what were we being fed for? All the time they complained. But I did do a good thing for our school. So when, you know, some people got promoted to cadre positions, no matter whether your Party committee, your propaganda department, your organizational department, your various workshop heads or deputy heads, all these jobs, but they didn't have the diplomas. A lot had junior high, at most vocational secondary school, or technical school, just that level. Some who didn't have their junior high diplomas did catch-up to earn those; those who didn't have senior high school did remedial work to get those. After I'd left, in '84, they had a senior high class that then helped these people catch up and earn their high school diplomas. […] Not just in our factory, this was all over the country, all over. They had tests, four subjects, Chinese, politics, history, geography, so basically having them pass through a simplified senior high education. Then when we lectured, after I finished, [they said] "Hey! That was really great!" They said I actually taught pretty well.

[…] So I've been a teacher my whole life. What wasn't so good? Well, I never got to teach excellent students. Let's just say the students at the Eight-Five Steelworks, they weren't too great! There was this vicious cycle, you know? Good students thought it wasn't good, so their parents transferred them elsewhere. The students weren't stellar. The poor ones weren't good in Shanghai and came into the mountains. So the quality wasn't high. Really, we asked of ourselves to teach [them] well. But the amount of teaching duties we had was much, much bigger than the amount of knowledge we had to teach. So it was a real struggle, really!

Transferring all around Tianjin, I taught all these vocational school grads. [...] In '84 I didn't leave [for Shanghai], we went to Tianjian, we went back together. I kept teaching there at a tech school. [...] Just a few years later [we came to Shanghai].

Actually, after my formal retirement, I taught for another decade. I only stopped in '06. That was all in private schools. No, ah! No, I mostly didn't do history. History made you not much money. I did politics. That, and for a few years I did geography at a secondary school! [...] History is very annoying [to teach], you know? So you have to give them [the students]—the ones who get it, they get it. The kids who don't, I kept teaching this kind of student, you have to really put a lot into it. You have to think of a way to give them a—a way to explain the key words; when you ask them questions, you have to think that question through. Geography is simple. A few phrases, ta-da, that's all. Yes, it's very clear, as long as your geographic knowledge is very rich, no problem.

At the Eight-Five Steelworks, well! You felt like "heaven is high and the emperor is far away," and the most annoying thing was that specialties didn't get covered. They'd give you chances for training, but you were left alone, you know? So no one to guide or oversee you well. I feel like a lot of times, at that school, you just relied on good faith efforts. Actually, the simplest thing I have to say is, my consciousness is really not that high; I just say that, forget all the highfalutin stuff, just make sure you're earning your keep. You have to deserve what money you're getting. Also, you have to be responsible to your students, right? You have to be that.

[...] In junior high [today] they really press you hard. But that's not actually good. I feel that's bad. For students, really, how do I put it! Sure, going to the next level [of schooling] is good, but you've ruined them for life. I always championed, students studying should be filled up [with knowledge] by end of senior high, and then in college you can study by yourself, you wouldn't have issues, right? [...] I think the most important thing is how you treat the students. Do you like them? Or do you reject them? This is very key. If you really treat them like your own, treat them like your own kids. How'd you teach them [your own children]? Right? You'd never be cruel, never manipulate them!

Another thing I think is very key—if you were a very good student as a kid, you'd not get it. If you weren't a good student, you'd understand. Because when I was young, growing up, I'd tell them, they are all good students. But I wasn't. Not exactly disruptive, just not very obedient, not very good grades, teachers didn't really like me. So when you grow up and

Image 5.1 B&W photograph of a secondary school classroom at the Eight-Five Steelworks, late 1970s/early 1980s, collection of Xu Youwei

become a teacher, you know really well what those kids are thinking. [...] Sometimes I think, in the vocational schools they say this a lot too, there's nothing wrong with the students. They just don't like school. Just this, no other issues, no character flaws, maybe they made mistakes? But no, they just don't like to study. [...] But their tinkering skills were good, and technical schools are also pretty good. You study your technical skills, what's wrong with that? Nothing bad about that.

[On why she went to teach at vocational schools after the Small Third Front]: Ahh, let me tell you, my mistake was right here. Some kind of aftereffect from the Cultural Revolution. After I went to Tianjin, my classmates were all in [public] secondary schools, you know, because we were all teachers. They all said, absolutely don't come work in a secondary school—why? The pay was too low! I was in the factory still, and they kept giving us goodies all the time in '84 and '85, and we had high bonuses too, all that. So that was my own shortsightedness. Then there were a few opportunities, actually none of them public secondary schools. Once was a public security office school, another time it was a police academy. This kind of school, but I turned them down (Image 5.1).

* * *

葛鼎学 Ge Dingxue, male, worker at a Small Third Front steelworks.

Keywords: art, camaraderie, conflicts, education, entertainment, living conditions, nostalgia

Most people were bored most of the time, with nothing to do. Usually, we ate all three meals in the canteens. A group of us who got along pretty well set ourselves a plan: back then I also liked reading and studying and would make up these puns and jokes. The kids who were kind of studious, we'd study and train something for three months at a time. Like, this quarter we'd do brush calligraphy, next quarter we'd learn to take photographs. My calligraphy was trained in the mountains, from the first I was doing calligraphy. A bunch of people were practicing along with me. We'd save the paper from the day's practice and take a look over them three months later, and feel pretty great: oh, we've made progress, and we'd feel rewarded and more interested (Image 5.2).

Image 5.2 B&W photograph of the PA control room at the Shaoshan Electronics Factory, 1978

At the time I helped classmates and colleagues write stuff. After I'd done that they'd say, Little Ge, why don't you help us make seals [TN: a distinct stamp with one's name or other inscriptions used in lieu of signatures, often associated with classical literary culture and calligraphy]? I was like, where would I get my hands on those? Then I did give it a try; I tried carving a little on my own and I thought I did a pretty okay job.

I also like reading, so whenever I came to Shanghai I'd buy a lot of books. Just about all of my cash was spent on books. It was pretty good in the mountains back then, they'd have book shows and whatnot where you could also buy some books. The Xinhua Bookstore [TN: a national, state-owned chain] they didn't have until later. At first there were no books at all; at first they'd hold these book shows that the factory arranged for [the vendors] to come out to us. They had a library in the factory and I'd hang out in there, reading.

Of course, I'd make fun of a few colleagues who were studying for diplomas. I'd say, what good is this diploma of yours? And they'd say, what's the good of what you're practicing? I'd say, no matter whether it's useful or not, this skill would always be my own, but after you all do your studying, you'll just be throwing it away. Each to his own. Later on, some of them took the university entrance exams and such. We were all sorts.

I also knew how to give haircuts and a lot of workers and cadres in my No. 2 Workshop came to get haircuts from me. I'd be barbering from after work all the way until it was too dark to see. I'd cut so much hair that I got blisters on my hands. Now they all have electric trimmers, but back then it was all by hand. A lot of people came to me for haircuts. I did a lot of things back then in those mountains. I even wrote love letters for a lot of people. Some people got married and the wife would be all puzzled. How come your handwriting was so nice early on, but now your characters are ugly? So then someone gave me away saying that it was me who'd written the letters. Not only were my characters pretty, my content was great too.

* * *

季美华 *Ji Meihua, female, kindergarten teacher at a Small Third Front steel mill.*

Keywords: camaraderie, education, living conditions, men vs. women, nostalgia, performing arts, rural vs. urban

I didn't apply to be in the kindergarten. Others recommended me, and I thought I'd kind of like it, so I left [the workshop]. Things like [training, selection], I don't remember well. After all, it's over 40 years since then. I was only 21 then; I went to be a kindergarten teacher. When I first started, I think I came to Shanghai to take a look. We were all women. All the kindergarten teachers were female. No men. Three female teachers came out in the first batch. In one workshop, there were three of us teachers. Very few of us, and we had very few classes too. We three also went to Shanghai. Someone escorted us, yes, let me think—but I forget who. We weren't part of the Logistics Department; we were supervised by the Education Department.

We had an Education Department [at the steelworks], yes, because there was an elementary school. This factory of ours was very orderly. There was an elementary school, a technical school, a daycare, and a kindergarten. They were very regimented from the start, and everything came along. Unlike other factories, we didn't merge the daycare and kindergarten; we were separate in our organization. The daycare and kindergarten were never merged because one's part of the educational system and one's part of the logistics system. Different systems. Because we were part of the education system, we were subsidiaries to the Education Department. Training and study were all part of that.

In Shanghai, we took a look at how other people ran kindergartens. We took tours and had a good time of it, but mainly we were trying to see how people ran the place. [...] The school building was built a little at a time, then we took in children. At this point there weren't so many children to be taken in; there weren't many workers either. Just one grade. Later on there were kind of more. The entire education was really organized. Our factory was large scale, plus it was all Shanghainese. The kids would follow ma and pa. When they went in [to the mountains] they were all youths, then at a certain point they all got married and had kids. Our training in Shanghai wasn't so long [...] more than a week, about half a month.

'Cos we were young, we picked things up quick. Afterward the school began to be more regular. The teachers were good to start with, and then gradually more teachers came in. Very few teachers actually graduated from early childhood education [programs]. Then some years later on, in Shanghai, before they went into the factory, they picked out some people to go study intensively, then come be teachers in the kindergarten. I was the first batch, yes, a veteran. In the first batch we didn't have this training.

But we did well later too. Because we didn't have official certification, the Ministry of Education then gave us the option to do distance learning by mail. Four teachers from the Shanghai Specialized Institute of Childhood Education taught us and helped us improve our work. We also took exams, and the certification we got was the same as [other] early childhood educators [have]. Our factory really was very good, training us teachers for these kids. Because in the end it would always have to be properly formalized. If it wasn't, the kids we nurtured wouldn't be proper either. Our professional skills had to be endlessly improved. So, the factory helped us set up such a great chance, [...] and four teachers were tasked by Shanghai to guide us. So, our factory's kindergarten had an environment of female comrades; it was all female. Kindergarten teachers have distinct traits; they can talk, they can sing, they can dance and even perform; they're all pretty lively. And whenever our factory had some kind of activity, some kind of performance or show or something, we kindergarten teachers were very active participants.

Our first batch of students were great. I can't remember exactly [how many students we three teachers led] but each class had at least 30-some. Yes, [in three classes]. [We each took care of one class] and there was an auntie, a caretaker. I think not [an older woman] from the factory, probably of a slightly lower educational level, I think. The caretakers weren't one to a class. Oh yes, teachers were two per class, one early shift and one late; one person would cover two classes. Caretakers were part of logistics and also cafeteria staff. We also had a cafeteria, very proper; you could say it was the same as Shanghai kindergartens now. Before, our kindergarten had no caretakers in the mornings, just cafeteria staff, so you had to be teacher and caretaker both.

The kindergarten students would arrive at 7 a.m., and adults would have to be there then too. In the morning there'd be a teacher on duty who'd get there a little earlier; in the evening there'd be another teacher on duty who left a little later. At first it was just three people, then we found some others, then we began to grow bit by bit. [...] We followed the Shanghai curriculum. Materials were all given to us by Shanghai. These days, Shanghai [kindergartens] don't have a formal curriculum, but back then we did: language arts, English, art, math, physical education, [...] we all followed the textbooks to lead classes.

There were two types of classes in a day: one teacher would tell stories, do music, teach "common sense" [TN: a combination of basic natural knowledge and civics or social studies] physical education, art, and arithmetic was another. They divided it up. I taught music, stories—language arts and "common sense." I specially taught these. [...] Yes, each of us was responsible for three classes. Yes, it was very complete, and the kids were all quite outstanding. I feel like nowadays, the kids are happy, but it's not so good for the kids' development. Children aren't allowed to study the most basic things.

I'd just do the language arts, the "common sense" and the English, those three classes. Monday morning there was language arts, common sense, then music, common sense. Free activity time in the afternoon. Sometimes we'd have classes too. We used to only have the "middle" and "upper" classes, no "lower" classes [for the youngest children]. Yes, the "lower" classes were part of the preschool, then later they had them [as part of kindergarten]. Saturdays we'd have to hold classes, because the dads and moms also had to work, you know. Kids' intellect are based on what they inherit. Those with high IQs from birth, they are just smart. Those who aren't smart as kids, they are just not smart. Nothing you can do about it.

[I took care of my colleagues' friends, all of them], yes, so we were all very close.

No, I don't think it was easier to work in Shanghai than in the Small Third Front because I had to take care of more things in the Front, but we had it tough back then. Back then, to keep warm in the winter, we'd have to go pull our own coal. The first thing we did when we got to the kindergarten in the mornings was to light the stove, and you had to drag in the coal from way far away, then put it in each classroom. At the time waxing the floors, wiping the floors, that was all done by the teachers, no caretakers. At first there weren't any caretakers, we only got them later.

At first the kindergarten wasn't so big, but later we built more onto it. Three rooms, [one for each class], yes. Yes, yes [we had to take care of lots of things, not just educating children]. Not like Shanghai parents; they drop the kids off in the morning, pick 'em up in the evenings, they didn't have contact. We had 24-hour contact. Parents would ask [after the kids], and we really trusted one another. We did a good job with them, and we related to them like our own family members. The factory that we thought was so big then now seems very small.

I should have worked until 55, but the factory wasn't doing well, so everything got merged. It used to be that the No. 5 Steelworks had two kindergartens, but they combined into one. There were too many teachers, so they said that anyone who didn't want to work anymore could retire. I live here and it was too far to get to work, and I really couldn't take it anymore, so I said I'd go ahead and retire, so I retired early. I don't get teacher's benefits. Teachers in factory schools don't get teacher's benefits, but we don't count on that anyway.

[…] There were unexpected emergencies, for sure. One kid had asthma and couldn't breathe when sleeping at night. I scooped him up and rushed him to the clinic in a panic. It was a ways. [Just I] took him, because the [other] teachers were working. […] The doctors in our clinic were very good. Each department in our factory had its specialties, no less than a miniature town. Everything was very outstanding. [The clinic] wasn't all female comrades. There were male doctors, and also traditional Chinese doctors. There were also female doctors. Both internal and orthopedic medicine, they did very well.

[…] The Education Department was responsible for choosing teachers after us, then we'd take care of them a while. I took charge of the four and five year olds. The first batch of kids to come in were relatively older, about the "higher" class. Nowadays they're all 40-something. This [closeness] isn't like anything else. We were colleagues with their parents, so the kids were also [close with us]. I still have a deep impression of Xu Xiaoying's two sons. Real smart, and almost 40. We are still in touch. [We're close] mainly because of the adults' relationships. The kids would have to go to school and would leave; how would we have any impressions? Some [kids] directly went to elementary school, others went to Shanghai. The latter was the majority. Everyone more or less thought the same way.

[...] No matter for whom, [kindergarten teaching] is very suitable. I think young girls are best suited for kindergarten teaching, the adults getting to spend the days like children. Yeah, [your heart is very young,] and you just can't imagine how people who go to work every day think. I can't think of that even now.

[…] [At first] there were lots of teachers at the No. 5 Steelworks. Half of the kindergarten teachers at the Shanghai No. 5 Steelworks was from our [Small Third Front] factory. Very few [teachers] at the Shanghai No. 5 Steelworks had certification. But basically all of us from the Eight-Five Steelworks had certification. The Eight-Five Steelworks did a very good thing, which was to have us do distance learning, go get training outside, and get our certificates. I was one of them. Later, the retraining, because people didn't have certifications at the time, they did by their own intuitions. In the end you had to have a certification. The factory provided [us] such good conditions. Our factory was really great. The factory education department proposed this plan. So I say that our factory was really, really humane. They really thought on behalf of the kids and the workers.

Every year I returned to Shanghai twice, during winter and summer break, for training and classes. I went to lots [of different schools]. Nanxi Kindergarten, Bingchangling Kindergarten, all good kindergartens. No, those kindergartens weren't on break, it was the in-between time; we rotated out to do training and study. Everyone had a chance. [...] And so many Small Third Front [units] weren't as good as our Eight-Five Steelworks. Advantages included it being big, having everything, and being organized really well, not like some factories that were small, lacking many things. And you can't blame their leadership because it was just a size issue.

After the factory kept raising our work skills, year after year our teaching level and abilities really got better. After going back to Shanghai, they all said that the teachers from the Small Third Front, they felt that we were really impressive. That we were able to plant ourselves in the Shanghai No. 5 Steelworks was really mainly because of the Eight-Five Steelworks teachers. Why were we so impressive? That was all the factory taking care of us. The emotional bonds between teachers, this kind of harmonious getting along among female colleagues, truly could only be like this after an experience like we had [on the Small Third Front].

[...] Many activities were organized by female colleagues. Singing contests in the factory, we participated in all of them. Sports, jump-rope contests, we won awards. Yes, [we competed as a kindergarten teacher group]. ...We kindergarten teachers had an advantage. We could sing, dance, talk; we were better off than workshop workers. [Workers in the factory] really respected us; they were really good. So, this experience I didn't feel to be a waste at all; I didn't feel any unhappiness. I was really happy. Yes. So I say, if you have daughters, if they're willing, being a kindergarten teacher is the best. [...] They are really happy, and even happier these days.

Things are even better now. Back then our sense of responsibility was much stronger than now. Nowadays many duties are left to parents, left to society. Back then it was us teachers who took the burden. Even a little trivial thing, we'd really feel responsible for it. So, there are some things we don't like, some things these days. From when I was a kindergarten teacher, to when my son entered kindergarten, to when my granddaughter started, that process, if you compare it, was totally different. [...] Many things, you can't blame the parents and you can't blame teachers either. You gotta blame society. You can't get to that level like on the Small Third Front. This history is really valuable. [...] My deepest feeling was that I put my heart into every lesson when I was delivering it. Teachers would observe each other's classes, for critique. We'd do critiques of one another. At the end of each year we'd rate the active teachers, the best workers. I often got these [titles]. In Shanghai I was even rated "Excellent 'Gardener' [TN: a common metaphor for teachers is as gardeners of young plants] of Shanghai City." After going to the Shanghai No. 5 Steelworks, the first time they were touring to give the "Excellent 'Gardener' of Shanghai City" title, I got it.

The factory organized teacher ratings on the Small Third Front. Not the Education Department; the entire factory rated the best workers. No, there was nothing specially for teachers. We teachers would decide among ourselves who was the leading worker, then report it up. We'd all make our suggestions then they'd rate it. We didn't rate education[al outcomes], we rated for work attitude. It'd be how the classes were, if they were lively and interesting, how the kids took it in, and we'd also give some suggestions. We'd speak freely [in our meetings], by the grades we taught. There were the intermediates and the uppers. Also groups like the language arts education study group and the mathematics education study group and such. There weren't very many teachers in each group, a total of ten-odd teachers...

I had to make my own teaching props; you had to make everything yourself. [...] Also, the arrangements for the classroom, the setting, teachers had to make all that themselves. We'd do it in different classes, each class being responsible for their own things. We also rated classroom setups for awards. Right in our kindergartens, and also done among the teachers. Basically yes, every year I got an outstanding worker award. The other teachers would nominate people and the list would be sent up to the factory. Every department in the factory would have an outstanding worker; the kindergarten had one, the elementary school had one, and other departments had several too. Smaller departments had fewer, bigger ones more.

Yeah, kindergarten teachers who got the outstanding worker award got rewards, like going for rest breaks to Beijing, Amoy, and Shanghai, to the Forbidden City, and also to hospitals. When I was young my temperament wasn't good. I was really impatient and didn't put up with things, so I couldn't be a bureaucrat like an office manager. [...] I never thought about taking a leadership role, I just wanted to be a teacher. I've never thought about turning toward an administrative role. I think I feel like I wouldn't be good at administration; I should stick to my specialty. I feel like I met my own standards and was at peace and didn't give any child short shrift.

* * *

瞿惠相 Qu Huixiang, male, worker, cadre, and educator at a Small Third Front machinery factory.

Keywords: conflicts, critique, education, frustrations, nostalgia, pay and benefits

The problems in education were very obvious. A lot of the workers in our factory were graduates from vocational secondary schools and colleges. They felt that they were already here in the mountains, so the key was educating their kids. But schooling conditions were bad here and information from the outside didn't get through much. These parents really made noise in requesting a school from the factory. Then the factory decided to set up a school for the workers' children with kindergarten, elementary, and secondary school, plus education and training for the workers, all together and unified under the Education Department. I managed the department and the schools and was also the school assistant principal.

At the time the greatest pressure on me came from the promotion rates for elementary and secondary school students. In the process of setting up the schools, we had first to find good teachers. Some of the people already at the factory used to be teachers who had followed their spouses to the factory. Some had graduated from a formal normal college. We gathered these teachers first, and where we still had need, we went outside to bring in some good teachers. There were some workers who'd learned foreign languages [TN: likely English] pretty well, so after a short training period they were asked to be foreign language teachers.

So why the pressure on us? Because the parents had very high demands of the school. Like, if one day a student didn't do well on their test and went home to talk about it, their parents would ask our teachers, saying, "Why do some students get 90-somethings but my kid, who's also really smart, doesn't do well?" They wouldn't blame the student, they'd only blame the teacher. "What did you teachers teach them? How is the school leadership running things?" Some parents even called the school leadership asking for new teachers. To improve the quality of our teaching, we linked up with the Kongjiang Secondary School, the Songjiang No. 2 Secondary School, the Jiading No. 2 Secondary School, and other magnet schools in the city. Every summer and winter vacation we'd have our teachers go to Shanghai for training. We also invited Shanghai teachers to come give public lessons and improve our pedagogy. But the parents were still not having it. The tests were being written up by our school, so higher or lower scores were all in the hands of the teachers and our school. The parents weren't satisfied? So we came up with a plan: we took the standardized midterm exams from a magnet elementary school in Shanghai—Beijing East Road Elementary School—and had our students take them.

Doing this wasn't just testing our students, but also testing our teachers [to be able to mark the exams properly]. For secondary school we did the same; we took Kongjiang's exams and had our students take them. With this, now our teachers had things to say: you're testing us. The pressure on them was huge. Really, they were already very hardworking. Back then when teachers gave extra lessons or worked overtime, there was no compensation. The teachers would say, "We're working like dogs and the school is testing us." They had criticisms toward the school too, especially when test scores were bad, and the parents blamed the teachers. Once we used a magnet secondary school's English test on our students and one student did badly. Their parents blamed the English teacher and that teacher got upset and didn't want to teach anymore. In a huff, he said he wanted to take a holiday and go back to Shanghai. If he left, our third-year junior high kids wouldn't have an English teacher. So, we had to come out and patiently work with him and have many conversations with him. Later we found out that his wife was sick back in Shanghai, so the school union actively delivered him some assistance money. He was really touched by this and said he would absolutely prioritize the big picture and take responsibility for the students and do his work well.

The school leadership took extra care for the teachers' living situations and work lives. In 1983, not many of the factory's pay raise quota slots went to the school. There were three tiers, three, six, and nine-yuan raises. Average performance was three, enthusiastic workers six, and especially good performance got nine. To increase the number of people who got pay raises, the school split the six-yuan awards into two so two people could both get raises. Even so, some teachers didn't get anything. I, as the school principal, voluntarily gave up my chance at a pay raise and gave my allotment to other teachers. When I told my kid, she really didn't get why I'd give up a chance at more pay.

Running a school well needed coordination on many fronts. We also requested that parents and students work with us to do education better, together. Though there were a lot of issues with the school, there was no way around it; we had to do it this way. A few years of toughing it out forced everyone to do a better job. Then everyone slowly got used to it and the gap between the education we delivered and on offer in the city shrank. After a while our caliber went up. After a few rounds of standardized testing, we found students' grades mostly went up. One student got into the Secondary School Affiliated with Jiaotong University [back in Shanghai]; several got into Kongjiang Secondary School, too. So parents started thinking "oh, your teaching isn't bad," and we also grew more confident. The other time I bumped into a student who called me "Principal Qu" on the street in Shanghai. I asked who he was. Turns out he used to be the biggest little troublemaker at our school, a real champion bad boy. Now he was working at a bank with a very nice salary. These kids all grew up studying in the mountains. They also really miss their childhoods in the mountains. Some of them have gone back several times to the Small Third Front.

* * *

汪福琪 Wang Fuqi, male, Anhui native and county-level cadre in Jixi. Helped oversee transfer of Small Third Front to local control.

Keywords: art, camaraderie, education, entertainment, movies, nostalgia, performing arts, rural vs. urban

Well, with cultural exchange, first, the Third Front factories would play movies every week. Back then there were no movies here. Yes, every single week. Each of the factories would put on movies, and farmers from about a mile or two in all directions would go to watch. It really made the local farmers' extracurricular lives more interesting. [...] For example, the Brightness Factory over in Yingzhou, my family came down from Yingzhou, we lived next to this big bridge you'll go over. I remember back then that everybody within a mile or two would run over to the Brightness Factory.

And then also, they had a batch of amateur artists in the factory too back then. At the end of the 70s and the beginning of the 80s, that was when it was developed quite well. Back in the day I also worked at the county cultural center and helped them specially train a group of people who could draw, talents in artistic work. For instance, this large [landscape scroll] painting in my parlor here, this was by someone named Wang, Wang Hequan, back in the day at the Ignited Plains Factory. He's now the head of the Yunjian Art Academy in the Songjiang district of Shanghai. Yes! Yes, he painted this himself. At the time, there was one in his factory, another in the Ten Thousand Miles Factory, two in the Seapeak Factory—including a woman artist; there was a woman artist who made pictures over at the Central Youth Factory. In our county, at that time, we were over-age university students who'd train them in making pictures after graduating and other fine arts. The biggest [name] of the ones who trained back then is Zhang Biao; he's the chairman of the Anhui Provincial Arts Association now. Back in the day he was one of our students. Training, photography, drawing, we interacted in all of these ways.

And, the biggest silk-reeling factory in our county in the 70s, they put on two performances. One was a silk-reeling dance. Back then I was doing propaganda work in the factory and put on a Yue drama [TN: a genre of traditional musical theater from Shaoxing, Zhejiang province] and an opera. [...] The dancing, the silk-reeling dance, that reflected the workers' lives. They interacted with the locals. At the time, going to the [Third Front] factories, they would invite us over and provide us with a meal—back then you had to use grain ration tickets to eat, you know. Then everybody—the local folks—would go themselves to the factories for dancing and putting on performances, but if they wanted to go, they had to go through the [Party] organization, because the Small Third Front was a secured unit and not everyone could go willy-nilly. That was the cultural exchange.

* * *

王金忠 Wang Jinzhong, male, Anhui native and farmer who worked in a Small Third Front chemical factory.

Keywords: Cultural Revolution, movies, nostalgia, political training, rural vs. urban

Yes, [the impact of the Cultural Revolution on the Small Third Front Factories] was very big. The factory wasn't finished back then, so we were constructing it while doing political study. As a whole, when they were building the factory here, we local folks, we were a bit more open than people elsewhere in Xiangyu. Why? Because they've got more contact with

Shanghai people, with the movies and such they showed in the factory, they [locals] watched a lot of those. Where would ordinary folks get movies to watch? Culture is all really backward here. After Shanghai people came, we folks around here were relatively progress-minded.

* * *

王世益 Wang Shiyi, male, Anhui native and villager near a Small Third Front machinery factory.

Keywords: communications, education, entertainment, movies, nostalgia, performing arts, rural vs. urban

Their entertainments were usually singing and dancing and such, and local folks didn't know [how to], so we wouldn't participate. They also often showed movies, usually once a week, usually in their factories. We locals would go watch too. At first they didn't even charge for tickets, but later they would charge a fee. Workers paid ten cents and local folks, I guess it was five cents. They had it cheaper for locals. We could go into the residential areas of their factory but not the workshops. You didn't need a permit or proof of anything to go. You could go into their residential areas. They had a basketball court there too that you could play on, and you could go watch the movies and operas. Back then the Anhui Provincial Opera Troupe even came to perform, and every time some of the younger folks locally would go watch. [...] When they played basketball, it was just the Shanghainese playing themselves. Occasionally, some of the sent-down youths from Shanghai would also go play with them. When their factory was doin' well, some of the sent-down youths got put over here with us. Well, usually we used Putonghua [TN: Beijing-standardized Mandarin Chinese] to communicate, some people who didn't speak it could understand it by listening after a while.

No, we didn't send our kids to their kindergartens or preschools, mainly because we weren't used to it. We had schools locally, so we never thought about that.

* * *

王文青 Wang Wenqing, female. Worker and propaganda cadre at a Small Third Front steel mill.

Keywords: art, camaraderie, communications, entertainment, movies, nostalgia, pay and benefits, performing arts

The Workers' Committee [compared to the Youth League Committee] was a bit broader, giving assistance stipends to struggling workers, organizing work contests, labor protections and so forth. Of course, now the Workers' Committee is broader. It included workers' entertainment, because it was very dry and boring on the Small Third Front. We had to do television rebroadcasts; many [programs] couldn't get rebroadcast [because of poor signals], so then we went on the hilltops to install relay stations. At the time we also had a library, a television room, a photography room, special people to do the work contests, special people to do the labor protections, propaganda people for propaganda, radio people for the radio broadcasts, and also Birth Planning. It used to be under the workers' union, but then it was given to administration. It used to be also a Workers' Committee [duty], all these things to do with the masses, including that time we organized several small teams. Wasn't there a play called *In the Land of Silence* [TN: a 1978 play by Zong Fuxian]? It was really popular in Shanghai at the time. We also put it on once at Eight-Five; several of the actors were from our factory. You could say that we had a lot of talent.

Then at New Year's and holidays, we'd organize some activities. At one point we specially organized smaller teams. At the time, we had to go to the Shanghai No. 5 Steelworks, and we specially had our small teams get together and do one big show and put it on at the No. 5. It was hardest to be in charge of the small teams. All of these people putting on performances were staff and workers. [The smaller teams] varied in size. The entire band was ten-odd, twenty-odd people. Our band was very complete, too: clarinets, the *yangqin* [TN: Chinese dulcimer], the *erhu* [TN: Chinese fiddle], and the string bass. We all played on our own [without an instructor]. And among us one comrade was really talented, he came from Xuzhou, name of Zhang Jun. He was the team leader. We didn't have a director or anything, so everyone among themselves, everyone rehearsed together, rehearsing a few programs. We danced what was called the "Little Knives Society" dance, and some People's Liberation Army dances. Anyway, we'd discuss the popular stuff and would give it a go. What we could do ourselves we'd do ourselves (Image 5.3).

So back then before the Small Third Front came back [to Shanghai], lots of Shanghai leaders would come to Eight-Five, and we'd often put on shows for them. And the movies there were endless. We didn't originally have an auditorium, but then when it was finished, then we had one; we used to have a fabric screen in front of the office building. Sometimes when the audience had filled up, we'd go behind the screen to watch. The

Image 5.3 B&W photographs of the Sun-Facing Factory performing arts troupe, 1970s

auditorium was built up like this too [by us]. We also built a basketball court and participated in events through the whole Rear Base. The Small Third Front had several regions. There was the Jingde area. Tunxi was a bit far from us, but us in Guichi were relatively closer to Dongzhi. Guichi also had several factories, and among us we'd also do exchanges. On New Year's and holidays we'd also go to the local military garrisons to perform and play movies. One year, I remember I'd just gotten to the [Youth] League Committee, '73, I took a couple people from the [movie] projection team over, then after I came back, I told my mom, "I really can't handle drinking with the soldiers. Those light liquors, they put them in cups the size of bowls and toasted me and toasted me until I was all woozy.

Mm-hmm, I think just two people [went with me], one Chen Jiang, one Wu Yibing, and another person maybe, someone. We went to show [movies] in the daytime. At that time, I should say, I hadn't really been made to hold some kind of production labor job. [...] then including after I came to Shanghai, I was still doing [HR work], and I was pretty happy helping workers resolve difficulties, so I don't regret this period. I feel like I did quite a lot of stuff, pretty valuable and pretty necessary.

* * *

许春华 Xu Chunhua, male, Anhui native and worker at a Small Third Front steelworks.

Keywords: entertainment, food, men vs. women, movies, nostalgia, performing arts

At the steelworks, our main entertainments were watching movies and various kinds of cultural performances and competitions and such. The ticket price for villagers to watch a movie was five cents and for workers, ten. You went to watch in the auditorium. There were chairs, 40 rows, about 1040 seats in all. They had them showing every night and mostly they were [World War II] flicks. A lot of people turned out to watch. You could also buy ice pops there, four or five cents for one, and each movie would run for an hour or so. Sometimes there'd be cultural performances put on by the steelworks, all of them young workers singing and dancing. Free admission for those. On March 8th, International Women's Day, they gave us a half-day off and women workers got free movie tickets, so we could go have a show.

* * *

徐小英 Xu Xiaoying, female, cadre, teacher, and office administrator at a Small Third Front steel mill.

Keywords: camaraderie, children, critique, education, frustrations, rural vs. urban, work assignments

No, I didn't stay the whole time in the Propaganda Department. In '76 I was transferred to the secondary school, to work at the Party branch. Not as the secretary, just an officer. Then in the secondary school, I remember it was '76, '77, I was visiting my husband in the military with my son, they asked me to be the middle school physics teacher. At the time people were just careless—our branch Secretary, he mailed an eighth-grade physics textbook to me on the military base, and the teaching guide, he mailed me the lessons he told me to teach for the eighth graders, so I had to bite the bullet and do it, and also look after my son. It ended up that after I had my son with me in the mountains, I'd be looking [things] up in books every day, about physics, and doing all the problems in the teacher's guide and lesson plans. [...] Because I'd forgotten all the physics I'd studied 18 years before that, I had to review it all again, do it all again, and I read over and did all the problems in the textbook and *Ten Thousand Whys* [TN: a popular-science series for young readers], then I went to teach other people. Like that. So I did teach. For a school year.

After a year teaching physics, the plant main office—well, during that year, because there was an unused typewriter in my office, when I didn't have other things I began to learn [to type]. After I learned, other people knew that I could type, and the main office happened to need a typist, maybe they were taking care of a married couple living apart and transferred one away, so after that there wasn't anyone. When there wasn't anyone, the main office staff began to think; they came to discuss with my school to get me over there to help them type [...] At the time I was the physics teacher and deputy head of the academic affairs office. I didn't want to do it [working in the school] back then; you wouldn't know, but things were a mess in the school at the time. The students weren't studying in school, it was really ridiculous. So, you have these middle schoolers, lots of middle schoolers weren't even at the level of first and second graders; I say this but you wouldn't believe it.

Twenty-six letters, a bunch of people didn't know them. Mm-hmm, none of them wanted to study. No, they thought studying was useless. Plus, the parents, even if you went [to visit them] they wouldn't cooperate with you. The kids didn't want to study, they took up cigarette smoking instead. We went to visit the parents, and the moms and dads would be playing cards and such at home. You go talk to them and they seemed not to give a care. Anyway, it was like—I can't express it clearly—nobody felt much interest in studying at that time. So then, I thought, well, main office then, it's easier. Then not long after I began typing at the office, they had me actually go work in the office. I did have kind of a lot of experiences. Mm, then I was the confidential secretary for the factory offices. The confidential secretary would manage the department heads, the factory head, plus documents and stuff; I oversaw all of it. [...] Then I directly moved to doing document work for the factory head's office. Yup, I worked in the factory offices until I left.

But my son, why did he go to Shanghai for third grade? There was going to be a major renovation in this school in the mountains, and they would delay the start of class for one to two months. So I thought, that's going to set him back. My son got very good grades in first and second grade, he was very self-motivated. Then I put him with my mother. Until that point, he was always the first or second ranked student in his class, his grades were always very good. He was the brigade captain [of the Young Pioneers]. Then he tested into Kongjiang Secondary School, a municipal magnet school. [...] Plus, telling him to go try for [...] Shanghai High School [TN: a highly regarded public school], well, his teacher said that there was just one spot in our district. If you didn't make it, you wouldn't be admitted into any school. There were more quota slots for Kongjiang, so you should just put down Kongjiang for your top choice.

In the end my son's grades were really—he for sure could've gotten into Shanghai High School. That year the cutoff for the three main subjects [TN: Chinese language, math, foreign language] was 283 points, and my son got 289... basically one of his essays got nearly perfect credit. He got a 91 on that essay, it was very good. He was writing about the Small Third Front, that's what my son wrote about. He was kind of funny. He picked one of two prompts. One was from "a new thing," the other was "an exemplar." So my son chose "a new thing," because it was easy to write a hackneyed [essay] about "an exemplar." That would definitely not get a high score. So he wrote about a new thing: he wrote about how television was brought into the mountains, how it got into the mountains. He wrote about this process. My son kind of liked going into the mountains on his winter and summer breaks.

When they connected the television [network], this was a big, rare thing in the mountains, in the mountain gullies. So then this essay got a 91. So, we ended up surpassing [the cut off] for Shanghai High School by this much. In their class it was my son and another person, a little girl, who was always his rival in studies. Then my son got nominated to be the

District "Three-Good" [TN: good grades, good athletics, good character] student by his teacher in fifth grade. In sixth grade, he [the teacher] encouraged my son to study and get in, and surpass that little girl, because if you get the "Three Good" rating in sixth grade that would add extra points onto—that would be bonus points on your exam for middle school. But my son didn't get that bonus. The teacher told him to do his best; in the end he got 289 points, that young girl got 282, then she got the 6 bonus points to 288, still lower than my son.

If he'd had the bonus at the time, he'd have put Shanghai High School for absolutely sure, yes. Yes, but in the end it was pretty okay. Then at Kongjiang Secondary School, well, my son had pretty good grades. After he graduated from Kongjiang Secondary School, my son went directly to the high school; basically he waived the entrance exam. After he finished high school…mm, then he tested for Tongji University. After he got into that, then he went into urban planning […] Then my son was at Tongji, five years, he got in in '93 and graduated in '98; they had five-year undergrad, Tongji construction [degrees] had always had five-year degrees. No, the other majors at Tongji are four-year, only construction is five. Pretty good. My son is pretty good now. Basically, from when he was small—when people like us eat bitterness like this, that affects the next generation.

Look at the kids from our Small Third Front, they're all pretty good. Yes, yes, last time that Ji Meihua and I were talking, she said, take a look, even though we're all from a mountain gully, we all really put in a lot of effort and really suffered, and we got through it like this for ten-odd years, 20-odd years, but our kids all came out pretty well.

* * *

章亚光 Zhang Yaguang, male, Anhui native of a village neighboring a Small Third Front factory; later a local historian and lawyer.

Keywords: entertainment, movies, nepotism, nostalgia, performing arts, rural vs. urban

[…] [The Small Third Front work units] often showed movies. But most older films had been labeled as "poisonous weeds" at that point and were forbidden. So-called fragrant flowers, like *The Legend of the Red Lantern*, *The Red Detachment of Women*, *Shajiabing*, *Tracks in the Snowy Forest*, and the like; also older pictures like *The White-Haired Girl*, *Tunnel War*, *Heroic Sons and Daughters*, *Behind Enemy Lines*, and so forth, those got played regularly. The local folks didn't give a fig about "fragrant

Image 5.4 People going to work in the Cooperation Factory residential area, 1980

flowers" or "poisonous weeds," they just wanted a spectacle. After "the wise leader Chairman Hua [TN: Hua Guofeng, successor to Mao after Mao's death in 1976] smashed the 'Gang of Four' in a single blow," old movies were gradually allowed. More movies than ever got played at the 703 power plant, the 683 driving team, the No. 3 Industrial Area (the light industry area for the Shanghai Rear Base), and other Third Front units (Image 5.4).

My wife and I were young then, so when we heard some place was going to have a movie, we'd rush to it. I remember the Brightness Factory was playing *Flower Girl* [TN: a very popular film from North Korea], and my wife and I rushed by night to see it, then rushed back to the county town by night, of course walking both ways. There were tremendous crowds of people there—maybe not 10,000, but definitely over five. When the famous Peking Opera performer Li Bingshu (from Su County, Anhui) led a troupe from Shanghai to perform at the Jixi Theater, our entire family got to go see. It was very hard to get tickets, but I "ran a back door" to get three standing tickets so me, my wife, and my old mother all went and borrowed a wooden bench to sit in a corner in front of the stage. We could only see the actors come out and couldn't see them go back in, but we were still thrilled. I heard that the troupe had come to perform for the Third Front workers, so we got to benefit from those workers being around.

* * *

赵惠瑛 Zhao Huiying, female, worker and kindergarten teacher at a Small Third Front steelworks.

Keywords: camaraderie, children, education, frustrations, living conditions, medical issues, nostalgia, performing arts, work assignments, work schedule

My work was a bit Jack of All Trades, and I also oversaw the logistics, because you could say things were quite tough at the time, including the [...] stoves. We used to use firewood, and coal—coal-ball stoves, because you had to cook the food for the children. An auntie did cook, but if the wood was out and the coal was out, Teacher Zhao, the firewood's gone, what do we do? I'd say I'd think of someone to contact. We used to have a coal field; we'd try to contact them and report it. After they approved the request we'd have to go make contact. After that no one would deliver it to your door. We'd have to go get it ourselves. So, what can we do? We'd get the teachers' spouses involved. We had one person whose man was a driver [...] she was in the Mechanical Department. One auntie in the cafeteria, her man was a driver too. Basically, whenever he had to go transport something, get something, he'd help us drive over. Who'd help us pick it up? Well, we teachers, the aunties, we'd all move out and do it ourselves. Yes, we did it all. We didn't have a specialized caretaker to help with the logistics and such.

Then bit by bit it got more organized. At first there wasn't anything. Basically, we teachers did it all. You had to lead class well, following the state curriculum. Requirements then weren't as complex as now. It was just language arts, "common sense," music, and another teacher to do math, art, and PE, just these six subjects.

There were about ten-odd teachers when I went to the kindergarten. Yes, the first batch only had three. I was about one or two years after that. Yes, they expanded pretty quickly. Then there were nine classes, two teachers a class, so that made 18, plus people to look after the auxiliary stuff—cooking, finances, the nurse, just about 20-some people. Right around that. No, I didn't lead class after becoming principal. If a teacher got sick or had to go back to Shanghai temporarily, situations like that, I'd substitute in. So back then I'd call myself the Jack of All Trades, or a firefighter. Wherever someone needed me, I'd be there putting out the fire. Including the three aunties who cooked in the cafeteria; if time was short or an auntie was sick, I'd go in and help them stir-fry dishes. I would do all of it. Yes, we had a cafeteria for the kids' lunch.

At that time, we teachers didn't have a lunch break. We'd bring it all from home. [...] We didn't eat with the children. We were strictly separated. We teachers brought our own food. We didn't go back to our home cafeterias to eat because it was too far! So, we'd stint a little. We'd only have 30-some yuan for our monthly salary, so we had to budget it out. We'd bring food we'd cooked the day before. We all did this. The children's cafeteria had a designated steamer, so at noon we'd steam our food up a little, eat it for lunch.

[...] [I] didn't go to many meetings at the [Shanghai] Education Bureau and such as principal. Typically, we'd be in the holidays—teachers would do training during the holidays. Sometimes I'd do training too, coming to Shanghai. The educational work and Huangpu District were linked; back then we were directly linked to them. When we began doing the kindergarten the teachers didn't have any certifications, or employment licenses, no job titles, nothing at all. They were all transferred over from positions as workers, or other jobs, if you liked singing and dancing.

After I started, we hired twice, two batches of teachers, because we kept expanding. Some people were swapped out. When we were hiring we'd put up a notice; the kindergarten was hiring people at such and such a time, and people who wanted to would come apply, and we'd pick if there were a lot of applicants. We'd pick them ourselves, the teachers who were already there. She'd sing for us, dance, or tell a story, to see how her expressiveness was. We interact with little kids—to put it kind of bluntly—with teachers and the kids interacting, the teacher had to be like a performer, singing, dancing, telling, and tricking the kids to get them to like you. You had to have this ability.

Meetings at the Education Bureau would basically be assigning tasks, discussing education-related issues, like that. No, I wouldn't be there to report on my kindergarten; if I came for a meeting in Shanghai, it'd be typically listening to education-related topics, how to treat the kids, how to lead our courses, how should teachers' attitudes be? I'd listen and then bring these things back to the teachers. What attitude should teachers have? What should you control during class? How should your sitting and standing positions look? How should teachers be in front of the kids? You can't get used to "children, you must do this and that"; we can't do it that way. And now our rules are more and more [...] you have to crouch down when you speak to the children. The kids have to be in your line of sight [...] safety comes first.

So, these kinds of ideas, the common rules of education, you had to frequently tell the teachers. Sometimes I came to Shanghai for a meeting, listened to some reports, and there was a relatively large amount of information. For example, about safety issues and accidents in a kindergarten somewhere, how it happened, really, like acts of God. This would be intended to cause us to be more aware and conscious. Then I'd relay it to the teachers, and in our work we'd as much as possible avoid these things. I'd often relay things like this to the teachers. Every week or two we'd have an all-faculty meeting. Yep! All together!

Sometimes we'd have a teacher meeting, and it was the afternoon, the kids were all napping, and we'd have the logistics aunties go in to take a look, in case they had some issue, then for the teachers I would seize the hour or half hour to give them a meeting. On the one hand I'd summarize what was going pretty well recently; I'd encourage them on the good things first, then where we weren't doing enough, I'd also talk about that, about what to avoid. Each time we had meetings, safety was always first. Do you want to live? When parents give [the kids] to you, you are legally responsible, so the kids are everything you, as the teacher, had to be responsible for.

We didn't have any big problems with safety, but we did have a couple of emergencies. The doctor would say, you guys, very good, after lunch you have to have the children exercise a little, then have them lie down for nap time half an hour later, then you must inspect to see if the children have anything in their mouths. Once we had an incident; I don't know what happened with that child. One kid was slow in eating. The others had all finished and he was still eating. After eating he went to nap, then when he lay down I don't know if he choked or something; the food blocked his nose when he sneezed, the teacher heard the commotion, then he also had symptoms, so she quickly carried him over to the clinic.

Yes, these sorts of things can often happen in a kindergarten. These things would happen. We'd also tell teachers, the kids' nap time is not your break time, it's also your work time. You must keep looking, keep patrolling. Sometimes when napping the kids will take their toys and play, and put something small into their noses, then stuff it in there, but then try to dig it out and start crying when they can't get it out. This kind of thing would happen all the time, and the teachers would encounter this a lot. They'd know the situation, and we'd told them how to handle it. If the teacher saw a nosebleed, they'd pinch one nostril, and push on the other nostril to squeeze out the object; if they don't get it out then things can get very frightening.

Sometimes these small things would happen, so we'd take care of the teachers. If you saw the blankets moving, you had to pay attention to what the child was doing. You had to be careful of their safety. And at lunch, if you keep telling them to hurry and hurry, what could happen? The kid might keep some food in their mouth and not swallow it when you urge them to hurry, then if they trip while walking then something could easily happen. And with the kids peeing, if the teacher is very harsh in her attitude, the kid will try to hold it and not dare to ask to go to the restroom, and they end up peeing themselves. And another thing to be scared of, I'd often tell this example to them, of a kid, who was holding their pee in for some reason, then tripped and ruptured their bladder, and a bladder rupture can be fatal. This was actually me scaring them so that they'd be careful in the future.

Yes! I'd tell them examples. The teachers who taught on floors two and three—basically teachers who had to go upstairs to teach—kids were easy to lead back then too; they'd line up to go to the restroom; I'd say you teachers can't just say "line up to go pee" then sit in your classroom, no, you must follow the children. Some teachers were really bold, and I'd say, you might be training the children to act independently, but where the kids get to, you must be able to see them. You might have to follow behind the kids, see if they were lined up right, see if they had any situations. I'd often have to remind them that water made the bathroom floor very wet, and if it were very wet you'd immediately have to take measures and wipe it, so not only did teachers have to lead classes, they'd also have to do things like this. Our [caretaking] aunties weren't one per class, they were one per floor. Yes! Yep yep, the aunties, if something happened, if a kid wet themselves, if a junior class child just came in, didn't know anything, cried and made a fuss, and peed themselves and the teacher didn't have time to help them change, they'd hurry and call in an auntie, "this child has wet themselves, hurry and help her change," the auntie would help out. Basically, the teacher would be doing educational work and also caretaking work, so the teachers were pretty hardworking too.

Well, this was our work duty, to relieve the extra concerns of the workers. This was one of the basics of kindergarten education. One is learning some basic abilities and skills, like singing, dancing, exercising, calculating, these are very basic things [...] the techniques and skills for studying. The second mission is to lighten the burden of worry for parents. So, when parents go to work, the kids are put here, so we have the children be very happy in the kindergarten and be able to learn some things—parents really care about learning things; even until now, this is the idea, like learning something is somehow meaningful. Even though the Department of Education emphasizes that kindergarten isn't for children to study or learn anything, but instead to have them be happy how they want to be happy, but many elementary schools in society don't link up to kindergarten. Elementary schools' requirements are very high. So, parents are keeping such tiny kids busy studying this today, studying that tomorrow. We all taught very basic, rudimentary things, so I should say that in this area, our kindergarten did a very good job, because we were a Rear Base leader [...] other factories also had kindergartens. In all these very many kindergartens, ours was the best.

We had contact with other kindergartens. Tours! Yes! Exchange tours. Other teachers would often come to tour us. We were like a model [...] they'd come here to see how we led our classes, then see some shows put on by our children and such. Every year we'd do a big event. On June 1st [Children's Day], each child performs. Every class puts on a program in the show, a cultural performance! [...] Parents are really glad that their kids can go onstage to perform. There should've been other factory kindergartens that put on an annual show like we did, but possibly their scale wasn't as big as ours; because our factory was big, and we had a lot of kids, it was easier to get it out.

Some factories we went to see, their [kindergartens] were small, only ten-odd or a handful of kids in one class; some would have blended classes, some would have the bigger and littler kids mixed together. [...] We were relatively organized. Yeah! So our care conditions were especially good, so the kids from our kindergarten—this isn't me just praising my daughter—they were all very good. Including Ji Meihua's son, he's very good too, really all very good. When we meet up we say that our kids were all very good. There were some that weren't, but growing up in that environment—nowadays they call it positivity education, and they're all doing very well now.

These unpleasant things in kindergarten work were impossible to avoid. Some parents don't understand you and come to talk at you. Not yelling, no, it used to be that us teachers were really respected, and it was really good. But it was hard to avoid, sometimes, relationships—why, you ask? Parents and teachers were next-door neighbors, because we were all in the same factory, but give them three to five minutes and it'd be all right. Possibly when they got off work, they'd be seeing you face-to-face, just like that. Some bad relationships, saying things [like] this teacher steals the kids' lunch, maybe there were those too, but [...] this kind of thing wasn't too common back then. After I came to Shanghai as principal, instead, I feel like this kind of conflict is more common. Yes, people [over there] got along pretty harmoniously.

[...] Being a kindergarten principal on the Small Third Front was relatively straightforward, no really, really complex things. Now, in Shanghai the sense of law was stronger; the kids being together with other kids, unavoidably they'd bicker and fight and yell, but back then [in Anhui] everyone would be understanding and not take this too seriously, no matter. But now, the kids can't be touched. If they get a little scratch, the parents will come after you. Yes, I've had this happen! When I was at Baiyulan, one parent even wanted to take me to court.

[...] Yep! After I retired...I worked another seven years at a private kindergarten. So then the boss said, don't worry [about the lawsuit]. The kid transferred; the parent had the kid transfer to another kindergarten. [...] When selecting Model Teachers, we superiors would have quotas. In our steelworks' Education Department, there'd be quotas about how many model personnel you could choose, for example two from the primary school, two from the kindergarten; they'd give the vocational school some too [...] if they, say, gave us one, then we'd all choose together. Yes, once we had the quotas we'd select someone. So, you'd write out her actions and résumé. We'd hold a meeting, with the quota, then we'd name people. The people wouldn't all be concentrated, but dispersed, so at this time there'd be some weighing of factors. The teachers, I'd say there's one for the quota, they'd name two or three people, but not very spread out; this everyone could see, they wouldn't be so dispersed. They'd name two or three, if there were some specific things that they could tell, or write out, they'd go up, and then for just our kindergarten there'd be a couple of models too, just like this. Yes, we organized our own model personnel—the factory also gave a quota for this. Because the factory had different grades. Factory-level model personnel, department-level, kindergarten-level, like that. [...] We were pretty good [at having a full set of these evaluations]. We gave out these serious-looking red certificates, too.

Yes, we all passed the exams for our teaching certifications [after a correspondence course and training with visiting Shanghai experts], basically all of us [...] our factory was like this, but I'm not sure about other factories. At that time, people all respected teachers a lot. Nowadays the kids that are doing well, when their parents see us, they're like, Oh! Our son is really doing well! Yes, it was really all thanks to you! You educated him! So [I] do have a pretty good sense of accomplishment.

[...] Yes, [I did feel that being kindergarten principal] could be lonely. You don't have many friends. In the end, when our kindergarten was disbanding, everyone came around to my office, not wanting to go back. After work, people would naturally walk to my office and start chatting. After going home, they wouldn't cook dinner. It would get to be six or seven p.m. [...] they didn't want to go [home]. Yes, being kindergarten principal means not having a day off. On Saturdays and Sundays you might have to do home visits [...] During winter and summer break, you have intensive renovations. And when I got back to Shanghai, I'd do reports; if superiors ordered that the classrooms had to be renovated, I'd have to arrange it, so I'd not rest. With the construction team in there I'd be worried; the kindergarten was like my home, so I'd stay in there day and night. The teachers, you had to let them rest up, so basically, I'd stay in the kindergarten straight through, because the distance back to home was pretty close, a shorter trip, so I basically camped out in the kindergarten.

* * *

Further Reading

On Literature, the Arts, and Popular Culture

Brian DeMare, *Mao's Cultural Army: Drama Troupes in China's Rural Revolution*. Cambridge: Cambridge University Press, 2015.

Maggie Greene, *Resisting Spirits: Drama Reform and Cultural Transformation in the People's Republic of China*. Ann Arbor: University of Michigan Press, 2019.

Perry Link, *The Uses of Literature: Life in the Socialist Chinese Literary System*. Princeton: Princeton University Press, 2000.

McDougall, Bonnie S. *Mao Zedong's "Talks at the Yan'an Conference on Literature and Art": A Translation of the 1943 Text with Commentary*. Ann Arbor: Center for Chinese Studies, 1980.

Barbara Mittler, *A Continuous Revolution: Making Sense of Cultural Revolution Culture*. Cambridge, MA: Harvard University Press, 2013.

Nikolai Volland, *Socialist Cosmopolitanism: The Chinese Literary Universe, 1945–1965*. New York: Columbia University Press, 2017.

Emily Wilcox, *Revolutionary Bodies: Chinese Dance and the Socialist Legacy*. Berkeley: University of California Press, 2018.

On Education

Emily Hannum, "Political Change and the Urban-Rural Gap in Basic Education in China, 1949–1990." *Comparative Education Review* 43: 2 (1999), 193–211.

Denise Ho, *Curating Revolution: Politics on Display in Mao's China*. Cambridge: Cambridge University Press, 2018.

Shi Ming Hu and Eli Seifman eds., *Toward a New World Outlook: A Documentary History of Education in the People's Republic of China, 1949–1976*. New York: AMS Press, 1976.

Peter J. Seybolt, *Revolutionary Education in China: Documents and Commentary*. White Plains, NY: International Arts and Sciences Press, 1973.

Mun C. Tsang, "Education and National Development in China since 1949: Oscillating Policies and Enduring Dilemmas." *China Review* (2000), 579–618.

Eddy U, "The Hiring of Rejects: Teacher Recruitment and the Crises of Socialism in the Early PRC Years." *Modern China* 30:1 (2004), 46–80.

On Media and Information

Harriet Evans and Stephanie Donald eds., *Picturing Power in the People's Republic of China: Posters of the Cultural Revolution*. Lanham, MD: Rowman and Littlefield, 1999.

James Farley and Matthew D. Johnson, eds., *Redefining Propaganda in Modern China The Mao Era and its Legacies*. Abingdon: Routledge, 2020.

Nikolai Volland, "Cultural Entrepreneurship in the Twilight: The Shanghai Book Trade, 1945–1957," in Christopher G. Rea and Nicolai Volland eds. *The Business of Culture: Cultural Entrepreneurs in China and Southeast Asia, 1900–1965*. Vancouver: University of British Columbia Press, 2014, 234–258.

Y. Yvon Wang, "Yellow Books in Red China: A Preliminary Examination of Sex in Print in the Early People's Republic." *Twentieth-Century China* 44:1 (2019), 75–97.

CHAPTER 6

Gender and Sex

Translator's Note

Small Third Front workers were expected, like other good citizens of the PRC, to set aside their personal relationships and desires in favor of dedicating themselves to collective goals set by the Party-state. Men and women alike were enjoined to participate in productive labor. Women and girls who took up physically demanding roles associated with male workers, such as operating machinery, loading cargo, and heavy agricultural work, were praised as "Iron Girls" who "held up half the sky." Some of our female narrators strove to do exactly that, and they still speak many years later with pride of their accomplishments and those of other hard-working women. From the perspective of the state, the feminization of formerly "masculine" tasks in rural agriculture after the Great Leap Forward freed men from constant field labor and may have crucially underwritten heavy-industry-focused economic campaigns like the Third Front.[1] At the same time, some of the women among our narrators express anxieties and fears about the tasks they were asked to perform on the Small Third Front, which they describe as "not suitable" for their gender.

[1] Hershatter (2011), 265–266.

Y. Xu, Y. Y. Wang, *Everyday Lives in China's Cold War Military-Industrial Complex*, Palgrave Studies in Oral History,
https://doi.org/10.1007/978-3-030-99688-8_6

Regardless of the work women did and how they felt about it, the normative expectation was that all adults would marry and have children. In spite of the rhetoric of women offering themselves selflessly as workers for the Motherland alongside men, they were still expected to take the lead in childrearing, cooking, and other domestic tasks. The contradictions between apparently radically gender-equalizing policies and discourses versus familiar misogynistic, patriarchal expectations and conditions in daily life have led some scholars to call the PRC's gender politics a "revolution postponed."[2] Indeed, the vast amount of unremunerated and even belittled domestic labor that girls and women performed in cities and the countryside was also indispensable to the developmental agenda of the PRC from the 1960s through the 1980s.

Sexuality was another central arena of life on the Small Third Front that was marked by many apparent contradictions. Early Chinese Communist thinkers had participated in open discussions of human sexuality and calls for sexual liberation. Mao Zedong himself had written famously on the need to end arranged marriages and had fled one set up for him by his parents.[3] But heteronormative, monogamous marriage and reproductive sexuality were not widely challenged; they remained the default socially permissible sexual relationship in the era of the Small Third Front. Sexuality outside this form was socially disapproved of as immoral at best and punishable by bureaucratic or criminal punishment at worst. However, this did not stop people from pursuing socially and even legally risky desires. Nor did social disapproval and the risk of official sanctions entirely prevent extreme feelings and violent actions stemming from sexual and romantic relationships.

[2] Margery Wolf, *Revolution Postponed: Women in Contemporary China*. Stanford: Stanford University Press, 1985.

[3] See, for example, Christina Gilmartin, *Engendering the Chinese Revolution: Radical Women, Communist Politics, and Mass Movements in the 1920s*. Berkeley: University of California Press, 1995; for Mao's early feminism, see Delia Davin, "Gendered Mao: Mao, Maoism, and Women," in Timothy Cheek, ed., *A Critical Introduction to Mao*. Cambridge: Cambridge University Press, 2010, 196–218.

Questions for Discussion

1. What are some assumptions about gender and sexuality in these testimonies? Do these assumptions differ from those you hold yourself—if so, how?
2. Do you think the people whose testimonies about sexuality and gender appear in this section would've spoken differently of their experiences if they had been interviewed during their service on the Small Third Front? Do you think they would speak differently about their experiences to male versus female listeners?
3. A common view of the Mao era portrays it as one that tried to reduce gender difference and that tried to limit citizens to ascetic, "sexless" lives. Do testimonies in this section support or contradict this view?

* * *

陈金洋 Chen Jinyang, male, doctor and obstetrician for the Rear Base Health and Hygiene Team starting in 1975

Keywords: birth planning, conflicts, crime, critique, entertainment, frustrations, marriage, medicine, men vs. women, travel and transportation, violence

[TN: Please note that this narrative contains references to self-harm and a homicide that may be disturbing.]

When I went down [to the factories] with Wang Zhongping to survey [matters], some workers would say to us "our life here in Anhui is really boring." The most they had was a movie or two outdoors for everyone to watch, and then there wasn't even a TV; they didn't have TVs then; only in the final stages did they have TVs. So, it was just an open-air movie. Without anything else to do, you'd drink, you'd smoke, and then you'd date around. One [unmarried worker] dorm room would have four people, and all of them would be dating somebody, so you just pulled a bedcurtain around your bunk and the couple would be lying there together. The factory next door, they were also sleeping in pairs. That's how they got [pregnant].

These days we talk about abortions and such openly but not back then. When you first got to the Rear Base, there wasn't any other way. That was just what you had to work with. These young kids are all that age;

biologically they have these needs, and their work was dull so with nothing better to do so they'd date around, and it was hard to avoid developing feelings while dating around. With feelings, it was hard to avoid having a sexual relationship. This was all very normal. Some people's bellies started getting big, so they had to get an abortion or get married. Those were the choices, nothing else. So, we felt like Birth Planning work was very important.

But there was an age limit on doing birth control then. If you weren't old enough, you couldn't get married. No way. You couldn't get married early and have kids early. So you could only get an abortion, and you could only get married when you were old enough. This was a special issue on the Rear Base, many people don't realize. The Bureau of Health had us following the late-marriage, late-childrearing rules for Shanghai, but our lives were so tedious on the Rear Base and even seeing a movie wasn't easy, much less anything else. From what I know, there was a man who wasn't successful in love at the Eight-Five Steelworks who killed the woman and jumped off a smokestack himself. That affair rocked the whole Small Third Front.

There were quite a few people who got abortions. We didn't have the specific numbers since that wasn't part of our scope. That was a management problem for each factory, not for us the health and hygiene unit. [...] The thought work, the educational work, the problem of a boring lifestyle, that was all for yourself [to deal with], or for your factory, or for the Rear Base headquarters labor union or the Women's Federation. [...] Because the Rear Base was so boring, there'd be these issues around sexual liaisons, but all these various related issues weren't in our purview; all we could do was promote contraceptive measures, that was key. We had to ensure the provision of [contraceptive] drugs to do a good job with contraception, so when we made our reports, we had [the factories] send us data from their clinics [about the ratio of men and women of reproductive age]. After we collected them, we left room to request more [drugs and devices]. Every factory clinic guaranteed provision of these without fail, because this was the key to doing Birth Planning well, and also a way to avoid abortions.

You kids dating, sleeping together, go right ahead, but you can quietly go to the clinic to get some meds; that way you won't end up pregnant and you won't need an abortion. The objective cause [for unplanned pregnancies] on the Rear Base was that it was boring and there wasn't anything to do except work, eat, with nothing to do after work. And at that right young age they all wanted to date, and it was totally normal, and with a skewed sex ratio, with so many more men than women, so from our angle all we could do was take professional measures so they wouldn't get pregnant.

The drugs were all free. It was a planned economy, but basically most things were free. Our targets included women of childbearing age and those who were dating or had partners, but the specific operations were left up to the individual clinics because the few of us in the team headquarters couldn't oversee all of that, all the nitty gritty. But we knew the situation, so we had them report their numbers, leaving that up to them. You'd report up a number at will and we'd apply [for the items]. The factories had a lot of vehicles, from Jixi to Ningguo, She County, Tengxi, Jingde…so it was relatively easy to get to us. A place like the Changjiang Hospital that was farther, well, we'd have our own cars to go down every year for our big hygiene "clean-up," so we'd take the stuff along, enough for a whole year, and pass it to them. Same for Dongzhi County.

* * *

丁秀玉 Ding Xiuyu, female, technician at a Small Third Front steelworks who later rose to cadre positions in Small Third Front Party organs, including head of the Birth Planning office.

Keywords: birth planning, children, conflicts, frustrations, men vs. women

Yes, doing the statistics would mean going to work in the mornings, to work and from work, to work and from work, a set schedule. Only three months a year would [I] have to go down [to the workshop floor] to do the three shifts. …Just me. Yes, one workshop had just one person [to do production statistics], me. [In other workshops] it was also female comrades [doing this job]. Typically, production statistics was [done by] mostly female comrades. I belonged to the production group and the production group had just me, one female comrade. Some oversaw equipment, some did water samples, some did production scheduling, you know? All kinds of people, together, together. And those who did equipment and machine maintenance, overseeing them […] the equipment often broke down, so you had to look after it. Our production team were all male comrades, just me the one female comrade. So, I did production statistics like this for about over a year, then I was transferred away.

[… About a difficult colleague:] What was she like, then? She was in the No. 2 Workshop, and me in No. 4. They were right next door. She, well, she was also transferred really early to the factory admin offices, then at first she was in the library. At the time we didn't have a library. She began with the planning and construction. Then she was transferred from the library to the Birth Planning Office. Her work was no problem, but her personality wasn't good. She had issues when communicating with people. Not issues in communicating per se, but personality problems. I feel like I didn't like her personality. In our work, basically all the people we contacted were female comrades. There were some things that were good, but also not good.

I had a person I really admired. After meeting her, I felt like she was a talent. She's a good writer and a good speaker... her name is Hu Jin. Her dad used to be the district head for Changning District and her mom was a worker for the Shanghai Workers' Union, a leader too. Now both have passed. [She's] one year younger than me, [born in] '49. She had a fierce mouth, and she was a fast writer too. She was a female worker at the Eight-Five Steelworks, and again at the Shanghai No. 5 Steelworks. I had relatively a lot of contact with her. I really like her kind of personality.

[...] I didn't have any consciousness of [getting special treatment or being held suspect when receiving promotions as a mid-level cadre or leader]. I feel that men and women are equal. I can compete in work with men just like them. What advantage do women have? Their work is different from men's. Take my work. It's not the same as men's. Some work we can't do. But work like teaching or Birth Planning, we can absolutely do an outstanding job. No, these weren't just empty words [about gender equality], I feel like that was how it was. Our generation, Chairman Mao said, men and women are the same, women hold up half the sky, we fully exemplified this, definitely fully exemplified that. But now, I feel like there's a bit—on the job market these days, it's often men who have an advantage and women are relatively speaking the worse-off group. Men rule in today's society. Maybe these words aren't correct. Nowadays it's men in charge. Many policies do say it's men and women being equal.

Yes, things were all right in our time, but now when young women have a kid after working, they encounter a lot of—I had 56 days [off], and asked for some extra sick leave [when I had my daughter]. There wasn't this issue [of maternity leave endangering your job] before.

* * *

伏如山 Fu Rushan, male, worker at a fuse explosive factory.

Keywords: conflicts, family, frustrations, living conditions, marriage, men vs. women, nostalgia

[TN: The below translation comes from a written recollection penned by Fu.]

Love in the mountains wasn't as complicated as in the city, with going shopping, going to restaurants, or strolls in the park that would cost a lot of money, and often with money poured in but getting broken up with anyway. It was simpler among us in the mountains. As long as there was a go-between, you could come and go between your dormitories and be basically glued at the hip, and you'd "go public" by eating together at the canteen. And this kind of relationship, as soon as it was confirmed, would typically not have some bad outcome. The combining of daily life like this was a prelude to planning for marriage; we absolutely didn't spend a lot of money to meet the expenses of the dating period. Because both sides were aware that one had decided for the rest of one's life as soon as the relationship went public, the relatively unassuming people in the mountains wouldn't stir up drama and enemies in this little microcosm.

From 1970 on, my classmates began to get married. People wanted to introduce me to women, too. And since it was the first time in my life getting involved in romance, I was really a little flustered and unprepared. I had a lot of angst and conflict: I wanted to find [someone in] Shanghai, and I also wanted to delay things a little; I worried about my low salary and was just constantly indecisive. But then I also thought that my parents were getting up there in age and they hoped their youngest son would quickly settle his marriage and help them get rid of one of their many worries. I couldn't not try to satisfy them. Plus, since I was away from home, if I married sooner rather than later, I could even get a bit of help from my parents, so why not?

How did love descend on me? I find it hard to explain to myself. I was still on the steel-forging team at that time. During breaks I'd habitually go to the nearby security office [...] and sit a while. Because she was often unwell, [my wife-to-be]'d gotten a post tending to the security office, so unavoidably we'd get to idly chatting. Before we got romantic, these chats were just very casual and unconstrained. But fate had it that Cupid would quietly come to us, and our little chats got even more casual, but we got a little flustered every time we had them. What this gradual, subtle change in our emotions meant, of course we both knew in our hearts.

She came from a family of workers. Because there were so many children, they weren't at all well-off. She was the oldest and had experienced even more of the difficulties of life. She wasn't really beautiful; she was very slender and petite, and often in poor health. I couldn't explain why I'd fallen for her. Was it because other people were all getting married? Or was it a man's weakness, which I just couldn't overcome? Maybe this was all fated to be! Her forthrightness and her young woman's warmth and gentleness, and her plain and unadorned character affected me from the first time we met. She rarely primped herself up but still had all the traits of a young woman. She was small and slender but had a kind of feminine beauty. I saw in her eyes that she really needed warmth, kindness, and care. Some of her weaknesses were exactly what told me she would become a gentle, warm wife who would make a man content.

Not long after we met, she went home [to Shanghai] for a visit. I took the chance to ask her to bring some things to my older sister (though this wasn't really necessary), because I was staying at the factory. But for whatever reason, after she left, I felt something missing and was restless all day. Though at this point my family disagreed with my intentions, I still went back to Shanghai and decisively made a first step toward our romance. As soon as I was back in Shanghai, I called her on the phone. She was surprised, but in our conversation, I could tell that she felt happy about my arrival. If our conversations in the factory had been comradely, then this first romantic phone call and the first time we conversed while walking around town was when we made our official debut on the social stage as significant others [TN: Fu uses the word "friends" here]. I felt so happy; I'd never felt so at ease in my life. Because now I had a girlfriend, and it didn't matter if she'd be mine forever—at least for the moment, she was mine. Our dating confirmed my feelings; we had a great time around town in Shanghai and also talked about our plans for after we returned to the factory. Of course, we couldn't understand everything about each other in a few months, but I already understood her, comprehended her, and deeply loved her.

The joy of first love is unforgettable. We weren't dating fashionably like how people were around town, but our two hearts grew closer and closer. She wanted us to go public after a delay after returning to the factory and I consented, because [our relationship] was an already undeniable reality. We didn't return at the same time, nor did I go to the station to see her off—that was a special kind of separation that was actually an expression of being head over heels.

Very quickly after I returned, the agreed-upon five days of delay was abandoned by me; with our mutual efforts, the feeling between us grew with unusual leaps and bounds. On the street, in the dorms, at the canteen, we were inseparable. The first time we publicly ate together at the canteen, everyone stared at us. Some concerned people even told me privately to reconsider. Perhaps they were well intentioned, or perhaps they thought I shouldn't have a wife like her, or maybe they'd been asked by someone to introduce a "beauty" to me. But I didn't care about all that. When a woman matures, why shouldn't she be able to fall in love with a man near her side? Before she's married, any woman could be claimed by any man. Since I'd fallen for her, I would resolutely continue to love her and never regret it. Love brought enormous joy to our lives and I was completely immersed in this bliss. But this love relationship meant we couldn't continue as we were, so to ease her anxieties and reduce the pressure on her, we finally married on Lunar New Year, 1971, and formed our own new family.

* * *

胡进 Hu Jin, female, cadre at a Small Third Front-associated farm, then transferred to a transport department.

Keywords: camaraderie, manual labor, men vs. women, nostalgia, politically correct, rural vs. urban

There was one workshop that had an Iron Girl, called Wu Yuzhen. She was propagandized about very well. She did a man's work. She was a "Three-Eight" [TN: International Women's Day] Red Flagbearer. [...] She was a crane operator. [She was good] because when the crane stopped, she'd help the people below with things. Doing the male comrades' tasks. She was very willing to "eat bitterness." Another one in the administrative department called Pan Xiaoya, she was pretty good too. She was in the cafeteria. She also did the work of male and female comrades.

I don't think there are any other big things. Just when we were heading back, when the factory was going back to Shanghai, they had us escort the things in batches. The factory had me escorting other people's furniture and house goods, making sure that each household's worth got to their homes. [...] Just me alone. Tiring. [...] Our [male] loading workers were mostly loading coal, so this thing nobody was doing, so it was me—logistics—and the workers' union. We managed it together. A new logistics person, she wasn't strong. Me, I counted as pretty strong, so I would get the driver to work with me, loading [the truck], pulling ropes and tarps; in Shanghai, we'd unload, and the family would come out to help unload. So everyone said I was like a man, doing a man's job. On the farm, I'd also carried fertilizer on a shoulder pole. So people like us, we can pretty well "eat bitterness." [...] So I just trained myself, and my personality was chiseled out like this.

* * *

季美华 Ji Meihua, female, kindergarten teacher at a Small Third Front steel mill.

Keywords: frustrations, manual labor, men vs. women

When [I first got to the Eight-Five Steelworks] I wasn't a teacher, because then there was no kindergarten. They hadn't built it yet. I was among the first group of kindergarten teachers. I squatted in a workshop [in the factory] for about a year, then they were hiring kindergarten teachers, so they had me go. [I was in] the No. 2 workshop, doing stuff below the cranes. What do you call it? It was really scary. They would be moving the crane above. I was young then. While they were moving the crane above me, I'd be below helping them to move things. I got hurt on the job too. A round steel bolt took off one of my toenails. I was terrified. I didn't want to do it, I really was scared to death.

Yeah, [this kind of work doesn't suit a young woman.] Driving the crane was scary enough, much less working under it. I was really very afraid, because truly I'd never seen it before. It was the first time I saw something like this. [...] After a year, I left and became a kindergarten teacher.

[...]Of course there are advantages for women comrades as teachers; how could male comrades be kindergarten teachers? The parents were very respectful. [...] Workshops were too frightening [compared to the kindergarten work]. Even if I hadn't gotten hurt I'd be afraid; I feel like I'm just not made to be suited for that kind of work. [...]

* * *

刘存龙 Liu Cunlong, male, head of the Planning Team for a Small Third Front steelworks; later, worker and cadre, then staff at the Small Third Front Shanghai offices.

Keywords: conflicts, crime, critique, family, frustrations, marriage, medical issues, men vs. women, policing, violence

[TN: Please note that this narrative contains descriptions of self-harm, sexual assault, and a homicide that may be disturbing.]

Image 6.1 The Red Star Lumber Factory's firefighting team, 1975

There was a kid, Guo Mingchen [TN: the original name has been altered throughout this narrative]. His daddy was an engineer or assistant engineer at the Minhang [District, Shanghai] Water Pump Factory, and his mom died a long time ago from diabetes. Then his dad married his mom's younger sister, thinking she'd be nicer to the son, but his stepmother ignored him. So he started working and entered our No. 8 Workshop. I was in the unmarried men's dorms so I got to know him early on. I thought this kid was very smart and fast at his work. But the one thing was that he had a temper. If you butted heads with him face to face, he wouldn't give you an inch. So, among the cadres, he only listened to his Party branch secretary, Zhang Heming, the head branch secretary for that workshop. When I left that workshop, he was still okay [Image 6.1].

[...] When I got to the factory headquarters, well, once Guo Mingchen came to tell me, I'm dating Tan Kailin [TN: the original name has been altered throughout this narrative] from the No. 2 Workshop. She was very pretty, slender, tall. I told him, you two aren't a good match; your temper is too bad, she's too introverted. In reality, I didn't say this next bit, but I thought, "she likes you no doubt because you're pretty good-looking."

Mingchen was over 5'7", medium build, very clean-cut. I saw that girl and I talked to her, too. I said, this thing, you have to consider carefully. I said, this old cadre here just hopes that you kids are going to be all right.

Not long after, Mingchen found out he had diabetes and he told Kailin. He also came to me, asking me what he should do. I said, it's not like your mom's day anymore; there's medicine you can use, but you have to watch what you eat too. When the girl found out he was sick, she dumped him. In the end, one night Mingchen called her to meet him somewhere and murdered her with a pair of scissors. I saw the scene. I don't think it was that he stabbed her to death, but that she died of fright. There wasn't much blood; just from that, I don't think it was the direct cause of death. So, this thing happened.

There's another thing that I want to talk about; I want to talk about it along with this case. There was another worker, Cui Bingfang [TN: the original name has been altered throughout this narrative]. This kid came from Hubei, over 5'7", skinny, very clever, and he could speak some Shanghainese too, and would say some humorous things. Suddenly I got a call from the Shanghai office saying that he and some others had gang-raped a sent-down youth in Shanghai. I said, "not likely." But they said it was true and the woman had already described the people and what happened and so on. Then we asked what we should do, and they said to go lock him up and put him under supervision. So we reported this to the Security Department and they sent a pretty capable man, a Wei Yuegen, who showed up and took Cui away, probably to some security department place to talk. They talked for half a day. Near the end of the workday, Wei came to find me, saying this thing wasn't going anywhere because Cui was denying everything. I said, go try again. He said, I think you should go show your face.

Now to be fair, I wasn't too willing, because this was an affair for you guys in the security department to look after, not for me. This was clearly illegal. He said, help me out. This got to me, so I said all right, I'll come after I get off work. I went right over there, and when I arrived that kid (Cui) saw me come in and kind of gave a start. I talked for five hours with him, and he admitted he'd done it. I told him, now that you've come clean, I can tell the public security people that you confessed and that your attitude was quite cooperative. So, he told me everything and it was already nighttime. What to do? We called the person on watch. There was a military representative—I've forgotten the name—who said you all should put him under guard. So we took Cui to the workshop and put him in a room where they play ping-pong and sent a veteran Party member to guard him.

The next two days, he wrote down his self-examination; he confessed everything, all of it. Then on the third day he fell asleep—this was definitely investigative isolation now, but we hadn't openly called it that. From today's point of view, this'd be also illegal. The old comrades guarding him were on three shifts. Probably at four or five in the morning, one old comrade went to the bathroom and Cui made a break for it. After he ran, we looked all over the world for him but couldn't find him. There was a path behind our office, and we looked there; we looked in the woods on the hills, but we couldn't find him. By chance, one worker looked up. There on that smokestack that was 200, 230 feet tall, there was a shirt. Then we knew things had gone really bad. He'd climbed up the smokestack, put his clothes there, and jumped. Oh, my God! That horrible scene! It was really tense, then. If it were today, that military representative who did us a bad turn would have to leave.

It's not that he [the representative] ignored what'd happened. But he just gave a speech of all sorts of gobbledygook. And then he blamed us, in reality he was just shuffling the blame to us. With nothing else to do, I wrote a self-examination. But before I'd even finished it, they climbed up and looked at the clothes. Great, I was off the hook. Yes, there was a note in the clothes: I don't blame the leadership, I don't blame my family, this was all my own responsibility. So with this suicide note, I was in the clear. So, we immediately reported this to Shanghai. They were going to send a bailiff out here, but now he didn't have to come. We asked [Cui's family] if they wanted to come, but his family also didn't come. So this thing just passed very quietly.

I was just talking about Guo Mingchen before. Well, Mingchen also jumped. It was Cui Bingfang's jumping that inspired him. After he killed Tan Kailin, he also climbed onto that smokestack and jumped off. A lot of folks talk about how the factory looked after the workers and looked after the sex ratio and so on. Actually, it was a huge issue. These were lessons in blood. [...] The steelworks had very few girls. Out of 100 people, there were maybe ten or twenty female comrades, right for production. When I first got to the Machine Repair Factory, I saw only five women comrades in the entire factory.

I was married, but when you mention this, I have a sad story. I was also divorced. This is kind of off topic. About when I went to the Rear Base in '69, she [my ex-wife] got pregnant with our second baby. I said, you should get an abortion, you can't manage two of them alone. But she insisted on carrying to term. Six months afterward, she gave the kid to my mom and dad. That was fine. But then she and another worker—she was in the No. 5 Workshop, I was in No. 8. She was in the steel-rolling workshop, I was in casting. My old Party branch secretary had introduced us, that was how we met. When we met, her character was pretty good. But being apart for a long time, well, eventually she found someone else. When she had this side man, she'd ignore me when I went back. She ignored me all the way until '77, when I got divorced. After the divorce I was there in the mountains, and whenever someone's relative came, I'd go visit on a Sunday evening. Then a worker introduced his older sister to me.

[…] So the Cui Bingfang affair, his parents didn't want to come, they asked the Party organization to take care of it. So, we just buried him in an empty spot in front of our offices. And then for the Guo Mingchen case, his daddy and stepmother would obviously not come either; they also asked us to take care of it. There were two other incidents, even more atrocious. One was a worker named Ni Renhao; this guy was a pretty good worker and was one of the better ones in our old factory [in Shanghai]. In the mountains, he coordinated pretty well with the Party branch secretary. But the long separation from his wife made him develop a need that couldn't be satisfied. In the end he did it with a mentally disabled girl that a worker had brought in. Well then, the girl spread the word around, but at first [Ni] didn't admit it. She was only 20-something, but Ni was nearly 50. When they found this out, they weren't easygoing about it at all, they gave him three or five years [in prison], I can't remember which, for the crime of "seducing a disabled person." Her daddy was an honest guy, a very decent heating worker. You think he could still stand up straight in that factory? After three or five years, Ni came back to the factory, but his wife ignored him. Not long after that, he died.

There was another guy, Jie Shengxi, who was 40- or 50-something already at the time too. Tall, Shandongese. His work was top-notch, and he never got on the wrong side of anybody. But then we found out a weird thing. After work he'd run all over the place. But we didn't see anything wrong at first. Then some villagers came to tell on him, saying he'd hand out some steamed buns, some cash, or some meal ration tickets and then do it with people. The youngest were in their teens, the oldest 40s or 50s. So we investigated and found out he was sleeping with over ten people! He admitted it, admitted to this thing. So that got him a sentence of over a decade or so, and after that I don't know what happened to him.

These four events illustrate a point. I'll give an old example. When Admiral Zheng He went to the western seas [TN: a reference to Zheng's seven imperially sponsored Indian Ocean voyages in the fifteenth century], he didn't only bring men. He brought along a lot of women to sew up shoe bottoms and clothes and cook. In ancient times they all knew this. This [gender] balance. When minority people were defeated in battle and ran into the mountains, they had the women running in front and they ran along behind. Why? When the Three Years of Natural Disaster happened, everybody was hungry as could be, but the men didn't eat first [and let the women eat]. They died from hunger, one after the other after the other.

And then we neglected this problem. You might say, well, they didn't think about this in the city. But they did; they wanted to move a textile factory out here, but they did a survey and the conditions wouldn't work, they really wouldn't. [...] I also knew the daughter of a dentist for the Shanghai No. 5 Steelworks. Her daddy asked me to help [her find a spouse], and she often came over [for dinner] on Sundays. I'd say to her, how about I get you a cadre? She said, I don't want one, I want to go back [to the city]. Just to demonstrate that the conditions there really didn't suit Shanghainese staying there for the long term. So these four incidents I told you about, these were living lessons. [Like the saying goes,] "men and women paired off together, work'll feel light as feathers."

[...] Oh, one more thing. I forgot just now. There was a Party branch secretary; this guy had been moved from the steel-rolling workshop, the No. 3 Workshop. He seemed pretty good. The old secretary in the steel-rolling workshop, he was my first secretary, that is to say I entered the Party under him. He's dead now, too. His children are doing pretty well. So he told me to take in somebody and of course I had to say yes. Your mentor, after all, no ifs and buts there. After [the recommended man] came to us, he did pretty well; you could count on him for things.

Then, once I was away on business in Shanghai. In the middle of the night someone came looking for me. [...] He said one of your Party branch secretaries got grabbed by the "Attack with Words, Defend with Force" crew; you need to hurry over there. I went and asked what happened, and it turns out this guy—of all the things he shouldn't have done—he'd taken his wife in [to the mountains] with him, and he'd come out and gone to sleep with his girlfriend in the city. If you're going to sleep with her, fine, but have a mind to the date! He went to spend the night with her the day Chairman Mao died. And he had his wife back in the mountains, and here he was sleeping with his Shanghainese girlfriend. If it weren't the day Chairman Mao died, the "Attack with Words, Defend with Force" people wouldn't have been so strict in their inspections, and it'd have just been water under the bridge. But when they did go looking, they found him. Yes, they'd be monitoring everywhere; even if two people were hand-in-hand in the park they'd have words for you. This guy just happened to do this on that day of all days.

Well then, great, the 507 [Rear Base] HQ got a report on this; it was no good; this was a political matter; he needed to be kicked out of the Party. I thought this was problematic. I told the Party Committee, this is adultery, not rape, and you shouldn't magnify this. No! They insisted on kicking him out. So there was nothing for it. I had a lightbulb moment. I said okay, what if each of us on the main Party branch committee wrote a written memo on this and put it in [this file]. After "reform and opening," it was all overturned. Well, I got on this guy's wrong side, but he doesn't hold it to my account.

* * *

徐小英 *Xu Xiaoying, female, cadre, teacher, and office administrator at a Small Third Front steel mill.*

Keywords: camaraderie, manual labor, marriage, nostalgia, men vs. women, Party members, politically correct

[Female comrades] weren't given special accommodations. At that time, you'd see who behaved well. They had one rule: those who behaved well during training-through-labor would be hired into the plant, those who didn't wouldn't be hired in, so we all nearly killed ourselves, really gave it all we had; we didn't care back then. The No. 2 Workshop, we were building the foundation below, right; you took concrete in a wheelbarrow, you poured it in and couldn't stop; there was a line of people pouring it, glug glug glug, doing that; we were all pushing a wheelbarrow by ourselves, full of concrete, pouring it, because the engine on the foundation would have to pour [water on the concrete] for 20 hours or 26 hours without stopping. If it stopped and the cement dried, then that wouldn't work, that would affect it. So, we did the cement like this, we carried the yellow sand [...] we did it all. Mm, both men and women, yep, working like our lives depended on it.

[...] Then after organizing the ranks, I was the [Youth] League Branch Secretary for the Infrastructure Department, [beginning] in '71. I was in the first group. Like the veterans of the factory. Then after the Infrastructure Department was founded, I was the Department's Party branch officer. I'm one of the luckier ones; in reality I wasn't ever a worker or anything. [...] Not many [females were mid-level cadres on the Small Third Front]. Mm, I didn't count as a mid-level cadre. Yeah, the office of teaching affairs—the secretarial level in the school were mid-level cadres, we didn't count—we were a grade under the school [administration]. In the Small Third Front, well, at the time when we [female comrades] came to the Small Third Front, I thought it was really good [in terms of social status and respect].

Good people, good supplies, good tools, and our family backgrounds—our [foundations] were all pretty good. Our performance in our work units should—because I was the grade's Youth League branch secretary in school, and a League Committee member, so I was always pretty upward-looking, and in school my older sister and I originally entered the Party too, so [I was] pretty good when I got to the steelworks too. All along it seemed like people relatively respected me, treated me seriously.

It should be said that in our Small Third Front there wasn't [inequality between men and women]. I should say that in our Small Third Front, in us batch of people who just opened the factory, there were relatively few women, and we also were treated well. Mm, and the [brides who answered] marriage ads, the other female comrades all got treated well.

Really, in our Eight-Five Steelworks, several pretty fine women married out, all of them looking for military men. All of them found [spouses] outside; they didn't take care of [their marriages] in their own factory; they all went to take care of people outside. So look, Wang Wenqing, Yang Xiuzen, and so on, they all married into the military. In that time, the military was pretty good. Mm-hmm. If you found a spouse in the military in those years you'd be treated well.

[...] Mm, yes. I feel like [women] had a pretty high position in the work unit. Yes, women were treated pretty well in the Small Third Front. Especially at a steelworks, right. If it were instrumentation or something, that wouldn't be the same. I thought we seemed to be treated pretty well. If you had a bit of something going on, especially in our factory offices, if you talked about it, you'd not talk to the mid-level cadres, because the people you were in contact with were all a level lower, all [grassroots] level. If you had some difficulty and needed something done [for you], it seemed pretty easy.

* * *

王妙才 Wang Miaocai, male, head of the Sun-Facing Factory, former head of the factory security department. Interviewed together with 张福信 Zhang Fuxin, male, Wang's successor at the factory's security department.

Keywords: conflicts, critique, frustrations, marriage, men vs. women, policing, politically correct

[Before I became factory head,] while doing security work, you also had to make sure to keep the workers calm and their mood stable. We had relatively a lot of single workers and there were issues around sexual affairs. Because it was boring in there and some didn't have their spouses or family around. So, these issues were pretty common in the factories. Not a lot, but in ours there were about six or seven incidents. They were between workers, not with locals. There were two issues. First, apprentices and full-fledged workers weren't supposed to date. But we on the Rear Base, we opened that rule up, because if they went into the mountains but you didn't let them date, what were you going to do down the line? Are you going to be able to help them resolve the problem of finding a spouse? The marriage difficulties on the Small Third Front were very serious. But our factory was a little better because our [Party] secretary had some prescience, so our sex ratios were a little better and there were quite a lot of couples among the workers [Image 6.2].

Image 6.2 Eight-Five Steelworks young men and women at a party, early 1980s, collection of Xu Youwei

But there was another problem here. If I liked the looks of you, and you me, and we hadn't gotten married but one of us was an apprentice, then we could date, sure, but we couldn't get married. We let them date but not marry. So then we had problems. One unmarried apprentice got pregnant. For her, this was going to be a reputation problem. The two of them, they came to talk to me on their own accord. After our chat, I talked with the factory head. To protect them, we wrote a letter to approve her going to get an abortion. We didn't say she'd gotten pregnant out of wedlock. In the end she did marry that worker. This was a thing between the two of them. So this kind of thing, we usually tried to help cover for them and we didn't try to break up their marriage. In the mountains back then, marriage was a very big issue. If there really were something up, we'd go to the political work team and find a leading cadre to help.

[...] There was another incident. One of our workers got injured in a vehicle, so he went home to recuperate [in Shanghai]. So then his wife was in our factory. One of our other workers was a carpenter on the side and we had a lot of lumber around there that could be made into furniture. So she, well, invited this carpenter to help her make furniture. And with all the back and forth with the furniture, the two of them started a relationship. After they started, at first they didn't know, but then she had an ectopic pregnancy and started hemorrhaging. That was really serious; she could be in mortal danger. So we sent her to the military hospital. She needed a blood transfusion.

Zhang Fuxin: At first we didn't know and just thought she needed a transfusion, so our workers lined up to give her blood. Nine people gave blood.

Wang: At first we didn't know, we didn't say anything. After the transfusion, though, people found out. Then they were upset, saying "how could I have given blood to someone like this?" Actually, we were keeping her secret at first. Saving the person was the priority. Another thing was, me and the [Party] secretary had gone to talk to the carpenter guy. He wasn't married himself, but he was an "Aid Agriculture" [TN: a program to help employ peasant farmers] worker. His native place was in Wenzhou. Me and the secretary found him and at first he wouldn't talk. We found the woman and at first she wouldn't talk either, but then she told us everything. We were asking, if your husband's home recuperating, how'd you fall pregnant? So later she did tell us. After that we found this carpenter guy again and he admitted it. Then he got demerits and had to pay her medical bills.

These issues between male and female workers also affected the overall mood of the factory. Another worker, he and his wife were both in the factory, but maybe the two of them had some conflict. So then this male worker and the wife of another male worker had an affair. It was summertime during the siesta rest period when another worker caught them in the act and ran over to tell us. For that case we mainly had to educate them.

Zhang: We called it criticism then. A few of us gathered for a meeting in the [workers'] clubroom and held this criticism session. That was "criticism education." This kind of stuff, we'd also manage. Nowadays it'd be fine, but then it was treated like a problem.

Wang: We really wanted to avoid having their two families be broken up, so we did try to take care of these things. See, the propaganda department wouldn't handle it, neither would the union, so it was up to us in security. We were just this autonomous body that had to oversee everything. Things like this, in Shanghai, would get sent to the police precinct. This is a pretty difficult issue to talk about. Even some of our relatively high-positioned cadres in some of our stations, his wife hadn't come, and some workers went to have a chat about him with the secretary and the factory head. This cadre went to eat dinner at somebody's home, and afterward was coming onto the girl there. It wasn't a local's house but a worker's. So this pertained to the worker and also to the optics for that cadre. So, after discussing this with the factory head and secretary, the priority was put on stabilizing the workers. If this got out, then things would really be a mess.

Nowadays sexual affairs are mainly a question of personal morals, but back then they were very troublesome. When I was in the military, my commander would say, you could make all sorts of mistakes. If you make a mistake in your work, that's inexperience. But "lifestyle" problems, you can't have. If you do, then your entire political life is shot. But in consideration of the stability of our factory, a lot of these problems we didn't handle this [harsh] way. Instead, we relied on internal, private education. So these sexual relationships became affairs that the security department had to get involved in. If a cadre had "lifestyle" problems, it'd influence his political career a bit, when it came to promotions. [...] You all came to interview me today so I'm mentioning these things, but at the time the workers wouldn't have known about them. The worker who had the ectopic pregnancy got transferred away, both of them got transferred. She requested the transfer.

Zhang: At first she was still in the Rear Base, to another factory. Then when the Small Third Front came back they also came back to Shanghai, to our old factory.

Wang: These kinds of incidents didn't just happen in our factory. Other factories had them too. This was a widespread phenomenon. We were a little better because our sex ratios were a little better.

* * *

王文青 Wang Wenqing, female, worker and propaganda cadre at a Small Third Front steel mill.

Keywords: birth planning, camaraderie, manual labor, men vs. women, nostalgia, politically correct, work assignments

[...] At the time our Shanghai No. 5 Steelworks even specially made a booklet about the stories of model [staff], me working in the cafeteria, and even an essay about me inside. Someone else wrote it, "cooking her whole life for the revolution." My son-in-law jokes that because I was very busy, my husband always did the cooking for the family, saying "cooking her whole life for the revolution but never cooking at home" [laughs].

[...] We used to have several female comrades who were called "Iron Girls" and such, quite a few of them—one was Zhang Huihui, another was Wu Yuzhen. At the time they were below in the workshops, our No. 4. You'd have round steel cylinder; first you drill into it to make it hollow, then you stretched it bit by bit. There were several stages in the process. Basically, you had to move this solid steel onto the machine. It was pretty tough. Zhang Huihui would do this work too, so she was called an "Iron Girl." After she came back [to Shanghai], she worked in the Workers' Committee; after she stopped working there she, well, she began brokering real estate and it was pretty good [...] at the time, well, she was always in Workshop No. 4 at Eight-Five.

[...] [Interviewer: Were there more female comrades in the Workers' Union? Because they're a bit more detail-oriented?] Just talking about female comrades, there were three in radio, two in finance. More in the library. Doing lifestyle work, like giving assistance and such; one was doing that, then another came along. Two in Birth Planning. Not so many. Because there weren't that many people in our steelworks' Workers' Union to start with.

Definitely, female comrades were definitely more detail-oriented. I think probably not really other differences, possibly due to the situation of our Eight-Five Steelworks. Yeah, [about the same as men]. Yeah, [over there], pretty much the male comrades respected the female comrades.

There wasn't really suspicions of female comrades' work abilities. We were all very capable. We didn't have young people who weren't settled, who would make trouble.

[…] We should say—the numbers I'm not clear on—but later on, the [proportion] should've been about the same between the sexes. At most it was 40/60. Because most people had families. Yeah, our plant had over 6000 people. There were kind of a lot of contributions from female comrades; I don't really remember any really outstanding ones. […] No, they didn't used to do things like assigning me easier jobs. Just these things to do, and you just did them.

* * *

杨秀珍 Yang Xiuzhen, female, worker and cadre for a Small Third Front steelworks.

Keywords: camaraderie, frustrations, manual labor, medical issues, men vs. women, Party members, pay and benefits, politically correct, sent-down youth

Doing purely physical labor on the docks was pretty tough. Back then my deepest impression was that it was really very hard. Because back then the conditions were all pretty bad. And I ate pretty badly. Work, you had work hours, but—back then there were a lot of "shock troop" or "concentrated attack" duties. For example, a boat arrives on the docks, but if there was still something not yet done, we'd all have to organize a "shock attack" team. Party members would often organize these teams, and Youth League members would do it a lot too. The team would get together a bunch of League members or Party members. This was regardless of whether you were a cadre or a worker; you'd all go down below to knock out all the coal, then this attack would be complete. This left a really deep impression on me. The shock attack.

Some cadres were really there among the front lines. Apart from their own responsibilities—the Party branch secretary would have branch secretary work, doing some thought work for the docks, cultivating new Party members, and the work of the team. Apart from this, well, these shock attacks would need a cadre to head them. Back then—they worked alongside us, especially Party members. Zhang Sumei, the branch secretary of that time, she's already passed away. She got promoted to deputy factory head later on. Then she was made a Leading Worker of Shanghai. She was branch secretary but led the troops—she was already 40-something then.

You know, every time we had to shovel coal, she'd give 120%, really working until she was exhausted. Back then we'd be shoveling coal below deck, and people like me, I don't know how we were able to shovel at all. Shovel by shovel, we put it into a big net [...] then the crane would pull it up. I feel like the most stand-out thing of that time was that our team was led by a cadre, and they got nothing else for it—this was standard—no matter their pay, no matter what. The only [difference] was their title as a Communist Party member. [Their compensation was] even lower than other people's. The workers' reward money would be seven bucks—that was later on; they didn't get rewards before. The cadres would get five bucks.

[...] Hard physical work had to be done by all the female comrades on the loading team. Afterward I was given special benefits because I worked hard [...] and also in consideration of the situation of female comrades. [...] At that time, I was switched to controlling the crane after not too long. While doing that, I had a fall. [...] You had to check that you had put the coal onto the boat. One time, it was rainy, I was young. There were no loading workers, it was just me, the driver. Just the crane driver operating. So I jumped onto the boat. It was a big jump. I slipped and fell, because it was coal. I fell. I slipped and broke a bone. But I was young then. I didn't really take a break, or just for a few days. So, this back problem, I've had it all this time. When I was young, I wasn't so careful. [...] It's not like arthritis, but my back often hurts. If I don't watch it, my back is chronically sore. [...] About 20 or 30% of the dock workers were female comrades doing this type of work. Some were locals who were brought in.

[...] There was no thinking that female comrades needed to be especially taken care of a little. Men and women were the same. We at the time didn't think that we were weaker, or needed to have less to do; we'd do the same things as men. Because in this respect, we didn't have that awareness. We only thought about working better or doing more than other people. At that time my body was at its limit. [...] I just wanted to perform a bit better, show my upward spirit. I was really progressive then. Becoming a Party branch secretary, I actually felt that I was a little too young for it. I was 24. And then with the sending down, and on top of it, we people didn't have a lot of book learning.

* * *

张薇薇 Zhang Weiwei, female, worked in various positions in propaganda, education, and technology inspection at a steel mill.

Keywords: conflicts, crime, frustrations, marriage, men vs. women, nostalgia, Party members, politically correct

At first, when I was graduating, I had a classmate of mine at school, one class above me, who wanted to date me. He went to Sichuan; he was assigned to the Great Wall Steelworks [built there by the Shanghai Metallurgy Bureau]. We kept up our correspondence all through that. After a year or two, in '72, I joined the Party. He'd left for the Great Wall Steelworks in '69, and I left in January '70 for the Eight-Five Steelworks in Anhui. The letters he sent, people knew about. A stack of mail arrived and other people would always rifle through and see them. All these letters from the Sichuan Great Wall Steelworks; people knew this was my boyfriend, and I acknowledged it too, I never denied it. But we never saw each other during that time. We'd see each other once a year when he was visiting family and I went to visit mine; we'd meet up. Our feelings did cool off a bit. Because when we were in school—well, we were naïve. Mm-hmm, so we got along pretty great. Because of that, when we had to be separated, there was this reluctance to be parted. So then he said he wanted to be boyfriend and girlfriend and I agreed.

Then in '72, my factory wanted to cultivate me to join the Party, so they went to do their investigations. They'd also investigated your boyfriends. We weren't married, so I thought that was weird. But then they showed me the results, they asked me, you know what they said about him? I said I didn't. Turns out he'd gotten a major demerit out there for theft. Yep. I had not a single clue about it. I asked what he'd stolen. They said it was lumber or something, wood. Probably [he took it] because he was dating me and wanted to make some furniture [for getting married]; I figured it was that. Mm-hmm, not really ill-intentioned. Early on they were very strict with this sort of thing. But later, taking small things from the factory, mm-hmm, that was very common.

But at first they were pretty strict, so he got counted as theft. And he was the shift supervisor for his workshop. [...] The impression he gave me was pretty good. Because it was the Cultural Revolution then, I'd also participated in [political] organizations at my school, so we were together. We were often together, so we got along pretty well. How could I have known that after he went out there, he'd do something like this? Then our branch secretary advised me, since he's this kind of person, and you're living apart, there's not much reason [to continue the relationship]. I said I'd think it over. After thinking it over I wrote a letter to him [my boyfriend] saying, let's split; this thing you did, such a big thing, but you never told me, I had no idea. This was in itself disrespectful to me. Then I also wrote another nice letter asking [to break up]. He immediately wrote me back and cursed me like crazy, just a string of curses.

Mm-hmm, he didn't try to comfort me at all; he didn't admit he'd done anything wrong, or try to make any explanation. He just cursed me out. I was angriest when he accused me of having a "petit bourgeois consciousness." Yep, because back then he'd come over to my house [in Shanghai]. My family had a pretty big place. Back then that was my maternal grandpa's house; it had an upstairs and a downstairs, and was a standalone wing [of a courtyard building]. Yeah, so he said I had a "petit bourgeois consciousness." Then I just ignored him. He didn't try to explain himself at all. He didn't do that and didn't seem to want me to forgive him, there was nothing soft in that letter at all. Yep, and then we really did split. It was pretty comical too, when we did. All the presents he'd sent me and the stuff I'd sent him, yes, we sent them back to each other.

Since we were both away [from Shanghai], him in Sichuan and me in Anhui, he called his younger brother to get the things and I got mine to help get them. When I went to visit my family, [I gave back] the gloves, scarves—really all just small things—that he'd given me. Yeah, not like he gave me any big presents, just some small stuff. I gave them all back to him and he gave [presents I'd given him] back to me. Our two younger brothers stood around outside doing the handover, each of them with a bag [of things]. My brother still makes fun of me these days, "you broke up and made me be the go-between." Mm-hmm, it was really pretty funny. Such a small thing…

Well then, at the time, there weren't many female comrades, so I had a pretty nice time out there. Back then there were several guys [interested in me]. Some of them didn't dare come talk to me, and some wrote letters to me, things like that. Well, it's not that I was hard to approach, but they were kind of afraid to raise the request [to date me]. Would you turn them down? But then the people who did really come ask me, I did turn them all down. I didn't like any of them. And then a few others—I'm just saying what comes to mind with you [the interviewer], just chatting now.

There was one guy, we got along pretty well. He sang pretty well. And I was arranging the programming, and he was always the star. Because I was always doing the programming and he was always the lead, we always got along very well. Then he said he had a girlfriend back in Shanghai at the No. 5 Steelworks. He'd come to "Support the Interior" from the No. 5; he was three years older than me. Then his girlfriend caught wind of something going on. He told me at first that, after he'd come to Support the Interior, the girlfriend's parents opposed their marriage and wanted [her] to break it off with him. But that girl was still pretty into him, but then she heard some rumor and—well, she came looking for him. She came over to visit, basically she had, with him—well, then we started hanging out less. He was a pretty good writer back then too, writing things that other people didn't know about. Poetry; he'd stuff them in my office desk drawer and I'd write him one back. Back and forth like this. There were two other guys who I didn't consider for a moment.

My husband, well, back then we were all getting married pretty late. How naïve we were. When people started dating at 23 or 24, we'd be like, oho, they're dating now. How shameless, we'd say. Even when someone put on a bra we'd say, that's so shameless, she's wearing a bra. We didn't know anything back then. They [our busts] were all pretty big by the time we were girls, and we were wearing [bras] by the time we got into the factory. But in school we'd gossip about other girls. Yes, you'd wear a vest back then, a little vest, with buttons. Mm-hmm, we all thought the kind of person [who wore bras] were kind of loose, we'd think that. Later, thinking about this, you realize you were incredibly dumb. And when people wanted to get married we'd also be like this. Like, oh wow, she's already dating? [Late marriage] was more "progressive." So we all waited until very late to start [dating].

[I married] when I was 29. Around when I was 26, everyone had found [their significant others] and started to pair off. Then, back then, I couldn't tell you if I liked anybody in particular. I thought a few guys were pretty good and they were pretty nice to me, too. But then they went to be with other women and didn't dare bring it up with me; none of them brought it up. So then our syndicate head, Master Ji, he said, "aren't you on pretty good terms with Ma Yunyao?" Well my husband's name is Ma Yunyao. So then I said I didn't really have any feelings toward him. He [Ma] was very respectful to me then, very admiring.

Then he also joined the Youth League and the Party, and he even became the deputy League branch secretary, but everything he wrote he'd have me look over and ask me to help correct it. He kept calling me Teacher Zhang, so that meant we had some distance between us. So when he [Master Ji] brought it up, we were both shocked. We never thought about it. So I thought, I'll just wait on him then. After a couple of years, Master Ji asked us, how's the dating going? And I said what dating? We never dated.

He said, "What? You never dated?" I said, yeah, we never did. He [Ma] never brought it up and neither did I. When we went to Shanghai we also didn't meet up. He visited his family and I visited mine; we were both busy. So then Master Ji formally pulled us together, formally said to us, to Ma Yunyao, "you're a man after all, you have to be a little more proactive, you have to ask her out." Then he did, and I agreed. Mm, he's two years younger than me.

* * *

张燕芳 Zhang Yanfang, female, teacher turned production statistics and logistics cadre at a steel mill.

Keywords: camaraderie, children, conflicts, family, frustrations, manual labor, men vs. women, pay and benefits, politically correct, travel and transportation, work assignments

Oh. The female workers had it worse than I did. They were all junior high graduates, or senior high—the better ones were high school grads; some were only junior high. I don't really know much about this aspect of them. Then we came to the factory and were together, so there was more contact. About Yang Xiuzhen, that comrade really was...she was the [Communist Youth] League Branch secretary for the piers, then the Party branch deputy secretary. Let me tell you, when the factory was holding a routine meeting—the mid-level cadres' routine meeting, [she was wearing] an incredibly tattered old padded cotton coat, and she was black all over [TN: unclear if the narrator means from sun or from dirt], not at all like a young girl.

So hard! What didn't she do on that pier! Our pier was [shipping] scrap steel and was 27 kilometers from our unit. She had it really hard! When the scrap steel arrived, she had to go organize other people to unload it. That scrap steel could be used by other people; the trucks had to carry it in. When coal came, she had to organize [people] to move it. The cadres of that era, really—like Yang Xiuzhen, Wang Wenqing, Ding Xiuyu, back then they were all Iron Girls. What didn't they do in the factory? They did it all. Yang Xiuzhen was moving coal, moving scrap steel, moving the heat-resistant materials. The refractory materials in the steelworks were in pieces and very heavy. She did it all. So when she came for a factory meeting, she was like—not at all like a girl. So I was very impressed by Yang Xiuzhen. She really put in the work. I worked in a workshop; I did production statistics.

No, no special treatment [as a female comrade and transferring from a school into the factory]. Who'd do that? You should do it actively yourself. Even if they took care of me, I'd ...yes, [be embarrassed]. People thought differently back then. Take Yang Xiuzhen. When she talks about the people in her department...what was she doing, such difficult work. Right? Everyone was like this. Not just me. Of course, it could be that people were on different levels. For example, among mid-level cadres, everyone really wanted to do more, go above and beyond, right? Among the workers—well, if you stick out your ten fingers, some are short and some are long. You can't demand the everyone else is the same as yourself; that's impossible. Right?

Yes, meetings big and small were held regularly. [My husband and I] always took care of [eating] at the cafeteria! We didn't cook for ourselves. No, not at all. No time to cook. Where would we get the time for cooking? Yes, yes this helped reduce the burden a bit; no need to buy food and cook. Once in a while, Saturday or Sunday when they felt like it, others—so, apart from fish, meat, these products in bulk, and also poultry, was always shipped in from the outside, vegetables, fresh produce; you had to take Yang Xiuzhen and them to buy [it] on the piers. Seventeen miles. We had a truck specially for buying produce. Two of them.

At that time, men and women didn't seem to be separated. Everyone worked together. For instance, we also had the "three tickets," meaning grain [ration] tickets, and national grain tickets. If you were going on a business trip you needed [...] gas tickets. These were the "three tickets," you know. And the stationery warehouse, all those many departments of the whole factory, the stationery they needed to work, we supplied it. Getting it in—back then you had cards to pick up [supplies]; the safety and protective equipment warehouse, all of that was our responsibility. Dividing the tasks—we had various groups.

Female comrades' effect on the Rear Base were big. One, first, female comrades could stabilize the situation on the Rear Base. You're talking about a factory full of bare sticks [TN: slang for unmarried men] [...] from the bigger picture, don't you agree? Stabilizing the people's hearts. So then lots of people came [...] Like, the handful of us weren't like that; Yang Xiuzhen wasn't like that; Ding Xiuyu wasn't either. Some [women] were younger, later on, they were from all over the country and answered marriage ads to come. Right? So for stability, the effect of female comrades can't be taken lightly, right? If you were really [all men], the plant wouldn't be able to hold on. The situation couldn't have possibly been maintained until that time. This is on the bigger picture side.

On the smaller side—especially us in logistics, we depended on female comrades. You talk about the commissary retail clerks, all of them were female comrades. Those clerks were really hardworking, honestly. Standing behind the counter, right, not even the No. 1 Department Store in Shanghai had so many products, right. You had to know all of them, all of their properties, their prices, accounting, keeping books. And including accompanying shipments—the commissary came to Shanghai to buy goods; there was always someone with the trucks. Here's your list, my truck brings in four tons of stuff; you'd receive it and have someone else take it? Of course it was you the commissary that came to accompany the trucks. Two female comrades who really could work hard, honestly.

There were only one to two male comrades at the commissary store [...] those old liquor jars, they'd move them one by one, these female comrades, really [...] our female comrades in the "three ticket office" were comfortable, the stationery warehouse female comrades were comfortable. But when the truck came, the "three ticket office" was like "whatever," but if stationery supplies arrived, they had to move them and settle them just the same. Like you, whatever, the telephone office's female comrades were all right; the most comfortable [job] in logistics was in the telephone room, and also the "three ticket office" [Image 6.3].

Everything else was pretty difficult. The female comrades in the cafeteria had it hard too; they had to do shift work. All those people you've got, especially in the plant administrative offices' cafeteria. The cafeteria for the workshop was all right. There weren't many men. The men were the few senior cooks. Female comrades also were in the medical clinic. Men too. The men in our clinic were the two heads, Lu Yichang and Tao Changsheng, men. Then they changed the roster, and I don't know, because I'd left, right. The two heads were men...and another volunteer was male. We also had a traditional Chinese medicine pharmacy. The story of that pharmacy was, he was the heir of their ancestral tradition. He was a very good traditional Chinese medicine doctor, a man. Also X-ray [technicians]. Later on, two college grads went in there, both male.

Basically all the [doctors and such] were female, yes, not young girls. Some were a bit [younger], nurses from Shanghai. Yes yes, nurses worked like doctors, and doctors like nurses, out there. No way around that. When we'd just gotten out there, just arrived. Yes, doctors would have to do

Image 6.3 Hu Qinying working the switchboard at the No.260 Communications Station's Jixi Branch, 1970s, collection of Hu Qinying

their jobs if anything unexpected happened. Our Shanghai Steelworks Hospital out there was a "Support the Interior" [branch] of the Shanghai No. 1 People's Hospital [...] Your little problems or illnesses, you'd get taken care of at your own factory clinic. Our clinic, under the [main] clinic—each workshop would have their own small clinics, following the three shifts. Because if you had a work injury or something—for example, Workshop No. 2 had a clinic, the No. 4 Workshop had one, and No. 1 and No. 3—all the bigger production workshops—would have little clinics. They followed shifts. Yes, and the factory had a big [clinic], like a small hospital, like the [...] neighborhood hospitals now. So for really big deals, then you'd go [...] to the Shanghai Steel Hospital. Yes, yes, the clinic [doctors] would have to follow the patients over to relay the situation. Very tough, in the clinic, for the female comrades.

[...] Yes, female comrades worked relatively more in the daily life aspects. Production [work], well, the intermediary testing room, the central laboratory—like when the steel was made, you had to immediately test it then and there. And then a lot, like forging, when you forged round steel bars, or you pulled steel cable, or pipes, all of these had to be tested, like if the steel material met the standards or not, was the annealing up to standard. And also if the [steel's] properties were good. Physical and chemical properties all had to be tested. There was intermediary testing just for all this, lots of female comrades there. Relatively high-end [work], relatively technical. Yes, not brute strength work, the central laboratory. They didn't need to take shifts. Mm, unless there was a special urgent [task], like if this batch of steel needed to get out, but if the samples hadn't come out, the examination reports hadn't come out, then special urgency—that was once in a thousand years, you know.

Yes, if female comrades had their kids in Shanghai with their parents taking care of [the kids], that was relatively much easier, because you just had two ends to run between, dorms, factory, dorms, factory; the work might have been hard, but anyway it was all over there [in Anhui]. But, yes, if you had your spouse and kid by your side, that was also okay. Because later, a very good nursery school, a kindergarten, all got established. School, from elementary to secondary, they had them. Yes yes, yes yes, teachers were mostly female, and had a significant effect, they had to work pretty hard, especially the teachers of the little kids, they had to watch them a bit more. Like now, some students, some students in Shanghai, still remember their kindergarten teachers, their elementary school teachers, they still recall them.

Nowadays we all get along really well. At that time they kept making trouble for me. Our drivers' team captain, a really great person. [Interviewer: A woman?] A man. One of the drivers under him was a woman, really skilled. So you know the drivers for the Shanghai No. 5 Steelworks, if their tires blew there was a tire mechanic, if their battery went out there was an electrical mechanic and such; like everyone else was looking after them, and you only had to look out for the car and turn the steering wheel. Not us. When our trucks went out, for example if you went to Jiangsu to bring in ducks, if your truck stalled out there you had to do [it], you always had to fix it yourself. Just one other worker accompanying the truck, following you, the driver.

This female comrade of ours, I really looked up to her. If it was snowing heavily out, other people's trucks couldn't make it back, but she could still drive it back just fine. You know, when our trucks are away, [we're] real nervous, right? Like if you had a flash flood, I'd be worried. How were our trucks that were out? There weren't cell phones or telephones really then; there was no way to get in touch. If she had gone out, you could be 120% assured. If anything broke, she'd be able to fix it. I really admired her. But then our driving team captain was also really good. Even now we're still thick as thieves. But back then there was a time he'd pound the desk and curse me. Why? The two of them were carrying on an affair. Because each of their spouses was in Shanghai. Yes—so there were big, big outcries among the others.

[So I intervened.] Who else would take care of it? [Interviewer: Shouldn't this go up to the Workers' Union or something?] But then you'd be making too much out of this thing, everyone would [...] so this thing could only come to us, right? Even if you were the [work] team captain you couldn't take care of this kind of thing. It had to be us directly coming in. So directly coming in, old Chi [my boss] talked it over with me. "Little Zhang, transfer that woman away." I really didn't want to let her go. I really—I said, I'm a female comrade too. I see this kind of female comrade and it's really a shame. [I did] go try to mediate. No use. Other people [put pressure on...] because this kind of affair—you wouldn't understand it—especially in a mountain gully.

[Interviewer: Did this kind of thing happen frequently?] No, people at the time were pretty good, pretty okay. But because he was a driver, a captain, and she was a team member—yes, they were together all the time. So, the rumors and gossip really grew and grew. Some people talked about it as though it was—and, you know. So old Chi talked it over with me. "What to do, little Zhang?" Transferring her away, I really didn't want to see her go; I said no. He said there's no other way; if it keeps on like this it's really not fair to their spouses, right? So in the end there wasn't anything for it. I had to go talk to this woman and transfer her to the "Big May Seventh" [TN: Mao's "May Seventh Directive" of 1966 resulted in the creation of industrial and rural work units for urban cadres]. At that time some places had the May Seventh [cadres] work the fields, you know. So, transfer to the Big May Seventh.

She didn't want to go. Every day she came to my office, bang-bang-bang, knocking [on the desk]. I said don't knock it; this is public property; if you break it you have to pay for it; don't bang on it. She said, "I won't go!" I said, "You have to go; from the day that I talked with you, I already don't have any more work hours for you here, no salary either. You can only go to the Big May Seventh to get your salary." "I won't go!" "If you don't go, lemme tell you, you still got to go." I called old Chi's people again to do work on her. Right?

So, everyone knew what was what. This kind of thing wasn't glamorous, and you couldn't talk about it openly. So the excuse was "the demands of work." She said, why do I have to be transferred? I said, work requirements. Not—not saying you have something else! Right? Yes, she was embarrassed. She couldn't talk about it out loud either, you know. I said you have got to go, this was decided by the organization. People back then saw the organization as bigger than the sky, not like now; who'd care? Wouldn't you say? [...] She wrangled for more than a month! She wangled for more than a month before going. The man didn't come yell at me. Yes! Only this woman came, because she was getting transferred.

[...] So then later, what's-her-name, after yelling at me, she began to ignore me. The man wasn't happy to see me either. Before, to arrange work and such, we'd chat and talk, right. I'd say, Ahui—his name was Guo Lihui, so Ahui, [as a diminutive] what do you think of this day [for a shipment]? Can this truck go out? Can you arrange to go over and have a look? You know. If something was a special-priority assignment, sometimes people in the Disciplinary Department needed trucks to pull bamboo, so we'd go. I'd go with them, I'd go with Ahui to load the bamboo, go out to load the bamboo in a mountain gully. We really talked often. Back then, the situation was, everyone knew without saying why she was being transferred. That [affair] was the reason. After I came up [to Shanghai] I ignored him too.

Then later, this woman's son was in Shanghai; back then he was sitting for school exams, exams for vocational high school. He got into the Shanghai Cement Factory Technical School in Xiajing. His own family came to Baoshan, because the Shanghai No. 5 Steelworks was in Wusong, right. Three older sisters in Shanghai and just one son. We thought that wasn't right. She brought it up herself: could the organization help? At that time her husband had gone in [to Anhui] too and there were only three older sisters and one little brother in Shanghai. Then later me and a comrade from our Shanghai office, and a comrade in the Labor and Salary

[Department], the three of us were going to the Shanghai Cement Factory. They'd started school already. We moved his dossier out and arranged for him to go to the Baosteel [TN: Baoshan Steelworks] Technical School. So the older sisters could look after everything. The parents were at ease. How great: the Baosteel Technical School, a great work unit like Baosteel. That cement factory, well, it was dirty and out of the way, with no one looking after [him].

So that's how we helped her. This was her own son. Her husband was also in our cafeteria at the Shanghai No. 5 Steelworks. They had Albanian foreign students back then in the plant; he cooked for the foreign students. He was very good. Well, the husband went in [to Anhui] because of this [affair]. [...] Nowadays everyone gets along just great. There's no way around it, handling this sort of thing, being the public face, being stared at and thought to be doing things badly or being blamed, even though this was a conclusion reached by negotiation. There was nothing else to do, after all. I couldn't very well say, this isn't my business, this is old Chi's business. I couldn't say that kind of thing, wouldn't you agree? So whatever, whatever you [think], if you want to wheedle, wheedle, if you want to talk, talk—yes, later on you'll understand. So now our relationships are all very good. Few days ago, I went to Wusong and bumped into Ahui at the station and was very glad.

* * *

赵惠瑛 Zhao Huiying, female, worker and kindergarten teacher at a Small Third Front steelworks.

Keywords: camaraderie, education, manual labor, men vs. women

No! At that point, no! Kindergartens didn't have [male teachers]. Really, doing education work, really women comrades were more careful. But in our kindergarten, there was a really nice thing. I said before. When we ran out of firewood, or coal, the teachers would call over their husbands, get their husbands and go look, go pick up firewood, go move some coal, move it all over and do everything well. Even—not like now—even with periodic maintenance and such, I honestly started feeling like my classroom was looking bad; what to do? I'd paint it and clean it up. I'd go find some lime from the mechanical department, soak it myself, then on Sunday paint the walls with my husband. Like this, everything you did yourself.

No, I don't think, being female, that others would be prejudiced against me or think I couldn't handle this kind of thing because I was a young woman. I think that in work, they didn't look down on me. I thought I wasn't good enough…I didn't feel like because I was a young girl, I can't do this kind of thing. [On special treatment for women teachers:] If you needed something, I'd go over to discuss it with others, and probably they'd say, "A kindergarten teacher? Sure, sure!" Basically they'd all help. […] In physical tasks, our teachers could handle it, or pass it to our husbands, to our boyfriends, or have male comrades come and we all work together to carry [things], like that.

* * *

赵连洪 Zhao Lianhong, male, security department cadre in a Small Third Front company

Keywords: conflicts, critique, frustrations, marriage, men vs. women, Party members, politically correct

[TN: Please note that this narrative contains references to self-harm that may be disturbing.]

My wife is also an "Old Small Third Fronter." She went in in '68, I think. No way, we didn't meet in Shanghai first. I almost didn't find myself a wife! Don't know if you'd heard of the Rear Base's Cao Wenjing—she was in with Dai Liqing and their posse. They all came out of the National No. 17 Cotton Mill, Wang Hongwen's factory. Dai had a few henchmen, you know, including that Cao Wenjing. She was the Party Committee Deputy Secretary for the Rear Base; at first she was the Youth League Secretary and a Party Committee member. She was one of Dai's underlings. She [and my wife] were in the same dorm: my wife, Cao, and a Li Li, and a Zhang something. All one dorm room. They'd all come out of that cotton mill. We [my wife and I] met by being introduced. How do I say it—at the time, the girls in my work unit, I never thought I'd be looking for a girl among them.

[Pan Jinfeng, Zhao's wife, chimes in:] Same here, no thought of looking in my work unit. I came from the East Wind Factory, tons of male comrades, and people would introduce me to them, but I never thought I'd seriously consider someone from the factory. Sometimes when you know someone too well you don't want to consider them. Hard to say, this stuff.

[Zhao:] There were [cases related to affairs], yes. At her [East Wind Factory] there was one. Someone jumped into the reservoir. [Pan:] A love suicide. I don't really know why, but it happened in the No. 3 Workshop in the eastern branch factory. [Zhao:] It's been a long time, 30 or 40 years.

If you found a factory-level cadre with "lifestyle problems," they'd be fired. [Pan:] If you got pregnant out of wedlock, you'd have to leave the company. The people who got pregnant all had to leave the factory if they were in the factory. If you were in an administrative office you'd get sent down to the factory. [Zhao:] Now with the "reform and opening," it's not like adultery cases go away. No, it's just that now we don't care anymore. Yes, now we don't count these as cases, but before they counted as administrative discipline cases. No, if a cadre were fired, we usually handled it internally [without publicity].

[Pan:] I have an example, actually. Not a lifestyle problem. They just were dating. They were pretty good all around, but then they got pregnant without being married; yes, they didn't have a marriage certificate, but then they got pregnant. But that wouldn't do, so you had to do something about it. They were handled internally. By that point it was no good to go pick up a marriage certificate; it was useless to get married. [Zhao:] [It was] pretty "Left" back then.

Further Reading

On Gender

Gail Hershatter, *Women in China's Long Twentieth Century.* Berkeley: University of California Press, 2007.

Gail Hershatter, *The Gender of Memory: Rural Women and China's Collective Past.* Berkeley: University of California Press, 2011.

Emily Honig, "Maoist Mappings of Gender: Reassessing the Red Guards," in Susan Brownell and Jeffrey Wasserstrom eds., *Chinese Femininities, Chinese Masculinities: A Reader.* Berkeley: University of California Press, 2002. 255–268.

Elizabeth Perry and Nora Dillon, "'Little Brothers' in the Cultural Revolution: The Worker Rebels of Shanghai," in Susan Brownell, Jeffrey Wasserstrom eds., *Chinese Femininities, Chinese Masculinities: A Reader.* Berkeley: University of California Press, 2002. 269–286.

Y. Yvon Wang, "Heroes, Hooligans, and Knights-Errant: Masculinities and Popular Media in the Early People's Republic of China." *Nan Nü* 19 (2017), 316–356.

Zheng Wang, *Finding Women in the State: A Socialist Feminist Revolution in the People's Republic of China, 1949–1964*. Berkeley: University of California Press, 2017.

Zheng Wang, "Gender and Maoist Urban Reorganization," in Bryna Goodman and Wendy Larson eds., *Gender in Motion: Divisions of Labor and Cultural Change in Late Imperial and Modern China*. Lanham, MD: Rowman & Littlefield, 2004.189–209.

On Sexuality

Emily Honig, "Socialist Sex: The Cultural Revolution Revisited." *Modern China* 29:2 (2003), 143–175.

Wenqing Kang, "Male Same-Sex Relations in Socialist China." *The PRC History Review* 3:1 (2018), 1–36.

Other Materials and Resources

Weili Ye and Xiaodong Ma, *Growing Up in the People's Republic: Conversations Between Two Daughters of China's Revolution*. New York: Palgrave Macmillan, 2005.

Xueping Zhong, Zheng Wang, and Di Bai eds., *Some of Us: Chinese Women Growing Up in the Mao Era*. New Brunswick, N.J.: Rutgers University Press, 2001.

CHAPTER 7

Marriage, Reproduction, Family

Translator's Note

Given the pressure to prioritize production over personal relations, even normative, heterosexual, work unit-approved marriages were celebrated with a minimum of fanfare. Spouses frequently lived apart due to the exigencies of educational or work assignments. Cadres in work units routinely intervened to prevent "bad" matches, upheld rules about legal ages of marriage, and, as some of the testimonies in this section show, also closely surveilled people's reproductive lives as the One Child Policy began to be rolled out nationwide around 1979. The main targets of the Birth Planning Policy, as it is known in Chinese, were women. As scholars have argued, the policy had differential impacts on people based not only on gender, but also their socioeconomic standing and their location on either side of the sharp urban/rural divide; many of these effects were personally traumatizing and led to unintentional negative outcomes for China's sex skew and age structure.[1] Adhering to the new policies closely also became a badge of pride and accomplishment for some; doing so could also bring material rewards. Disobeying, on the other hand, could come with severe

[1] Susan Greenhalgh and Edwin A. Winckler, *Governing China's Population: From Leninist to Neoliberal Biopolitics*. Stanford: Stanford University Press, 2005; also Greenhalgh (2008).

Y. Xu, Y. Y. Wang, *Everyday Lives in China's Cold War Military-Industrial Complex*, Palgrave Studies in Oral History,
https://doi.org/10.1007/978-3-030-99688-8_7

repercussions like being dismissed from prestigious, stable employment [Image 7.1].

Small Third Fronters' relationships with older kin and with their own children, like those between spouses, were also supposed to be put on a lower priority than their work assignments. It was not unusual for workers in these remote factories to have family elders in Shanghai look after young children for years. Some workers who could return for official purposes took advantage of that privilege to carve out more family time. Even so, traveling back to the city was laborious and vacation days were limited. Some of the recollections that follow attest to the logistical and emotional challenges that these separations entailed.

As was the case for sexuality and gender roles, the kinds of family relationships and feelings that the Party held up as ideal often dictated the constraints on people's lives on the Small Third Front, but they could not reshape the actual relationships and desires that people had. Being able to deprioritize marriage, children, and extended family may have been a relief

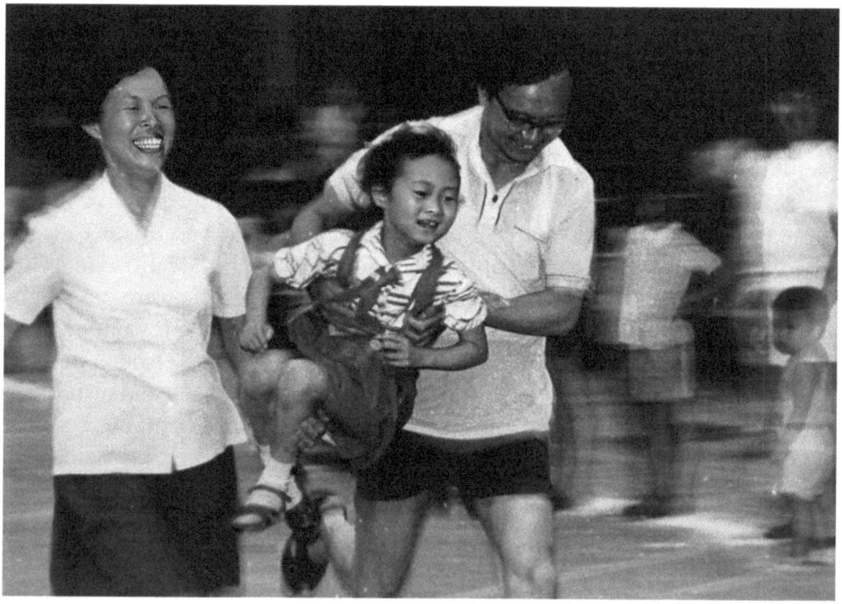

Image 7.1 Parents and their daughter playing a game at the Eight-Five Steelworks, early 1980s, collection of Xu Youwei

to some Third Fronters. The trauma, regret, and distress that others experienced still comes through in their testimonies many years later. For those in positions of responsibility in Third Front work units, the potential demoralization and discontent of people kept from forming or maintaining marital and family relationships led them to make special exceptions and concessions. These ad hoc workarounds should remind us that there was no singular "Party-state" even in these secretive military-industrial complexes. Instead, political authority always existed in tension with individual motivations, internal contestations, and deeply felt values that extended beyond the dictates of any political party or leader.

Questions for Discussion

1. Are there any broad commonalities in how Small Third Fronters talk about their marital and family relationships? Where do they differ? Why do you think these differences exist?
2. What do you think the people whose testimonies about family and marriage appear in this section thought of the possibilities and limitations for their marital and family relationships in their time on the Small Third Front?
3. What, if anything, surprises you about these Small Third Fronters' testimonies about relationships that many consider the most intimate and personal ones in life?

* * *

卞建华 Bian Jianhua, female, driver for the Rear Base militia headquarters.

Keywords: children, conflicts, critique, family, frustrations, men vs. women, rural vs. urban

During the big retreat [back to the city], even if I can't say that the divorce rate was really high, at the very least it did break up some families. Nothing for it. Like when you were young, you'd date around, [but] it was very dull. There weren't really places to go have fun there [in Anhui], just the county town or the nearby town to stroll around. Staying together every day, it was very pure and simple. Like, in the Jing County seat, there was just one big street to stroll up and down. Life was relatively boring. In this boredom, the woman might help the man wash his laundry.

When we left, even though a lot of families didn't divorce, a lot of them barely scraped by. Nowadays you do see this kind of family. Then there were some, well, the idea of marriage got changed up to something new, they got to thinking that a dead marriage is a painful thing, and they came back and split; there are those too. In terms of marriages, some cases you could say were failures. That was the special situation of the time. In Anhui, you were bored, so you were together. Once in Shanghai, in this big colorful world, you take a look, and wow, is this how it is, then the marriage hits the rocks.

[...] No matter what my household registration was, I was stationed there. My kid was little then, you know. The tyke was really small, but nothing for it, I had to work, so the little one was in a full-time nursery school. My husband was working outside the home then too. Two people working outside, then there was no time to tend to the home, so the kid was in full-week nursery in Shanghai. Once a week we'd go pick her up. At the time we'd come to Shanghai, pick [her] up on Saturday, my husband would take her back on Sunday morning, and I'd go back to Jinshan. From four years old, she was put in the nursery, so I owe a debt to my daughter.

* * *

陈金洋 Chen Jinyang, male, doctor and obstetrician at the Rear Base Health and Hygiene Team starting in 1975

Keywords: birth planning, children, conflicts, critique, family, living conditions, medical issues, men vs. women, poverty, rural vs. urban, travel and transportation

[...] Some Rear Base workers came to Shanghai [to have kids], but some had their whole families "go down," so there was no way the woman'd come to Shanghai to give birth. Where'd she stay if she came? Who'd take care of her? For sure she'd come to our Rear Base hospital. And then there were locals. My deepest impression was of a local woman having a difficult labor. They carried her over on a litter, lit their way with torches in those mountains and ran with her for half the night to take her to our hospital. She was hemorrhaging and ended up dying. There was nothing we could do. By the time they got her here she was already lost, she was already a dead woman. Then the baby was born but the placenta hadn't detached fully. The bleeding wouldn't stop. In their mountain gully they didn't have any way to deal with this and they knew we had a Gutian Hospital, so they brought her to us.

She died after she arrived at the hospital. This was her second baby. The first had been a girl, and this one was too. After the woman died, her man didn't even want this second baby. We had a pair of workers on the Rear Base who were infertile, so we gave the girl to them for adoption. That man didn't want much, just 200 bucks. That was in 80-something, and 200 bucks was worth a lot. When the patient was brought out there was blood all over the cotton blanket, and he still wanted to bring that back with him.

Then I didn't go, but others did; they went to have a look at his home. He was so poor, all he had was a table, a bench, and a bed, nothing else really. Very very bad conditions. So this bloody blanket, he was going to take that back with him. Those 200 bucks were huge for him. Now I've heard that he went through someone at our hospital who was hired locally; he found this guy and says he wants his daughter back. Of course, they're not going to discuss it with him. Back then everyone talked it out clearly and signed their names. Plus, this kid is doing very well right now. We know where she is, because we also kept track of the people who adopted her.

In the mountains, it was very backward, very remote. If you had a difficult labor, there wasn't much to do. If the baby came out but your placenta wouldn't, they had nothing to help you. They couldn't manage it. The midwives couldn't do something at that level. They could only handle a normal labor. Unusual circumstances, they couldn't manage. It was always a hemorrhage, and they'd see it was bad and rush the woman to the hospital. Going anywhere in the mountains meant going over them. I heard from a training class for the captains of the National Women and Children's Health Stations from a Sichuanese guy. He said that when women had a difficult labor, they'd have to yell from one hilltop for someone on the next hill top to hear, and going down and then up again to that mountain top could take a whole day in those huge mountains in Sichuan. I shared some at the class about our Rear Base situation, but after I heard him, and comparing our situation to theirs, we were thousands of times better off. We had a Rear Base hospital, such a great setup, and when I say mountain, I really mean hills. Those mountains in Sichuan were real big mountains, and it'd take a whole day to run from one to another, and it was a long, long way too.

Peasant farmers who lived near the hospital would come for [normal] births, too. In the obstetrics department our joke was "we'll never be short on eggs." When those women came to have babies, especially after having sons, they'd be happy as anything. The family who came to see her, because there wasn't much else to give as a gift in the village, they'd bring their own hens and eggs. Now these things [fresh-laid eggs from a hen] are rare, but then they weren't. When they left, they'd take the hen with them, but sometimes they'd leave the eggs because they had more at home. When we were there, eggs were five cents each. They'd give us these eggs and we'd share them through the department. It wasn't like they gave them to me, the doctor, and I took them all. No, we shared them and all had some eggs. Because taking care of the laboring woman wasn't just all my work, the nurses did a lot of the heavy lifting too.

Usually, we only got eggs when it was a boy. When they had a girl, their faces would be long. The favoritism for boys locally was a very serious thing. If the heavens gave them one girl and then another, then there's nothing to do for it, that's just what you got. If they had two girls and the man still wanted to try for a third and a fourth, their local People's Communes would bring them forcibly to us to have the woman's tubes tied. With tubal ligation, no matter how mighty you were, you weren't going to have another one. That was how they did Birth Planning locally.

* * *

丁秀玉 Ding Xiuyu, female, technician at a Small Third Front steelworks who later rose to cadre positions in Small Third Front Party organs, including head of the Birth Planning office.

Keywords: birth planning, children, conflicts, critique, family, frustrations, living conditions, medical issues, men vs. women, politically correct, post-Mao

[TN: This narrative contains descriptions of coercive reproductive policies that may be disturbing.]

I was about 25 when I joined [the Party], 26 when I was made a cadre. Not yet, I hadn't married. I married very late.

[…] I fooled around like this [in the Propaganda Department] till I got married in '78. After I got pregnant with my daughter in '79, they transferred me to the July 21st Worker's University to be the deputy Party Branch Secretary. In reality, there was some accommodation there, because I was pregnant, and because I was pregnant, the factory admin offices had too many people and wasn't too safe. After I got [to the July 21st University], because they were all adults there, it was like being a kept pet. I'd just chat with the teachers, have conversations, not a lot of time [spent there]. I got there in March '79 and by August '79, I was about to give birth—my daughter was born in August '79—I went back to Shanghai to have her. I had her at the No. 1 People's Hospital because my superiors weren't comfortable letting me have her in Anhui. I needed someone to look after me, after all.

After I had her, I stayed a while in Shanghai, until about the end of '79, then I went back to Anhui. [...] Our birth planning work began in '79. [...] Originally the Eight-Five Steelworks had two people doing this work, but they were members of the Workers' Union.

[...] But, you know, the national Birth Planning initiative and the workers' unions were two [separate] lines [...] [namely,] the Birth Planning Committee and the Labor Committee. The Labor Committee was a mass organization, and the Birth Planning Committee was a state organization. So these two people had to be made separate from the union and form a Birth Planning Office. When they were separated out, they needed a leader, so they had me go be that leader. I worked there in the office until I came back to Shanghai. After coming back, I still did this work, all the way until I retired [...] at the Shanghai No. 5 Steelworks.

For me, I really liked this work on Birth Planning. To speak from the heart, I didn't like doing propaganda. Propaganda people have to be good at talking things up; they have to be able to make a sesame seed into a watermelon. I'm just "one equals one, two equals two," very straightforward. I can't exaggerate like that, make things up, or just say whatever. I can't do it. I'm a person to do real work. At the Birth Planning Office there was lots of real work to do. At that time, you needed to pick up a permit to have your only child; we had to monitor the Birth Planning rate, the abortion rate, the late-marriage rate, all really concrete things; I really liked it.

I was the office supervisor. Just two people below me. No, no more people came later. Yes, just us three the whole time. To say it was two people, it was really just me leading one person. The other was on long-term sick leave in Shanghai, but was on our roster. She didn't work. I even went often to check on her at home. Two people could do the job. The office wasn't affiliated under the Union but was directly under the factory administration. [...] Me and my subordinate comrade would be responsible for the entire factory, over 5000 people. We had a lot of young people, and they had a lot of kids, so we had to pass out the Only Child permits, and sometimes we had to go to the Rear Base [HQ] to hold meetings.

Yes, the other office staff member was also female. Definitely it's better to have women comrades doing this. For sure, it's more convenient than having male comrades work on it. If you think about the abortion rate, the rate of IUD insertions, how could men go talking about these things? The abortion rate counted the female comrades who got pregnant and went to get abortions; this was an indicator for us to consider. In reality, we always asked female comrades to give birth before putting in an IUD. This came from a specific policy. There was also the birthrate for first and second children, and the rates for abortions after IUDs, and repeated abortions after IUDs; all of these were very specific and needed verification.

Anyway, after '79, the nation enacted Birth Planning initiatives. As an enterprise, we began mainly by focusing on the rate of [having] only children, then on late marriage and late childbearing—we had quotas. At that time, you had to guarantee that the only child rate was at 100%. Which is to say, after having one kid, you had to pick up a certificate. If someone didn't pick up the certificate, that quota wouldn't be met. Yes, if someone didn't come get it, we'd go look for them. At that point, we didn't actively go seeking out people yet. So we were at the factory level and below us there were the workshops, and female workers in the workshops. These female workers were our "feet"; they'd go [after the individuals]. We'd also release only-child rewards. After you picked up the certificate, you got five bucks, and it was specially from us, not from the HR and Salary Department. It was only later that it went to the HR and Salary Department to be given out.

[…] On June 1st [TN: Children's Day], we'd also give out only-child rewards. We did these kinds of things. The leadership would allot money to us, and we'd estimate how many only children there were. If everyone got 10 yuan, we'd buy lunchboxes, buy a scarf, then distribute them. Everyone was really happy, like [it was] an encouragement. Then, this got canceled. After all there were some who didn't have only children. Some had two kids. […] In the same department, I got something and you didn't, then you'd be unhappy. So just a few years later, these [rewards] were canceled.

If you were an IUD abortion, we'd oversee that too. What it was, was that you had one kid, then you'd have an IUD, but then after the IUD you had to get another abortion. So the IUD quota was reached, but after inserting the IUD, the abortion rate was still really high. It wasn't 100% effective contraception. So, in this situation, we'd have to buy things [for the person who had the abortion] and go tend to her. [...] If you didn't have an IUD and you got an abortion, the first time, you wouldn't be looked into. But if it were the second time, you would. That first time might be from inexperience, or ignorance, but some people did it twice, even three times. Only the first time after you got the abortion would we go to you and give you some money. For the second or third time, you wouldn't get a leave. The first time you had a 12-day work break. Then later you wouldn't. If you applied for sick leave, they'd even hold back your bonus, and even your bonuses. It was all tied together. The work of the leadership and the personnel's abortion rates, late marriage and late childbearing rates, were all linked.

The policy at the time was that women [could] marry at 23 and men at 25, the standard for late marriage and late childbearing. [...] 25 full years for men, 23 for women [TN: as opposed to the old style of counting ages by the Lunar New Year, with babies counted as one year old at birth]. If a woman had a kid at 24, that was late childbearing, and could get a reward. If the woman had a kid before 24, that wasn't late childbearing, so they didn't enjoy the leave or the late childbearing policy['s rewards]. The reward varied. State-awarded vacation days, for late marriage, meant you get seven days instead of three. If it were a late marriage, you'd get ten days [for the wedding leave]; if you weren't late, it was only three days. [TN: This inconsistency is in the original interview; Ding seems to mean seven extra days.]

For late pregnancy you'd get an extra two weeks [maternity leave]; if it wasn't late, you wouldn't get those two weeks. The state vacation was given as a standard reward, but the enterprise didn't have any standard. When we had more money, more was given; when there was less money, less was given. We formulated these rules, and in the end, it was up to the workshops to execute them. In the workshops there were female union members, and periodically we'd hold meetings. So it was these people who went to reward [the women who were marrying and getting pregnant]. There were differences among the workshops too.

Some workshops had high adherence and got more money. The leadership took this work seriously, and they'd put more effort in. At the time, Birth Planning [follow-through] was a progressive thing; if you did it you'd become a Red Flag Unit. The leadership would be honored, and you'd get more [bonus] money. Some units' leadership didn't take it seriously; they just weren't willing to use money [as reward incentives], then the unit's quotas wouldn't [be met], then the Birth Planning work wouldn't [be followed through], and they wouldn't get the progressive rating.

Once a month we'd meet with female workers in the workshops. There were emergency meetings too. You asked me about incidents at the Eight-Five Steelworks earlier. When I was [there], I encountered a pregnancy outside the Birth Planning directive. Pregnancies outside the directive were really a headache for us. It means that she had one child, then got pregnant again, but she doesn't get an abortion and wants instead to have the baby, but the policy doesn't allow it. This was called extra-directive childbearing. If it fit the policy, actually she could have the second kid. If both [parents] were only children, or if one of them had been married before and hadn't had a kid, there were specific exceptions. But she didn't fit any of those, so this was an extra-directive pregnancy. We had to do work around extra-directive pregnancies. We had to get her to get rid of it, no matter how big her belly was; even if she was about to give birth, she had to get rid of it. That was the policy then.

When I was at the Eight-Five Steelworks, I had one incident like this. This was a female worker in the cafeteria; she already had one girl, then, you know, she got pregnant again, but she didn't know, herself. Such confused women, there were lots of them. Well, she was fat, and her belly was big; she thought it was her period being irregular; other people might have just thought she was kind of fat; they couldn't tell that her belly was big. Only until she was about to give birth did she know. [...] After we found out, we had to do work on her and not let her have it. She was a cafeteria worker and kept working anyway. People like her—Shanghai wouldn't perform an abortion on her. After seven months, you couldn't get an abortion in Shanghai. In the end they let her [carry the pregnancy to term], but at the time it was a mandatory policy, by force; all our rules were mandatory. If it was an extra-directive pregnancy, you would get fired[...]. The punishment was very harsh. Then, she got scared, you know. She said she went elsewhere to get [the abortion] done; she went to Haining to do it.

Fortunately, [she was] fine. She said she wanted to go do it in Haining and we just pretended not to know anything. We were afraid too. We said, you can go; we won't do anything about that. We didn't tell her to go. This was her own thing. Then she did it and she was all right. [...] This left a pretty deep impression on me. Then, at the Shanghai No. 5 Steelworks, I was still in the Birth Planning Office. There were 30-some departments at the No. 5 Steelworks, and one was called the Research Office. There was a college graduate in the Research Office; his wife was at the cotton textile factory. His wife had one daughter and wanted to have a son; under his parents' influence, they had to have a son.

That woman also had [a] low consciousness. She said if she didn't have a son, she'd have no place in their family, so she wanted to have one too. Then we found out and started to do work on them, I can't even tell you how much work. The materials from our discussions with them was this thick. But then in the end they still had it. [...] After having it, the college graduate left; he got fired. The kid was born at the Quyang Hospital. It was a son. [...] Yes, they went to check; anyway they had to have it. The doctor told them it was a boy. In the end both left their jobs. The woman left too. We definitely contacted her work unit. That factory didn't want [her] either. This college grad at our Research Office, 30-something at the time, they didn't want him either. It was useless [to ask for concessions]. The factory rules and disciplinary code was right there, very clear.

Another from when I was at Shanghai No. 5 Steelworks was an old man, already 60-something, who found an unmarried woman, 40-something. He had had seven kids. At that time, it was pretty normal for a 60-something person to have seven kids. His wife died, so he found a 40-something woman for a wife. Then this woman got pregnant. For this woman, it was her first pregnancy, but for this man it was his eighth. So we had to do our work. [The policy at the time] did not permit this. [...] At the time I was traveling out of town. There were two people in our office, and they kept their eyes on that 40-something pregnant woman. She went to Wuhu in Anhui, going back and forth. In the end this woman had the baby. This 60-something old man had retired already, so there was no way to punish him. He couldn't be fired. [...] This woman, 45, after she had the baby, she went to take care of the baby; basically she retired early too. So things ended like this. [...]

[Interviewer: If someone her age went to get an abortion, if there were serious danger, whose responsibility would that be?] Not the hospital's, because when you go [get an abortion] you sign all the forms. If there were anything unexpected, the family members had signed too. The hospital had no responsibility, and we didn't either.

My daughter's a long story too. At first, I took her to Anhui and put her in the nursery. Yes, about 100 days [after I had her], I went back to Anhui; before that I was in Shanghai the whole while. After I went back, the kid had no one to look after her and that wouldn't do, so I put her in the nursery. She cried a lot. It didn't use to be disposable diapers but cloth ones, and she was wet up to her back. I felt really awful. So I put her in the kindergarten for a week. Then I called my mother. My mother was already 70 then. She had me when she was 39, and I had my daughter when I was 32. I had her very late. I married when I was 31. So my mother came to help me take care of the kid, until about when my daughter was eight months old, when my husband took our daughter to one of his brother's houses in Shanghai and my mother went with them. My mother took care of my daughter [...] until [my daughter] was about three years old. My daughter being in Shanghai, I wasn't ever settled in my heart, but there was nothing to do about it, because of [my] work.

I was working at the school then, and we had the rule that kids could enter kindergarten at three, so I took my daughter to Anhui and put her in kindergarten. That was all the way until [she was in] first grade. Then that elementary school was torn down and I took her to Shanghai. At that point, my mom was already gone. Oh, no, my mom was still around then, she [died] later on. When my daughter was ten, and my mom's health wasn't good, I'd often go back to Shanghai and had my older brother and sister-in-law watch [my daughter]. This was how my daughter went to school in Shanghai until I returned in '88. I was in the last batch to return. Why? This Birth Planning work of mine was based on people. When our factory was moving [back], it was in batches, not all at once. So us researchers would hand over the Birth Planning materials and such batch-by-batch to the Shanghai No. 5 Steelworks. When one group returned, we'd hand over that batch of materials. The Shanghai No. 5 Steelworks also took Birth Planning work very seriously. It was a national leader, a 25,000 [-person] factory with flying colors. This was well known throughout Shanghai and even nationwide. Those were the days. Now the Shanghai No. 5 Steelworks doesn't exist anymore.

[I was] young, you know. I remember when I was 40. That May, my mom died. I went back to Shanghai. From 39 to 40, in that year, my ma was sick. In those 12 months, I went back and forth 11 times. Every month, I came back. Well, of these 11 times, about nine were for business. So I'd bring back some materials and hand them over to the Shanghai No. 5 Steelworks, go make some reports, then stay a couple days then go back [to Anhui]. Every time I came back, I'd ride the long-distance bus for a whole day. This bus was really scary. The seats were hard and it'd be bumps all the way. It was from early in the morning all the way to nighttime. We set off at seven in the morning, bump our way along, and at noon there was nowhere to have lunch. [I'd] eat what food I brought. The bathroom was very, very dirty; I won't talk about it. That kind of bathroom, you all would definitely not go into these days. On the way back then, I'd take the boat. The boat was actually a bit more comfortable.

After my mother fell ill, my younger brother was at the time still in Shanghai. His health wasn't good [...] he had gone to Jiangxi, class of '69. To a [...] farm in Jiangxi. Once he had a bleeding ulcer. After the surgery he stayed in Shanghai. But he didn't take care of things. After my mom's health declined, we hired a nurse. Because my older sister was in Hong Kong, she paid for the nurse to take care of my mom. My older brother returned to Shanghai from Gansu, then, good, there was also big brother and big sister-in-law, who could often go tend [to Mom]. Me, I'd also often come back. I'd help my brother and sister-in-law. That's how we got by. As for the kid, she also was with my older brother and sister-in-law, that's how it was. At the time, well, we only thought about our work. When my mom was sick, she wished we could be at her side, she wished we didn't have to go work, wished that we could stay beside her. But there was nothing for it. On May 22nd, my mom died, at night. From about May 1st to 12th, Labor Day plus a few days of paid leave in exchange for overtime, I stayed in Shanghai for 12 days. After I went back on the 12th, my mom died on the 22nd; it was ten days later. My older sister was in Hong Kong, and she came to see [our mother] before the 12th too. When it finally came to cremating Mother, my older sister didn't come, just mailed some money to us.

My older sister went [to Hong Kong] after the Reform and Opening. Her parents-in-laws were in Hong Kong, then my brother-in-law went, in '78. So in '79, my sister went. After she went, well, she took her son and daughter. The consideration then was to go for the kids, for their future. Hong Kong's better than Shanghai. When my sister went, she was already 40-something. Then my mom got sick. It's because my mom had bad teeth. She wanted to remove all of them and put in a set of good [dentures]. She went to Hong Kong, to my sister's. Then, [my mom] didn't understand medicine, she was ignorant. All at once she got two teeth pulled. After she came back, she should've rested, you know, and eaten soft things. She didn't understand that and kept on eating her fried dough sticks in sticky rice and doing the laundry. Usually, my mom's health was great. At 70 she was still helping me look after my kid, then at 74 this happened, then she got sick and never got better. [...] After that her stomach started giving her trouble, and she didn't understand medicine, so she got ill and stayed sick for four years and died when she was 78. After Lunar New Year, you know, she wouldn't eat or drink. Actually, she wasn't very ill or anything. We took her to the doctor, and it was gastroparesis, gastritis, common things. She felt like, "Oh, I'm never going to get better, I'm suffering so much." So she was sick like this for four years. We had a nurse for four years. My sister thought, Mom went to her place to get her teeth out, then she got sick. I have to take responsibility.

[...] For sure, in some cases, there were woman comrades who [...] refused to pay attention to the Birth Planning policy and wouldn't listen even if you went to work on them. Most people did heed the state's call and felt that this Birth Planning policy was good. It was a policy that couldn't be helped in our country. Our population base was high. If everyone had two or three [kids], the population would explode, wouldn't it? Overall, there weren't especially selfless people who left a deep impression for following the campaign, either. For example, Wang Wenqing had a daughter. Her husband was an only child. But she had no more. Someone like me could do this work, because I was late to marry and late to bear kids. I only had my kid when I was 32. I was very persuasive. Who could compare to me? That's what I thought. I felt like [not having more] was very normal. Birth Planning work had an effect on us, too, and on our family. There were many flaws and drawbacks then. And I realize this too and admit that the self-centeredness of the only children generation is one. The environment in which they grew up, relatively speaking, has been pretty well-off. So they are very self-centered, but they also have many good points. Their educations, their environments, have been far better than our generation.

* * *

伏如山 Fu Rushan, male, worker at a fuse explosive factory.

Keywords: consumer goods, family, food, living conditions, marriage, men vs. women, nostalgia, rural vs. urban

[TN: The below translation comes from a written recollection penned by Fu.]

My aged parents spent so much care on me. Because of the limitations of her family's resources, my parents picked up the financial burden of our wedding; they transported a five-compartment armoire and a bed to us from Shanghai and put on a banquet in her household and ours. Though it wasn't a huge affair, it still cost my folks dearly. I felt uneasy at this:

without their help, how could I have set up my own household? We didn't have assigned housing in Shanghai, so we stayed in my older brother's room. Society wasn't so into the pomp and display back then as today, and people from outside Shanghai were even more casual about it, but we still had a bustling feast. Many friends and family members came to celebrate.

[…] We didn't have much money to get nice new clothes. I just wore my old blue twill student uniform. If it were today, I'd definitely be a laughingstock. Our furniture wasn't much either. We didn't even have a nightstand, much less a [sewing] machine or radio. This wasn't because I couldn't make us some—wood was cheap back then and so was furniture, a lot of choices too. But the atmosphere of the time didn't emphasize these material goods; for a "poor groom" like me this was perfect. I was so glad to find such a well-matched wife at the right time in the right place. After marriage we've gotten along very well; we rely on each other and are inseparable. She listens greatly to my advice, and I fulfill her needs as much as possible. For example, she thought the first apartment the factory gave us was too far [from work], so I found a way to trade us to a unit below a cadre's apartment. She wanted to eat "thousand-year eggs" [TN: a type of preserved egg] so I bought a whole basket from Yichun. The days seemed to pass quickly after our wedding. With our joint efforts and the support of our parents, we gradually added new furniture and bought a bicycle and a radio though we were both low-paid and she was actually a [pay] grade above me. But with frugality, we managed to make our little home look the part.

* * *

葛鼎学 Ge Dingxue, worker at a Small Third Front steelworks.

Keywords: conflicts, frustrations, marriage, medical issues, men vs. women, violence

[TN: Please note that this narrative contains descriptions of self-harm that may be disturbing.]

[…] There were a lot of young male workers then. People said that we men were like the pebbles in Baiyang River: the female comrades could grab a big handful of us to pick and choose. See, there were very few female comrades. Then the Youth League Committee of the factory did a good thing to help this problem. […] They tried to arrange for some female comrades [to come], but in the end it was still mostly men. Plus, there was only us in terms of big factories in Guichi, and we were a ways off from Huizhou. Some people did marry local peasants, but very few. I had a friend who married a little lady from the local township. Her father was a cadre in the town, working in the local court. No way would [he have married] an ordinary person.

[...] I began dating my wife in 1981 and got married in 1982. We had our son in 1983. I hadn't dated at all before her; she was the first. I said just now that the League Committee did a lot of work around the problem of unmarried male workers and put personals ads out in newspapers for us. And they were national newspapers too, or else how would the women know [about it]? Actually, it was my older sister-in-law in Nanjing who saw this in the newspaper—if you were interested in a young man on Shanghai's southern Anhui Small Third Front, if you were willing to be transferred to the Eight-Five Steelworks, you could come give it a try.

Per the League Committee arrangements, all we had to do was fill out a form, and they'd help sort us with people, and whoever you got, that's who you got. They saw that I was pretty nice, so they helped me make a match. Everyone got matched like this, so the divorce rates after coming back [to Shanghai] were pretty high. Of course, after a match, the pair had to actually make contact and see if both parties were willing. At the time, there were a lot of guys who were older than me and still single. Once new women came in, these older workers would definitely want to have first dibs on dates, so many women who came in went with the older workers. The factory also hoped to help out the older workers first. When older workers couldn't find a partner, they'd go fight other people for their girlfriends, a lot of fighting back and forth. Some people even developed mental illnesses. Pretty extreme was jumping from one of the smokestacks.

I "met" [my wife] through a photograph. She saw my photo, I saw hers, and then we wrote letters to each other. We still have these letters; they're my treasures; I hoard them.

We met up in the Nanjing train station. We had a secret signal and everything. This old story I haven't written down, but if I wrote a book about it, it'd definitely be a bestseller. Not long after we met in Nanjing, they transferred her over; we got married back in Shanghai. All in all, it was a little over a year. My marriage certificate was written out in Mongol. It's not that I went up to Inner Mongolia for the certificate; my wife [working in Inner Mongolia] had someone help us get it. Because you had to first get that certificate. Back then by the rules when you went to the Eight-Five Steelworks you had to have a marriage certificate. So we had someone help us. Inner Mongolian licenses didn't have photos on them, at the time. After we got it, then we began the request for her transfer. If you wouldn't make the transfer, then don't marry me and we won't worry about the transfer. At the time we used this certificate to hurry up with the transfer order. Nothing else would do much. With the certificate they'd agree; the factory would rush to help move her.

[...] My wife's ability to look after herself was pretty high. Coming from Inner Mongolia, she was totally able to adapt; both of us could. It was pretty easy to settle in. Like me; I also suited that environment. A lot of people thought the food there stank of dirt, but I was fine with it. We didn't have conflicts in day-to-day life either, because she adapted quickly and it came naturally to her. I remember when we were dating, she wouldn't care much about what we ate and I also don't care much; I'm okay no matter what. Even though she spoke Mandarin and I spoke Shanghainese, when we first met, she'd speak Mandarin and others would too. After she was with me, she started to understand Shanghainese. When we went out and people heard her Mandarin, they said it sounded beautiful.

[...] Plenty of people came to get married in Anhui like my wife; a lot of successful matches were made back then, but the divorce rates were high too. I saved a woman once. She was in our steelwork's offices; she found a young man who worked the furnaces, a short, small guy, and not great in various aspects. When they got matched up there must've been a mistake, because that young lady was high-spirited; no matter from looks or various aspects, she was very good. They lived just below us in the [dormitory apartments], and we had just this long hallway in front of our rooms. I'm a pretty careful person; I'd used copper wires to make a five-stranded rack for sunning our bedding. In the end this young lady tried to kill herself by jumping off the building, and she landed on my copper wires. She hurt her back. This woman was ruined by this guy; in the end they got divorced. This caused a pretty big stir in the factory; it was really an example of an unsuccessful match.

So this story was a not-so-great example, a pretty extreme one. There weren't many extreme cases. A lot of divorces, but not to the extreme. Some got divorced back in Shanghai. Mostly it was women who wanted to get a divorce, and they'd negotiate about the kids. Because we all used to be colleagues, we all know about these things. Because that was a special time then, as a man, you thought, "whatever I get is what I get, good or bad." And for women too, there wasn't much room for picking and choosing. But after you came back to Shanghai, your world expanded, your contacts changed completely, and then getting divorced was understandable. People like us [who stayed together] are truly pretty rare. It's good fortune that we could be together this long.

* * *

胡进 Hu Jin, female, cadre at a Small Third Front-associated farm, then transferred to a transport department.

Keywords: children, education, family, frustrations, living conditions, marriage, men vs. women, rural vs. urban

I had my kid in '81. I got pregnant in '80 and had to climb this mountain every day with my belly. I lived at the foot of the mountain. The family dorms, just under Mt. Xihua. Every day I had to climb up to go to the May Seventh Farm to work. No special concessions for being pregnant; I kept going to work every day until I was about to deliver and by regulation I could go back [to Shanghai]. After I'd had the kid, I brought her back [to Shanghai]. Back then [my husband] was in Shanghai at the July 21st Industrial University, a technical school, a workers' school. So he was in Shanghai, and until the kid was one, 18 months, a little over one, we kept her.

[Her husband interjects:] At first we put her in the nursery of the Municipal No. 3 Secondary School.

Yeah, from 18 months we put her in the nursery, "full-day." She was put in Shanghai. Not in Anhui because there was no one to watch her; how'd we keep her there? I had to go to work on the May Seventh Farm. Plus, I took a one-year leave in Shanghai. That was just when the One-Child policy was coming out; I could take a year in Shanghai, so I stayed in Shanghai a year. At 18 months we put the kid in a residential full-week nursery, then we went to Anhui. Then later we took her back [to Anhui] and asked a worker's wife to help me look after the kid. Every morning we dropped her off in their home. We didn't put her in the factory nursery school because it was no good. They had the kids sitting on spittoons [to use the toilet]. Yes, we weren't comfortable, and the kid was too little, but the kindergarten was okay. But the quality of our kindergarten [in Anhui] wasn't very good, so we put her in a Shanghai kindergarten.

When she got to elementary school we came back [to Shanghai]; she was six; we just about were coming back. We came back in '87. Yes, just in time for her elementary school. Before it was all residential full-week kindergarten, then my mother-in-law took care of her in Shanghai. Ordinarily people like us, we could pull ourselves away though we worked in Anhui and the kid was put in Shanghai, but it was just when we saw her about to leave us in Shanghai that we didn't want to leave her. Once we did it was all right, because we felt secure having an elder take care of her.

It was pretty tough back then. Back then when visiting her, we'd take her to the nursery, take her out on a bicycle, and she'd say, "Mama, where are we going?" and I'd say to her "to the funnest place," basically making things up to her; my heart was very sore. She was only 18 months old, the youngest in her class. In theory they weren't supposed to take her yet. Nothing to do about it, I insisted that she go; I couldn't have her think that, because Mama was back [in Shanghai], she didn't need to go. When I went to get her on Saturday, I'd see the other children with their clothes all on already, but she'd be sitting on the ground, still not dressed, not yet very able to do it [get dressed] yet, and I'd watch her and my heart would be really sore, but I really held it back.

I got transferred out. Back then I had the kid, well, then I thought, every day would be like this. The kid put down below [the mountain], and every day I'd have to rush down to take care of the kid, cook dinner, and do other things. I began to feel like it was an inconvenience. I raised it and again asked an acquaintance to help me arrange things. [...] I held it back for three years, then I requested to switch to the transport department. People like us never take our work casually; we are very responsible. So doing that for a while, I built some good rapport, so they told me to do the workers' union work.

[...] When I went back to Shanghai No. Five Steelworks, work–life balance was for sure tiring. We were living at Xinhua Road then, living in [my husband's] home. Then we moved to Xijiao Park but I was still working in Wusong, and the kid was going to school in Wusong too. So, every day around four a.m. I'd drag the kid from bed with a little stool [for her to sit on] and get on an express bus to Wusong. There were no seats, because we'd be hurrying and still only get in the back of the line, so we had to stand. She'd sit on the stool and rush over to Baoshan. Every day it was like that, until we truly couldn't take it and rented a place in Baoshan.

[...] In our settlement fee there was a housing budget. So we stayed at a farmer's house in Baoshan. But [...] well, we couldn't cook; they had one stove and two families cooking on it, the two brothers. Of course, we couldn't build another stove to cook on. So we ate at the cafeteria. We were staying in a home that wasn't far from the factory, so we'd ride our bikes to buy food from the cafeteria and bring it home. The kid lived with us, and also ate the cafeteria food. Saturday and Sunday [we'd] go for a trip back to Shanghai city, on the weekends; well, when she was at home she ate cafeteria food, so then we'd go to Shanghai to upgrade [her diet] a little. It didn't affect my work. When she was at school during the day, no impact at all. After school I had her wait until I was off work to pick her up; it was a regular daytime shift anyway. It was just dropping her off and picking her up that was pretty tiring, but the rest was all right.

* * *

季美华 Ji Meihua, female, kindergarten teacher at a Small Third Front steel mill.

Keywords: children, education, family, frustrations, living conditions, marriage, men vs. women, nostalgia, rural vs. urban, work assignments

I married in '74. I also put my kid in the preschool, then one year in kindergarten, then because I had to run about for work, I took the kid back to Shanghai. Yes, yes, I put him with my parents. It was okay to take care of the kid and work, not too hard. The pace of work before wasn't the same as now. Nowadays the young kids work at a fast pace, you know. ...Truly, it's like they're working for dear life. No, no matter how hard we worked it wasn't like the kids today.

Because I could put the kid in Shanghai, I did. After all there was nowhere really that fun in the mountains. If I had the ability, I'd definitely put the kid in Shanghai. This was the thinking of every adult. I came back to Shanghai in '85. [...] The kid was in sixth grade. Then I took care of the kid myself. Of course there were differences when I came back. I had to take care of the home and the kid. Another point was that, when I came back, the rhythm was faster than in the mountains, and the way to work was farther. Back in the No. 5 Steelworks I was still a kindergarten teacher; yes, until I retired, I was there for several decades.

Pregnancy leave was only 56 days long. Our 56-day-old son was sent to the nursery. Nursery work was pretty annoying too. The teachers were slightly older, aunties with a bit more experience. They were about the same age as me, yes. Some were wives [of workers]. The men came and the women followed, [...] our factory did a really great thing by brokering marriages for young men who couldn't find girlfriends. I'm not sure how the women comrades who married in were allocated work, but some did get put in the kindergarten. The man would be in the factory, and if she had been a teacher outside, then she'd be assigned to be a teacher in the factory.

[...] My husband was in the same factory as me. We met during "training-through-labor." He worked in a workshop; carpentry, welding, he did 'em all. Then when he was transferred back to Shanghai No. 5 Steelworks, I came back first, then he came back, we were one year off. Because he was at the Geological University and hadn't graduated yet. Yes, we lived in the family residences of the steelworks. At first we ate at the cafeteria, then we cooked for ourselves. At that time we didn't think so much about the inconveniences of cooking for two and portioning.

Life was just simple and plain, and it went year by year like this. At first he did a lot [of the housework]. Then he got sick once and I began to do more. [...] Every woman had something to give. No [it wasn't very tiring for the female comrades who had their kids with them to take care of work and family at once]. Work tempo wasn't so fast back then, and each family arranged matters well.

[...] No, I wouldn't come home with my husband. I worked the two-end shifts and he was on regular hours. Two-end shifts were 7 a.m. to 3 p.m., or 9 a.m. to 5 p.m. [...] Being a kindergarten teacher meant no Children's Day off on June 1st—that my own kid didn't get Children's Day. No, [I didn't really feel regrets]. As the kid got older, it was just how it was.

By the time I came back [to Shanghai], my own kid was big, in sixth grade. I never had to discipline him. Kids didn't used to have so many things going on. [...] He was a real good kid from the time he was little. [We] didn't have time to monitor him. Yes, I put all of my energies into work. I think a lot [of other teachers] were like this.

* * *

史志定 Shi Zhiding, male, Communist Youth League cadre at a steel mill.

Keywords: communications, conflicts, crime, critique, family, frustrations, living conditions, marriage, men vs. women, nostalgia, politically correct, political problems

[TN: Please note that this narrative contains descriptions of self-harm that may be disturbing.]

I became Youth League Branch Deputy Party Secretary in 1973. From 1975, I began to write study reports for the Shanghai Municipal Youth League Committee, reporting on problems like the severe sex skew among our youth. Because they weren't able to find spouses, the Eight-Five Steelworks had some young men who were carrying on improper relations with married women. This kind of phenomenon happens everywhere, but it was a bit worse on the Small Third Front. Men and women alike have these biological needs, but if they can't find them in society, then they'll look among their coworkers. As for problems in affairs with local farmers, there was one homicide case, but because there was insufficient evidence, they let the person go. There were quite a few people who had incidents because of marriage issues. There were people who killed themselves by jumping from the smokestack.

[...] Out of the 5400 people at our mill, there were over 700 "above-[marriage] age" young men. If you looked at the entire Rear Base, it'd be about ten times that, nearly 8000. After we led the way in putting out personals ads for our above-age young men, other factories all followed suit. By the time the steelworks was being transferred back to Shanghai, over 600 of the 700 had found a spouse, with 112 "older, difficult" cases remaining. The factory leadership decided to let them be in the first wave to return to Shanghai to help them find partners as soon as possible. All in all, it all worked out well.

[...] Once I saw a report from the Shanghai Ocean Shipping Bureau about how they helped their sailors find girlfriends and wives by holding parties on their ships and inviting young women to attend. That was really inspiring to me. Then they restored commercial ads [in periodicals], so I thought, maybe we could put out a personals ad? By the way, the New Light Factory's ad on August 5, 1980 seeking female workers in the *Liberation Daily* was earlier [than us], but the nature of what they were looking for differed. At the time, the Ministry of Labor gave us a quota for hiring people. Our factory had 880 slots, but we only ended up hiring 660. Why didn't we hire more? Because there were regulations at the time that, in order to ensure Shanghai's stability, 10% of hires had to be people who'd gone to reform-by-labor or who'd served prison sentences. So they called on me to go and help pick out hires. At the time my kid had just been born and was five days old, and it was honestly too difficult to pick, so we opted to let that quota go partly filled. And we didn't want to hire too many people, either.

This batch of workers were mostly male; basically they were all vocational school graduates who'd graduated in 1974, '76, and '77. So, the New Light Factory used the fact that the quota hadn't been filled to hire female workers via a newspaper ad. In reality, that move also gave us an opening. They ended up only hiring ten-odd women, but it gave us new ideas and shook us up.

[...] In August 1980, during a holiday trip I was granted to the Hangzhou Pingfeng Mountain Workers' Retreat, I passed through Shanghai and went to the offices of Shanghai's *Youth Daily*. Ling Jiaru, old-hand journalist and director at that time of the communications department, greeted me warmly and listened patiently to my story. [...] Mr Ling listened and then said, compassionately and supportively, "[...] Our paper is for Youth League members and should help serve young people by truthfully and accurately reflecting the needs of Rear Front League members. But the paper's space is limited. If the Municipal Youth League Committee agreed, we could print an ad, but only in the seam of the paper, and we'd need to charge some fees for printing it. I said, "Of course!" As long as they'd run an ad, the money and the place where they printed it didn't matter at all. Mr Ling reported to the Municipal Committee, got their permission, and finally approved my request. We took the limited funds the factory League Committee had earned from selling castor seeds and spent 120 yuan and 200 yuan to run two ads in the *Youth Daily* on October 10, 1980 and August 7, 1981. [...] The results were terrific. No correspondence from Tibet or Taiwan, but flurries of mail came from all other cities and provinces.

So we'd have the women write in a letter telling about themselves and their situations, then we'd mail her a form and ask her to fill it out and include a photograph. Then we'd take a first look at her form and photo to see if she would be a good fit for our single young men, then we'd make recommendations to the youths: "We helped you pick one out, have a look to see if you think it's a good match, if not there are other forms and photos laid out on the table, you go take a pick yourself." If the man was happy about a pick, he'd also fill out a form and have the factory League Committee mail it back to the woman. The form would include basic information about his situation, his preferences and hobbies, and so forth. If the woman were interested, she'd write back and then we'd let them go sort it out on their own. If they were successful, we asked that they inform us so we could make a record.

We also intensified education about views on love among youths. At the time, the political czar of the Eight-Five mill even personally led lessons for the young people. *Youth Daily* even ran a "Six Firsts" guide with tips about dating, with topics like "the first visit" and "the first date" as their main content. Those whose relationships succeeded, the youngest men were about 20-something and the eldest was 53; the youngest women were around 20 and the oldest, 49.

The young women we matched our workers to were mainly living outside Shanghai. In fact, one was even the head of the Organization Department of a county Party Committee. All had been "sent down" from Shanghai. Some wanted an urban household registration. Some wanted to transfer to be nearer to Shanghai. Then we stopped hiring women from the Big Third Front, because when the Rear Base Management Bureau expanded over these large areas, they had difficulties [with unmarried men] there too. The problems we had on the Small Third Front, they had them there as well.

[...] The record for us was over 100 letters in a day. Typically, we included a blank form in our reply letter to have her fill out and return. Some girls were pretty cute about it; they'd include some commemorative stamps with their letter to help us save on postage. Back then we were all very frugal and honest—we'd return these stamps when we replied to them.

Liberation Daily had a feature about the collective wedding we held for an orphan, Little Sun. Little Sun had lost his parents and was fairly economically poorly off, so we helped him throw a wedding and did a pretty fancy job of it too. We also started encouraging workers to form "Five-Good Families" [TN: a campaign originating in the 1950s that promulgated "honoring elders and caring for the young," "equality between men and women," "harmony between husbands and wives," "frugality in housekeeping," and "solidarity among neighbors"]. [...] We started these earlier than they did in Shanghai [Image 7.2].

[...] A lot of people, you'd graduate junior high, you wouldn't have anywhere to go, so you'd go to a factory and be an apprentice for three years before graduating from that. But the Small Third Front needed labor, and the master workers didn't want to go, so these apprentices would be sent off without completing their three years. Of this group of people, a lot ended up having trouble finding partners. Cai's wife we found for him via matchmaking, then she got colon cancer. For over ten years, with a lot of difficulties, he patiently nursed her. He has a son in university—sending his kid to university and looking after his wife. A classic good man.

Image 7.2 Wedding at the Eight-Five Steelworks arranged by factory Youth League cadres, 1980–1981, collection of Shi Zhiding

And there was another Shanghai-based worker whose wife was also found through our matchmaking. At the time his family had a really tough financial situation. He lived on Xinjiang Road, in a really tiny place. His parents had a bed, and he had another bed laid on top of theirs sideways like a drawer. With these kinds of prospects he wouldn't ever have been able to get married. We helped him fix that with our matchmaking, and he even had a son. There were lots of examples like this. There was a furnace captain whose wife was also introduced to him by us. She ended up working in accounting in the mill. I did these real things for real people one step at a time, but if I hadn't seen the New Light Factory's example, if it hadn't been for Deng Xiaoping's "reform and reopening" and for Zhao Ziyang, there wouldn't have been this role for me.

There was also a rightist in our factory who married a university graduate. This was a woman who ended up working in our clinic. This was also thanks to our marriage matchmaking service and ads. The woman university graduate was 13 years younger than the man, but she was also an old maid; she was almost 40 when she married and had a daughter. The woman's still alive, but the man's passed. Because he'd been sent to reeducation in Qinghai for over ten years, by the time he got to our factory he was already 52. At the time, the oldest workers tended to be the "supporting agriculture workers," that is, the workers who'd been "sent down" to the Shanghai suburbs from the city during the Three Years of Natural Disaster [TN: the years of famine and economic shortage following the Great Leap Forward campaigns]. When the Small Third Front needed them, they were called back [to the urban work units]. This oldest man, this 53-year-old, was named Wu. He was a bamboo construction worker in the construction department, and he married this university student who'd been sent down to Xinjiang. That was thanks to our making the match, too.

A woman from Quzhou, Zhejiang, was also brought to us through matchmaking. She worked in our logistics department. She said she had a great head for business—a lot of people from there do. After she came out here, she became the manager of the concessionary store, which made her the equivalent of a team leader under the administrative department. When we went back to Shanghai, she worked in the logistics department of the No. 5 Steelworks, then rose to become deputy section chief, section chief, then a manager of the No. 5 Steelworks Tertiary Sector Economic Development Company, then she went into her own business. Now she's really made it big. Her marriage was matched up by me personally. The man was a vocational college graduate and worked in the chemical testing room of the same workshop where my wife worked. He hadn't been able to find a partner; I think he was over 30 already. Then they married.

[…] In the end there were still 112 who didn't find a partner. These people were all mostly around 32, all fairly older, not the best-looking, and their families not the best-off in economic terms. This kind of person would be a tough customer wherever they went. After they went to Shanghai, some of them resolved their problems, because the range of potential partners was bigger in the city. Why did the Xinjiang heavy industrial factories have textile plants built beside them? Just for this marriage problem for men and women. […] Before [the matchmaking], our Party Committee Secretary and other leaders would try to do one-off matchmaking out of their personal concern, but then after that they couldn't be sure if the women would be able to be transferred to the factory. [...] But the marriage matchmaking [policy] made it clear that you could have unilateral transfers in.

There were issues with some of the matches we made, too. One time I caught sight of a young fellow on the 507 docks who wasn't the best looking. The woman in this case was from Heilongjiang, also not the best looking. Our factory's young man was very honest, a little naïve even, and this young woman really liked to sleep in. One early morning in the snow, he bought some nice meat buns from the canteen for her and took them to the residential area, and also helped her with the laundry and such. But then this young woman got involved with a local man and fought to divorce our factory's young man. I was very angry and helped the fellow with the divorce suit, but in the end it went through. But when the Small Third Front retreated back to Shanghai, this young woman couldn't return to Shanghai. She suffered the consequences of that "burned bridge."

When serious incidents happened [in Anhui], the local police would take care of things. Then when the Rear Base set up a Rear Base Management Bureau, they had their own public safety department. Arrest and detention would be back in Shanghai—they arrested you locally and transferred you back to Shanghai.

There was a young man in the factory who loved to gamble. We also helped him make a match. At first, the factory housing hadn't been expanded, and then they built the Eight-Five bridge and over 200 units of new housing across the Baiyang River, and these newlyweds got a unit in the unmarried building, first floor. The woman ran up to the fifth floor and jumped, trying to kill herself, but thank goodness that when she leapt down, there was an electrical wire that people were drying their blankets on; she bounced on this and then underneath her was all trees and green space, so she survived, but she broke two bones in her lower leg. Why was she attempting suicide? Because her husband loved gambling and went off to gamble even on his wedding night. In the three days after the wedding, he still didn't keep the bride company, so she got desperate. She had a boyfriend back on the farm [she was working on], and he'd even bought furniture [for their future home] and was ready for the wedding, but she didn't want to keep staying at the Dafeng Farm and wasn't the most satisfied with that young man, either.

So, she changed her mind and didn't want to get married. That young man, in a fury, smashed up all the new furniture, really barbaric. This girl was shocked and had to take a holiday in Shanghai. When she saw our matchmaking ad, she came over to us, and was pretty satisfied, but she didn't realize she'd married a gambling addict. She was furious. She was pretty ambitious; she was a Youth League member, a pretty good, productive worker. She couldn't see her way out of it, essentially sitting home by herself. This shows that our work wasn't sufficiently careful. In the youths who came in [after graduating between 1974 and 1977], about 10% were problem youths. We reformed about half of them, but there was still another half who were badly behaved, you know. Then this young man cut off one of his own fingers, swearing to quit gambling. When he was in the hospital, the two reconciled. Things between husbands and wives, "fighting at the head of the bed and reconciling at the foot of it," are always complicated and tough to handle.

Most of the marriages we made were good, but some problem youths, well, we also had to help them look for wives. Some had hooliganish ways, like they'd take a screwdriver and stab themselves in the leg, meaning "I'm tougher than you," and they'd do this to get the other party to pay their bills. I also had to be in touch with this type of person. I requested of them: you can't be all over the place like this, you have to reform yourself. Most of them listened to me. Most of them would see me and greet me. Even though I'm old now, I look pretty different, if they bump into me they still recognize me and even from a long ways off they'll greet me. When they think of me, they even ring me up to say hello. I feel like this is the way to live like a person. In the beginning, some of them even threatened me. Some individual cases fought to get divorces, but most of them were good.

[…]

[Text of marriage ad placed by Shi Zhiding:] Eight-Five Steel Factory League Committee Notice:

Seeking Partners for our Factory's Young Men—Transfers into our Factory Possible after Marriage

We are a state-owned enterprise led doubly by the Shanghai Metallurgy Bureau and the Shanghai Rear Base Management Bureau located in Guichi County, Anhui. There are over 5000 workers in the factory and over 3000 family members. At the moment, the factory has over 200 young men above the age of twenty-seven years who are unmarried. In order to resolve these urgent issues for these men, we have decided to publicly seek partners for them.

Our factory is equipped with all living needs. Salaries are 33 yuan per month for a First-Grade Worker, 39 yuan for a Second-Grade Worker, with extra prize bursaries and so forth. After marriage, every year accumulated vacation days can be used to holiday in Shanghai. The young men seeking partners on this occasion are all those who have come to the inland areas from Shanghai.

All young women with city or town *hukou* and have grain rations who are working in state-owned enterprises in metropolitan or suburban Shanghai or in other areas around the nation, if interested with good intentions, may write to us. If your romance succeeds, then you may transfer after marriage to work in our factory (approval has already been granted by the relevant organs). Please mail correspondence to the Youth League Committee, PO Box 419, Guichi, Anhui, mail code 247175. Girls or their families may both write to inquire of the situation and solicit forms for completion. Please indicate a mailing address, personal situation, and desired attributes in a partner, as well as a recent photograph.

* * *

孙继雯 Sun Jiwen, female, worker at several different Small Third Front factories.

Keywords: communications, family, frustrations, living conditions, marriage, men vs. women, nostalgia, politically correct

Seeking Spouses for Our Factory's Young Men

Our factory is under the double jurisdiction of the Shanghai Instrument Factory and the Rear Front Base Area as a state-owned work unit, mainly manufacturing radios and electrical record players. Currently, we have nearly 200 young men in our factory without a romantic partner. They are mostly around twenty-seven years of age. We are placing this public advertisement to seek partners for them. Unmarried young women with urban household registrations and commercial grain entitlements affiliated with state-owned work units (including in agriculture, forestry, husbandry, and fishery) of good intentions may write to us to solicit a registration form. Please describe your personal situation and requests and attach one recent photograph. Following marriage, you are permitted to transfer to work in our factory. Mailing address: Youth League Committee, Postal Box #402, Quande County, Anhui Province.

—Shanghai Electronic Materials No. 2 Factory Youth League Committee

This personals ad was placed by the Jinggangshan Factory in Shanghai's *Youth Daily*. That was in 1984. A common phenomenon across all the factories of Shanghai's Small Third Front of that time was young men outnumbering young women, and the Jinggangshan Factory was no exception. When the Small Third Front began construction in late 1969, 80% of workers were those of us "old three cohort" sent-down youths whose younger brothers and sisters had been "sent down" to the countryside and were therefore given "special treatment" by being assigned to the Small Third Front. When we first came to southern Anhui, we were only 20.

[...] In the blink of an eye, almost five years passed. Pairs of boyfriends and girlfriends began appearing around Jinggangshan Factory. Strange to say, they really moved pretty efficiently. Often, you'd see pairs of youths eating together in the dining hall, and basically that meant they were going to get hitched. [...] We used to joke that this was "fishing in a stagnant pond, one less for every one hooked." The time rolled past, and they sent another batch of nearly 200 young people from Shanghai in the cohort of 1971, of which most were men. As time went on, problems became obvious: some young men couldn't repress their loneliness and picked fights and caused trouble; some worked with low spirits; some— [TN: Sun trails off here, perhaps referring to the most infamous incidents attributed to singledom: self-harm and violence]. Then, with the approval of the Rear Base, the factory management decided to seek young women of suitable age in society at large. That was how this personals ad came to be.

[...] One week after we put out the personals ad, we gradually began receiving mail from young women all over the country and all of a sudden, the union office began to really bustle. We recorded and numbered each of these young women's personal information. Some were the children of those sent to Xinjiang to "support the frontier"; there were women from Sichuan, Shanxi, and Gansu. In a flash, this "stagnant pond" got a burst of fresh, flowing water, and we two became the matchmakers for these young people.

We first had the young men pick from the girls' information and then made adjustments based on the conditions and requirements of each party. Though we weren't perfectly successful, but the first-round success rate wasn't bad. Similarly, when the young women mailed out their information, they were eagerly awaiting a response from us. Some got a letter and immediately rushed to Shanghai for a meeting. Our factory's young men would go with pomp and circumstance to Shanghai and meet [the girls] at a park they'd agreed on. I remember once the young woman that Ma Jian from the No. 4 Workshop had picked out decided to go to the meeting in Shanghai and her parents accompanied her by train all the way from Lanzhou [TN: capital of the northwestern province of Gansu]. That day, me and the Party Branch Secretary of the No. 4 Workshop, Lu Zhijing, held a sign waiting for them at the Shanghai North train station until they arrived in the middle of the night. Her parents were very moved by our dedication. After a while to get to know each other, they quickly confirmed a romantic relationship.

A daughter of workers who had gone from Shanghai to the Big Third Front in Chongqing [, Sichuan] told us warmly that "you all have really done an amazing thing. I don't know how, but when I saw his face, it was like meeting an old acquaintance. We had just endless things to say to each other, it was totally a fated match." I also remember another young woman whose mom went with her to Shanghai and met up with the young man at the Naval Defense Secondary School in Shanghai. Her mom found our factory's guy reliable and trustworthy after meeting him and kept praising us for doing a great good deed for her family. She knew how to play the piano and couldn't stop herself from walking over to the piano at the school and playing the main theme from the movie *Intimate Friends* [TN: a 1981 film about the love between a patriotic courtesan and a young warlord from Yunnan in the Republican era[2]], "seeking a soulmate over high mountains and across flowing waters...."

Before long, one young wife after another appeared at the Jinggangshan Factory. Some were assigned to factory workshops; some continued being teachers at the elementary school for workers' children. There were quite a few workers' children at the factory who were in this age group, so they also managed to hop the wagon and benefit from these efforts. Their parents were all my colleagues, and sometimes when we ran into one another they'd always ask solicitously whether better young women had sent in letters; there were also those who'd already found an agreeable daughter-in-law.

* * *

徐小英 Xu Xiaoying, female, cadre, teacher, and office administrator at a Small Third Front steel mill.

Keywords: children, conflicts, critique, family, frustrations, living conditions, marriage, men vs. women, violence

[2] Paul Clark, *Chinese Cinema: Culture and Politics since 1949.* Cambridge: Cambridge University Press, 1987, 164.

At the time my partner was in the military. Then in '73 I got married [at] 26 years old. I met my husband after I'd gone there. Because he was in the military, he had to stay where he was posted. At that time his posting wasn't even there [in Anhui]—he'd stayed on Hainan Island, in Qingdao. Hunan was the training air base for them in Naval Aviation. After I married him, I got pregnant. After getting pregnant, if I had duties, if I had so many social work obligations, that'd—yeah, that wouldn't be too convenient. Then I had the kid. After I had the kid, there was no one to help me raise him, so I had the kid with just me in the mountains. I had to go to work and look after him.

[...] Then having him there, I really couldn't take it anymore; my mom saw that I couldn't take it anymore, so [I] put [him] in Shanghai for a little bit. My mom had to work, my dad too, so in Shanghai they gave me a little help and [I] put [him there] for a while, then when that was no good, I took him back to the mountains. We traded back and forth. My son went to first and second grade in the mountains. [...] I had [the kid] in '74, when I was 29 [TN: inconsistency in ages from original transcript; Xu is possibly counting in traditional style, where a baby is one year old at birth, in the second mention of her age]. After the 56-day maternity leave, I went on sick leave. When my son was three months old, I took him into the mountains. I just put him in the nursery. In the mornings I'd finish all the [household] tasks early, get him over to the nursery; after doing that, I'd go to work. It was hard, it wore away half my life. Yep, I kept working at the Propaganda Department after having him.

[...] [My husband] came back [to Shanghai] about '81. He could come back to Nanhui [District, Shanghai], because he had left from Nanhui. When he went back to Nanhui, I could have too, and at the time Nanhui also wanted me. Then when Ma Tianshui was mayor [of Shanghai], he said that not a single one of the Small Third Fronters could be moved. After "not a single one could be moved," it turned into [my husband] going alone to Nanhui; I couldn't go, and we were separated again. Then he came to the home Steelworks. '81 to '87, I stayed about five or six years [alone].

[...] By the time [my husband] came back [to Nanhui], the kid was already in second grade. Me alone, it was really hard, really hard. [...] Once I took my son; at that time my son was seven months old, he had a fever, 102 degrees. It wasn't so easy then to get to the Shanghai Steel Hospital; there were no cars. After the kid started running the fever, I hitched a ride with someone else; there happened to be a car going to the hospital. After we got to the hospital, it turned out he had to stay. He had to stay a week. On the day I'd taken my son [to the hospital], it was the rainy season, I'd cooked porridge in a little pot at home, and after we got back, the fuzz [of the mold] was this long.

At the time it was really very hard, very hard living alone. Getting through alone, you had to go to work, you had to work and participate in [political] study; back then Mondays, Wednesdays, Fridays you had to go to meetings. Political study from 6 p.m. to 8 p.m., no exceptions. Mondays, Wednesdays, Fridays, three study sessions a week. And [I] had to go to work and look after my son. It was really a lot during that time. Other people say, "we couldn't look after [our kids] well between the two of us, you've got special powers to do it alone, [your son] got through with you." [...] I was really on the brink, toughing it out. Bathing, I'd carry my son in one hand, a jumble of stuff to wash with the other hand, and the wash basin, the wash basin too, running down 78 steps—basically my house was on the hill; I went down 78 steps to take my son for a bath. Afterward, I had to go back up.

No, [I don't think I ever slacked off with work], because of these things; if it was my task, I would always finish it. Yes, it was pretty tough when I was at the school and raising the kid. [The kid was] put in nursery school. Well, my son truly was pretty well behaved from the time he was little. Sometimes he got sick, and I'd lock him in alone at home and put some food out there for him, [...] and he never made a fuss, all by himself. That's how it was. That saved me quite a lot of worry. From when he was little, my son also adapted to this type of setting. He really is pretty well behaved. Well, once when I came home it was a mess, he had drawn a mess on the wall. I had to do the housework. Really, the clothes I wore and the shoes I wore were all made by myself in the mountains there. There wasn't anywhere to go buy them. There was a commissary store at the time, but it didn't carry everything, at most condiments and cooking oil. At most. They didn't sell clothes and such. That I was able to make it through that time really wasn't so easy. Well, me, that's to say, in terms of work, I was always a beneficiary of Chairman Mao's [...] I really put my heart and effort into it. In terms of work there wasn't really anything big. No mistakes and no slacking off. I toughed my way through.

[And back then] there was no place at all to talk about it. Mm-hmm, couldn't complain, I felt really wronged. I already had it tougher than other people. Plus the assignments you give me, the work I do, I actually didn't do less than other people. Not many women took care of a kid alone while working [...] basically none. [...] When I was doing nighttime study, I'd still have my son at my side. I did send him to Shanghai; my mother saw that at one point I really couldn't handle it, I really couldn't take it, so my mom took care [of him] for a while [...] just temporarily.

Mm-hmm, he went to two years of school in the mountains. At the time there weren't better options; at the time my parents were in Nanhui, the suburbs, no chance of good schools there either. Where my mom and dad were, both of them had to work, and my younger brother lived there too. That is to say, after this younger brother of mine got married, that one flat with two bedrooms had my younger brother in one [bedroom] and my parents in the other. Beginning in third grade, I put my son with [his uncle] at the Shuangyang Road Elementary school in Yangpu District. At the time, my younger brother's household—my sister-in-law wasn't so...it was a grudging place there, it was always like my son was an outsider, temporarily staying there.

Anyway, my son never made a fuss. My younger brother and sister-in-law would fight, and my son always—he saw a lot. Why would my son have been so well behaved from such a young age? [...] Once my son was in their room playing with my niece. My sister-in-law wanted to hit my son; when she hit him, my mom heard the sound. After she heard that, my mom thought, after all, she's got to be sweet on her own nephew, she couldn't [bear to hit him]. [...] So, she waited until my sister-in-law went to work and asked my son if his aunt had hit him in [the room]. My son was very clever and said she hadn't; this hadn't happened. [...] He was very well behaved from a young age. [...] Later my mom told me the story, and it made my heart very sore. Mm-hmm, because I couldn't take care of him.

Yes, there is a relationship between that environment and kids being precocious. Every year afterward my son would come into the mountains during summer vacation. He wouldn't go out, he'd just study [at home]; he wasn't like other kids, behaving badly. The laundry we put out to dry, after we came off work, he'd have taken the clothes—his daddy's and my clothes, folded them, mopped the floors, cooked the dishes and cooked the rice too. From the time he was little he was really well behaved. [...] My son is really—you know—really good. [...] Mm-hmm, yes, my son's temperament is like a young lady's, very careful, very caring. So now [...] the wife he found, my daughter-in-law, is also living pretty well, and it's all my son. My daughter-in-law is also pretty good at things, she was his classmate at Tongji University. [...]

My husband [...] In '81 he changed to a civilian career; he changed ahead of time; a bunch of cadres were changing jobs, you know. He was one of the better cases. He had it good; he was earlier than two other cadres changing work [...] He was among the earlier [people], and he was older than them. This was much better [after he came back]. Because my husband is very good at things too, so I would go to work in the mornings, he could help with cooking meals, buying groceries, then my son was with us too, Xihua Elementary School, first and second grade. By third grade, the quality [of schooling] there wasn't good, so then [my son] came to Shanghai.

Teachers, well, our elementary school's first and second grades were okay. Mm-hmm, in higher grades, if you could go to Shanghai, then you'd go to Shanghai. If he weren't very self-motivated, I wouldn't necessarily be at ease. From when my son was small I'd observe him. Other kids would finish playing before doing their homework, but my son would finish his homework before going to play. I felt that he was pretty self-motivated, so I put him in Shanghai. Mm, so I put him in Shanghai, and he did get pretty good grades after all.

* * *

袁彩霞 Yuan Caixia, female, Anhui native who married into a Small Third Front factory.

Keywords: children, critique, family, frustrations, marriage, men vs. women

In April 1984 I arrived at Steep Cliff. I lived on the Huaibei Plains but these Small Third Front factories were all in the mountains. As soon as I got into these mountains my heart went cold. Oh no, I had to spend the rest of my life in these mountain gullies? After I arrived, Ma Pinjun introduced me to my husband, Zou Jianchong. He was a benchworker and started at the factory in 1976. He was pretty dark-skinned. If you asked me "Do you feel repulsed?" Well, I didn't feel that. But if you said "Do you like him?" Well, not necessarily. I'd graduated from high school, but he only had junior high.

When we met in person, Jianchong actually already had a girlfriend from Heilongjiang. She was very pretty, and they'd already been writing each other for three or four years. But this woman just refused to meet up in person. After I went in to meet him, Jianchong suddenly left me behind and ran to Shanghai. I thought, what game is he playing! What'd actually happened was that Jianchong wasn't able to make up his mind and had gone home to Shanghai to ask his parents for advice. I thought, well, it's over, better head home. But then one morning, his parents made a long-distance call to Ma Pinjun to say, "We're so sorry. This marriage [with Caixia], we approve of it, we're sending Jianchong back right away." So he came right back and settled things with me: on May Day he came and took me to Shanghai to meet his parents. They were very pleased and gave us their approval. On National Day [October 1], 1984, we were married in Shanghai and had a wedding banquet, then we went to my folks' home and had one there. My daughter was born in 1985.

* * *

赵惠瑛 Zhao Huiying, female, worker and kindergarten teacher at a Small Third Front steelworks.

Keywords: art, children, education, family, living conditions, marriage, men vs. women, nostalgia, politically correct, post-Mao

After I went in [to work at the kindergarten] I came to Shanghai for training, you know. When I went [to the kindergarten] I was already pregnant, so [the superiors] said, you're fine, you don't need to lead classes, so I went directly to Shanghai for training, to Hankou Road Kindergarten for training.

I [married] in '76. Yep, yes, me and my husband met in Anhui. He was also a vocational school graduate; he went over from the Shanghai No. 1 Steelworks...yes, he was also at a steel mill, the hardest work. I think he really liked writing a little here and there. His prose was pretty good. Then after about two years he was moved to the Politics and Propaganda group. There was a Propaganda Department in the workshop too. [...] Relatively speaking, it was much easier [work]. Because he was a good writer, so people had him do this, write stuff for propaganda work. So then it was really lucky, because I also like writing and talking. I was one of the more radical ones, a person nurtured by Mao Zedong during the era of Mao Zedong, very radical. When they held various activities I'd enthusiastically participate. And once there was a poetry contest—everybody writing poems, you know! Everybody was letting their creativity free and writing poems.

[My future husband] thought my poem was pretty well written, then when both of us chatted a bit and got more familiar, we were both in the same team, so after some time passed—yes yes yes! We began to date. Back then you really wouldn't look into how much money someone's family had, or if he had housing. Back then everyone had it tough; we were all about the same! Everyone's family was very economically hard up. So then from us dating to marrying, it was all us counting on our own hands, because our parents didn't help us; we relied on ourselves.

After I'd had my daughter, my mother-in-law went over [to Anhui] to live for a while, and my mother also went over for a while, then the kid was brought to Shanghai. [She did] stay [in Anhui]; the kid was put in Shanghai for two years or so, and I took her [to Anhui] when she was around three. I carried her over to Anhui because I happened to be working in the kindergarten, so I put her in the kindergarten. It was a bit easier having her at my side. When she hadn't been weaned yet, my mother-in-law and mother helped take care of her, for about one or two years. Then when she was three, I thought she could go into kindergarten, so I took her with me, and it was easier going to and leaving work. So I just kept taking care of her myself [Image 7.3].

[…] For this we have to thank Deng Xiaoping. Didn't Deng Xiaoping want all the Small Third Front people to go back? So local property and stuff were all given back to the locals, and the personnel, we came back. So the nation? We just gotta thank Deng Xiaoping for this. First the kids could come back; children of the Small Third Front could move their registrations back to Shanghai to go to school. Also, our middle school, elementary school, kindergarten, and nursery school were very complete. Our educational system was very complete. So later, in the 80s, when Deng Xiaoping put out this directive, the kids gradually went back to Shanghai […] We came back two years later. Back then we were already really happy that the kid could come back, even though it was pretty happy over there too, but after all it was in a mountain gully, and you wouldn't see the world. We wanted after all for the kid to come see the world a bit. We were already very, very grateful that our child was able to come back! Then two years later, Party Central said that Small Third Front people were going back to their original places of residence, and we were jumping up and down, we were so happy! So we gradually came back. I should say that in this process, the state took real care of us. After we came back we went to the No. 5 Steelworks, which helped us take care of housing and such.

When I brought my daughter back to Anhui, I was already head of the kindergarten. It was all right to take care of her at home while working. With her in kindergarten, it was basically the same as me having her alongside me, and I could take care of her a bit. It wasn't like now back then, taking an hour to get to work. Three to five minutes riding on a bicycle,

Image 7.3 A toddler eating noodles at the Eight-Five Steelworks, 1970s–1980s, collection of Xu Youwei

and you'd arrive. So if there were anything, I could call [my husband] for help. So between us we raised the kid.

It was okay, in terms of having a lot of things to look after as kindergarten head. My daughter also did pretty well, was pretty good. The kindergarten was also very good. I should say that she was a really obedient child, and we had pretty high expectations for her too. From age three she could already read some characters and do some other things, so when the kindergarten held activities, shows—oh! Shows in the big auditorium, several thousand people, she wasn't afraid. She'd take her script and pow pow pow, she'd start announcing the events. She was the MC, you know? The primary school was right next door. We were together. Her homeroom teacher really liked her, always patted her on the head. Her forehead was really big, so she got called "Little Sprite," "Little Sprite." Anyway, they really liked her.

Then in third grade there was this [new] policy, she came back [to Shanghai]. She was clever, and a quick study, and she came to Shanghai to study. We said to Shanghai schools that she was a [Young Pioneer] brigade captain over there [in Anhui], but hey! All you people coming from outside, [the schools said], you all say your child does well at school, but you come here and you can never catch up. I said that we're only saying that this kid did pretty well over there, not a very bad kid. Some schools really suspiciously asked how the kid was. We introduced ourselves, I said we weren't necessarily coming to be some [Young Pioneer] brigade captain or something, we just have this policy to come back to go to school. Then not a week after she went back to Shanghai, the teacher had her be brigade captain again.

She really is good at school. She was real clever at her books; she didn't need anyone looking over her; she was real self-motivated. So then my daughter, I truly didn't really have to discipline her for anything. She was in her maternal grandmother's house and I was in Anhui. She went to school in Shanghai, while grandma and grandpa only made sure she was fed, but she really worked hard at school, always the first few places in the class. [...] She got into East China Normal University's No. 2 Affiliated Secondary School. She was the first person in her school to get into this kind of secondary school. We didn't expect it. The principal was laughing herself to death, she was so happy. It was like earning glory for their school.

[...] After she got into the No. 2 Affiliated Secondary School, middle school, high school, college, then to graduate school, she rose straight through, she didn't have to take any exams. Yes! She took not one exam! She just counted on herself. From middle school on she lived in the dorms; I didn't go see her very often at all. It was all her on her own until she graduated grad school. She spent very little time at home. When she graduated grad school, she'd also gotten herself a boyfriend. He was from outside [Shanghai], a classmate, and after time went by, they developed feelings for each other. I'm really open-minded. In college, if you were dating, if you had a boyfriend, then the boy and the girl can complement each other. You got to be aboveboard, no shady dealings, everyone's proper and aboveboard. Communication and topics of conversation are shared because they study the same things. You can talk about these things, and when interacting with the opposite sex you can complement each other, you can help each other out. She majored in finance. In grad school she all along studied insurance, but then she took an actuarial exam, and now she's got her license too.

[...] Nowadays if you say you're going to one-handedly take care of things [like I did], it might be a bit difficult, but now requirements are higher and higher; in the past, it was all right. [I think I did] all right. [I also looked after my family] all right. Because there weren't overtime hours back then, it wasn't much. By 5 p.m. the children would've all been picked up. When I went [back home], well, I'd cook. My husband would basically have come home from work too. The kid would be coming back too. One of us would mind the kid, one of us would cook, just like that. Basically, it was pretty good.

Further Reading

Xiaoping Cong, *Marriage, Law, and Gender in Revolutionary China, 1940–1960.* Cambridge: Cambridge University Press, 2016.

Neil Diamant, *Revolutionizing the Family: Politics, Love, and Divorce in Urban and Rural China, 1949–1968.* Berkeley: University of California Press, 2000.

Susan Greenhalgh, *Just One Child: Science and Policy in Deng's China.* Berkeley: University of California Press, 2008.

Yuxiang Yan, *Private Life under Socialism: Love, Intimacy, and Family Change in a Chinese Village, 1949–1999.* Stanford: Stanford University Press, 2003.

CHAPTER 8

Politics, Social Order, and Military Affairs

Translator's Note

As developmental centerpieces in the PRC's economic and military strategy, the Third Fronts, including the Small Third Front, were closely enmeshed with existing military and political institutions from the People's Liberation Army itself down to local people's militias. Testimonies here demonstrate the depth to which daily life was militarized, with workers being trained in wartime skills like throwing hand grenades and using firearms.

Workers on the Small Third Front were also witness to the upheavals of the Cultural Revolution and its aftermath, wherein leadership and power could change hands seemingly overnight as contending factions fought for supremacy in Beijing and throughout the nation. Factories sometimes became arenas for public struggle, though Party Central sought to control the degree to which Red Guards and other self-appointed revolutionaries were able to access Third Front facilities due to their secrecy and Cold War national security concerns.

Keeping order was a major concern for the CCP; actions that would be called crimes in another context also carried a political valence, as there was not much of a gap between the Party-state and society at large. Despite people's later recollections of a less crime- and instability-ridden society, the years of Mao's supremacy were far from tranquil, even leaving aside the

Y. Xu, Y. Y. Wang, *Everyday Lives in China's Cold War Military-Industrial Complex*, Palgrave Studies in Oral History,
https://doi.org/10.1007/978-3-030-99688-8_8

many campaigns against "counterrevolutionaries," "class enemies," "rightists," and others under political suspicion. In the early days of Communist rule in Shanghai, workers striked and protested at high rates and relatively autonomous workers' militias—one of the forces that helped the Party rise to power in China's most industrialized city—were disbanded.[1] National authorities were alerted to food shortages every year between 1952 and 1958 that displaced sometimes tens of thousands of people who left home in search of a living; of course, conditions further worsened in the aftermath of the Great Leap Forward. Students were often forced to leave school due to limited quotas for advancement, and young people often struggled to find jobs for similar reasons. Resistance and non-cooperation at the grassroots took on many forms. Farmers covertly traded food and handicrafts in private and ate crops before they were ripe rather than letting their produce be harvested and centrally redistributed.[2] Urban people formed gangs that stole and harassed women; others fled from perilous, remote, or otherwise unwanted work assignments. These violations of the sociolegal order, despite official condemnations linking, selling one's own crops outside of the collective to "counterrevolutionary" activity, may have actually made the regime's continuation—and the survival of people who lived under it—more possible by meeting needs the state was not fulfilling.

Moreover, constant challenges to the authorities in the "New Society" do not mean that people wanted to overturn the state, or that they were impervious to the Party's rules and rhetoric. The vocabulary of politics and revolution, as we have already seen in other chapters, became fully integrated into people's everyday language. Terms like "struggle," "rectification," and "rebel" are inseparable from how former Third Fronters understand their personal histories, though they are not necessarily used in orthodox ways. Finally, narratives in this chapter also demonstrate how deep political tensions and campaign-style practices persisted after Mao Zedong's death and the Party's turn away from Cold War enmities and toward global markets.

[1] Elizabeth J. Perry, "Masters of the Country? Shanghai Workers in the Early People's Republic," in Jeremy Brown and Paul G. Pickowicz eds., *Dilemmas of Victory: The Early Years of the People's Republic of China*. Cambridge, MA: Harvard University Press, 2007, 59–79.

[2] Wang Chunying and Y. Yvon Wang, "Gray Markets in the Great Leap: Prosecuting 'Profiteering' in Liangshan County, Shandong, 1958–1960," forthcoming in *Modern China*; Ralph A. Thaxton, *Catastrophe and Contention in Rural China: Mao's Great Leap Forward Famine and the Origins of Righteous Resistance in Da Fo Village*. Cambridge: Cambridge University Press, 2008, Chs. 5–6.

Questions for Discussion

1. What are the attitudes that the Third Fronters in this chapter seem to have held toward the militaristic, highly politicized atmosphere of the Third Front and of the time period? Whom or what do they blame for the bad, and whom or what do they praise for the good?
2. What were the primary tasks and priorities of Small Third Front public security and order-keeping institutions?
3. How do you think more recent politics (i.e., since the era of the Small Third Front) may have impacted how narrators remember and talk about politics and social order in their experiences of the past?

* * *

卞建华 *Bian Jianhua, female, driver for the Rear Base militia headquarters.*

Keywords: Cultural Revolution, militias, policing, politically correct, weapons

At the time, militia firearms and ammunition had to be applied for. The Shanghai Garrison Command Militia Command Center later had some dalliances with the "Gang of Four." Back then you had to make a report, and with the Garrison Command's approval, then the arms and ammo would get sent to you. Local training, well, you'd get together with the local garrisons. Back then you didn't think about it. Including Shanghai's Armed-Grassroots-Cadre-and-Militia union, ordinary militia, all of 'em would conduct drills. Back then in Tunxi, we'd have a division of tasks internally, but from the outside it looked like all one group. If the Public Security Department had some action or situation, those of us doing the militia stuff would do it all together. Back then we'd also do firing-range training, in the Rear Base; we also drilled by ourselves (Images 8.1 and 8.2).

Because they were armed, we were really afraid when they were coming after Dai Liqing [TN: a leading Shanghai "rebel worker" during the Cultural Revolution who fell from grace for being associated with the "Gang of Four" in October 1976]. We were afraid that they'd really bring the guns out. But you couldn't just grab the guns. There were rules. If you wanted to get a certain weapon, you had to be approved.

Every factory's guns and ammunition had to be approved by us. In each Industrial Area there was a detachment, a matching one, and they all

Image 8.1 Drilling militiamen at the Cooperation Factory, 1971

had their own guns allotted to them. They couldn't just take and use them. They had both guns and ammunition. An armed company, the number of guns were matched to how many were in it, they'd have a designated arsenal. Back then there was this buddy system, meaning that you couldn't go alone to get 'em [the guns and ammunition]. If you wanted them, you had to get someone else to agree to go with you to get 'em together. During training, if you were planning to do a certain kind of training, you had to report that too. You needed approval, and sometimes the superior units would send people along too. Sometimes it was with local armed units. Training wasn't just whenever you felt like it; especially armed militia, you definitely needed training. Grassroots cadre militias got

Image 8.2 Militiawomen from the Red Wave Factory, 1977, collection of Li Shouren

more training time than the ordinary militia troops. [The Militia Command HQ] was in command [of the factories and enterprises' armed units.]

Usually every Industrial Area would have [big drills]. Well, each wouldn't have what you necessarily call a big drill. Just a standard drill [...] So, army crawls, standing, shooting. Everyday military drills. Things were pretty anxious back then. They'd say that if war came to Shanghai, we'd move to the Rear Base. So back then we had to "prepare for war, prepare for famine, prepare for the people," "dig tunnels deep, store grain everywhere," and so forth. [TN: These are slogans attributed to Mao from the Third Front era.] So at that point Shanghai took the Rear Base pretty seriously [...] at first it wasn't called the Rear Base. At first it was the 812 Command Headquarters, and the 812 HQ's personnel transferred to the Rear. So the Rear Base's Party political cadres' abilities, in retrospect, was really pretty good. Dai Liqing was a cadre sent over by Shanghai, and he'd had some key roles there, so you can see how important the Rear Base was to the city back then.

The militia command HQ in the Rear mainly was responsible for training. Otherwise you couldn't pull out. At the time the requirement was to be able to "pull it out, hit it loud, do it tough." These slogans. Training wasn't so frequent. We all had to go to work. [...] I couldn't say exactly [when the police station was set up]. All this work was done in increments. But the Public Security Department was set up in 1975 or early 1976, and the police station was set up after the Public Security Department had been operating a while, also between '75 and '76. All the household registrations moved to the Rear were managed by the Public Security Department. We also selected a few young people from each of the subsidiary industrial areas to help manage them. Whichever industrial area you were from, you'd oversee that area. No. 4 would oversee No. 4. That's my impression of it. That was one of our tasks.

[We in Public Security] wouldn't really go arresting people, but we did carry out missions. We were very circumspect, because after all we had limited personnel. Later on, we even had a police station. Lots of household registrations were managed by the station. For the later times, I don't know. [...] Definitely there was no way we would let the locality oversee [the household registrations]. The police station was for the entire Rear Base industrial district. The subsidiary areas would send people over too.

* * *

卜晓明 Bu Xiaoming, female, internist and attending physician at a Small Third Front hospital.

Keywords: conflicts, critique, Cultural Revolution, frustrations, medicine, nepotism, Party members, politically correct, violence, work assignments

The Rear Base Health and Hygiene team saw my dossier and one of the leadership recognized my mother. He said, "Oh, isn't this so-and-so's daughter? Well good, let's have her go to the Rear Base Party Committee, they need politically reliable people there." So that was how I ended up at the committee. There, well, it's not like you're doing much clinically. I was 100% against going, I was definitely not interested at the time. But I couldn't do anything about it. Then my family also said, why don't you first go and fix it later, so I went. All in all, I maybe worked there for a month. So I was their primary care doctor there. There was a guy, Dai Liqing, in the Rear Base hospitals, a henchman of the Gang of Four. He was there so I really didn't want to go, I really didn't want to work for them. I thought this gaggle of people were always going after senior cadres and really fearsome, so I really objected to them. But there wasn't anything I could do.

The Shanghai Public Security Bureau also sent a bunch of people that set up a Public Security Office in the Rear Base Party Committee. There were a bunch of veteran public security officers in there from Shanghai. I thought they were so old at the time, but now thinking back on it, they were 37 or 38 at most. These people and I had great relationships. There was a boss too; the head of the office was called Li Mingbao, a pretty showboat sort, but then he was taken down as part of the Gang of Four; he was gotten rid of by the people at the public security office. He was also in Dai Liqing's posse.

How do I describe a man like Dai? I don't know what he used to do before. They say he used to be a little street peddler and had gone to prison and then rebelled along with Wang Guowen [TN: Bu may have meant Wang Hongwen, a leading figure during the Cultural Revolution and a member of the "Gang of Four"]. And then this and that. I was still pretty young then, just over 20, but I didn't think much of Dai.

But Dai was pretty okay looking, not like I'd imagined him. He'd stayed at the senior-cadre sickroom of the Ruijin Hospital, and before going to work at the hospital I'd see him there. The rumors about his past were like this and that, so I kind of looked down on him. He was pretty tough, he wasn't like how people thought he was, he was very good looking, and his way of talking was pretty macho, but you couldn't say he was a bumpkin with no charisma either. He was a main leader [for the Rear Base]; another was a Secretary named Wang, an old Shandongnese, I've forgotten his name. This was a veteran cadre who'd come down south. From our view today, we'd say he picked the wrong team. So, he was working together with Dai Liqing, and I know that when the Gang of Four was completely toppled, both of them were caught up in it. Old Secretary Wang could still say some righteous things; I felt he was the type who could still say some fair stuff out loud. I feel like he had no choice; others decided for him and so he was [sent to work with Dai].

Anyway, at the time I was just their primary care doctor there and pretty idle. If they got sick, I had to go proactively fuss over them, but I really didn't want to do this kind of stuff, so I made such a big stink. Every day I went to talk to the Organization Department saying I wanted to leave, saying that I was letting my training stagnate there. That was already the very end of the Cultural Revolution. By then, a lot of veteran cadres had been set free again. So in the end it was through some backdoor connections with some older cadres that I got transferred to the Rear Base Ruijin Hospital. Dai Liqing was apparently not too happy at the time and didn't want to let me go. He said some displeased things. I ignored it. I was just a kid, so I just up and left.

When we got there, it was the mid- to late Cultural Revolution so there weren't very bad problems. Many of us medical staff had been affected by the Cultural Revolution: they'd all been struggled, punished, beaten up, had "big-character posters" posted about them, but in the end it was all cleared up, or else they wouldn't have been allowed to go [to the Small Third Front]. I remember our Old Zhou, Zhou Quantai, I thought this old cadre was pretty much on a higher spiritual plane. He was the HR department head for a long time at the Ruijin Hospital before the Cultural Revolution and knew a lot of confidential stuff in a lot of people's dossiers. But after the outbreak of the Cultural Revolution, the people who'd been in HR before had a really hard time. They got beaten up by the Red Guards. The ones who beat up Old Zhou were from the No. 2 Medical College. They beat him so badly. Then these kids got work assignments and a lot of them got sent to be factory doctors in Third Front factories, or the ones who got sent to the Big Third Front tried to find ways to get transferred back to the Small Third Front because the conditions in Yunnan or Guizhou or Sichuan were even harsher. Compared to that, life here in Anhui was much better. First off, in southern Anhui food wasn't a problem, plus this factory still belonged to Shanghai.

Later on, these students maybe got a little older and a little more mature and felt some remorse for their childish, ignorant behavior during the CultRev, so they came to visit this Old Zhou. He even took them out to lunch. Then the medics began to have a different view of things. Some thought this Old Zhou was a truly impressive veteran cadre. But some would say to his face, "Back then they beat you so badly, and you're still taking them out. People like this should just be grateful you're not coming to collect accounts on them." But Old Zhou's heart was pretty open, and he'd say, "They were just kiddos then. It's been such a long time, what's past is past, why bring back all that?"

* * *

储瑛娣 Chu Yingdi, female, Party cadre at a precision optics factory.

Keywords: conflicts, crime, critique, Cultural Revolution, frustrations, living conditions, pay and benefits, politically correct, political problems, violence

[TN: This narrative contains descriptions of assault and allusions to violence that may be disturbing.]

In Jingde where we were, there were five factories: Guarding the East, Worker-Peasant, Erecting the New, Yan'an, and us, the Steep Cliff Factory, each in a gully with a rough road. We had it relatively developed where we were, with road lights so you could walk to places at night. Each factory was about one kilometer apart; two of them were pretty close, just half a kilometer or so. Enterprise names at the time were all "revolutionary" names, a hallmark of the Cultural Revolution.

Our workers were veterans "sent down" from the city, vocational school graduates from the late 1960s, junior high school grads from 1972, a few junior high grads from 1973, and those who'd been "sent down" in the 1960s to help with the nation's difficulties [TN: a reference to the fallout of the Great Leap Forward] to be peasants.

[…] In 1973, we were all of a sudden sent 300 people, all of them kids around 18 years old. With them coming, the factory got really exciting. Because of anarchist influences, some of them had really bad characters. Often, they'd be pilfering this or that, fighting, gambling—we really had a lot to deal with. When they all arrived, they were mutual strangers. Those from different [city] districts would gang up together with nicknames like "Charger," "Scab-head," "Big Bamboo," and all this junk, all the habits of a pack of little hooligans. The first night they got in a fight so bad that some of them ran off. Then we had to root these people out. We didn't even know their names because they only called one another by nicknames, so we had to use their nicknames too. We called them into the conference room. Before they'd gotten to the factory, people didn't latch their doors at night; nothing like this had ever happened before. After they got there, then suddenly someone would have something go missing, then someone else got something stolen. We solved all these cases at the time, too, all by our own security department. Some received punishments. When some of them didn't get pay raises, they even came to put up a fuss. I asked, "What're you yelling about? You got yourself a major demerit and you still want a raise?" Then when they got a little older, got married and settled down, they got better.

[...] At the time I was the deputy Party committee secretary and was in charge of the political work department, the militia department, organization and human resources, the workers' union, the Youth League, and day-to-day thought education. Back then it was class struggle as the foundation; you'd be "Criticizing Lin Biao and Confucius" one moment, then doing something else another moment. You couldn't not take care of it [political work], but you also couldn't let it affect production, and you'd have to organize the militia for nighttime patrols. Not everyone could become a militia member—you had to be between 20 and 35, and there were more male comrades and fewer female comrades. You needed courage to go on these night patrols too. We also had guns, pretty heavy ones. And we had to drill; every month we spent two days doing target practice. We had a few people who were very good shots. There were wild hogs in the mountains, and one ran into our factory compound, so the company commander had some militia members shoot it and got the canteen to cook it up. Everybody got a little for a taste.

[...] The Cultural Revolution meant that we all had to take part in mandatory study campaigns. When our bosses held a meeting at the office, we'd go to Tunxi—our Rear Base offices were in Tunxi, in other words, where Huangshan city is these days. To get there we'd have to ride 90 minutes in the car. After the meeting, with our assignments set, we'd have to come back and execute our orders. Each branch secretary would hold a meeting and write a few pieces once they went back, for reading aloud on the PA. Sometimes there'd be a bigger meeting and each branch would talk about their situation, do a little bit of exchange. Meetings at the [Rear Base] office were on an as-needed basis. Sometimes you went out there twice a week. A lot of people hated this in their heart of hearts; you had to work on production *and* write these pieces. If you couldn't write something original, you'd just copy the newspapers, one big transcription of everything out there. Big papers copied the smaller ones; the smaller ones copied the commentaries by "Liang Xiao" [TN: a pun/pseudonym for the Critique Groups at Peking University and Tsinghua University during the Critique Lin Biao and Confucius Movement; "Liang Xiao" sounds like a person's name but is homophonous with "two schools"].

Extreme "left" thinking was the order of the day and the "rebel" cliques were all boss. All of them were hot-blooded youths. Then later when we were "cleansing the class ranks" [TN: 1968 campaign that often targeted populist upstarts from earlier phases of the Cultural Revolution], we also made distinctions between the rebels. Some were young and foolish and full of passion, different from those bad elements deliberately causing trouble. Someone joked at the time: the mountains here are pretty great; if things go south later, we can all go into the hills to do guerilla warfare. But the person who said that got pinned as a "counterrevolutionary." They later reversed that.

[...] In 18 years, we got two raises. The first came in 1976. [...] there were "half-grades" and "full grades," 3.5 yuan was half and seven yuan for the full. Those being paid over 64 yuan [per month] didn't get anything because they counted as "high income." Most people got this raise, unless you'd been absentee a lot over several years. That first time there weren't too many conflicts. Most got a half-grade raise; a minority, 10%, got a full raise. A lot of people were really pretty good, but our quotas were limited, so they only got half. Then the second raise, there was the "3, 6, 9" policy. That was in 1979; our old factory head died in 1979. It was this raise policy that wore him to death. [...] nine yuan was the top level, and again about 10% of people got that. The majority got the middle six yuan, and another 10% minority got the three yuan. Those who had performed poorly, who hadn't completed their assigned tasks, who were often absentee and who'd gotten infractions and punishments got no raise at all.

The people who got the three yuan thought it was too little. Some of those who got three could've gotten the six, but the mandated ratio couldn't accommodate that. Everyone started sniping at one another behind their backs and making comments, getting pretty seriously disharmonious. Oh, how they fought! A few young guys were like, if you don't give me a raise, I'll get violent, I'll bring out my knife. I got sick with a fever around then and was at home with a saline drip. One young kid rushed into my house and even smashed one of my flowerpots. I had them sit there. I couldn't even muster the energy to talk that day. I said, "I'm sick anyway today, you can have my life. Why'd you come here? If you want more pay I can't give it to you, everything's been announced. If you want, go ahead and kill me. Let me tell you, if you kill me the factory'll hold a funeral for me tomorrow and plenty of people will come to attend it, and you all are going to have to pay the price. Your own mothers will have to pay for that bullet they use to execute you. How could you all be so stupid? Tell me honestly how good your performance has been." So these kiddos fooled around for a long time, but none of them was bold enough to do anything. Then they all left. The doctor helping me with the saline was scared to death, saying "What if they beat you up?" I said there was no way they'd dare.

Two kids got sent to prison because they were gambling and lost, and one informed the authorities on the other one. The one who was told on hated that other kid to death and stabbed him in the dormitory building. And there was a political work cadre who had some [interpersonal] conflicts in his job. On the way to work one day, some guy took two thermoses of boiling water and threw them at him, wounding him. For that, the perpetrator was arrested by the local public security bureau and then locked up in the Qingpu Reform-by-Labor Center back in Shanghai. After that guy went back to Shanghai, he got married, had a kid, and then died of liver cancer. He was only 37. After he died, they held a funeral, but no one was willing to go or write a eulogy. I wanted to give the family some face so in the end I wrote the eulogy. The guy went all alone in to the Small Third Front, lived independently, and could do some work. All that should be recognized.

* * *

丁秀玉 Ding Xiuyu, female, technician at a Small Third Front steelworks who later rose to cadre positions in Small Third Front Party organs, including head of the Birth Planning office.

Keywords: camaraderie, Cultural Revolution, Party members, politically correct, work assignments

Yes. I joined the Party on September 5th, '71; just before the September 13th Incident in '71—the Lin Biao Incident—I entered the Party. After I joined, in '72 the class [of cadres] sent me [to the administrative offices], and they kept me on in '73. Basically, I joined the Party, they trained me a while and promoted me to a cadre, to being a mid-ranking cadre. I was very young at the time.

[...] There were some old comrades in the Propaganda Department; they guided me. After all, I was still young, I'd just entered society, I had no real experiences or résumé. At that point in the Propaganda Department, we were "Criticizing Confucius, Criticizing Lin Biao," so I did that. Basically, the Propaganda Department faced outward as well as inward, all of it. At that time, it was like this—though we were in Anhui on the Small

Third Front, some things sent down [as orders from] the Central Ministry offices [of Propaganda] we'd still have to carry out. At that time it was "Criticize Confucius, Criticize Lin Biao," and such. Political things, that's what the Propaganda Department was all about working on. Let me give another example: when they destroyed the Gang of Four in '77, when the radio station announced it, I had to go. I had to go organize materials and make slogan banners. No, not alone, others would help. At the time I'd go make arrangements and organize [others]. Then sometimes I'd write some materials, situation reports, sometimes I'd go to the workshops to give a speech, to go attend a meeting.

* * *

伏如山 Fu Rushan, male, worker at a fuse explosive factory.

Keywords: communications, conflicts, critique, Cultural Revolution, frustrations, manual labor, nepotism, politically correct, political problems, violence

[TN: The below translation comes from a written recollection penned by Fu. This narrative contains descriptions of assault and allusions to violence that may be disturbing.]

[…] They were still building the factory, and workshops were all temporary buildings, with huge distances between them. The furthest were half an hour's walk apart. It wasn't peaceful here; the remnants of the Cultural Revolution still simmered here and the conflicts between factions were still intense. Class struggle slogans [on megaphones] periodically transmitted tension above the factory. Nearly every day, there were new directions announced and new "class enemies" being singled out. We naturally served only as bystanders. No one wanted to be sucked into such dangerous whirlpools. […] Days seemed to pass very quickly in the mountains. There weren't really many things worth recording; life passed with regular routines every day, very dully and monotonously and certainly without any moving things. Whenever there was some kind of Campaign or some Important Document was read over the PA, the typically very silent mountains would gain a bit of energy. They'd put on a parade about something or other, stick up a few slogan posters, as if to remind people that we were not cut off from the world and that the tides of politics would reach even here. We "intellectuals" fresh from school weren't familiar with the situation in factories. We thought, well, at least we can learn something new (Image 8.3).

Image 8.3 A Worker-Peasant-Soldier Factory group saluting revolutionary martyrs, 1972

But there were too many campaigns. The blasts of class struggle shook the mountains. The military representative at the factories held the real power. One man named Hu was even more so a self-proclaimed "revolutionary faction" leader. If he called you out, you were bound for sure for the "cowshed" [TN: nickname for the often improvised holding cells where cadres and intellectuals were kept during the Cultural Revolution], but if he wanted to promote you, you'd rise three grades in an instant. His word was law and many innocent cadres and ordinary people received inhumane abuse at his hands. I saw with my own eyes a scene of a woman comrade kneeling on a board with nails in it, getting punched and kicked, with her hair all cut off. Anyone could go up and hit her a few times. Even more cruelly, some hooligans and violent thugs ferociously kicked her privates, causing her to take off her pants and kneel on the ground whenever she saw these people. She was tormented until she passed out and ended up disabled. I saw this kind of tragic scene and was distressed for a long time. I was filled with outrage at these thugs. Was this "revolution"? Was this "class struggle"? I really couldn't understand it. Were these thugs still human? Would they treat their mothers like this? What a crime, what a total loss of basic morals.

So I spent the first three years of my time in Jiangxi among the periodic gongs and drums of "class struggle"—the three years before I got married and started a family. I counted as one of the luckier ones. In 1968, just three months after arriving, I was sent by my workshop to Manchuria on business to ask them to expedite some equipment. [...] The mission was to rush along manufacturing equipment in Changchun, Fuxin, Yingkou, and Dalian, while traveling with an older comrade from the Supply Department. I was very careful and deferential to my senior comrade, thinking that I had to complete the job well. Fresh in the world, how could I have imagined the complexity of human relationships and how to be an upstanding person? On the trip, he left me behind on purpose in order to travel more freely.

Of course, I wasn't happy to be dropped—and as a student who'd been through the "exchange of revolutionary experiences" [TN: paid travel for Red Guards and students during the initial years of the Cultural Revolution], I wouldn't be scared off by something like this. So I directly contacted the factory about the remaining business and managed to complete the job anyway. But who knew that action would get on the wrong side of a bunch of gentlemen who decided I was insubordinate and arrogant? So I got into trouble. I really couldn't make sense of it. So just putting my all into the work wasn't enough? I also had to consider these personal relationships? [...] I think if I'd been a little cleverer then, maybe I'd have a new promotion. I see now that they were testing me. But I didn't take the hint, so I didn't have that nice luck, so back I came to pounding the iron!

The workshop officially began production in late 1969. We were responsible for machine operations for forging parts [...] the team members were us few students, a few older master workers, and then discharged soldiers. We did the dirtiest and most tiring work in the factory. Because people who had "problems" were sent here for reeducation, people humorously called it the "reform-by-labor area."

* * *

葛鼎学 Ge Dingxue, male, worker at a Small Third Front steelworks.

Keywords: communications, conflicts, critique, Cultural Revolution, entertainment, frustrations, marriage, men vs. women, politically correct, post-Mao

[Because it was so boring], when it came to fights and such, it was really easy to set something off. It was just the beginning of "Reform and Opening" then; you couldn't even play mahjong and you couldn't listen to Teresa Teng's music. We brought a semiconductor ourselves in there—there was actually a radio signal in there. I remember back then you weren't allowed to listen to Voice of America. We kids back then were pretty good, pretty rule-abiding. TVs came along later. After I had my son I'd take him to go watch TV. [...] The environment was truly mind-numbingly tedious, with nothing to do. You weren't supposed to play mahjong so people who wanted to play did it in secret. Cards, you were allowed to play "Winner." Drinking, they couldn't control us, life was just too boring. What to do about the lack of entertainment? The factory worried about this problem and they took the fact of "over-age," unmarried young men as a work project to resolve. If they didn't resolve it there'd be no way for stability. We didn't know that the Eight-Five Steelworks was going to come back to Shanghai. If we'd known, I figure they wouldn't have worked on this.

* * *

瞿惠相 Qu Huixiang, male, worker, cadre, and educator at a Small Third Front machinery factory.

Keywords: communications, conflicts, critique, Cultural Revolution, frustrations, nostalgia, politically correct, political problems, political training, travel and transportation, veterans, weapons

When I graduated junior high in 1965, they happened to be looking for [military] pilots, but at the last test my eyesight didn't pass grade, so I was cut. Then the East China Confidential Bureau in Shanghai hired me to train in confidential translation. After working for a while beginning in August 1966, Party Central issued a document in December 1967 that eliminated our unit and asked the provinces, cities, and military regions to make work arrangements for all of us confidential staff. There weren't that many of us in Shanghai. [...] In the interim, the city also thought of having us go to the Public Security Bureau, but ultimately, they decided to have the head of the Organization Department of the city Revolutionary Committee, Yao Baogen, be responsible for our work arrangements.

During that Cultural Revolution era, things were very chaotic. So in the end we were on Point Island [TN: an island in the Huangpu River downstream from downtown Shanghai with government and military installations] doing nothing but studying politics and Chairman Mao's latest directives. The East Sea Fleet oversaw our work unit during the Cultural Revolution. The rebel factions had gotten rid of all the veteran cadres, so they needed to find people to take charge. Then they saw that we had good political backgrounds, were young, and were pretty good all around, so they had us go guard the "cowsheds" [TN: nickname for the often improvised holding cells where cadres and intellectuals were kept during the Cultural Revolution].

I was watching over a hero of the Menglianggu campaign [TN: a major 1947 victory for CCP forces during its civil war with the Nationalists], Company Commander Pang Hongjiang. The rebels had locked him up, so I was responsible for guarding him. But really, we didn't do much guarding. I was polite as could be to him. If he wanted cigarettes, I'd go buy them for him. If he wanted to play some chess, I played with him. He was a very tough man. He'd be like, I've gone to the battlefield, why would I be afraid of these rebel factions? Late in the Cultural Revolution he was rehabilitated, and after being liberated, was restored to his leadership positions.

We wrote endless petition letters to the city to ask for them to arrange work as soon as possible for us, but the city Revolutionary Committee Organization Department chief Yao also got sent down to a May Seventh cadre school for labor, so nobody was looking after us. They pushed us over to the Labor Bureau for assignments. We were originally under the Organization Department and were assigned as cadres, but under the Labor Bureau we were assigned as if we were workers. They saw that we were pretty good all around, and the Small Third Front needed people, so they decided to send us there.

We were supposed to be settled like cadres, but now we were being handled like workers. So, two opinions appeared among us. Some of us thought that the Labor Bureau were treating us like ordinary workers and weren't treating us by the spirit of the Central directive that said, "appropriate arrangements," so some of us resolutely requested new assignments from the Bureau. Another group thought we were probably not going to be able to stay in Shanghai, and if we didn't go to the Small Third Front, then we could very well be sent to the Big Third Front. Thinking that the Small Third Front was at least a little closer, they agreed with the Bureau's assignments. The Bureau saw we had two sets of thinking and did thought work on us, saying, no, the superiors have decided, you must go. So it was without choice that we went down to the Small Third Front.

On January 30, 1970, after the Party Central's *Notice on striking counterrevolutionary destructive activities*, the "One Strike-Three Anti" campaign was launched nationwide (striking counterrevolutionaries; anti-graft, theft, and embezzlement; anti-profiteering, extravagance, and waste; anti-bureaucratism). [...] Our factory set up a factory-wide campaign office and I was transferred there to write reports. Someone at the time said that the big storerooms were an archetype of extravagance and waste, and a worker wrote a "big-character" poster criticizing the factory leadership for it. With the deepening of the campaign, the factory also exposed some problems among some workers. They became the living targets of the campaign and were sent around to the workshops for round after round of criticisms.

[...] In October that year, the factory had a Party rectification; by early November, Party members began "struggling against private interests and criticizing revisionism," undergoing a "self-revolution." January 6, 1971, the factory's first wilderness camping field training began. Seventy-five workers set off first thing in the morning, shouting slogans like "training well our feet, to hand imperialists, revisionists, and counterrevolutionaries defeat," "be determined, don't fear sacrifice, achieve victory," and singing the "Three Disciplines and Eight Attentions" [TN: a list of disciplinary items for the PLA based on a wartime directive to the Red Army] at the tops of their lungs. They got to the village that afternoon and had a "recalling bitterness, thinking of sweetness" meal [TN: politically ritualized meal of low-value items like rough taro and corn buns or wild vegetables] while watching the village ladies dance the loyalty dance [TN: a Cultural Revolution choreographic fixture].

They slept that night on hay spread on the ground, ten people to a room. Some got a terrible night's rest from being bitten by fleas and were covered with red and purple blotches. They got back to the factory on January 20, after two weeks' training. People said gravely that "we've tanned our skin and reddened our hearts."

Based on the Americans' 88.9 mm M20 Super Bazooka, our nation duplicated the "Model 51" 90 mm rocket launcher. Production began in 1951 and mainly equipped the People's Volunteer Army [in Korea], launching anti-tank rockets. [...] After the "Resist U.S. Aggression, Aid Korea" conflict [TN: the official PRC name for the Korean War], these weapons were behind the times and Chinese troops began to look to the Soviets' weaponry. [...] In early 1960, after the Soviets' new RPG-7 anti-tank grenade launchers were successfully created, China got a sample and reverse-engineered it. This grenade launcher, which also had a 40 mm barrel, we called the New 40 grenade launcher [TN: also known as the Type 69 RPG].

August 1964, they did a demonstration of the New 40 that was still in R&D to the chiefs of the Central Military Commission, and General He Long said, "this little gadget can shoot tanks from 300 meters away, we should be shouting 'hip hip hooray.'" Sino–Soviet relations were worsening then, and the Soviets hadn't shared their technology with us, so the R&D work for the New 40s was progressing slowly. After the incident on Zhenbao Island [TN: also known as Damansky Island, the site of a seven-month undeclared border conflict between Beijing and Moscow in 1969], production for the New 40s was fast-tracked. As soon as we got the assignment, we began to develop it. Back then everyone at the factory took the Party's priorities to be their own and the Party's directions to be theirs. We were united as one, with revolution plus determination, and worked unconditionally. There were some good equipment in the factory then but not enough. We had to make our own, so we designed and built some of our own clamps. We didn't have ready-made equipment or blueprints.

Technicians and workers ate and slept all together in the workshops, working around the clock on the attack together. To have the New 40s ready as soon as possible, the entire factory was put on 12-hour shifts from 6 a.m. to 6 p.m. Many workers put nation over household and worked themselves to the bone, day and night. The frontline workers were like this but so were the logistics and support staff. Their MO was "everything for the frontliners." So they brought warm food and warm hearts to deliver meals to the workshops.

The factory's transport department wouldn't be beat—when the frontliners needed vehicles, they were on call, absolutely resolved not to be holding things up. Factory driver Fei Shimin had an early and midday shift, and sometimes worked through the night shift too, forgetting all about his own needs. Once his small truck used for delivering to workshops broke down and he couldn't deliver a truckload of half-assembled products from the No. 1 Workshop to No. 3 (general assembly), so, in order not to cause a delay, he took a fire-extinguishing sack, loaded the half-assembled New 40s onto his own shoulders and jogged the two kilometers between the workshops.

The New 40s' regulator ring and body tubing needed argon arc welding, but Shanghai didn't provide much argon to us. In urgency, the drivers drove all day to Shanghai, loaded the argon, and immediately drove it back. Because the road surfaces were bad, they couldn't go fast and arrived only the next morning, working an exhausting, continuous 24 hours. At the most pressing period of producing the New 40s, a giant banner with the slogan "develop the new product, strike against imperialism, revisionism, and counterrevolutionaries" was hung in the No. 1 workshop and the entire factory threw itself into production for the 56 days it took from commissioning the launchers to the first finished product. On December 15, '68, the New 40 grenade launcher successfully sent off its first shot.

[...] June 25, 1969. A big "Liberation" brand truck with a canvas tent above its bed departed from our factory carrying the New 40s. First, we'd gotten an introduction letter from the Shanghai Garrison. Three of our gunners from the testing range went along, plus a cadre supervisor from the workshop and technicians, altogether six or seven people. June is the rainy season and it happened to be raining heavily that day. We were almost at Jingdezhen [TN: a city famous since the imperial era for its ceramics] when we hit a flash flood. Soon the water had passed the driver's seat. We were stranded with no villages nearby and still a long way from Jingdezhen, but there was no way to keep driving, so we had to shut it down and just await our chances. The day was pretty cold, and we younger folks went ahead and jumped into the water. The engine was still warm, so we huddled near it trying to keep warm.

Around evening, a rescue team from Jingdezhen saw our truck there and approached in a small boat with torches to pick us up and had us stay overnight in a kiln; they sent militiamen to guard the truck. Our bedding, carried on the truck, had been soaked, so we dragged them to this kiln in Jingdezhen and dried them off there. We managed to pass the night in that kiln. After the flood receded a little, we continued toward Hunan. We hadn't gotten to Yichun yet when, due to rain and a slippery road, the truck's front tire slipped into a rice paddy. With the truck leaning sideways and the tire slipping, no matter how hard we pushed or pulled, the truck was stuck. The only way to move was to put something under the tire, but the ground there was soft and there wasn't so much as a rock nearby; what to do?

Someone yelled, "there's a grave up ahead!" By this point no one was afraid of anything, so we dashed over and moved some bricks and stones from the tomb mound and put them under the tire. It took over two hours for us to free the truck and get back on the road; by the time we arrived in Yichun, it was past two in the morning, and we were starving. We knocked at the first little eatery we saw, but the owner was so afraid that we were rebel faction Red Guards, "beat, smash, loot" types, that he wouldn't open up. Finally, after we spoke to him, he welcomed us in and made us some noodles with donkey meat. We got going again after 5 a.m. and arrived at the No. 282 Factory on June 28th.

We all took our places at the national testing range just past 8 a.m. on July 7. Anxiously but carefully, we made all the preparations for testing the New 40 grenade launchers. Various leaders, experts, and the chiefs of the Wuhan Military Region as well as Commander Kong of the PLA Artillery [TN: Kong Jizhou, posted to the Southwest Military Region, whose son married Mao Zedong's daughter] all arrived. Hua Guofeng [TN: later the successor to Mao], who was serving as the chair of the Hunan Revolutionary Committee, came in person to supervise the tests despite many demands on his time. Over 30 work units—the Nos. 197, 317, 3302, 9383 Factories, the Beijing Scientific Instrumentation Factory, the Shanghai No. 5 Steelworks also among them—came to witness the tests. The first shot of the New 40s went off past 9 a.m., with balance, armor-piercing power, and velocity all within the "pass" range. Immediately the range was filled with cheers of "Long Live Chairman Mao!" and "Long live the Chinese Communist Party!"

The armor-piercing ability of the New 40 was very strong. At a 45-degree angle it could pierce a steel plate 160 to 180 [mm] thick, so clearly it wouldn't have a problem against the Soviet T62 tanks. After some more test rounds, Deputy Commander Kong said very happily, "Very good, go back and hurry to production." [...] Chief of Staff Luo Ruiqing also said, "Rush to production and deliver them to the front lines."

So we returned to the factory and began rush production; our first batch of New 40s got sent immediately to our warriors on Zhenbao Island, demonstrating their power in the fight.

* * *

沈嘉麒 Shen Jiaqi, male, People's Navy veteran and Party cadre on the Rear Base.

Keywords: communications, conflicts, critique, Cultural Revolution, frustrations, politically correct, political problems

When I arrived on the Rear Base, I was first working on the Political Work Unit Propaganda Team. In late April 1973, Dai Liqing, who'd risen through the ranks by being a rebel, came to take up the post of Rear Base deputy Party Secretary. The Party Committee decided to set up an office for the "Criticize Lin Biao and Criticize Confucius" campaign, with people drawn from the Party Committee office, the propaganda team, the workers' union, the Youth League committee, and other political work departments.

One afternoon in February 1974, the head of the propaganda team notified me that deputy Secretary Dai wanted to talk to me, so he took me to Dai's third-floor dorm housing and, while we walked, told me, "The Party committee wants to tap you to work in the 'Criticize Lin Biao and Criticize Confucius' campaign office. After you get there, do a good job. This is a badge of the trust the committee has in you." We got to Dai's place and saw that he was shaving. He saw us and said, "sit, sit." The team leader introduced me. Dai kept shaving and said to me, "Oh, you're Shen Jiaqi? Welcome, you need to do your best. Whatever the leadership arranges, you've got to do well. Be a bit freer in your mindset, learn to intuit what the leadership intends. The campaign office is a small team, but we'll be doing big things, taking charge of big things. This is the committee's trust of you all, so you all need to do well." After about five or six minutes, we left. From February 11, I joined the campaign office.

Dai Liqing would often give speeches to us during the "Criticize Lin Biao and Criticize Confucius" campaign about things like "the Cultural Revolution hasn't yet swept enough through the Rear Base," or "there are places in the Rear Base that the broom can't reach," stuff like that. The night of February 15, 1974, I was in contact with the Electronics and Instrumentation Company campaign office, talking about the campaign's kickoff with them. The Zunyi Factory had a Party branch committee member and another branch committee member from the same factory's No.3 workshop who each put up a "big-character poster," the main contents of which were exposing the factory Party branch secretary's lifestyle corruption issues and also some of the deficits and problems in his work. The morning of February 18, during a work meeting for the campaign office, each comrade reported the situation at various work units according to their assignments. That day, Dai Liqing and Han Kexin (the Rear

Base Party Committee Secretary and bureau chief at the time) heard my report. After I told them about the Zunyi Factory, Dai shouted, "Great! Write up this situation immediately into a report for various Party organizations on the Rear Base."

So Dai also raised key points about how the report was supposed to be written. (1) The Party Secretary's errors were grave: he neglected the main issues politically and neglected class struggle; he didn't study the works of Marx, Lenin, or Chairman Mao; (2) his will was severely degenerate and complacent; (3) his morals were corrupt and depraved; he played around with women. So according to their tone, I also added information about the campaign kickoff at the Zunyi factory and drafted a report. That appeared later on in the No. 21 *Situation Report* for 1974. After that went out, because the situation was poorly understood, it diverged from reality. Cadres and the masses at the Electronics and Instrumentation Company and the Zunyi Factory were very put out; they thought the report was wrong and asked the Rear Base Party committee to retract it and reduce its impact. I heard this and was very nervous, so I reported this immediately to the head of the "Criticize Lin Biao and Criticize Confucius" campaign office. Dai heard my report and said, "getting a reaction with a report is a good thing, what are you afraid of!" And I heard that and was reassured.

On March 28, the Rear Base Party Committee held the "Again criticizing the 'suppress the self, restore ritual propriety' meeting" at the Unite Factory, launching the "Criticize Lin Biao and Criticize Confucius" campaign on the Rear Base. The Unite Factory produced torpedoes, land mines, and hand grenades. When these items were successfully manufactured and after they'd passed an inspection meeting, the Party Secretary of the factory had invited some relevant people to have a small banquet. The Production Team leader of the Rear Base was also invited. But after finishing his meal, the team leader came back and reported that the Unite Factory secretary was doing excessive wining and dining and was so subjective, prideful, and etcetera. After Dai Liqing heard this, he sent out a team to investigate at the factory. After the team returned, they wrote up a report saying that the Unite Factory was enacting complete capitalist restoration. After Dai saw that, he sent this report with this conclusion up to Wang Hongwen [TN: one of the so-called "Gang of Four," important figures during the Cultural Revolution; Wang was second Vice-Chairman of the Central Committee at this time] in Beijing, and reported it to Ma Tianshui of the Shanghai Party Committee.

Dai said then that he was going to make the Unite Factory a negative model of the "total capitalist restoration" going on in the Rear Base Area.

After Ma Tianshui saw this, he said at this point no work unit has been raised as an example of "total capitalist restoration," and he didn't really commit to Dai's intention to make an example out of the Unite Factory. But Ma also dared not reject it directly. All he said was "the higher-ups are talking about placing Chairman Mao's revolutionary line in the ruling position, not talking about total restoration." Actually, he was disagreeing with Dai. But when Dai came back to the Rear Base, at a meeting of the standing committee of the Rear Base Party Committee, he said Comrade Ma Tianshui of the Shanghai committee had approved the plan to make the Unite Factory an example of "total capitalist restoration" for critique. So the Party Committee decided to hold that "Again criticizing the 'suppress the self, restore ritual propriety' meeting" at the Unite Factory, and also decided that the various heads of all the Rear Base work units would be in attendance; all of them would be brought there to participate in the criticism meeting. Plus, they'd use the Rear Base's telecommunications system to broadcast the meeting live to every unit. Han Kexin was upset at how Dai Liqing was handling things, so much so that he had a developed an acute heart condition and had to be hospitalized.

To monopolize political power in the Rear Base, Dai Liqing wanted to push out Han and others. Dai happened to get a notice to attend a meeting in Shanghai and thought he'd take the chance to bring along Han, who was at the Ruijin Hospital in the Rear Base. In order to trick Han into going to Shanghai, Dai and others held a discussion in the campaign office. In the end they decided to have the campaign office draft a "telephone record" and write in it that Ma Tianshui himself had called and asked Han to go to Shanghai for the meeting. They worried that Han wouldn't believe it, so Dai himself wrote up the "record" of Ma's "call." They decided that the next morning, they'd rush to the Ruijin Hospital and drag Han from his sickbed to Shanghai.

I rode along with them to the hospital. Dai then showed his "telephone record" to Han. After Han looked at it, he asked me, "Little Shen, did this happen?" I knew it was fake, but it was very hard for me to say anything, so I demurred, "I didn't answer the phone, I'm not sure!" Then I immediately left the hospital room and paced in circles in the hallway. I saw Dai and the driver and others forcibly putting clothes on Han. Han had realized Dai's intentions and threw his arms around a pillar in the room, refusing to leave, shouting "I won't go, I won't go!" Dai, however, ignored his cries and half-dragged, half-shoved Han into the car. In the end, Han had a relapse of his heart condition on the way and Dai could only put him in the Gutian Hospital.

So there was nothing for it. Dai Liqing had to be the MC and give the speech at the "Again criticizing the 'suppress the self, restore ritual propriety' meeting" at the Unite Factory. Once he got back that night, Dai cursed Han as an old slippery weasel. After that meeting, this surge of an evil wave to fully usurp the Party's power had risen and could no longer be suppressed. But this wasn't in line with the Gang of Four's goal to "stir trouble around the country but keep Shanghai peaceful." So Dai was rebuked by them. He tried to clean up his act, using the execution of Party Central's Document Number 12.

On the morning of May 22, Dai came into the campaign office and gave us a spiel. He wanted us to summarize and review the immediately prior experience of the campaign, and to remember to embody the spirit of policy, to protect Shanghai, and to protect key interests within the city. Basically, we had to think of ways to stabilize the Small Third Front. Then on the afternoon of May 24, he came again to the office to tell us that, in order to carry out the spirit of the municipal committee's directives, the committee was going to hold a radio meeting. He asked us to write up what he had said two days earlier as a draft that he could read out as a report during the meeting. After discussion, I was tasked with writing this draft. I composed a draft around three main points that Dai had made on the 22nd: first, recognition of the great significance of the "Criticize Lin Biao and Criticize Confucius" campaign, our current campaign efforts, and what we should do when the nation was defending Shanghai and Shanghai's priority areas. Because this speech affirmed the meeting at the Unite Factory and again trumpeted rebellion and struggle in the Rear Base, there were people who raised concerns with it during the [Rear Base] standing committee's discussion of it. But Dai had an ally on the Party committee who knew that he wouldn't ever take that criticism, because they were his own words. Dai slapped the table and said he'd never change the draft; it was set. So one member of the Rear Base Party committee standing committee read it aloud during the Radiance Factory radio conference on June 1.

After that conference, the cadres and masses of the Radiance Factory were very angry about what they'd heard. They raised strong protests and even walked late into the night to the Rear Base headquarters wanting to debate matters with the Party committee and duke it out with Dai Liqing.

* * *

王根富 *Wang Genfu, male, PLA veteran and Small Third Front military representative.*

Keywords: conflicts, critique, Cultural Revolution, frustrations, living conditions, politically correct, political problems, veterans, water and irrigation, weapons

In the early days of the CultRev, the Small Third Front was something of a mess. Shanghai organized a batch of military representatives to go to southern Anhui to do military oversight [of the factories]. At first there were only ten-odd of us, like the deputy department chief Zhang Kekuan of the Shanghai Garrison Logistics Support Department. Then, a lot of military cadres went in succession. I went to Anhui in June 1969 with Sun Ziyu, deputy political commissar of the Shanghai Garrison. "Military representative" had two meanings: one, a management and coordination role overseeing various administration and management affairs. Two, doing the quality control and receiving for military-industrial products. The quality control and receiving representative was affiliated with the Nanjing Military Region. These representatives were posted at the factories. For us [managerial representatives], some were also posted to the factories. Some military representatives even joined the factory revolutionary committees and such at that time.

A lot of people wanted to rebel in the early days of the CultRev and wanted to go back to Shanghai. Some of the leadership in factories couldn't even look after themselves. Without sending the PLA in, who'd listen to you? If you're a "capitalist roader," how could anybody listen to you? Military cadres went in there in uniform and were relatively better able to manage things. Under these conditions, the military control committees were formed.

Why did they send me to the Rear Base? That's a long story. In the early CultRev they wanted to rebel; the Red Guards were "exchanging revolutionary experiences" [TN: free traveling throughout the country by Red Guards and youth in the early Cultural Revolution], and this affected the troops. Most of the cadres in the three main branches went to Beijing to do study classes but I didn't go. I stayed behind in the department and kept working. Each department had one or two people. Why'd they leave me? Supposedly at the time the Shanghai Garrison was reviewing each of our dossiers and saw I'd been born poor, spent time herding cows, was a poor and lower-middle peasant, and I hadn't done anything that stuck out during the rebelling.

So, I stayed behind in the offices. There was a lot of stuff to look after, weapons and armaments and such. I was just one of the two people left at the Military Equipment department. The others were at the study classes for more than two years, because they had to wait to be reviewed in person by Chairman Mao—they couldn't bear to come back before being reviewed. After a couple of years, they came back, and just then the southern Anhui Small Third Front military control committee needed staff. They'd all just come back from Beijing so they couldn't be sent out, so they sent me. I couldn't refuse to go. That would've been impossible. A lot of military cadres were in this situation; if they told you to go you couldn't say no. At the time it was rotations, typically two or three years before a switch. In the chaotic situation of those days, this had a certain stabilizing effect.

All the personnel who went over had to go through a political review—based on the political angle of the time and professional standards. All of them were reviewed. The cadres were mostly good and so were the workers [...] but the political background and context didn't exclude the possibility of some old work units in Shanghai pushing out these comrades. They put it nicely then, "good troops, good horses, good weapons," but there were some cadres whose work abilities weren't very strong. Our military cadres were overall very good, but some cadres of course had some personal life problems, especially when it came to sexual relationships. Though there weren't very many incidents, the impact was very large. Then the young people, the workers, they were overall good. A lot of them were fresh secondary school graduates.

[...] I went in 1969. When we got there, it was called the 812 Command Center. The Rear Base was set up later, with a leadership cadre. We went to the command center, and there were representatives in the factories too. Later we organized a lot of military cadres to go into each factory. Basically, each had one to three military representatives. Some went into the factory revolutionary committees, meaning they had leadership roles. I'd go to these factories several times a year. Sometimes it was to check up on the conditions, sometimes it was to coordinate production. For example, if the cannon-making plant didn't have steel and they weren't making any there, then you had to coordinate.

I was in south Anhui for a couple of years, then Shanghai formed a Defense Industry Office, so I was transferred there in the Small Third Front department, mainly overseeing the production of conventional weapons. The Fifth Ministry of Machine-Building [TN: which controlled manufactures of artillery and tank equipment] would send down an order to Shanghai, and then to each military factory. The Rear Base was set up then, so production was organized through them. Because it was a planned economy then, especially with military goods, they gave you a certain amount and you fulfilled just that. These products had to be received by someone. Apart from relaying the orders down, you also had to ensure the supply of raw materials. For example, for the 57 mm shells, at first the cartridges were made with copper and copper was very expensive. Then they switched to steel. Military representatives received the finished goods.

From 1969 to 1971, I inspected and studied at each of the Small Third Front factories. First was picking a location. You had to pick a location against a mountain, like a chair—hills on three sides and with a lower piece of land in the middle. Not necessarily like that, either; there were a lot of different shapes. Another was to communicate with each factory and to relay it to Shanghai if there was something that couldn't be resolved locally. When I first got there, Xu Guoguang was the point person there. I was pretty young then, so I'd just follow the senior comrades around all day getting to know how things worked. It was after I transferred to the Shanghai Defense Industry Office that I really began to participate in managing production work. After I left [Anhui], the other representatives also gradually returned, not all at once but in batches. When one group returned, they organized another group to go out. Then, after Mao Zedong passed away, these folks all basically transferred [out].

[…] Contacting the Small Third Front factories for production, that was my job alone. They came to the military representative for coordinating technical and planning issues. If the representative and the factory had a conflict—like when receiving the products, the rep might say this doesn't pass inspection, it has problems—you had to handle it with them, you had to figure out how to resolve the situation, with a lot of coordinating and negotiations. If the steelworks couldn't bring out their products, then the guns couldn't be cast, then I'd have to get in touch with the gun factory, negotiate, so every year I had to go out there a lot of times.

[…] Mainly we went to the Rear Base to do thought work. At the time each factory had two factions. Though I'd gotten to the command center, the offices just had a few people in them and not a lot to do, so they sent me to the Cooperation Factory to resolve the factional disputes there. This factory's factions, one came from the electric welder factory [in Shanghai] and the other was from the blower factory. They'd formed these two factions and, in order to catch up on the production of military goods, the factory had to be stabilized.

At the time they were still building the Cooperation Factory; it hadn't gone into production yet. One of the rebel leaders from the electric welders' group went to the Cooperation Factory and made a real mess of the welder plant there. One night he suddenly gathered a group of people and stuck up "big-character posters" all over the factory saying "down with" the other faction. Everybody had been pretty settled before, but with him doing this it took a turn. I was the military representative sent to the factory from the command center, so I took him aside to talk to him. I said, "I heard it was you who did this?" He said, "It was me, so what?" I said, "Why do you want to 'down with' them?" He said that they had this and that problem. I said, "What if they also called you out for such-and-such and put up 'big-character posters' about you, saying 'down with' you?" There was an old cadre named Song; he was the number one over there. When the factory fell into a mess, he had to do his work with both factions. He said, "If you start fighting, how are we going to make our military goods? How are we gonna follow Chairman Mao's call? How're we gonna prepare for fighting a war?"

The factional fighting in the Rear Base wasn't as bad as in Shanghai, because things were relatively spread apart in the Rear Base, not like Shanghai; [others were] just one phone call away or one hour's drive away. The mountains of southern Anhui meant that forces couldn't gather, plus transportation was inconvenient. Also, a lot of the people who went were students. In the schools there were two factions, but once in the factories they were spread out and not as ferocious as in Shanghai proper. There were still factions, sure, but mainly from older factories. For instance, when several [Shanghai-based] factories co-built one [in Anhui], like the Cooperation Factory had some people from the electrical welder factory and some from the blower factory, then you had some people who thought that oh, your factory's people were taking charge, or were taking up a lot of the positions, and we were losing out. Over this, the factions had a lot of differences. A lot of factories had this kind of struggle—it was a fight for power.

Because it was the mountains, a lot of things in day-to-day life weren't planned out beforehand. With today's scientific thinking, building a lot of those factories in a mountainous area was not appropriate. For example, some factories used a very large amount of water. There's a saying, however tall the mountains, the waters run just as deep. Daily living and manufacturing all needed water. Guichi had an Advance Machinery factory. The number two hydrology team of the time was helping them find water.

They had an article on the front page of *Liberation Daily* [TN: Shanghai's main daily newspaper] (without naming which factory, because it was secret at the time). The headline of that piece I still remember clearly. The main headline was "Using Mao Zedong Thought to Find Water," with three subheadings, "From Waterless to Watered," "From Poor Water to Rich Water," "From Dead Water to Flowing Water." [...] They'd dug a well and found fish. They called it the "snake and fish pit." This pit was quite deep, and after they inspected it, they found water, so the first subheading was from waterless to watered. They found there was very little water in the pit but after drawing some out they found more, and then they found fish, so it was "dead" water becoming living water. But not really; it was just a hole in the ground. Because the factory demand was extremely heavy, several hundred metric tons of water a day, it took just a few days for them to exhaust this "snake and fish pit." They had no water again; it wasn't a question of poor water becoming rich water.

[...] Around 1979, the Rear Base had shifted to civilian production and made some light-industry goods like clocks and watches and electric fans, actually a pretty big variety of products. At the time it was still part of the National Defense Industry Office, so we managed it. We were mostly responsible for closures and wrapping-up work. In reality, after that, around 1984, the military-industrial goods orders were few and far between too. After all those years of putting out military goods without a war, we had all these things that have an expiration date—some you can't use after 20 years, so when the time came it'd just be useless. After manufacturing orders decreased, some of the Rear Base factories that were mainly making military goods didn't have anything to produce anymore, so they stopped; they didn't have anything to do. Without anything to do, the consideration was whether to keep [workers] at their posts, and paying wages became a problem. When workers didn't have work, all sorts of things would crop up, a lot more fights and bickering. Under these conditions, the State Council had a meeting to reorganize the Third Front, to turn military output toward civilian products. Our Shanghai Small Third Front formed a natural system within Anhui. According to the central directives, the city studied the issue repeatedly and had all of the Shanghai Small Third Front prepare for completely returning [to the city] and handing over all the equipment to Anhui.

To transfer the property involved handling the military goods appropriately. For example, there were a lot of munitions that hadn't yet been inspected and received by the Army, and some products hadn't been completed. These things couldn't be left back there. Some were complete but needed to be assembled through the Fifth Ministry of Machine-Building, like some fuses that had to be put on ordnance. But our Small Third Front had stopped making that ordnance and they were doing it elsewhere, so we took those fuses to match them up to those people's rounds. To do that matching we couldn't go ourselves, either, we had to go through the Fifth Ministry of Machine-Building. Some things had to be declared junked, some were given to militias for training, and some were destroyed. You can't just leave military supplies in a work unit.

Apart from doing the demolition work, I also picked spots in Shanghai for the Small Third Front staff. When they got back, they needed living arrangements. Shanghai built a million square meters of residences to arrange for the about 70 or 80,000 staff and family members who were returning. These were all in the suburbs of the time, which are now downtown, like Pudong and Minhang. Some factories just rejoined some of the existing factories; some workers got transferred to various work units. Only a minority of work units built up their own new factories. One, the Sea Defense Machinery Factory, did packaging equipment, so there was one that went independent. Some factories united; some merged and built a secondary plant. Just this kind of merging cost all together eight or nine hundred million [*yuan*].

* * *

王金忠 Wang Jinzhong, male, Anhui native and farmer who worked in a Small Third Front chemical factory.

Keywords: conflicts, critique, Cultural Revolution, frustrations, intellectuals, politically correct, political problems, violence

[...] Having fun in Shanghai costs money, getting here and there all costs money, so I just walk about nearby, go walk about on Nanjing Road, then go to Changhai Hospital to get a check-up. When I went to Changhai in 1984, it was still the Air Force Hospital, the No. 2 Medic Hospital. I heard Bao Kegang was there. His dad's named Bao Guohua, I think?

[...] Bao Guohua got struggled [during the Cultural Revolution] in the Red Star Factory. But he didn't get it too much. The one who got struggled was named Chen, Chen Guifa, and another one, a university student from Shanghai University, named Luo, Luo Xinhai. That person had a lot of learning. University students from back then, from before 1969, they were impressive. It didn't take long after Luo's getting transferred to this Small Third Front factory for him to get struggled against, and they kept struggling him without a break. Chen Guifa was a carpenter. I thought, what did he have to be struggled for? But back then, if you wanted to say what was right and what was wrong, you couldn't get clear on it. It was the "Gang of Four" back then. And Chairman Mao was getting on in years then; he couldn't manage so many things. When it came to the Rear Base Small Third Front, what people like Chen A'da and Dai Liqing said counted.

We had someone here, Xie Fugen, who was dissatisfied with the factory's leadership; there was also Yuan Genquan, who was the Party Secretary for the factory. So then Yuan was transferred to Dongzhi County's Small Third Front management department. The Party Secretary of the division then was named Jiang Fuhai [...] When Jiang Fuhai died, Yuan was transferred over as the Party Secretary. As for Xie Fugen, he wasn't the factory Party Secretary, but what he said counted. Even the Party Secretary was a bit afraid of him, otherwise he'd get you. He had a gang of henchmen; you could say he "wore the same trousers" as Chen Ada and Dai Liqing in Shanghai, so he struggled Chen Guifa so hard!

Another one was named Wang Minghzhen; he [Xie] struggled Wang until he became neurotic. Later when Wang went out, he wouldn't take the main road but only walk beside it. Back then the Small Third Front factory hadn't really been finished yet, so some roads were just through desolate countryside. Wang was struggled to become so afraid that he wouldn't dare walk on the main roads and would only walk in the grass.

* * *

许汝钟 Xu Ruzhong, male, deputy head and chief engineer of a Small Third Front steelworks.

Keywords: conflicts, Cultural Revolution, frustrations, politically correct, political problems, veterans

For a while during the CultRev we weren't doing the "Grand Alliance" [TN: a directive from Party Central in 1968 urging the cessation of armed factional conflicts]. The old rebel faction leaders didn't want to cooperate and wanted to grab power again. But at the Eight-Five Steelworks they didn't have much power because there were a lot of veteran cadres there plus military representatives, and everything was under the Nanjing Military Region. Deputy Commander Rao Zijian was the point person in charge; he oversaw the military-industrial complexes in the Region. The Shanghai Garrison sent a representative to be stationed in the factory and we called him Colonel Dong. There were three of them posted regularly with us overseeing logistics and overseeing organizational affairs, all of them in the factory offices. If rebel factions tried to start something, they'd go do thought work with the rebels.

* * *

杨秀珍 Yang Xiuzhen, female, worker and cadre for a Small Third Front steelworks.

Keywords: conflicts, crime, critique, Cultural Revolution, family, frustrations, Party members, political problems, violence

Back then there was an older worker; he was brought into the mountains by his kids, brought to work on the pier. He had two sons [...] the younger one was a bit more honest; he was on the mechanical team. The older one was real bad, like the kids today [...] The son was surnamed Yang, Yang Dongcai. Well, then he up and started a family dispute, and with fights we [cadres] would have to go do our reconciliation work. Why, he'd taken a knife like a hooligan, in Shanghai. That's why his parents took him into the hills, because he'd been sent to education-by-labor in Shanghai already. If they let him [go] into the mountains, his parents would be nearby. But his parents couldn't manage him. Then after he and his younger brother got in a fight, he took out a knife and was going to stab his own brother. So then we had to go work on him.

I was still young then. I was the Party branch deputy secretary. Gang fights. They were all young guys too. So I'd go to their homes to work on them. I really put a lot into it. I got there in the daytime. [...] It was real scary. For one, what was I going to say to him? I said, well, you two are brothers, aren't you? If you have something going on, you should talk it out with a better attitude. Nowadays I talk common sense, and back then I was trying to do my work this way, too. Then I got scared to death; he said, if you keep talking I'll kill you first. How do you deal with that? I said, if you kill someone, you're going to ruin your entire life too.

[Interviewer: Did you go alone?] Yes. I thought it wouldn't be dangerous, that he wouldn't—you know, right? I didn't think he'd be so wild. I still remember it. Yeah, I feel scared thinking back on it. He didn't care at all. He'd already stabbed his own little brother with a knife, his brother's hand.

* * *

张燕芳 Zhang Yanfang, female, teacher turned production statistics and logistics cadre at a steel mill.

Keywords: conflicts, critique, Cultural Revolution, family, frustrations, living conditions, Party members, political correctness, political problems, violence

[…] Oh, it was so hard. So then in '86 when they called me in [to Anhui] for the [Party] Rectification, well, honestly, I really understood [why they resented me], emotionally. For instance, if you're looking at all those people in Anhui, which one of them didn't have some difficulty back home in Shanghai? Like if my parents had health issues, my kid had no one to look after them, or if I had something going on. Right? So when the [Party] organization took care of me to let me come to Shanghai, after that, I knew that the conflict was going to be really big between me [and others]. Because everyone had difficulties, why take care of you, Zhang Yanfang, but not others, you know? I often heard this kind of talk in there [in Anhui] too…

[…] But I was willing [to go back for Rectification]. Why? The organization had already stood up to a lot of pressure to get me here; I had to know my place, right? […] This Rectification and whatnot at that time, the tone wasn't far off from the Cultural Revolution; if there's nothing [wrong,] they'd still find a little something. So they had a meeting, they were holding a big meeting. Well, guess what? Someone said of me, Zhang Yanfang had a few people in her family die; so what, why does she have to spend all that time in Shanghai?

My temper is really weird. I said, yes, I had someone die in my family; I had difficulties and I asked the organization to take care of me. If everyone in Shanghai died, I wouldn't have any difficulties anymore. Before anyone died in my family, I said, I'd always been holding fast in Anhui. The Lunar New Year, holidays, I never requested leaves. You all went. The two old ones [my parents], they really cared for me, and I should care for them too. Every holiday and New Year, you all went, I took up the slack here. No one being here at all wouldn't do, right?

I never went back during holidays. But our two leaders were very good; they really thought of me. After half a year, it was "Little Zhang, go back to Shanghai to see how the two old folks are." So only in Logistics was there this kind of opportunity. There weren't opportunities like this in the workshops. Who'd think of you? Unless you—husband and wife were both in there and you had no visitation leaves, only once every four years. Or you'd request a leave, right? They said about me, "What's so good about Zhang Yanfang?" That was the same person who used to talk about how good I was. How they talked! "Whoa, this female comrade's good, she can talk, she can write, she can do it all." I said I wasn't that great. And then he said of me that I didn't learn anything except wining and dining from old Shandong (meaning our old Chi [TN: one of her superiors]). My wining and dining wasn't even on the public dollar. When people came, I had no choice, I could only pull out my wallet to treat them, and I didn't drink or smoke.

[...] But at that time, at the Party Rectification meeting, [they] pointed at my nose saying—at the meeting, they said, how many people died [in Shanghai] that she needed to go for so long? I didn't care, I get it, you had difficulties too. What "good" was I, following old Chi, wining and dining? Damn, I thought I really was going to spit blood [I was so angry]. When I was good, they said I could talk, write, do things, could whatever, I was good without a fault. I mean, when I was good I wasn't that good, when I was bad I wasn't that bad, wouldn't you say so? I ignored him. A week later I left; if you didn't give me my salary, then don't give it, I have no choice, I can't settle [my family affairs in] Shanghai, right? Hard, oh, so hard. Just talking about it, really, my tears are about to come out.

[...] Well, we did this matchmaking, you all should know about this already. Shi Zhiding did more of them [than me]; I later went to have my kid. Yeah, Shi Zhiding is a talkative one, and he is one of those conscientious workers. He and I were colleagues on the Youth League Committee. When I went there in '73, he was already there. He was all along the deputy secretary; he had this knot in his heart, what was it? Well, he had a relative in Hong Kong. Mm-hmm, bad political background; it was this problem that caused him to never get promoted [laughs]. Once I got to the office and saw that he hadn't slept all night, I asked him what he was up to; he said he was writing a letter. He told me to drop it off at the post office. I asked "Who are you mailing it to?" He was writing it to Chairman Mao [about his situation], [laughs]; he was just that determined.

* * *

赵连洪 Zhao Lianhong, male, security department cadre in a Small Third Front company.

Keywords: conflicts, crime, Cultural Revolution, frustrations, nostalgia, Party members, policing, political problems, post-Mao, rural vs. urban, travel and transportation, violence

I was in the security department, which isn't the same thing as it is today. It was that all our household registrations got moved over [to Jingde, Anhui], but we weren't under the management of the local government, we were under Shanghai. [...] Being posted there, we should've been under the command of the local Public Security Bureau and police, but they didn't oversee us. We were under the Shanghai Public Security Bureau's Financial Security Department directly, so we were in a unique situation. Our company security department [...] had about five, six people, so relatively big. We had 19 factories attached to us, just under 20,000 people in all. Why so many? Because we didn't just oversee internal security to the factories, but also solved cases; all of that was us. Really this was different from a usual security department that doesn't take responsibility at all for solving cases. If there was something, they'd just call their superiors to take care of it. But we were too far away from Shanghai, so we also handled criminal cases and public order cases. Another thing was the property security of the various factories, so we oversaw their internal security offices too. So, our responsibility at that time was pretty broad, you could say.

Say you had a case; we'd have to go to the scene to take evidence, make observations, and then investigate. After we'd done all this according to the requirements of the public security system, we'd take that material to the Shanghai Municipal Public Security Bureau Financial Security Department; they had a few comrades there who were our point people, who were specially in charge of the Rear Base. And so, once we'd finished doing our paperwork, we'd take it up there to have them review it. If they reviewed and thought the conditions called for an arrest, they'd come with us to arrest or detain the person. I remember several big actions. The slogan at the time was "hard and fast." After Deng Xiaoping took over, there were some pretty bad security problems all around the country. In '82, '83, it was the "strike hard" campaign against crime. So we'd do these internal sweeps, all the personnel in all the work units, and if there were targets, we'd go gather information. When we reported to the city bureau and their people got here, [we'd move quickly.] Once we got six or seven people in a single night. So these were all the miscreants and baddies in various work units, or people with histories, people whose criminal actions we had good solid proof of. Basically we would investigate, and as soon as we got permission from upstairs we'd gather forces to take care of it.

We spent a lot of brainpower on the internal security stuff too. We made a lot of detailed rules and regulations and policies and such, including assessments for the factory security officers, including a lot of different requirements, all of them based on real-world experience. So we had several evaluations a year and a year-end review too. We did a lot of work on the internal side. Our Security Department was rated a "Top Unit" twice by the Shanghai Public Security Bureau Financial Security system. […] Now we think about it and it's almost silly. Like, for example, going after "lifestyle" issues [TN: usually referring to extramarital affairs or other disallowed sexual relationships]. Back then that was a case, and a very serious offense. Us at the company security department, we were in charge of the factory-level leadership. People in each factory were managed by their factory security offices. So once something like that happened, we'd be all very tense in the department.

One year, the day after Lunar New Year, I was eating at home when a phone call came saying "there's been a problem," so I left right away. No, I wasn't in Shanghai, I was right next to the company [on the Rear Base]. I didn't come back [to the city]; at first we all basically spent the holiday there. There were a lot of these types of situations then. For instance, there was this Sun-Facing Machinery Factory right next to us. They had a really urgent case. Today after dinner, they'd send someone and a car from their factory to us and we'd all drive to Shanghai, then we'd report in to the city bureau first thing next morning. The roads were hard to drive then, nothing like the highways today. It'd feel like your bones were cracking from all that bumping and jostling. After driving all night to report to the city bureau, they'd inspect the materials and make a decision by the afternoon. The chief of the Economic Protection Department then was Chief Ouyang. After his approval, they'd send people back down with us, and we'd be back on the Rear Base by the next morning. Transportation wasn't convenient and well-developed like now. Doing a roundtrip to Shanghai was exhausting. And a lot of cases were pretty urgent.

I remember our company pretty much had five or six of us working this security department, doing back-office work, field operations, case specialists, just like a mini police HQ. At first, we really did take the security job very seriously. The company Party committee and administration also took us very seriously, because we were key to them doing a good job, too.

[…] Because we were headquartered in Jingde, the farthest work unit was actually about 300 kilometers from us, in Qimen. We had two or three factories there, and factories along the way at the base of Huangshan. So our geographic range was pretty big; the distances were pretty big. Our relationships with the factory leadership was especially good, too. Why?

Because they wanted us to support their work. Being on call for them—they felt like we were really helping them. So we had great relationships with our subsidiary work units, and we were actually very close with the Rear Base Security Department too. They were also under the city's Public Security Bureau. When there were major directives we'd both get notifications to study them. Usually, crime and security issues and such, they didn't oversee those. We reported directly to the city bureau. [… The Rear Base Security Department was mostly responsible for studying the spirit of major directives and documents], and they were more focused on internal security, like the property and assets of each factory, and fire and theft prevention and such. Theoretically they were our superior work unit, but actually we reported directly to the city. They didn't ask for us to report to them and have them report on up to the city. […] Especially for criminal cases, we had relatively a lot of contact with the city. […]

I wasn't at the Instrumentation and Electronics Company at first; that wasn't until after I got married and transferred. Originally, I was at that Unite Machinery Factory, No. 825, under the Ningguo Machinery and Electronics Company. What were we doing at first when we got there? Well, we were all young and tough and strong, just past 20 after all. So the things we were making, that was right during the war in Vietnam. Actually, a lot of our products were for China to support them, otherwise they would never have been able to beat the Americans. So, what were we building? Well, like those timed explosives; you carried it on your back with two safety straps in front. After you pulled [the fuse], you aimed for the steel plate on those naval ships, and it'd stick on there itself from a meter and a half away. That's what we made, these things thick as a face basin, like a life preserver, with two kinds of explosives, yellow and black…the force from mixing them was especially strong. These explosives were crystalline, and you'd heat them to a certain temperature so they liquified, then you'd pour them, very simple—a copper pot, a wooden stirrer because you couldn't use a metal one; if you struck a spark it'd explode. The temperatures inside there on a hot day were at least 120 or 140 Fahrenheit, because you had to keep it at that level so it didn't easily crystalize again.

[…] I did [the explosives work] for about a month. We arrived just when they were organizing the Youth League. Our military factory there was a county-level Youth League unit and had over 2000 people, 70 or 80 % young people. So we participated in setting up the League. […] Then they formed League Committees and Party Committees, so I became League secretary and a Party committee member. Party committees then weren't like they are now. Each of us committee members was practically like a deputy factory head, even more powerful than them. There was a slogan back then, after all: "the Party manages everything." That was how it was then. I joined the Party in December '72; I started working in '70, you know. So that's how I joined the leadership team of the factory. But then they took down the "Gang of Four." This history you know about. Dai Liqing was a sidekick of Wang Hongwen [TN: a leading figure during the Cultural Revolution and a member of the "Gang of Four"]. Our factory's work output was quite good, so Dai found a weak point of ours and held a meeting for the whole Rear Base, live, at our factory. And then me and a classmate were brought into the Party committee as "model youth" representatives. After Dai held that meeting, and then the Gang of Four went down, the stuff he promoted became seen as negative and we got put under a ton of pressure.

[…] We had the whole set [of tools] for criminal detective work, like fingerprint dusting kits, cameras, tools to secure footprints, we had them all. Basically, the stuff for criminal detection by police, we had them. And we used them too. Like when a report came up that someone broke into our house. I experienced this case myself. One subsidiary factory, I think it was the Worker-Peasant Factory. Our lives were very boring then, but we had a film projection team in the company […] they'd drive to each factory in turn to show movies. All the workers had gone to watch—watching movies was like in the villages; every single person would go. And then one worker took advantage of the movie showing to run to one house, of course one they'd scouted it out beforehand, and stole all the gold jewelry in the house. Not a farmer's house, another worker's. There was no one home. There was quite a bit of it, about half a pound of jewelry. Yes, this was a very well-off worker.

So it was two people [who committed the burglary]. This counted as a fairly big case at the time, and the [city] public security bureau was also alerted, but the detective work was on us; we had to go do the fieldwork. After investigations from multiple angles, the guy's accomplice was found out when we were investigating something else. That's how you solved cases, half-tricking, half-scaring them. In the end the accomplice confessed to doing this. He said so-and-so had me be the lookout while he broke in to get the stuff. We asked this guy where the stuff was, but he said he didn't know; he really hadn't seen it. To solve the case, we needed hard proof. So after more investigating, we confirmed it was the two of them, so ultimately they got arrested on criminal charges. After that, the accomplice stuck to what he'd told us. But we knew this had been done by that other guy, but he—the main offender—he was seasoned, and he had experience putting off detectives. [...] So he was locked up in the pre-trial detention area for the Shanghai Procuratorate. They had this detention center, I think it was near Sinan Road then. We'd gone there many times. We asked him where the stolen goods were, and he just refused to tell us. The accomplice only knew that after he'd taken the jewelry, he'd put it in a gap in the prefabricated boards in his place.

The principal offender was locked up for half a year there without us being able to break through. It was just that we hadn't found the stolen goods; we didn't have direct evidence, so the court wouldn't take him. After a lot of hard work, we coordinated with a guy at the pre-trial center named Hou and got the principal offender to confess. He told us how the goods had been hidden in that gap in the wall, and how then he'd taken the jewelry. After his confession we asked where the stuff was, and he said after he'd gotten to Shisi, he'd sold it to some mafia people there. Shisi in Fujian was the worst spot in our New China for smuggling, and the earliest to really take off. Not only was smuggling really bad there, it was also generally chaotic. Later, Mr. Hou from the Public Security Bureau and I went there to take evidence. Through the offender's descriptions, with details like which wall, which turn to make all laid out, we invited the local police to come along and really found the guy [who'd bought the stolen goods]. After we found him, he also confessed: such a date in such a month, this person with these characteristics fenced off this gold on him. He'd melted the gold and made it into jewelry and so on. So we had our complete chain of evidence, and then they got sentenced. You see, the pre-trial center even took us in the security department with them to find evidence, so thinking back, we were really a bit like a public security bureau. ...And 24/7, too, and on holidays, Lunar New Year or the day after, if something came up, we'd have to go right away. [...]

Both offenders in the gold theft case were workers from the Worker-Peasant Factory—one the main culprit and one the accomplice, and yes, we slowly sorted out the main offender first. We did a lot of interviews with the masses and just screened them, figured out who wasn't present at the crime scene. Both workers were male, young guys, single. The main guy was really slick. He was only just 24, 25, but he had a lot of experience in society, lot of contact with some badly behaved characters. We at the

Instrumentation and Electronics Company didn't run study classes for people who had various errors and offenses, I think, but maybe others did. I don't think we did.

Militia, well, at first when we first got assigned there, there was a lot put into the militias. I was even a militia captain. But then they cooled off, little by little. I don't really remember exactly when, but it was like they stopped really bringing up this militia thing. In '74 and '75, the militia was still doing a lot of drilling, and going to climb mountains and things like that. But then later, I don't know, this concept just faded. I guess it had to do with the breakup of the "Gang of Four." And then the consciousness of fighting a war wasn't so powerful like it had been when Old Mao had been around. Because militia were about being battle-ready, and for catching spies.

[…] Dai Liqing, this guy, well I don't know what it was. I saw him a couple years ago, and it was totally different […] I felt like he used to be really capable, really good at giving speeches. Those speeches he gave at meetings, they really motivated people; the call to arms was really strong. I personally experienced this. When we had this live meeting, they called it the March 28th Meeting, for the entire Rear Base at the Unite Factory, when he was pushing the reorganizing of our Unite Factory leadership and talking about experiences of the "Criticize Lin Biao and Confucius" campaign, I felt like this person was really competent.

Our Party Secretary at the time was sent from above; he was named Huang Biao. Later Huang became the entire Rear Base Party Secretary. When Huang was around, it was five of us, me, one of my classmates, Huang Biao, one Organization Department chief, and one production chief. I should say these people were all pretty stand-up people. Huang Biao was my boss. Cadres back then did things differently from today. Huang said, Little Zhao, you hurry up to the town. The little town there…had a produce market. Huang Biao said, Little Zhao, hurry there to buy some garlic and dried tofu, Dai Liqing's coming tonight. Back then you wouldn't just order the canteen to make you a fancy table of food, no way. So we went to buy some food ourselves. After Dai got there, we just lit a kerosene stove in the single men's dorms and fried it all up as hospitality for our big boss.

And Dai gave you the impression of being unpretentious, too. He was a real chatterbox. And, when I was still a student, during the CultRev, there was an organization in Shanghai called the "Attack with Words,

Defend with Force," and they came to handle the problems at our school, because we also had rebel and conservative factions, what they called the conservative faction. And they were very impolite to my female classmates, even picking them up and throwing them onto the ground. This caused all of us to be resentful, and some students started a hunger strike. Four in a row, like this, they organized these protest marches to the higher-ups in the school.

At the time, Wang Hongwen was the head of the Shanghai Revolutionary Committee, and then he took the Committee's Arts and Culture Team to our school and gathered all of us, teachers and students, for a 15-minute speech. He got rid of all our resentment and hatred and everything. He was a real talker, really good at grabbing your heart. No matter what we say about him now, he was really an able person; he settled us all down in a quarter-hour speech, and we peacefully and willingly stopped what we were doing.

Dai Liqing was Wang Hongwen's sidekick, his follower. I thought he was very eloquent, very capable. But then I saw him a couple years back, and I felt like he'd changed. He wanted me to join some pyramid scheme, I was really turned off. How'd he end up like this? At the time all these people were very capable, you don't even know. Cao Wenjing, the deputy Party Secretary later on for the Rear Base, she'd come out of the National No. 17 Cotton Mill and the rest of them too. Wang Hongwen was from the security department in that factory, too. So Chairman Mao said he'd been a soldier and had farmed like a peasant. [...] and there was also Zhang Fengying, Li Li, and Fang Qing, they were all from the No. 17 Mill and came to the Rear Base. Zhang Fengying was with us in the Instrumentation and Electronics Company; Cao went straight to the Rear Base headquarters. [...] They must've had good relationships with Dai Liqing, sure, but they were promoted not without reason. These people all still had ability, and pretty good abilities too. This was all a matter of [partisan] lines. If you're talking about people in the past versus now, you really have to do some comparing.

They say that Wang Hongwen didn't get along at all with his own younger brother, because he wouldn't do favors and things the brother asked, like when he asked to join the PLA and Wang didn't let him. A matter of political lines. In terms of not being corrupt, none of the bureaucrats and cadres today can compare [to them].

[...] Yes, we at the Instrumentation and Electronics Company did go after gambling. Not directly by us, but the subsidiary factories. They'd confiscate mahjong [sets]. You had a hard time if you played mahjong back then. The factories would confiscate them and hand them over to the company security department. All those were bamboo on one side [of the tiles] and ivory on the other. Have you seen that type of old mahjong tile? They were very valuable, with bamboo stuck into the ivory. I think you'd treat them like antiques and relics today, very precious things. When they confiscated them and gathered them, so what did we do? We put them in the big furnace room and burned them all.

Let me tell ya, there wasn't really much gambling then, not like now—it's so easy to nab gamblers now. Back then there was basically none, just occasionally once or twice in the factory, and we the company didn't even have to show our faces. They confiscated them and got rid of them in the factory. After confiscating, they also gave out warnings [demerits]. I feel like, you know, Chairman Mao was really amazing, really great. How few people could be like him in the entire world? Look, no prostitutes. Maybe hard to say in the 50s, but in the 60s and 70s, prostitution, you didn't even hear about it. This kind of serious, common thing among the people, this was how tough they were back then. None in the open, none even underground. No gambling, there really was no gambling, I'm not just saying it. And drugs—very, very little of that. You wouldn't dare say none at all, like on the frontiers and borders, oh yeah, there was some. But normally there was very, very little. This was really an accomplishment. What other country on earth managed this?

Before Liberation [in 1949] these [people doing these things] were really powerful, but then they were all sent to reform-by-labor after, and had jobs and families, and they were all fixed up. And then there really wasn't any left. And more importantly, all the ordinary folks formed a shared view of values for all these things. Once there wasn't the oxygen for it, it just became very rare. As for feelings between men and women, well, all members of the animal kingdom have that. But without that—that hidden part from before Liberation.

* * *

Further Reading

On Social Order and Law Enforcement

Børge Bakken ed., *Crime, Punishment, and Policing in China*. Lanham, MD: Rowman and Littlefield, 2005.

Jerome A. Cohen, *The Criminal Process in the People's Republic of China, 1949–1963: An Introduction*. Cambridge, MA: Harvard University Press, 1968.

Michael Dutton, *Policing Chinese Politics: A History*. Durham, NC: Duke University Press, 2005.

László Ladány, *Law and Legality in China: The Testament of a China-Watcher*. Hirst, London, 1992.

Daniel Leese and Puck Engman eds., *Victims, Perpetrators, and the Role of Law in Maoist China: A Case-Study Approach*. Berlin: Walter de Gruyter GmbH, 2018.

Stanley B. Lubman, *Bird in a Cage: Legal Reform in China After Mao*. Stanford: Stanford University Press, 1999.

Klaus Mühlhahn, *Criminal Justice in China: A History*. Cambridge, MA: Harvard University Press, 2009, Ch. 4, "Reform through Labour: The Communist State," 175–283.

James D. Seymour and Richard Anderson, *New Ghosts, Old Ghosts: Prisons and Labor Reform Camps in China*. Armonk, NY: M.E. Sharpe, 1998.

Julia Strauss, "Paternalist Terror: The Campaign to Suppress Counterrevolutionaries and Regime Consolidation in the People's Republic of China, 1950–1953." *Comparative Studies in Society and History* 44:1(2002), 80–105.

Julia Strauss, "Morality, Coercion and State Building by Campaign in the Early PRC: Regime Consolidation and After, 1949–1956." *The China Quarterly* 188(2006), 891–912.

Harold M. Tanner, "Policing, Punishment, and the Individual: Criminal Justice in China." *Journal of the American Bar Foundation* 20:1 (1995), 277–303.

Harold M. Tanner, *Strike Hard! Anti-Crime Campaigns and Chinese Criminal Justice, 1979–1985*. Ithaca, NY: Cornell University East Asia Program, 1999.

Hongda Harry Wu, *Laogai—The Chinese Gulag*. Ted Slingerland trans. Boulder: Westview Press, 1992.

On the Military and Militias

Dennis J. Blasko, "Always Faithful: The PLA from 1949 to 1989," in David A. Graff and Robin Higham eds., *A Military History of China*. Lexington: University Press of Kentucky, 2012. 249–266.

Neil J. Diamant, "Hollow Glory: The Politics of Rights and Identity Among PRC Veterans in the 1950s," in Neil J. Diamant, Stanley B. Lubman, and Kevin

O'Brien eds., *Engaging the Law in China: State, Society, and Possibilities for Justice*. Stanford: Stanford University Press, 2005. 131–160.

Xiaobing Li, *A History of the Modern Chinese Army*. Lexington, KY: University of Kentucky Press, 2007.

Elizabeth J. Perry, *Patrolling the Revolution: Worker Militias, Citizenship, and the Modern Chinese State*. Lanham, MD: Rowman & Littlefield, 2006.

Mark A. Ryan, David M. Finkelstein, and Michael A. McDevitt eds., *Chinese Warfighting: The PLA Experience Since 1949*. Armonk, NY: M. E. Sharpe, 2003.

David Shambaugh, "The Soldier and the State in China: The Political Work System in the People's Liberation Army." *The China Quarterly* 127 (1991), 527–568.

David Shambaugh, "Building the Party-State in China, 1949–1965: Bringing the Soldier Back In," in Timothy Cheek and Tony Saich eds., *New Perspectives on State Socialism in China*. Armonk, NY: M.E. Sharpe, 1997. 125–150.

William Wei, "Power Grows Out of the Barrel of a Gun: Mao and Red Army," in David A. Graff and Robin Higham eds., *A Military History of China*. Lexington: University Press of Kentucky, 2012. 229–248.

CHAPTER 9

Shanghainese vs. Locals

Translator's Note

As the previous chapters have made clear, from the 1960s into the 1980s, the possibilities and statuses of people with urban household registrations differed, often greatly, from those registered in China's expansive countryside. Even in the remote, hilly areas of Anhui and Jiangxi, Shanghainese Small Third Fronters (who had the additional privileges attached to being state-owned enterprise employees) lived literally apart from those in the surrounding villages. On the level of dress, culture, and even language, there were considerable divides between farmers in the rugged areas of Anhui and Jiangxi and the Shanghainese they now hosted. This section of narratives reflects the complexities of the relationships that nonetheless formed between Third Fronters and their rural neighbors.

Some rural residents saw Third Front factories as a boon and their Shanghainese staff as friendly and generous, building close interpersonal connections with them. Some married Small Third Fronters and created families with them. But even in accounts of positive relationships, occasional glimpses of conflict can be detected. Shanghainese workers and their family members, though steeped in the culture of sacrifice and loyalty to their superiors' assignments, also evidenced a strong desire to return to the big city. This desire became especially obvious as the Third Front campaign drew to a close. With the end of the Small Third Front, the nature

Y. Xu, Y. Y. Wang, *Everyday Lives in China's Cold War Military-Industrial Complex*, Palgrave Studies in Oral History,
https://doi.org/10.1007/978-3-030-99688-8_9

of the relationship between locals and Shanghainese changed again. While military equipment could not be left behind, much of the factory infrastructure built up laboriously over the previous years and already transitioning to the production of civilian goods was transferred by Shanghai's municipal authorities to local governments at the behest of the State Council in Beijing. This, however, was not a smooth process in execution, as the city and the province sparred over valuable property and equipment.

Workers were supposed to be transferred back to Shanghai, China's most cosmopolitan city, with all of its perquisites and advantages for the people lucky enough to be registered as residents there. Many sought to return as soon as they could, using "back door" connections if they had them, as shown by some of the accounts below. But who was going to count as Shanghainese? For the cadres overseeing the transition, the very human complexities of Shanghainese–local relations made executing the State Council's order to end the Big and Small Third Fronts and turn over their assets to provincial and local control much more difficult.

Questions for Discussion

1. What kinds of conflicts between themselves and locals do Shanghainese narrators remember? Do these conflicts differ from those remembered by local villagers?
2. What are some reasons given by narrators for the mood and nature of the relationship between Shanghainese and locals? Did that mood seem to change over time during the Third Front years?
3. Divides between rural and urban places and people in the PRC are usually regarded by scholars as sharp, whether economic, political, or cultural. Do these testimonies reinforce or contradict that view?

* * *

毕文中 Bi Wenzhong, male, Anhui native, village cadre in Dongzhi County.

Keywords: camaraderie, electrification, manual labor, nostalgia, pay and benefits, post-Mao, rural vs. urban, travel and transportation, water and irrigation

We locals had really good impressions of the Shanghai workers. We felt like the Shanghai workers all came from a big city. Their clothes, the things they used, a lot of it we locals had never seen before, or had never used before. New things. Their technology was much more advanced than ours too. So without thinking about it, we'd all be learning from them, imitating their lifestyles and habits, imitating their clothes and presentation, imitating their way of working and such.

[...] When the Shanghainese came, they got along fairly well with us locals. When there was a problem, there'd be mediation meetings on both sides, we'd sit down and mediate and resolve it. If we had a difficulty and went to look for them, they'd help fix it. For example, during a drought, the rice paddies dried up and the river water too. Without water, paddies can't produce any rice. In that case, our village head went to talk to their factory head in person, and they turned on taps for the water pipes they'd run over from the Longjiang Water Plant and supported us in the fields by irrigating them. During the dry season, we folks had relatively inefficient ways of getting water, so they helped a lot. Then during the busy season, the factory would send groups of workers to the fields and help us plant or harvest.

I still remember in '79 that our village went to Tunxi, Anhui, to get a [power] transformer to get power, and the Third Front factory sent drivers and cars to help us bring it over. And, typically, if we needed to move something in the village, like government-requisitioned grain, bricks, cement—if the village went to ask them, they'd send trucks to help out. The Third Front factory would do this kind of favor a lot; I can't even remember the specifics.

Shanghainese take work pretty seriously, always operating by the factory rules, very solid and hardworking, never petty. The environment was relatively tough at that time, so they'd wear their dark blue work uniforms at work, then change to regular clothes after work, very rule-abiding. From their appearances and from the clothes that Shanghai people wore, they weren't so different from us village folks, except we talked different.

[...] Some Shanghainese went to nearby folks' homes to stay. We folks here were very supportive of the national Third Front initiative; we were all willing to board Shanghainese in our homes. Some stayed as long as a year or two, all the way until their factory buildings and dorms were ready. When the factory was going up, they were the designers and overseers. They did the fine work; we helped do some rough work. Anyway, there's no way they could bring a lot of temp workers down with them, so nearby production brigades, like villagers from Xincha, Laocha, and Hongcun, all went to help, [blasting] open the mountains, digging, all kinds of small

Image 9.1 Steep Cliff Optics Factory workers helping with local farm work, 1975, collection of Qiu Shanquan

tasks, some "coolie" work, tiring work. We did a lot of temp work, a lot of it for no pay. You could say that, for the Third Front initiative, we villagers also put in plenty of effort (Image 9.1).

[...] In my impression, quite a few Shanghainese came down here in the 70s, several thousand of them, then in the 80s they were gradually transferred away. I remember that a big group of Shanghainese came down, then they'd work in the factory and after work they'd go to the villagers' homes near the factory to visit. [...] There were exchanges [between the Shanghainese and villagers], but not too much. Sometimes they'd go to nearby villagers' houses to buy some veggies, some poultry, chat a little with the villagers, and such. This did happen. I often saw them strolling the streets after work. Some workers got along very well with the masses and would go to the masses' homes to visit.

* * *

卞建华 *Bian Jianhua, female, driver for the Rear Base militia headquarters.*

Keywords: conflicts, critique, family, food, frustrations, pay and benefits, politically correct, rural vs. urban, travel and transportation, violence

Sometimes relationships [between Shanghainese and locals] weren't very good. Because after they'd requisitioned land and taken in workers [whose land had been taken], some [local] people could come in [to the factory], but others couldn't, which caused some conflicts. Some physical fights too. Some people married locals, but then when the move [back to the cities] began, some people couldn't necessarily come back, and that triggered some other problems, with some big consequences for their marriage situations.

Conflicts weren't many. The ratio of people who married locals wasn't high, but there were some. There were good ones and bad too. After all, there were still differences in lifestyle and habits, plus us young people, when we went over there, life out there was boring after all. You got up when the sky lightened, but at a certain point, there weren't lights [at night], you know. But then later on the development was pretty good. After your marriage, they'd allocate housing to you, very nice. And the food and such was pretty good.

I was getting a Shanghai salary. I was getting a little more than them, 39 bucks a month, with 2% bonus. A few percentage points at a time, it'd go up a little at a time, then finally it got to 41.70 or something. Prices were extremely low there. People there were really interesting. They never ate pig offal; they always threw it out. Roasted chestnuts only cost a few dozen cents a pound. [...] When I was in Jing county, when my daughter was still not so big, they had middle-sized shrimp, all live, very cheap, only a few dozen cents a pound. It was because the Shanghainese came that prices rose. But then as time passed, and everyone came to know one another, the locals were pretty good. That was how it was where I stayed; I don't really know about elsewhere.

We're still Shanghainese, but that's useless. How important that Shanghai household registration was back then! It wasn't moved over to the Rear Base Public Security Department because at the time the Department didn't exist. So we were just [registered] locally. But it wasn't the same; we weren't moved to the locality; we didn't belong to the locality. This registration was like a collective registration, a bigger one, managed as a whole. They couldn't possibly be given to the local police. They couldn't oversee all that. But you also couldn't move it away. We moved our registrations away [from Shanghai]; our consciousness was so high, we wouldn't ever—the key was that you would have to apply to transfer back, you couldn't just move back on your own. So like with me trying to resolve our long-distance marriage situation, if at the time we didn't have that [registration] in the city—[if it didn't] just so happen that cadres and such were all managed by [the Department], it also managed us, and the two sides matched up and we just happened to have this open slot, then we couldn't come [together]. The big move [back to the city] later was another issue. Kids' registration at the time was with the woman.

* * *

陈克智 Chen Kezhi, male, Anhui native, accountant and Party cadre in a Guichi village.

Keywords: conflicts, critique, frustrations, men vs. women, pay and benefits, post-Mao, rural vs. urban

There were also conflicts, but not many. Like when they [the Shanghainese] came down here, most of them were young people; their wives and kids were back in Shanghai. In terms of relations between men and women, then, it wasn't so great with the locals. Some of them, with our local girls—and the local married women, you know. And also, when they were first building the factories, those Shanghainese would live in us locals' houses, right? Well, some would live with us for a few years at a stretch. And so, as time went on, if their lifestyles weren't so proper, then you'd have conflicts! There was an impact, but it was a minority of people who did that kind of thing. People come in all ways. So they had conflicts with us, if even just a little! Not in anything else, mostly in this area [of sexual relationships].

[…] No, [the Shanghainese workers didn't stay]; they all went back. I heard that during the transfer period, the Shanghai side was willing to keep some master-workers behind to help us locals set up the factory, but the Anhui side didn't really want the Shanghainese, saying that their salaries were too expensive, so they didn't want them. Plus they were afraid that it wouldn't be easy to manage the Shanghainese. So they didn't have the Shanghainese stay. I feel like if we had a batch of Shanghainese in the factory, then I figure maybe the factory wouldn't have been likely to go under. I heard a Shanghainese master-worker say, "If Anhui wants us to stay and is willing to transfer our grain and oil [rations] over here, and your local [government] is willing to pay our salaries, we're willing to stay here until we retire." But then at the end, Anhui didn't request [them to stay], so they all withdrew. Those Shanghainese were really technically good at steelmaking skills like rolling and forging!

* * *

陈兰志 Chen Lanzhi, male, Anhui native, head of the Anhui Third Front office overseeing the handover of the Small Third Front to local control.

Keywords: conflicts, critique, finances, frustrations, living conditions, marriage, post-Mao, rural vs. urban

The background to Shanghai transferring the southern Anhui Small Third Front to Anhui was a document from the State Council. It announced that the liquid and fixed assets held by Shanghai in Anhui on the Small Third Front were all to be turned over to Anhui. On the basis of that document, we formed a Southern Anhui Small Third Front Transition Leadership Small Group Office.

I was formerly the chief engineer at the Anhui Provincial National Defense Industry Office. In 1985, they transferred me to the provincial economic committee office to handle the [Small Third Front] transition work. At the time we thought, with the people gone, receiving these things shouldn't be much of a problem. But actually there were a lot of things to look after. I think it was a total of 54 enterprises, including the Huangshan Tea and Forest Farm. That didn't end up being handed over; Shanghai kept it. At the time the point person for Shanghai was Li Xiaohang, the head of the economic committee. Another person was the deputy head of the economic committee, Li Chuanqing, who later got transferred to Beijing to head the National Administration of Quality Supervision. Our [provincial] economic committee and the national defense industry office merged. Before that I was the chief engineer for national defense but afterward, I went to the economic committee. Mainly I was to do the transition.

At first, we thought, oh, there's a State Council document, no problem, but there really were plenty of problems, because Shanghai had their practical issues and Anhui had ours. The practical issue for Shanghai was that they had 27,000 people in Anhui, and over 90% were going back. Our thinking back then was, well, it's been so many years, all those Shanghainese came to the mountains in Anhui—you see, I'd stayed for 15 years in the Dabie Mountains. I'd worked in the military industry too. Before the Cultural Revolution I taught at the Hefei University of Technology. After they handed over the electronics industry to Anhui, I did radio at school, so they transferred me to a radar factory under the National Defense Industry Office.

[…] The portion of the Small Third Front that had come from Shanghai [as opposed to being set up by Anhui province], they came up with a principle during the handover: the people who wanted to go back, of course it was understandable that they wanted to return, but after being away all those years, their old housing was gone, and the elders they had had at home were gone. Some had a brother or another relative, but they couldn't just live with their relatives back there. So we thought they'd have a very difficult time, going back. When they transferred all the property to Anhui, we thought, truly there's a problem here. These several tens of thousands going back, how was Shanghai going to arrange for all of this crowd of people? Plus the kids and the old folks, the family members?

So we also thought about the pragmatic conditions. After all, there were intermarriages between the locality and the Small Third Front enterprises after all these years. Some were Shanghainese guys marrying Anhui girls; some were girls who'd gone to the Front who'd married Anhui guys. And another thing, the Shanghainese hired locals after they got here. So in terms of management, Shanghainese and the locals were all bunched together. Theoretically the Anhui people were supposed to stay where they were. Shanghai's burden was already so heavy, how could they handle you if you went too? But then some had gotten married; what if they left and their daughters and their sons didn't go?

Later on our attitude toward Shanghai was like this: respect personal decisions. If they were willing to stay in Anhui, we'd do whatever we could to help them settle down well and treat them like our own family in arranging them posts in Anhui enterprises. If staying were difficult and they had elders at home, what to do? In the past they were able to go to Shanghai, but if they stayed they'd lose their connections with Shanghai. People with these challenges would go back to Shanghai. Some enterprises at that time had very few who stayed.

We called our approach the dynamic transfer. What did that mean? Well, some enterprises were very small, like the Seapeak Printing Factory in Jixi. They printed all the university entrance exam papers for the entire nation over there, back then. Two months before the exams, they shut entry to the factory, no mail, no telephone, it was a real ordeal. We did dynamic transition with this kind of factory. When the people had left, if we had apprentices trained by older master-workers, we'd have them fill in. If we didn't have the personnel, we'd stop operating. This Seapeak factory is still there today. But these situations were rare. Another was the small-scale machine tool factory in Yansi, in Huangshan. They also did a pretty good job, a lot of [their products] were for export. Just breaking off their [distribution] channels like that was a real shame, so we wanted to take over their export channels. But it wasn't so easy to take them over after they'd gone. Production, craftsmanship, equipment, all these things the comrades from Shanghai were very responsible about, keeping everything tidy and clean. I was very happy to see that, because I had a technical background, so you had to be very responsible for that. A lot of equipment was set up in temperature-controlled rooms. Nowadays this is common, but it wasn't easy at the time; it was very valuable and was the treasure of that factory.

[...] So we negotiated with the factory and with Shanghai. In the 80s export channels were very few, so we wanted to preserve these connections. Some of the core staff, you can for whatever reason transfer out, but leave some of the core staff to help us bridge the gap. We could pay very well. Wages were very low then, so they were very willing.

When they left, back then, a lot of them were in Minhang [District in Shanghai]; I went to see it, because after they left, we also went to check out their situations. So from the get-go, I was really sorry for them. They happily came out to the Third Front, and then ended up so sad when they went back; all of us felt bad for them. Some people went to be entrepreneurial and set up a new factory. Key personnel had to go, so there were a lot of problems, a lot of problems for every one of them. They had some emotional attachments from working there [in Anhui], so they were willing to stay to help with this effort.

Yes, some key technical people, they had to stay behind. The timeframe depended: some stayed for one year, some two, some remained and weren't willing to leave because it wasn't easy to re-establish yourself again. We went to see their factory; they were specializing in electric fans; they'd changed their business. This I was very clear on, because we were doing a transition from military to civilian [products], but turning a military factory to a civilian consumer one was very hard. When putting out a new product, there weren't many skilled personnel who could do civilian goods professionally. And communications weren't very smooth in the mountains, and the transportation lines were pretty long. Could we compete with cities making sewing machines? Our costs couldn't be pushed any lower. [...] In the past we didn't care much about overhead; the costs were pushed very low, so you made the things and you got 5 to 8% profits, as long as the quality was guaranteed. As time passed, under the planned economy, folks stopped using their heads, so suddenly going to civilian goods was tough.

[...] There were some conflicts locally during the transfer. Huang Biao from Shanghai, at the time he spoke up more for Shanghai, and I represented the Anhui provincial government, so it was easier for me to speak for them. I lived in the 1960s in Shanghai for a year and can understand Shanghainese and can speak some too. Huang Biao and the others would speak Putonghua [TN: Beijing-standardized Mandarin Chinese] with us, then he'd turn around and talk Shanghainese with their colleagues from Shanghai, but actually I was able to stand beside them and understand. I was relatively empathetic toward the Shanghai Third Front workers, no matter whether they were Shanghainese or from Anhui; they'd all gone into the mountain gullies to do their bit. The first year [of the Third Front campaigns], I went to be the factory head at the Lida Factory in the Dabie Mountains; that was a factory from the Fourth Ministry of Machine-Building [TN: overseeing electronics].

The military representative there at the time had made a mistake, so I took his place and headed up the factory for one year and seven months there. When I went they said, "Old Chen, this place you're at is really too great, beautiful mountains and water, so pretty." But you got sick of it after just a week. After a week it was just high mountains and rocks everywhere and climbing up hills whenever you went out. All the workers were technical secondary school grads from the Nanjing Radio Industrial School. That factory of ours was the Nanjing No. 726 factory, moved out there.

Because workers were glorious at the time, everyone wanted to be a worker. We were all young, what could we do? I was only 30-something then; over there you couldn't do this, you couldn't do that, so we played movies twice or three times a week. So I was sympathetic to them suddenly going back and doing this [civilian transition]; it was pretty hard. We were "good people, good horses, good weapons" back then, so that Chairman Mao could sleep well at night. These people were all elites, but they didn't get any special treatment. Still, we were very happy at the time to be doing the Third Front. My salary was even a little higher then because I'd come back from the Soviet Union; I was in the last batch to study in the USSR.

[...] After we went to the Third Front, if this gang of people didn't wholeheartedly support the Party's policies, none of them would want to live in this place. After they came, wherever they liked, they turned it into a factory. Our farmlands got turned into asphalt roads in two days. A lot of our [local] people were working in the factories, so when your factories went, what were our people supposed to do? Huang Biao said, "good people, good horses, good weapons" came to Anhui, and I said we'd also chosen good mountains, good water, and good land to give to you. They

Image 9.2 Color photograph of the handover ceremony of the Burning Plains Mold Factory to local control, 1987

also had a hard time. Our transition office was just to help look after and coordinate between the two sides so that the State Council document could be carried out. I probably did that for more than three years. When I got transferred to Huaibei City in late 1987 to be the first deputy mayor, things were about finishing up then (Image 9.2).

[...] It was impossible [for the Shanghainese] not to have conflicts with [local farmers], but they also couldn't be segregated because everyone relied on one another. The locality couldn't work without the factory either. They sold vegetables, eggs; they depended on the factory to get by. So when the factory left later, they couldn't do anything. They [the Shanghainese] said, if you don't let us take anything at all, how are we going to live back in Shanghai? This was reasonable too, and there were a lot of these problems.

Shanghai already had a lot of challenges themselves, and if they had too many people, we locals could help settle them. It was really tough to get a household registration in Shanghai back then. One Shanghainese guy had a few kids with an Anhui woman—back then the One-Child policy wasn't very strict yet—and his wife and kids were all in the factory. The guy said, I can't [stay], my old mother is at home [in Shanghai]; if I don't go back I can't take care of her. Finally we followed the most humane policy and had him go back. When he came he was alone and when he went back there were a bunch; it's not like he could just abandon his wife.

Some people didn't want to go; they had pretty good relations with the locals. And some thought, they got along pretty well with the locals and they'd be very happy staying behind, plus if they went back they'd have a hard time getting along with their sisters-in-law or whatnot. Their places in Shanghai were really small, and if they stayed [in Anhui], their apartments were real large; one person might get two rooms. All of their housing was Third Front housing; when they left, the people who stayed could get two apartments. All the people who stayed had pretty good living standards. Some did real well for themselves here and also had contact with Shanghai. Plenty of folks in Ningguo County are like this, running back and forth.

[…] Long Nian was the deputy head of the economic committee; he later served as deputy provincial governor. He knew a lot. He often came with me, the two of us, to look at things and think about how these factories could be used and rebuilt, if we should do dynamic transfer or if we could partially rebuild them. The original products we'd try to use as much as possible, otherwise, when the people left, the craftsmanship would go too. Some took that with them. I said you can take some of the equipment, but if you take the crafting, without the crafting accessories, that wouldn't work. […] To process a set of things, you need a lot of accessories, furniture, molds, and so forth. Without that you can't make the thing. […] In the end we went to talk to Shanghai, to Huang Biao, saying, "If you want the equipment, we can work on it and let you take some, but you can't take all the crafting and process flow stuff; if you take them, that doesn't help you either. You'll have those, but not the equipment, but we'll have the equipment, but not the tools and accessories.

Basically, when we negotiated with them, all those things we said, they also thought were reasonable. I said, what good would taking this away do you? You can't sell it to anybody; they want a full set. Sometimes they'd also cause trouble. You're not going to cooperate with me? I'll take the model drawings, the process flow charts, the assembly drawings. Components made without the blueprints were no good.

We in Anhui didn't propose they leave their equipment; that was from the State Council document. They said, Shanghai built Third Front factories in Anhui, but from the current situation, this production is no longer needed, so it's been decided to do an adjustment; all fixed and liquid assets will be transferred to the locality. Shanghai [came to negotiate] with us; Shanghai said, if we're going back, well then, aren't all our fixed assets going to waste? What're we going to do about that?

* * *

储瑛娣 Chu Yingdi, female, Party cadre at a precision optics factory.

Keywords: conflicts, critique, family, finances, frustrations, medical issues, men vs. women, politically correct, post-Mao, rural vs. urban, work assignments

Then, later, a lot of people were getting unsettled. Some people had challenges, so we tried to help them. During the Cultural Revolution, getting assigned was par for the course; every family had this kind of situation: two [kids] sent down to the countryside, so one was "helped out" and assigned to a mine. One family had just one kid; they had [financial] difficulties, so the kid was assigned to a mine. So then he went, and then the two elderly folks had nobody to look after them. Getting sick, having a kid, and there'd be nobody to take care of you. Some husbands and wives lived in separate places and both made a fuss to come back [to Shanghai]; they weren't content to stay. They were pretty strict back then; you can't just go into the Small Third Front or leave it when you wanted to. Special considerations [and exceptions] also had rules. If you didn't have the transfer quotas left [at your factory], you couldn't just [have someone] come in.

Later, the conflicts were really sharp. Every factory had to make a report, and after that the main union would sort through them. Single guys, you could go out [beyond the factory] to find a wife. If you got married, she could get transferred in. It was a pretty good deal for those [women]. Some were sent-down youth; some were working on farms. These people all ended up as Shanghainese. Some young people really had family challenges, and some had allergies and physical trouble, so when they got there [to the Small Third Front], they couldn't adapt, they'd run fevers as soon as they arrived. We let all these people go, back to the original factory [in the city].

By 1988, the entire Small Third Front was in the red, and the Big Third Front wasn't doing well either, it wasn't making it. Zhao Ziyang set up an investigative group that went all over the country, and they found that there'd even been losses to the state's initial investment. Plus, the devices that got made would all become obsolete when new weapons came out. So he decided to modify things. Whichever province or city had set them up, they'd carry the [factories] back with them. This news, other provinces and cities found out first about—every province and city had Small Third Front factories—so they all returned and all left. But Shanghai's population was large. If you didn't get to go home, then all those staff and workers on the Small Third Front would start a rebellion.

After the Anhui provincial governor found out [about the State Council decision], he immediately reported to the Council, saying, if the Shanghai Small Third Front was going back, leave their stuff for us to help us out, Anhui's poor and backward, after all. After that was sent up, Party Central called over the Shanghai folks. Wang Daohan was the mayor then; he was called over and then they said the Small Third Front was going through an adjustment, your people are going back, but you're going to leave all your things. Then Shanghai was just stunned. All those people are supposed to come back; we don't need all those people. And all those things, leaving them behind, not a cent in exchange. What to do?

So then everyone opened up their bags of tricks, and the leaders also looked the other way. We were going back anyway, so how to arrange this transitional period? Everyone was in a burning rush to go back. Like our factory, we had this one scheme. What was it? Well, there was a village with a roasting plant that made roasted sunflower seeds and the like in Minhang, in Xinzhuang [in the Shanghai suburbs]. Their factory space was very big, and rent was cheap, so we rented a set of rooms, and a pretty big courtyard, and we just put the equipment we secretly took back with us alongside our furniture there.

The leadership didn't know. Like I said, everyone and their bags of tricks. So we left and those poor hardworking drivers were driving day and night, two of them to a truck, driving around the clock. Then Anhui found out, what, you're taking the stuff back with you, the equipment too? So they tried to block us on the roads. What could we do, they were blocking us? Well, we took a detour. We went over the Tianma Mountains in Zhejiang and not on Anhui roads. So they were like, what happened to all those people and why aren't we seeing their trucks? Our Steep Cliff Factory borrowed the trucks from the Jinggangshan Factory. Jinggangshan Factory wasn't under our jurisdiction, so they couldn't block them. Jinggangshan borrowed our trucks, so they couldn't block those either. They couldn't block us, so they began suspecting that we were packing our equipment with the furniture. Our factory head's furniture ended up being blocked in transit in the rain, and got all soaked. We all wrote letters to the Party Central to tell on them.

Then they opened up the roads. They were told they couldn't violate personal property, so they stopped the roadblocks. After that, we shipped back a lot of stuff, a lot of raw materials that were hard to source, like copper, platinum, that kind of thing, all pretty pricey to buy and useless to [Anhui] if we left them behind; it's not like they knew what to do with them. How'd we do it? Well, at night. We'd put these big-ticket, valuable raw materials in the file cabinets at night, and we'd seal them up ourselves, stick the sealed-file tape on them. Next day, the locals would check and see that the sealed-file tape was all on there, nice and neat, and would leave us alone.

After we got [the materials] out, we made do in Shanghai. When the workers came back and didn't have housing in Shanghai, they'd rent, or they'd live in the countryside. After a couple years of sticking to this, our output was unaffected, and we could finish our assignments just fine. Some people stayed behind to pack up and move house and continued persisting in production. Some of the equipment they didn't turn over; they stayed there working. We were working in both places. Then when we got to the end of it they took over and we handed over, we gave it all to them, and we also changed jobs here too. But there wasn't anybody to take us in; if we started our own, we would have all those workers and just a little bit of factory space. So the city then had the original factories take us back.

* * *

桂胜莲 Gui Shenglian, female, Anhui native and worker at a Small Third Front steel mill.

Keywords: camaraderie, communications, nostalgia, rural vs. urban

The Shanghainese who came to our place here were good, pretty good. When they first came down, we were given rules about not calling them "ol' Shanghais." And they weren't to call us "country folks" either. We were all village people, 'course. The leaders wanted us to call each other "master-worker," you know. They didn't let us call each other "ol' Shanghai" or "ol' country folks." We were all supposed to be "master" so and so, to respect one another. It used to be that people would call Americans "ol' Yanks," right? So when the Shanghainese came down, we locals would call them "ol' Shanghais." But then the leaders wouldn't let us anymore. When we saw a male comrade we were supposed to say "master"; for an older female comrade it was "auntie." People were all very nice at the time.

* * *

洪明来 Hong Minglai, male, Anhui native, former branch secretary of a village production brigade near a Small Third Front munitions factory.

Keywords: camaraderie, consumer goods, food, frustrations, living conditions, nostalgia, rural vs. urban, travel and transportation, water and irrigation

When they started building, it was basically all built by Shanghainese themselves, and then a few workers from other parts who were contracted on. Us locals would also go do some small jobs, some little things in there. Because at first not many of us here did construction work, and the Shanghainese wanted quality buildings, so they were afraid we locals wouldn't make good ones and the quality wouldn't be up there. So we only did some prep work and helped out. The main parts of their buildings were built up by them. I remember it was under construction for several years, and then after it was done, they began production. At first when the Shanghainese came to our parts, it was very hard for them. I remember at first their trucks would be stuck because they'd run out of gas. It was me who went into the county [seat] to borrow some gas for them. Yeah, they paid me, public money. [...] When they were first moving [in building supplies], it was all their own trucks. We didn't have automobiles out here. It was all trucks. They had a driving team, called the 683 team; they specialized in transportation. Those trucks went round 'n' round in our parts all day. We all knew that.

[...] This Satellite Factory, when it officially began production, apart from coming out on their days off on Sundays, the workers couldn't usually just come out. Ordinary folks [out here] couldn't go into the factory. If you wanted to get in, you had to go to our production brigade [HQ] to get a permit. The factory gave three passes to the brigade, so usually only three could go in at a time. Specifically, it was the village head, the [Party] branch secretary, and the [brigade] secretary. That pass was called an "entry pass"; it was red. If we wanted to go in, you had to show the pass first thing at the guard office, otherwise the guard wouldn't let us go in. If we were going in, to do or get something, like a water pump, we'd go to the Supply and Marketing Department. If we were looking for a car or truck, we'd go to the Administrative Department. Their department head would go report to the factory head. Once the factory head approved, it was a done deal. Like when we were fixing up the Daying River, we borrowed a lot of stuff from their factory. But then after we used the stuff, a lot of it got used up. We didn't end up returning them. But they didn't say anything. They really supported us in agriculture!

I had a pretty good relationship with the factory head! We went a few times, but not that often. We had meals with the factory head and had a very good relationship. We'd go to them for things, and they'd come to us too, you know! Like I just said, we came up with ways to get them gasoline for their trucks, because they didn't know people around here, but we did. And then the last time they were making their explosives, they needed cotton lint, this kind of material, and I even specially went to Chizhou to order them several dozen tons. I went to the regional committee to get the approval. For water, for drought prevention, they had tools to get water and they brought them out as much as they could for us to use.

[…] Yeah, they'd sell [stuff shipped in from Shanghai] to us, like laundry powder; sometimes we'd go to their store to buy [it]. They couldn't openly sell it. They didn't have enough to openly sell stuff; there were lots of local people [who'd buy it up]. Yeah, there was a clinic right in our brigade. When our commune members got sick, they had doctors, they'd treat us. There was a bathhouse in the factory too, and sometimes nearby people would go in there to wash. There's no bath in a farmer's house. Hot water, and big bathtubs they had in there [the factory bathhouse]. They wouldn't yell at us, no! Usually we'd go at night. Their bathwater was set up to flow, so after it got dirty, it'd get released out and new water would be put in. It was pretty clean. There wasn't just one. Every workshop had its own bathhouse, you know.

[…] I think [Shanghainese] weren't so different from us. They kind of liked eating sweets, not so much salty, savory stuff. They liked sugar. Their clothes and such weren't too different from ours, and sometimes we even had better clothes here! They had a hard time back then too, you know.

* * *

胡善莉 Hu Shanli, female, Anhui native hired into a chemical factory as a concessionary worker.

Keywords: camaraderie, communications, consumer goods, entertainment, food, living conditions, movies, nostalgia, politically correct, political training, rural vs. urban, work schedule

Overall, Shanghainese people gave me the feeling of caring about people, of looking after them. Secondly, I felt like they were pretty rule-abiding, orderly. [...] And their character and way of dealing with people was great! Once you became friends, they'd treat you extremely well. And their attitudes toward work were good too. Every week the factory would organize study sessions, Wednesday and Friday afternoons. If people had their work shifts, they'd take time at night. Every week there'd be these two group activities. They really focused on our politics. Twice a week. And then also publishing periodicals, newspapers. Our cafeteria had a place to publish things, talking about good people and good deeds, praising the "progressive," rewards and punishments, it'd all be written out. That was all militarized, very orderly!

And our extracurricular time was usually really full. Movies, they'd play several shows a week, and then some performances and art activities, all very nice. Back then in the mountains, the Shanghainese would say so themselves; it's not like being in a mountain gully. Aside from not actually being located in Shanghai, everything was just as orderly. Entering our Third Front factory was like going into Shanghai.

* * *

刘玉香 Liu Yuxiang, female, Anhui native, farmer near a Small Third Front chemical plant.

Keywords: camaraderie, consumer goods, food, living conditions, nostalgia, rural vs. urban

Around when my oldest daughter was 40 days old, that was when some of the workers hired into the Third Front factory came to stay in my house. She was born in '70, she'd just turned 40 days old and they came, living with us. Lots of housing was put up near my house for them to live in. The ol' Shanghais didn't come stay in my house. When they came, they ate in their dining halls. Their living [conditions] were much better than ours, by comparison. The ones in my house were all these hired temporary workers. Most of them came from Dadukou Township and Shengli Township, near those parts. But the ol' Shanghais and us folks didn't visit much.

Later on, when everyone got better acquainted, we had a pretty good relationship. [...] During the busy season, the ol' Shanghais would come to our [work] team and help out for a day or two doing some farm work. They ate produce they bought. They'd buy some [eggs and so forth from villagers], but that kind of situation didn't happen much. They'd always eat really big [cuts] of meat, a whole ounce apiece, that kind. Then when everyone got more familiar, they'd also get some buns, plain or stuffed, for us folks to eat. And then some Zhejiang people, they weren't authentic Shanghainese, sometimes we'd fry up some sunflower seeds for them to eat. They all wore big black cotton padded coats, the kind that was real long and big.

* * *

庞金来 Pang Jinlai, male, Anhui native, farmer near a Small Third Front chemical plant.

Keywords: camaraderie, consumer goods, food, living conditions, medicine, nostalgia, rural vs. urban, travel and transportation

There weren't that many people [living] near the Yangtze River Factory, maybe just a few hundred people. Of course the factories were really strictly run. You could only get in there if your village's production team captain gave you a permission note with a chop [stamped] on it. Back then, I was the team captain. Yes, I went inside [the factory] back then. At the time, the ol' Shanghais would use grain ration tickets for their meals. Each of them would have about five or six pounds of grain. Their tickets couldn't be traded for other kinds of tickets. They only had grain tickets. It's only peasants like us who had things like cloth tickets and such.

[…] Some [locals] knew [what the factories were making] and some didn't. They knew that the [Shanghainese] worked in there, but they didn't know what they were producing. …Actually, not that many actual Shanghainese came down to our place here. Most of them were from Zhejiang, Jiangsu, Sichuan, a whole mess of different places. They came here because they felt that our place here was better than elsewhere. In other places maybe there were production team peasants who were transferred into the factory to help out, but not among us here, because they didn't allow local farmers to go into the factory to work. They only transferred people from outside to work in the factory. […] We weren't familiar with the Shanghainese, plus we couldn't understand each other, so there were a lot of inconveniences.

The Shanghainese treated us pretty well. If you needed something, they'd give it to you. The things we asked for, well, there was plenty. Grain, machines for moving rocks and blacksmithing, and some rich ol' Shanghais would have electronics. No, you didn't have to notify the village committee; I was the team captain at the time; as long as the relationship with them was pretty good, you could borrow electrical machines like water pumps and such with just a note.

[...] The hospital isn't around here, but before, there was one. Yes, it was open to the public; if you were sick, they'd take you. The factory didn't allow that, but the doctors, if you were carried over to them, they'd treat you. Back then it wasn't like now, with cars. It was always people who would come carry you. But the Shanghainese had cars. If you needed urgent care, they'd use the cars to take you to the county seat to get treated.

They [the Shanghainese] all thought people in our village were a little better. They thought the people from the village across the way were a bit worse. Even Dongzhi people, even we all say that people from our village were better, because people over there were sticky-fingered; they like taking people's stuff. So they didn't really like people from that village across the way.

* * *

邱云德 Qiu Yunde, male, pharmacist and Rear Base medical cadre.

Keywords: communications, critique, conflicts, medicine, politically correct, rural vs. urban

[...] Some Small Third Front factories close to local prefectures, when their staff had acute illnesses, could only send them to the nearby local People's Hospital or county-level People's Hospital. Though the ill worker would express gratitude for having been resuscitated, they still felt unsure [about their treatment] and would request factory leadership to invite an experienced medic from a Rear Base hospital to go consult. At first these factory heads didn't understand the rules for consultations among different medical units and would directly telephone a Rear Base hospital to have them send a doctor to the local hospital, and the Rear Base hospitals would get this invitation from a Small Third Front factory leader and immediately dispatch a medic. This caused misunderstandings and frustration in the local hospital.

Actually, when factory leaders didn't ask permission from local hospitals to invite a Shanghai hospital to consult on a case, the local hospital would think this was a Shanghai doctor just barging in to examine the patient, which was disrespectful to them, and would not really accept the suggestions given by the consulting doctor. [...] The Rear Base Health and Hygiene team, through a conference, told the factory heads that they had to have the local hospital invite the Small Third Front hospital to send a consulting medic and emphasized that we had to respect the diagnostic rights of the local hospital and pay attention to make good relationships with the local hospitals[...] Rear Base medics must also humbly and attentively listen to the treatment suggestions of the local doctors, negotiate with them, and strive for close cooperation.

* * *

汪福琪 Wang Fuqi, male, Anhui native and county-level cadre in Jixi, helped oversee transfer of Small Third Front to local control.

Keywords: camaraderie, food, living conditions, marriage, men vs. women, nepotism, nostalgia, politically correct, rural vs. urban

Between locals and Shanghainese workers, their relationship at the time, well, it was exceptionally good! Back then, they [the Shanghainese] had come to build the Small Third Front; they had come answering Chairman Mao's call. No matter where they went, they were welcomed. You locals who got hired into a Third Front factory, you had to be a poor peasant; your [political] background had to be good. The political atmosphere of those years was different. Their whole factory was surrounded by walls, and you couldn't go in there. They were high-security factories; they made bombs. If they let you in, you had to go through layers and layers of clearance checks. So, speaking of the Shanghainese Third Front workers socializing day-to-day with the locals, the farmers typically couldn't go into the factories, but the workers could come to the farmers' homes. [...] They got along fairly well. Nothing [in the way of that] or anything.

Later, lots of them became great friends, you know. After the Third Front Shanghainese left, they'd come down here to visit every year, take a turn around the old factory site, go visit with the local farmers. These past few years there's been a little bit less of that. [...] At the time, it was really straightforward, we locals admired them! The Shanghainese came over here with their high salaries and good benefits, so at the time we admired them! Including the locals recruited to work in the Shanghai Small Third Front factories; we called them "local ol' Shanghais" around these parts. We all really admired them.

Oh yes, yes! Some local girls married the Shanghainese! The ones who married into the Small Third Front, I heard later on that they had kind of a tough lot. Why? Because after the transfer of the Small Third Front, the people who had been working on the Small Third Front, they could go back and get a Shanghai household registration, but [the women who married into the factories] had a hard time.

His wife chimes in: I thought they could take care of one person's registration? There were people in our factory [who got that].

[Wang:] I don't think so, that had to be approved. We approved them. It depended on the specific situation. Not everyone got a Shanghai registration if they went back together. Not many local girls went into the factory to work in the 80s. The factory didn't let people in. [...] The Shanghainese could come out and look for girlfriends. If you wanted to get married here, [the local spouse] had to pass checks—political background checks. If you fit the criteria, they could then marry you. You could only enter the factory after the wedding. Without the license, it was a no go. Let me tell you, some of the [local] girls, well, they liked hanging around with the Shanghainese, and they'd get to know each other that way. After getting to know each other, if the Shanghainese wanted to marry locally, the people in the factory in charge of politics, the political work department, they'd check the local's background. If it passed, then it was fine; if not, then no. Yes, yes! The girl's family had to be checked out first because it was a secured unit!

[...] Yes, there were Small Third Front workers who stayed in Anhui for 20 years. From '66 to '87. They'd say that their work experience was mainly here, but listening to them talk, after they went back to Shanghai, a lot of people didn't get by that well. They weren't able to get so well situated back in Shanghai. Not that many did well.

I remember the old 683 driving team from here, they were also originally from the Small Third Front factories. There was a worker in the driving team. His temperament at work wasn't that good. When he left for Shanghai, he left his kids here to go to school, going to school down here in the countryside. Me and two others took care of his little kids. After the Third Front was transferred [back to local administration], the next year I went to Shanghai, I went up there to see him. His work unit leader received me. I saw that his place was way too small! A whole family with his wife, daughter, and a son. This whole big family just crammed into a single little room. I took one look and said, "This situation won't do! How can you live like this, how do you pass the days like this?" His temper isn't that good, so I talked directly to his work unit leader: "Hey, this is my friend, you can't treat him like this!" Then I heard that the next month the leader sorted out his housing. I heard he got another room; he was happy as anything. That—that driver wasn't too good at speaking up for himself. He was from Subei [TN: northern Jiangsu province, a region often seen as impoverished].

* * *

王金忠 Wang Jinzhong, male, Anhui native and farmer who worked in a Small Third Front chemical factory.

Keywords: camaraderie, communications, consumer goods, food, living conditions, medical issues, men vs. women, nostalgia, Party members, rural vs. urban, veterans, weapons, work schedule

The Shanghai people and our folks had a good relationship. When the folks would be planting, irrigating, building dikes, and such, they would all help. They would help society without compensation. Especially one who was buried here named Zhang Qingyun, the way he treated the local folks was like family; he cared about us in every way. For example, if someone was having a tough time getting by, or if we were short on hands in the fields, or irrigating the fields, or helping us pump water, or getting their workers to help the farmers with the harvest, planting seedlings, he'd help with everything. This Zhang even would manage family and human resource conflicts among us locals.

This [Zhang] was a soldier who had gone to fight in Korea against the Americans and helped liberate Hainan Island. In 1966 he'd changed work and had been sent to Shanghai. But not long after, in 1969, he got sent to us here. He was a battalion commander in the army. He had four sons. [...] The four of them, the oldest comes down every year to do Qingming Festival here, commemorate his father, sweep the tomb. [...] Zhang had a wife who is still in Shanghai; she's 82, still healthy. A couple years ago I went to visit her and saw that she was still very fit, able to climb up to the seventh floor. I figure these days she's not such a walker. I asked her son, I asked him if his mom's health were still good. He said that she wasn't quite as strong, not able to go up seven flights of stairs, that her hair had gone all white.

[...] [Zhang Qingyun] died of cancer. He died of his stomach pains. He got checked at the Tianshan Hospital over here; he didn't go to Shanghai, just to the Tianshan Hospital next to the Daying Secondary School, a Dr Shao looked at him. He died in 1978 and was buried here.

At the time, moving his body back to Shanghai was no easy task. Here, the first thing was that it couldn't cross the river. Bodies weren't allowed to cross the river, only ashes. But actually, having his ashes moved to Shanghai wasn't as good as just asking for a gravesite among us, because he was on very good terms with our local folks, so it wasn't a problem. If it were someone else, we might not have given [a site] to him, but he had such a deep relationship with our folks here! Up till today, each generation of us here still talk about him. He helped us so much, and we feel so deeply for him! After he died, a lot of people stood by crying uncontrollably, you know.

[...] They had me do logistics work. At that point the workshops weren't really completed yet, so sometimes I participated in the Youth League logistics committee. The League branch secretary, the youths, all these people together would arrange daily volunteer work, or have League member activities. Me, well, I wasn't a League member, but they told me to make an effort to join. But Shanghainese, the young people do things differently from the older people. These people said one thing but meant another. They didn't do things firmly; they didn't do things well. They'd do this thing today, then chuck it aside, then do another thing tomorrow. In treating a worker or a job, there wasn't a very good "success rate."

[...] When I first entered [the factory], I spoke the local dialect, but as time passed, I began to talk Shanghainese. The day before yesterday, you called me and I, thinking you were a Shanghainese, began to talk in Shanghainese, using it to answer you. After spending a long time in the factory, I always use Shanghainese to talk to people from Shanghai. Not that many people here can talk Shanghainese; it's because I spent more time in contact with Shanghai people than those who went in [to the factory] along with me. They only started encountering Shanghai people after going in [to the factory], but I started when I was ten. Those Shanghai people saw me grow up. If I go to Shanghai now, I also talk Shanghainese.

The thinking of us folks here, well, you could call it pretty foolish and ignorant. They [the Shanghainese] basically moved their modern civilization into this mountain gully of ours. So, we began to slowly study their advanced things, and the quality of us people here slowly improved. Like [...] the people in the Dongzhi county seat, when the Small Third Front came, they couldn't even compare with us. We were much more advanced than they were. The lives of the folks were good too. The county seat people in Dongzhi, some of them were too poor to even feed themselves. But folks here were never in a panic; sometimes they'd go buy some meat from the cafeteria and eat it. The Shanghai people sold meat at a buck 30 a pound, and if some folks didn't have enough money, they'd say, "No problem, take it!"

Back then we folks here were able to eat meat but people in Dongzhi town couldn't; we were among the richer people in Dongzhi county.

Especially people in our production brigade. Even people in Nanquan village were a little worse off, because they were farther from the factory. In our production brigade, we saw Shanghainese every day; we'd pass by the cafeteria on our way to the fields; we'd always pass them on the road, and would encounter Shanghai people.

[…] The way that Shanghainese treat things and their character, well, this is my sense. They were very generous with food, clothes; any they had left, they'd give to you. But if you were trying to sell something to them, they'd argue over a penny; they'd pinch every ounce. If you shorted them even a cent, they'd not have it. Like, if you sold eggs to them, they'd pick only the biggest ones; they'd not want the small ones. What's funny is, when they were buying eggs, a bunch of them would crowd around buying. They were very clever. One would be buying, and one would be pilfering, passing the eggs from between their legs to somebody behind who'd catch it. Several of them would crowd around the egg-selling folks, and before long the egg seller would find that the eggs were all gone, but they hadn't earned more than a bit of money; it's pretty funny. I figure those were all young Shanghai guys. Older people would definitely not do this kind of thing. But Shanghai women when it comes to buying stuff are a little—they like to get tricky, picky down to the ounce. Men were a little better.

Some [Shanghainese] would go visit at local folks' homes, but not as many as Zhejiang people in the factory. Most of the Zhejiang people were also country folk; back in the 60s, Zhejiang was also pretty poor. Those Zhejiang people would be kind of struggling at home, so, well, they dealt more with us local folks, like with planting, harvesting, they'd all help with, but Shanghainese no, they couldn't even do it. But the Shanghai people's hearts were in the right place. They were wiser. Zhejiang people's characters weren't as good. The Shanghainese didn't really come visiting. The ones who did were pretty close acquaintances; the ones who had fun together were a little older, worldlier; like some cadres, they'd come over to folks' homes, take a look at how folks were living, like Wang Yunxiang, Zhang Yuguo; these folks would try to intervene with family conflicts and human resource problems among commune members and such.

Yes, they'd go to folks' homes to chat with them and talk sense [during a family conflict]. I had deep impressions of Zhang Yuguo and Wang Yunxiang. They really had character, and they were very understanding. Folks round here really liked them. But back then, they were very young.

So we had less contact with the upper levels in the factory; our contacts were mostly with junior people.

[Locals] didn't really dislike anything about the Shanghainese. Locals didn't dare get on the Shanghai people's bad side. Shanghai people are mean and tough. Older people were more reasonable; they didn't get in fights with us, but younger ones, if you disliked him, he might beat you. These folks were all afraid of the young guys from Shanghai. Those kids were very mean, badly behaved. They could fight for several days in a row. They might take a knife and try to kill you. If you got him really mad, he'd really take a vegetable knife from the cafeteria to kill you.

Those Shanghai youths fought with local workers in Xiangyu.

[...] But here [at Red Star], they didn't fight with local folks. They fought at that Daying Secondary School. Those Shanghai students would fight with local young guys, fight for days on end, and it took the Dongzhi County Public Security bureau moving out to settle it. Like Zhang Qingyun's son, the second one, he was a fight leader. Once he fights, he'd get locked up for several days in the detention center. Even the factory Party committee secretary going to plead for him didn't work. They wouldn't let him go. He was too wayward. Only when his father personally went to the county public security did that work, because his father's position was high and credentials deep. When Zhang came, you know, he could carry a gun, a real handgun. When I was little I used to sleep in the same bed as him, and he'd put his handgun under the pillow. Not only did he have a handgun, but also a submachine gun. At that point the factory's security team hadn't been officially formed yet, so he oversaw all the military stuff. If we're talking education and culture, he didn't have a lot of it; he was a straight shooter.

[...] When the Shanghainese came, they brought us many, many benefits. Especially our factory. Thank goodness for our old factory head; with him, there really were lots of benefits. I got hurt on the job on May 26th, '77. At the time I was riding a tricycle to the fields to get some vegetables and bumped into some young people from the factory having some fun after work. That driver, he was on real good terms with me. He was joking around with me, driving his mini-Jeep [TN: it is common to call all off-road vehicles "Jeeps" in Chinese] and chasing along behind me. I remember it was raining that day. When he started chasing me, the car's front bumper got caught on my rucksack. When [he lost control of] the car, it threw me, it threw me down on the road.

At the time my head was broken, the skull was fractured, and the factory sent me right away to the Tianshan Hospital to save me. The doctors at Tianshan said that they didn't have any way to help me there, so they had to immediately take me to Guichi. Then a mister named Wang who drove military vehicles— who'd driven in the army for several decades—he drove me for more than two hours to Changjiang Hospital in Guichi. This was another Small Third Front factory's hospital.

I was comatose for 14 days and on oxygen for seven days. After seven days, I was able to breathe normally, but I was still in a coma. I ended up staying at the Changjiang Hospital for 26 days, then got transferred to Shanghai. Old Meng—our factory head at the time—after I got transferred to Shanghai, he'd come to tend to me. He didn't make a worker do it, he'd come himself. He said, "Your head, you gotta go check it every day at the hospital. After coming back from your checkup, you got to come stay in my room here." His room was an office, and he'd fixed a room for me in the office. It was a real high-grade room. He sent over the stuff I ate and drank every day.

It was this factory's Party committee secretary, Old Meng, who brought me food, dishes, things I needed every single day. If he had a business trip, he'd make arrangements in advance. He'd say to me, he's got a trip, so he's got food here in the fridge, just take it when you want to eat it; I saw it was all pre-cooked food. Hot water, he'd boil it for me every day. He really took care of me down to the nitty gritty. When I got back from Shanghai, he even gave me some money, telling me to take good care of myself when I got back, nourish myself, buy some good supplements to take. And he didn't stint on my pay when I was recovering; not only did he pay me the full salary every month, he also gave me an extra 50 cents a day. I was hurt in '77 and all the way until '86, Old Meng would think of me, and give me a bit of extra support.

My head [injury], well, there's not really a "better" or "not better." Anyway, well, they took out a piece of the skull bone when I was in the Changjiang Hospital in Guichi. That is, they fixed it in Guichi. In order to prevent after-effects, I did another set of checks at the Changhai Hospital in Shanghai. I went twice to Shanghai, in '84 and '89.

[The driver at fault] was dealt with. Well, me at the time, I was pretty young and felt invincible, I guess; I didn't care. I didn't prosecute him; I didn't think about the after-effects or the question of moving. If I'd thought it through at the time, I wouldn't have gone to Huatai; I would have gone to Shanghai too. That was in '84; Old Meng specially told me, he said I could go with them [back] to Shanghai.

[...] Because my head was still not all better. I was unique among that batch of local workers they recruited, that is, the others couldn't' go to Shanghai, but I could. Now I think back and think, people, you can't live by looking at what's right under your nose. Because I'd married early, I married in '80, I had a kid, I had a wife, and I had an old father. If I said I wanted to go to Shanghai, I didn't want to leave them, so I thought, forget it, lots of Anhui people stayed local, so I thought I could too. At the time I did think about going to Shanghai, saying that if I went, life would definitely be happier, but I thought and thought and still stayed. Now I regret it! I regretted this for years and years. As soon as this factory shut down, I began to regret it.

Shanghai people used to joke with me, saying I was a mutt, saying "You're no different from us, who'd believe that you're from Anhui? Your Shanghainese is the same as us Shanghainese." A Wang from Shanghai, Wang Lianzhen, she told me, "I really can't figure it out, why'd you stay in Anhui. What good would staying there do for you? Why couldn't you just come to Shanghai?"

Last year Wang Lianzhen came, saw me, said, "You're old." I looked at her, said, "You're still the same." She said, "I'm still this way, I'm two years older than you." I said, "You look younger than me now." When I was little, my family was poor, and my clothes were all raggedy. Wang Lianzhen, well, she lived beside me, she always used to call me over, she'd take a needle and thread and help me sew up my clothes. My mom was ill. Back then, my mom got ill after having a baby, and my family struggled. We didn't have anything to eat, so [Wang] would give us things to eat. Sometimes when we were short on cash she'd give us some too; sometimes she'd come visit us. Last year she came down to see us, and I said, "You came, but where's your husband?" She asked, "You know who my husband is?" I said, "Hami!" She didn't think I'd remember.

Generally, when Shanghai people built the Small Third Front factories, this Red Star Factory with us here, they brought us many, many benefits, infinite benefits. My feelings for Shanghai people are so deep! I'm not well educated, or else I'd write a novel and record many things, I'd write down all the bits and pieces of bygone years; it'd make a novel. But I don't have a very good brain for thinking. You could say that the Shanghai people's help to and care for us was infinite, and I also feel deeply for them. They've gone to Shanghai for many years now, but I still think about them.

* * *

王世益 Wang Shiyi, male, Anhui native and villager near a Small Third Front machinery factory.

Keywords: camaraderie, consumer goods, food, living conditions, manual labor, medicine, men vs. women, movies, nepotism, nostalgia, rural vs. urban

[...] When they first came down here, of course they wanted to create good relationships with local Dongzi folks, so the factory head and the branch secretary would bring the workers from the factory to help us to do fieldwork. That was all organized. Yes, we were all very welcoming to the Small Third Fronters. The first time we saw them, it was pretty fresh and exciting, not like now when we go to Shanghai and don't really bat an eyelash. Back then at most we had one or two people in our village's work team who'd gone to Shanghai, and other [teams] didn't even have that many people. People hadn't even gone to Anqing [TN: a county seat in Anhui's mountains]. I went to Shanghai in 70-something. When I was there, my two sons were sick and my wife brought them to get shots in the factory hospital, because the Small Third Front hospitals were all open to the local folks. If you were sick you could go and they'd unconditionally treat you. [...] If locals wanted a shot, usually they'd go to Xiangyu Town for them, about three miles away. But the factory clinic, you just had to go over the dam over there, very convenient.

The Shanghainese had haircuts that were more fashionable than us in the villages. And in terms of clothes, they usually wore work clothes when they came to the village, these uniforms from the factory. Usually the women might be spruced up a bit, but the men were mostly in work uniforms and weren't so different from ordinary [village] folks. And when they came in, they didn't put on any airs in front of us folks. They'd always talk about the "worker class" then, but these workers didn't put on many airs. They wore "Liberation" brand shoes. And for hats, well some of them would have those safety hats, or those basket-hats, the kind woven [with grass]. When they first go here, their workshops would put on plays and operas and such, and some cultural entertainments. Yes, local folks would go to watch every time.

[...] Of course, the character and education of the Shanghainese who came over was very good, much better than local people. Locals mostly hadn't had much schooling. The most prosperous years for their military goods was probably '76, '77, '78, those three years. We locals didn't know very clearly what they were making. [...] About '70, their family members started coming in. Usually [single] dorms were five or six people to a room. I've gone in to look—just one big room with several bunk beds in it. Not a lot of extra furniture, just a desk in the middle. Every floor had two bathrooms on each end, and there was a big bathhouse for washing. The bathwater all came by the taps from the water plant, and hot water was made by steam pipes.

[...] A lot of Shanghainese got married out here, and their factory also hired some people locally to go in to work. And then they got married to Shanghainese and then went back to Shanghai, too. Later on the factory did hire locals, all official [not temporary]. Usually there was a quota for a village or a work brigade, but all that was set internally. Also some government cadres, veterans and such—usually veterans had priority.

[...] No, [we Dongzhi locals] didn't really feel put off by any of the Shanghainese habits. Usually us folks wouldn't do anything if we saw you having something not clean [TN: perhaps a reference to petty crime or extramarital sex]; usually it was some of the cadres, like the production brigade leaders, the village branch secretaries, you know, those cadres, they'd go get involved. We folks usually didn't get involved. No big conflicts. Usually they were pretty strict on workers back then, so if you had any kind of stealing or pilfering situation, you'd report it to the factory leadership and they'd handle it seriously.

[...] Their trucks were Liberation brand, with Shanghai plates. No military industry icons on them, just the character for Shanghai. Most of the roads, they built, and the ones in the village here too. But no, the roads didn't run to the county seat. [...] Locals could go buy daily things from [their factory commissary store], like some vegetables, eggs, poultry, and such; the workers could go there to buy these things. They ate in their canteens, where they went to Dadu township, or Anqing, or Dongzhi town to get the produce. If they cooked for themselves, they'd buy local vegetables. We didn't have a farmers' market or a street that sold vegetables or anything, but usually they'd come to us to buy [produce]. Like if they wanted to have a little extra food, if they wanted to have a chicken or something, they'd come to a local villager's house to buy one. Things were very cheap then, so no point in haggling or anything. [...] In the 70s a lot of people still used soap pods [TN: a type of locust tree whose fruits contain saponin, which can be used as a natural detergent]. Back then they issued you one or two bars of soap a month.

[...] They did all dress pretty well; at the time we couldn't buy clothes that nice around here. Locals would buy clothing from them—not only clothes, but also some daily things that we couldn't buy, we could get by having them bring them back for us, like white sugar or soap and such. We couldn't buy white sugar here back then. If you had kids or old folks at home you needed it, so you'd have them help bring some back for you. I once went with my older cousin by car to Shanghai and stayed at a Shanghainese's home for more than three weeks. I didn't buy anything else except a lot of sugar to bring back here.

Until 1994 I was still in touch with that guy [I stayed with], his name is Xu Qingsong. I don't really remember where he lived; I think where Luwan District is today in Shanghai. He was a driver and he was still a driver when he went back. The government arranged for him. His wife was at the petrochemical plant. I fell out of touch with him, but my oldest son went to go look for him [in Shanghai] before. In fact, my son found a job thanks to his wife making an introduction. My son is running a private school over in Zhejiang these days. Of course Xu was a great host when I visited. After all, he had come out here before, and I'd stayed at his place too. Yep, when I went up there he'd drive me around town to see the sights. Jiading, Pudong district, the City God's Temple, all that.

[...] When I went to [Shanghai] I didn't bring a lot of money. Most of my expenses, they covered. I just spent my money on sugar and such. Plus, when I went, his family let me have the bed and they slept on bedrolls they put on the floor in their living room. The place he had over there was small, and built of wood. Overall, actually, life out here was a bit better than in Shanghai. [When the Shanghainese left], they were sorry to go. Plus they didn't all retreat and leave at once. They left in batches, and before they went they'd come say goodbye at the homes of their local friends, and agree to continue visiting and being each other's guests down the line. When they first left, we'd correspond, and then there were some who came back for visits. But even those who didn't come back must've found this part of their lives unforgettable, because the environment here was really very good and they wouldn't be able to forget it.

* * *

汪援胜 Wang Yuansheng, male, Anhui native and communications staff on the Small Third Front.

Keywords: camaraderie, consumer goods, food, living conditions, marriage, nostalgia, pay and benefits, politically correct, post-Mao, rural vs. urban

Of course [the Shanghainese] didn't want to [come down here]. Who'd want to come down to this little mountain gully of ours? But there was no way around it back then. In the 60s and 70s, the policies put politics first. If you didn't come, you were a counterrevolutionary. By the 80s, it got less strict. In the 80s, they hired some local girls to go work in the factories, doing temp jobs. It was low-cost—their salaries were low. Lots of people—don't think that just because we're deep in the mountains here, I'm not trying to brag, but the girls who grow up here are all pretty, with good coloring, pretty. At the time if they could find a Shanghainese [partner] with a national registration or an industrial registration status [for guaranteed rations], from others' point of view, that was like jumping from the bran basket into the rice basket [a real upgrade]. Lots of girls paired up in the end with young guys from Shanghai. Then when the Small Third Front factories were withdrawn, they were all taken back to Shanghai.

When they were pulled out, a lot of the old workers didn't want to leave. They said they'd gotten used to it here and didn't want to go back; they said that the air and water were good here, and that they'd gotten used to life here. The tea was tasty here. Before they left, they all wanted a drink of our tea. They didn't want to give it up! In '09, Shanghai even arranged for a group of old Shanghainese workers to come back for a visit.

* * *

伍先权 Wu Xianquan, male, Anhui native and veteran, worked in Small Third Front factories as a worker and driver.

Keywords: camaraderie, living conditions, nostalgia, pay and benefits, rural vs. urban, travel and transportation, water and irrigation

Yes, I worked [with Shanghai people]. They were pretty nice to us! How? Well, their policies toward us locals were for sure pretty good. Back then we were pretty poor round here, definitely poor. Working in the factory, the Shanghainese gave us equal compensation in every way to themselves. The salary they gave us was the same as their own, plus, every month the money on their salary sheets was written clearly; they didn't separate local workers from workers from other places.

They treated work pretty well, relatively well. They were pretty careful workers. Here, they also pretty much followed local conditions, pretty much following local habits and such.

[…] Rarely, rarely would we have conflicts. Mostly we all got along pretty well. They did the best they could to follow the local customs and habits, assimilating themselves with local life fairly well.

Shanghai people are truly pretty good. When it comes to their character, they're fair. They don't stab people in the backs; they're humane. They don't bullshit you or do things that are out of line. They talk and act on rules and policy; when they want to have words, they do it to your face. They stick to real talk. In this regard, Shanghai people are pretty good. Near us, there's an ol' Shanghai guy, he used to work at the Self-Strengthening Factory. […] [He stayed] because his kids are here. They got married here, so he didn't leave. He could've totally gone back to Shanghai, but when the handover [to local management] happened in '89, he just stayed here.

[…] The Shanghainese are really pretty good. I'm being real, here. I've worked all this time under and alongside Shanghainese, helping them drive cars. I'm a driver. […] What I know of Shanghainese helping us with farm work is that, every year, when we here had to do irrigation, near the factory, the Third Front factory would turn on the taps to irrigate our fields. In the fields around us here, they all have these built-in valves. When it got too dry, they'd open the valves and send the water into the new-planted fields. They couldn't possibly irrigate all the fields. They only go along that road. But the fields near the road could all get water from the Third Front factory. Our county is predominantly agricultural, so them helping us irrigate was the biggest help.

If sometimes we needed to move things, and we went to the factory to ask for help, they would loan us a car. When I was driving for them, I'd help people move things, help people who were getting married; I never charged a cent. […] I belonged to the Self-Strengthening Factory driving team […] I began driving under the Shanghainese in '89; I started when they were leaving. There was only one team at the time, the 683. Dongzhi county didn't have one. Dongzhi just had one vehicle, an open flatbed truck. When the Third Front factory came, they brought income to us, and they brought a big group of labor to work for the Third Front factory, which helped resolve the unemployment problems we had here. When they were building the factory, it was pretty tough in the village to even get food. Our conditions were worse than in the factory. So back then, if someone in the family went to work some small job in the factory, they'd get paid pretty well. That way, this gave our families income. There were lots of good things that the Shanghainese brought to us. But it's been a long time, and I can't remember. The clearest I can recall are the water and the electricity. These are clearest.

* * *

许汝钟 Xu Ruzhong, male, deputy head and chief engineer of a Small Third Front steelworks.

Keywords: conflicts, environment, finances, frustrations, living conditions, movies, pay and benefits, pollution, rural vs. urban, travel and transportation

Our relationship with the locals was all right. We had a film projection team. All the peasant farmers would come to watch, the farthest from 30 kilometers away. They'd never seen a movie before. At first they didn't pay, because we had projections outside. After we built an auditorium, we charged them tickets at a discount price, but later on there was still conflict. They'd come to watch a movie and we'd warn them that our staff had priority, and if there were openings, they could go in. If it were a movie put on for just one or two days [and therefore popular among the workers], there wasn't anything we could do. If it were being shown for a longer run, we'd let them in.

I remember a particular conflict over the small produce market. The farmers wanted to buy vegetables, but this was an employment benefit for our workers, after all. So the local farmers dug a trench in the road and wouldn't let our trucks and buses pass. Then we had to have a talk with the county cadres and work through the issue. The county helped take care of the affair and we started having a closer relationship with the locals. During busy farming seasons, we'd help them out. Party Secretary Chen Suosuo advised us to be careful to maintain good relations with them and would give out assignments at meetings. Production would take a break and we'd go help them with harvesting and planting [rice seedlings]. Also, we compensated them for particulate pollution, and for streetlamps that caused them to harvest less rice. My impression is that we paid the locality 300,000 yuan a year in taxes. They still have very deep feelings for us even now, and they still remember the Eight-Five Steelworks nostalgically.

* * *

袁彩霞 Yuan Caixia, female, Anhui native who married into a Small Third Front factory.

Keywords: children, conflicts, critique, family, food, frustrations, marriage, men vs. women, movies, rural vs. urban

After the wedding, my relationship with my husband was all right. He let me be and I let him be too. My lifestyle wasn't the same as my husband's; back home, we'd cook eggplants and meat together; Shanghainese would cook them separately. When I made egg and tomato soup, he'd insist on putting in potatoes. Once I was cooking egg and tomato soup, he saw I hadn't put in potatoes and was so annoyed that he threw the pot on the ground. I was so upset. He had a temper and he kind of looked down on me. When he got upset he'd say, "If it weren't for me, how'd you be able to come to Shanghai?"

Two Anhui wives I know have gotten divorced. Those two were already yelling about divorces in the mountain. I figure it's that their guys weren't so smart. So they got divorced. Usually the girls from outside [the factory] were really capable, and the men weren't as much. They also didn't have kids. After we got back to Shanghai, people like me didn't get divorced. We all figured, let's make do for the kids.

* * *

张渭德 Zhang Weide, male, Anhui native, cadre in Guichi County during the Small Third Front.

Keywords: frustrations, homesickness, rural vs. urban

Just speaking of the leadership and workers in this Third Front factory, they were dying to get out of Anhui here, after so many years in the mountains. There was this saying, "Rather a single bed in the city than a whole house in the 'burbs." We're not even talking here in these mountains, but just in the Shanghai suburbs; they wanted that badly to go into town, much less stay out here. So then they wanted to quickly do the handover, do it quick, then leave sooner.

* * *

章炎盛 Zhang Yansheng, male, Anhui native, town- and county-level cadre in Dongzhi County., helped oversee transfer of Small Third Front to local control.

Keywords: camaraderie, environment, electrification, living conditions, medical issues, pay and benefits, pollution, rural vs. urban, travel and transportation, water and irrigation

Oh, the relationship [between locals and the Shanghainese] was really good! For example, the Satellite Factory handled relations with the surrounding folks really well. Though the Shanghainese worked in the factories, they still had very frequent contact with the locals. The impression that the Shanghainese gave me was of being just really honest, hardworking, and thrifty. Yes! These three words were probably their deepest impression on me! I went into the Satellite Factory a few times and saw that everyone was diligently working in there. The factory had a lot of rules, very strict. They were all very serious about their work! They came in about '70, staying all the way until they were withdrawn in the 80s. Lots of people came and stayed in our mountains here for ten-odd years; it was really something!

I'd been to see their dormitories. All there was in there were a few beds, a table, and then just their face basins and such, almost nothing much in there. You could say that the conditions were extremely difficult! People from the big city coming into our poor mountain gully here, but they still worked dutifully and hard; it was really not easy!

The clothes they wore back then were also very simple; I felt like it wasn't too different from us locals. They always talked to us in Putonghua [TN: Beijing-standard Mandarin], very warm and gentle, no superior attitudes at all. Lots of things they knew without being told; they were really sharp! They really got along well with us local folks. For example, I remember that one of the Third Front Factory drivers was driving to us in Jianxin Township here. But when they were close to the town, the vehicle turned over. After the accident, lots of people on it were hurt. At the time, it was our production team folks that came to help. Us folks helped each of the wounded people up. At the time, some of them were hurt very badly, and our folks rushed them by night to the clinic at the factory. If they [the Shanghainese] didn't do such a good job managing relations, then the locals wouldn't have been voluntarily helping them. The Shanghainese also helped us local folks do many good things! At the time, the Satellite Chemical Factory would dispose of this stuff that looked like it was some kind of synthetic fabric, really similar to cloth. The Third Front workers would tell area folks that "This stuff, you all shouldn't take it home. This stuff is poisonous, you can't use it." Yes, supposedly it was a chemical by-product that had poison in it and couldn't be used. The Third Front people were afraid that nearby villagers would take it to use at home, so they warned people around [the factory] beforehand. Their way of doing things was still very honest and very careful.

Also, the factory trucks from the Third Front factory often came to our Xiangyu town to buy produce. If the local folks stood by the roadside and just waved a hand, they'd immediately stop the truck and let the people hitch a ride. If the villagers waved, they'd stop; they never complained. You have to know that transportation at the time was very inconvenient. There were very few cars. The factory trucks were often out, and that often made it easier for locals who were traveling.

Did you know? Lots of the buildings in our Xiangyu township, including the buildings for the Xiangyu township government, all the bricks and cement, all of it was carried here truckload by truckload by the Shanghai 683 Driving Team. All of it was trucked over from the Longjiang Water Plant's riverside docks. There was a pretty long way between those docks and our Xiangyu town. I remember it clearly; I still have lots of good feelings about those workers from Shanghai! When locals had problems at the time, lots of folks would go to the Third Front factories to ask for their help. We felt that disturbing their work was not good, so we often instructed our folks, "Don't go bother them at their factory. They're doing their work, don't always go pestering them!"

[…] The tap water didn't get brought in from outside like electricity did. I remember that there was a river near the Satellite Factory; there was a reservoir there. They went and pulled water from that river themselves for the factory. But when we were irrigating our fields, they'd release water from the reservoir and help us out. I remember the Satellite Factory really helped with our Xiangyu anti-drought station! I recall there was this 1800-kilowatt-hour transformer; if it were nowadays, you'd have a crane just pick it up right there. But back then it was entirely pulled up [by hand]! The people from the Satellite Factory helped us install this transformer. …About 20-some people came to lift it and drag it up. [They moved it] about a kilometer. That transformer was very heavy. They toughed it out with their shoulders and poles, moving it over from the shore. The moving and installation took, all in all, about a week.

* * *

赵连洪 Zhao Lianhong, male, security department cadre in a Small Third Front company.

Keywords: conflicts, crime, environment, environment, frustrations, living conditions, nostalgia, rural vs. urban, weapons

At first things [with the local government and farmers] were intense, too. Because the locals had some wishes we couldn't fulfill, so—you might know about this already—there were a lot of things where we clashed with the locals. For example, like Jixi: the chemical engineering company had factories there. The farmers came and dug up their roads. Because each of these military factories back then had a military representative, so things got really tense, then. Some factories even brought out their guns; it was very tense. Why? Because the locals said, you gotta pay. You were gonna hire peasant workers, but you haven't hired them. You sucked up all our water and used our roads, all kinds of conflicts over these interests. Overall things were okay, because we kept emphasizing that we had to do well in relationships with locals. Like our company and the local county leadership had a very good relationship. Because if you didn't do a good job with this, then things would fall apart as you went down the scale.

It wasn't just some factories that didn't have surrounding walls—a lot of them didn't have those. Like our East Wind factory, working on radar. They had one gully for two workshops, another gully for the third, all of them in those gullies. No walls. The dormitories for families were just on either side of the road. We didn't have conditions like we do now. It was very hard then. The Small Third Front factories weren't all sealed off [because they're secret, unlike what archive documents say]. Like the Unite Machinery Factory where I started, our workshop was called the No. 2 Workshop; guess how far it was from factory HQ? You had to keep walking into the hills for half an hour. So you couldn't possibly have a fence or wall that big. So the workshop was in a gully, and then at night, not like now with special patrols and night guards and what have you, we didn't have anything like that. And we had one workshop that assembled hand grenades; that one didn't have a wall around it either. It didn't seem like we were worried about the farmers or bad guys getting in there to mess things up or anything. But the explosives storeroom definitely did have a wall around the building. Yes, that counted as a major security hotspot.

I feel like local farmers were pretty naïve and simple, too. They wouldn't be like how people are now, going for a stroll after work and snatching whatever they thought looked nice. I feel like that sort didn't exist; people back then weren't like they are now, I think; the question of self-interest wasn't treated as importantly like it is now.

* * *

Further Reading

On Workers and Industrial Culture

Elizabeth J. Perry, "Masters of the Country? Shanghai Workers in the Early People's Republic," in *Dilemmas of Victory: The Early Years of the People's Republic of China*, Jeremy Brown and Paul G. Pickowicz eds., Cambridge, MA: Harvard University Press, 2007, 59–79.

On Agriculture and Rural Life

Anita Chan, Richard Madsen, and Jonathan Unger, *Chen Village: The Recent History of a Peasant Community in Mao's China*. Berkeley: University of California Press, 1992.

Edward Friedman, Paul G. Pickowicz, and Mark Selden, *Revolution, Resistance, and Reform in Village China*. New Haven: Yale University Press, 2005.

William Hinton, *Fanshen: A Documentary of Revolution in a Chinese Village*. New York: Random House, 1968.

Huaiyin Li, *Village China Under Socialism and Reform: A Micro History, 1948–2008*. Stanford: Stanford University Press, 2009.

Sigrid Schmalzer, *Red Revolution, Green Revolution: Scientific Farming in Socialist China*. Chicago: University of Chicago Press, 2016.

On Rural–Urban Differences

Jeremy Brown, *City versus Countryside in Maoist China: Negotiating the Divide*. Cambridge: Cambridge University Press, 2012.

Tiejun Cheng and Mark Selden, "The Origins and Social Consequences of China's *Hukou* System." *China Quarterly* 139 (1994): 644–668.

Fei-ling Wang, *Organizing Through Division and Exclusion: China's Hukou System*. Stanford: Stanford University Press, 2005.

CHAPTER 10

Appraisals and Critiques

Translator's Note

We have already seen narrators implicitly assess different aspects of Shanghai's Small Third Front campaign and their experiences of it in previous chapters. Here, we turn to their direct comments on specific dimensions of the Small Third Front, as well as the entire project as a whole. As was the case when speaking of their family relationships, their work, and the political situation of the era, there is notable ambivalence in these accounts. Some narrators paint a positive overall picture even as they relate numerous deficits and harms created by the Small Third Front; others speak consciously of new, more critical perspectives afforded by hindsight.

Historical phenomena we might read about in scholarly texts or primary materials like government policies and laws can look very different when seen from a ground-level, personal point of view. It might still seem difficult to imagine how anyone could think that the Small Third Front (and the Third Front campaign as a whole) was a reasonable, efficient way for the PRC to defend itself against its Cold War foes; it might still seem hard to put ourselves in the places of the people who went to work and spend much of their adult lives in remote parts of the country on behalf of the project. However, looking back on the Small Third Front through the eyes of real people may help make more sense of how these massive campaigns were actually carried out and legitimized in their time. Individuals

Y. Xu, Y. Y. Wang, *Everyday Lives in China's Cold War Military-Industrial Complex*, Palgrave Studies in Oral History,
https://doi.org/10.1007/978-3-030-99688-8_10

have always had to contend and negotiate with huge forces outside their personal control in the course of making their own lives, and the stories they tell themselves (and others) to make sense of their experiences rarely match completely those recorded in official records or in textbooks.

In this chapter in particular, the gaps between personal histories of the Small Third Front and official ones should inspire us to be at least a little more empathetic toward people in earlier periods for making decisions or holding opinions that can seem alien or objectionable to us in the present moment.

Moreover, we should also think about how *we* might have acted if we took the places of these narrators—and about how we might be acting in ways every day that will come to seem, within our own lifetimes and to those who come after, unfathomable or even offensive.

Questions for Discussion:

1. What are the biggest positive and negative aspects of the Small Third Front, according to these testimonies? Do perspectives differ between locals and Shanghainese recruits?
2. The Third Front campaigns have often been characterized by historians as poorly planned and executed and wasteful. Do our narrators talk about the Small Third Front that way? How might they respond to such critiques?
3. How do the assessments put forth by narrators in this chapter of the Small Third Front compare to (and contrast with) the "official line" laid out by Yu Shunsheng in Chapter One? What do you think lies behind the similarities and differences?

* * *

毕文中 *Bi Wenzhong, male, Anhui native, village cadre in Dongzhi County.*

Keywords: camaraderie, environment, electrification, medical issues, nostalgia, pollution, rural vs. urban, travel and transportation, water and irrigation

When the Third Front came and began investing, it was good for all of us, too. When they were first building, we folks nearby chipped in plenty of work for the Third Front. It didn't use to look so prosperous like you see now around the Self-Strengthening Factory. Back then, this was a deserted wild area, weeds everywhere; you could say it was an uninhabited "place of thorns." Before they invested, there were stands of grass, trees, quite a lot. When the Shanghainese first came here to build their factory, whether in where they lived or how they lived, it was very difficult. They'd come down here from a big city, but when they were first building, there was nowhere to stay, so some people just built a simple shack out in the open. Living on an overgrown hillside, they often got bitten to no end by mosquitoes and insects. They could really "eat bitterness," because conditions back then were extremely tough!

[...] When the Shanghai Third Front factory came, it was a very beneficial thing for us local people. At that time we were a remote, poor mountain gully. When they came, they got our electricity, transportation, all that, up and running. The folks were really appreciative of them. When the villagers' land got, you know, taken by the factory, when they were building, whatever of our land they needed to use, we'd give it to them, and the folks were really supportive; they did it without a word. When the Shanghainese came, they also did some real substantial things for the local folks, like dredging the river and irrigating the fields. The folks were also close with them.

When the Self-Strengthening Factory was built, it didn't go into production, so for folks at the time, there was no source of pollution. Back then, there was no pollution, not like now with this chemical engineering zone. [...] People were very welcoming of the Third Front factory.

When the Third Front factory came and the high-power lines were put up, the nearby villagers could enjoy the electricity they put through. Workers from the factory helped us bring the factory's power to each home. With electricity, that was a big change for sure in our lives. At first we were still burning oil lamps. The Small Third Front factory changed our electricity-less, oil-lamp-burning history, and for this we are very grateful to them!

In terms of water, before the factory came, we all drank unfiltered well water, and gully water. That water had blood flukes in it. So lots of people nearby got snail fever [Schistosoma]. When the Third Front factory came, it began to supply the drinking water for several nearby villages, and the water all came from Longjiang Water Plant. The water was all filtered by professional treatment and delivered to us by underground pipes. At that time, the Third Front factory installed a public faucet in our villages, and if villagers wanted water, they could go get it from there, which also made it more convenient for villagers to get water. It didn't cost money, but more important, I think, is that we got to drink clean tap water. Then many fewer people got snail fever.

In terms of transportation, before, we used to have just a provincial road from here that ran east to Jiangxi, and very few other decent roads, much less the roads in these barren mountains of ours, where we had almost no decent roads at all. Back before, only muddy mountain tracks one or two meters wide ran through where we are. When it rained, it was just all mud when you put your foot down. It was really hard to get anywhere. After the Small Third Front came, they spent a lot of effort building roads. The mud roads became four- or five-meter-wide gravel roads, which really made communicating with the outside world easier and made it easier for us to travel. So, the Third Front factory, from these big areas of power, water, and transportation, were real, solid benefits, the three big areas that brought massive changes, and they're also what left the deepest impression among folks.

* * *

卞建华 *Bian Jianhua, female, driver for the Rear Base militia headquarters.*

Keywords: critique, family, living conditions, nostalgia, politically correct, post-Mao, rural vs. urban, weapons

From the time I graduated to now, among the people who graduated with me, I'm among those doing better. Nowadays a lot of people coming back from Gansu are really sad, really wrinkled and old-looking, really weathered, really sun-tanned, and very little money too. Some men come back looking like geezers. A few years without seeing them, and when I do see them I say "Looking good, looking good," but everyone knows in their hearts the truth. And some people are even there in leadership roles, but still it's no good.

Some people haven't come back. Some people found a local [spouse], so that's that. Some were ill and came back to Shanghai, and half their lives are gone now, and some have died. Remembering this time, there was a lot of difficulty, but also happy memories. The departed ones, they do make me shiver. They used to be pretty good in the class when they left, but nothing for it. Thinking back on it, people like us (in the Small Third Front) made it pretty okay. Not the best of the best, but definitely not the worst off.

[Interviewer asks if Bian thinks the Small Third Front was meaningful.]

Well, from Chairman Mao's war-preparation perspective, it was meaningful. Because you can't detach it from the historical situation of the time. If Shanghai really had a war, then the Rear could become an evacuation route; that would work. The Rear also had a certain purpose. After the Zhenbao Island conflict [with the USSR], the Rear also delivered some bombs to Zhenbao Island. It played a certain role in the war-preparation process.

Under those historical circumstances, you can't say that it had no meaning at all. You gotta say it was really tense back then. Shanghai was digging tunnels, anti-air tunnels. The anti-air tunnels and such were done pretty well in the Rear also. If they really had to put people from Shanghai into the Rear, that would've worked too. Now in retrospect it looks really wasteful, all these buildings built, then we left, leaving nothing behind, everyone came back. The feeling at the time was that everyone was running back to Shanghai. At the time everyone's household registration was moved over [to the Rear]; when we were moving over, everyone's consciousness was so high, we all threw away everything in Shanghai. If you were married, the kids' registration would follow their ma over.

* * *

陈兰志 Chen Lanzhi, male, Anhui native, head of the Anhui Third Front office overseeing the handover of the Small Third Front to local control.

Keywords: conflicts, critique, environment, finances, frustrations, rural vs. urban, post-Mao, travel and transportation

At the time we were in the Huangshan area, back then it was pretty poor. Third Front factories were all in pretty remote places. They're all now tourist paradises and the folks are all well-off. At the time it was "Go wherever you couldn't find anybody around." Mao Zedong said that [building in the] mountains, spread out, in caves meant we couldn't be bombed to pieces or broken up. So a lot of Third Front factories put their equipment into mountain caves. These were really damp inside. That was the directive and thinking then. Nowadays that wouldn't fly. Just one missile dropped, and everything would be gone. What did it mean, "couldn't be bombed"? Our one factory had just one workshop in each gully and the factory head had to ride in a car for a whole day just to go see all of them. These days I think, that was a really childish way of looking at things. If I don't bomb you to smithereens, I could just bomb that road you had to the outside. If you can't go out or in, what were you going to do?

[...] So we took this perspective to consider the difficulties for the Shanghainese. We in the Third Front localities told the cities clearly that these farmers had no choices; once you all left all of them would have trouble making a living. After you go, the land they were farming's all been turned into paved roads so they can't farm it anymore. After you go, nobody's going to be buying all their produce. We had to consider difficulties on both sides and make Shanghai understand [the farmers'] concerns while having [the locals] understand the Shanghainese concerns.

[In the end Anhui] thought we should try to use the factories left as much as possible and have them set up township enterprises among the farmers to solve some of their employment issues. Also, the places that were doing economically better with productivity could be transferred in part. But none of this solved the problem, really, so we felt very apologetic toward the farmers. From the standpoint of our government, at first when requisitioning land, whatever piece [the Third Fronters] wanted, they got. Then when they left, they just left it. Nobody even wanted their buildings. At the time nobody said they were willing to move into their places. The peasant farmers all had their own houses, their own households. If you ran up to the factory buildings or the factory residential areas in the mountains, they didn't even have running water or electricity there anymore. At the time it was all about production, and not about living.

* * *

储瑛娣 Chu Yingdi, female, Party cadre at a precision optics factory.

Keywords: communications, conflicts, critique, frustrations, living conditions, men vs. women, movies, pay and benefits, travel and transportation

When we were building up [the factory], we all knew that Chairman Mao's departure point was to protect the nation. Fighting a war would all be in the cities, and they'd be destroyed right away. So we were building in these mountain gullies and mountain caves, so that [the enemy] couldn't find their objectives easily. I think all the military industrial factories were hidden. This departure point was pretty good, but through our actual experiences, the evidence showed that you couldn't really go this way. Well, first, when we were doing the planning and construction, the nation's economic power just was too weak. All the construction projects were low quality. You couldn't arm troops that way. And second, building in those mountain gullies meant really inconvenient transportation, not like these days with highways, you know. Back then, even an asphalt road was very good. [The roads] were all just gravel from the mountains that we got down, mixed with some mud like this, and it'd be washed away in a snap. Whenever it snowed, you'd have to shut down the roads. Thirdly, there weren't raw materials locally. You had to go buy them in Shanghai and elsewhere. The transport [costs] were huge beyond belief.

[…] Also, there were a lot of inconveniences in day-to-day living on the Small Third Front. Our workers—the over 1000 workers in our factory were like one big family. We built two "Workers' Villages" for them. 24/7 you were together, families with other families: over here you had an old couple, then your son and daughter would be there married and forming their own households. If there was a conflict within a household, especially with pay raises, if one person didn't get a raise, the entire family would come to argue with you, asking me why their son hadn't gotten a raise! Plus, if there were conflicts between neighbors or workers, the parties would still have to see each other day to day, so it was really a pain to manage. Life was very boring. […] We bought a movie projector to show open-air movies, and local farmers would walk eight miles in the mountains to come watch. They even fought over spots to sit, and you had to resolve conflicts between the workers and the farmers.

The young guys were impatient; a lot of them couldn't find wives, so they made fusses about going back to Shanghai. But we didn't have a real work unit in Shanghai, just an office. The Shanghai Optical Instruments Factory basically didn't take any responsibility for us at that point, over production and so forth, yeah. Sometimes when we had problems, they'd help us out a bit. They gave us a room and we set up our office there. If our workers had some issue they'd go to that office in Shanghai, and then the office would contact the Rear Base. And it was very hard even to make a phone call then. It was all long-distance, and you had to go through the main switchboard in Shanghai, get transferred to the local switchboard, then to our own communications department, then to our factory. It was a real pain to make a phone call.

* * *

丁秀玉 Ding Xiuyu, female, technician at a Small Third Front steelworks who later rose to cadre positions in Small Third Front Party organs, including head of the Birth Planning office.

Keywords: conflicts, critique, education, frustrations, men vs. women, nostalgia, pay and benefits, politically correct, post-Mao

Yes, I had to control that situation [of disputes over raises], I had to talk with my subordinates, I had to propagandize the policy, do thought work. Face to face, back to back, whatever. A real annoyance. Not like getting raises now. It was a real bother then, big meetings and small, a lot of them. You know elementary school teachers, they're not of such high character. And then arguments and whining. Yes, [they thought it hadn't been divided fairly]. Some would yell that they should have gotten nine bucks, why did they only get six; I should have gotten six, why only three. Some people would be just off-balance in their minds. [...] I could only keep holding meetings, keep making guesstimates. All this put in today's terms seems way out of date and burdensome. Some people, for this, even yelled their way to the factory admin offices. After they went there, I had no face.

The clearest thing I remember of that time was, at the time we were buying national bonds, and everyone was asked to buy five bucks' worth. Well, I had this teacher, he wasn't willing to buy a single cent's worth. Teachers would compete among themselves, so some people were like, he's not buying any, so I won't either. So I told that teacher, you are a teacher of the people; when the nation has difficulties, you of course should help take them on. He just ignored my positive inducements like this. Actually, he had some emotional baggage. He felt like he was struggling [financially], and leaders weren't taking care of him, so he didn't want to buy [bonds]. That was what he thought. So, what were my feelings? I said to him, your not buying any will affect a large swathe of people. If you don't buy, everyone won't buy, so I dinged him this way.

I'm actually a really soft and weak person. But later on, people at the factory admin offices said, "Ding Xiuyu, we could never have told by looking at you, you're really tough, nicely done." I said, nothing for it. In the end this business got so that the factory leadership knew of this person too and knew that I had slammed my hand on the desk. I said that if he stayed on, I wouldn't; if I stayed on, he shouldn't. I said, as a people's teacher, when the nation is having a difficulty, he won't help, and it's only five bucks, plus it'll come back to him; after five years this bond will have interest, and he still refuses to buy it. I said that this man doesn't deserve to be a people's teacher; how could he get behind a podium to lecture to students? From this angle, I am the Party secretary, I should have this kind of attitude. Because if he doesn't buy [the bonds], nobody will. Not like nowadays: now, cadres muddle through. At that time, we were really upright. Wrong was wrong, we were very clear, no muddling at all.

But this teacher's character was just off. He just wouldn't buy it. So, he still refused to buy it and then this ended up going nowhere. I didn't leave the school. I really learned a lot in the four years I was at the school. I felt like I was a cadre who went "straight through" from school to factory to dormitory—I felt like I lacked grassroots training. Once I got into the factory, I was interning, researching, organizing study classes. All the people I contacted were of a certain level, all people who were cadres. I'd never contacted these low-level people, like those people of really poor character among the elementary school teachers. I felt like I had no way to deal with these people. That's what I think.

Yes! [Cadres overseeing cadres, that's easy]. Cadres have a degree of conscientiousness; they won't play shameless. Like that teacher was shameless, a typical shameless rogue. He just felt like the leadership wasn't helping him fix his problems. [They] didn't necessarily [pick the better people from the factory to become elementary school teachers]. Like our teachers in our elementary schools, they should be graduated from normal schools, technical schools, or have a master's degree. But the people who got picked for it were from different tiers too. Some had come over from Shanghai, not picked locally. For example, some followed their husbands over and were of really poor character. They weren't graduates of a real teachers' school. Teachers weren't the same then as they are now.

* * *

顾国籁 Gu Guolai, male, Anhui native, technician who rose to administrative leadership roles in Anhui.

Keywords: electrification, nostalgia, politically correct, post-Mao, rural vs. urban, travel and transportation

I think these factories, well, going in[land] by the Center's directive, I think that, first of all, they contributed to national defense, though the costs were high (Image 10.1), but they made very great contributions to national defense. Leadership cadres at various levels, works at the time, local peasant workers, and local farmers, all contributed immensely to the making of the Small Third Front. The farmers gave their land, and some also joined in many basic infrastructural projects, you know. I think that this had a very large driving effect on local economic development and sociocultural progress. Where there hadn't been a road, there's now one;

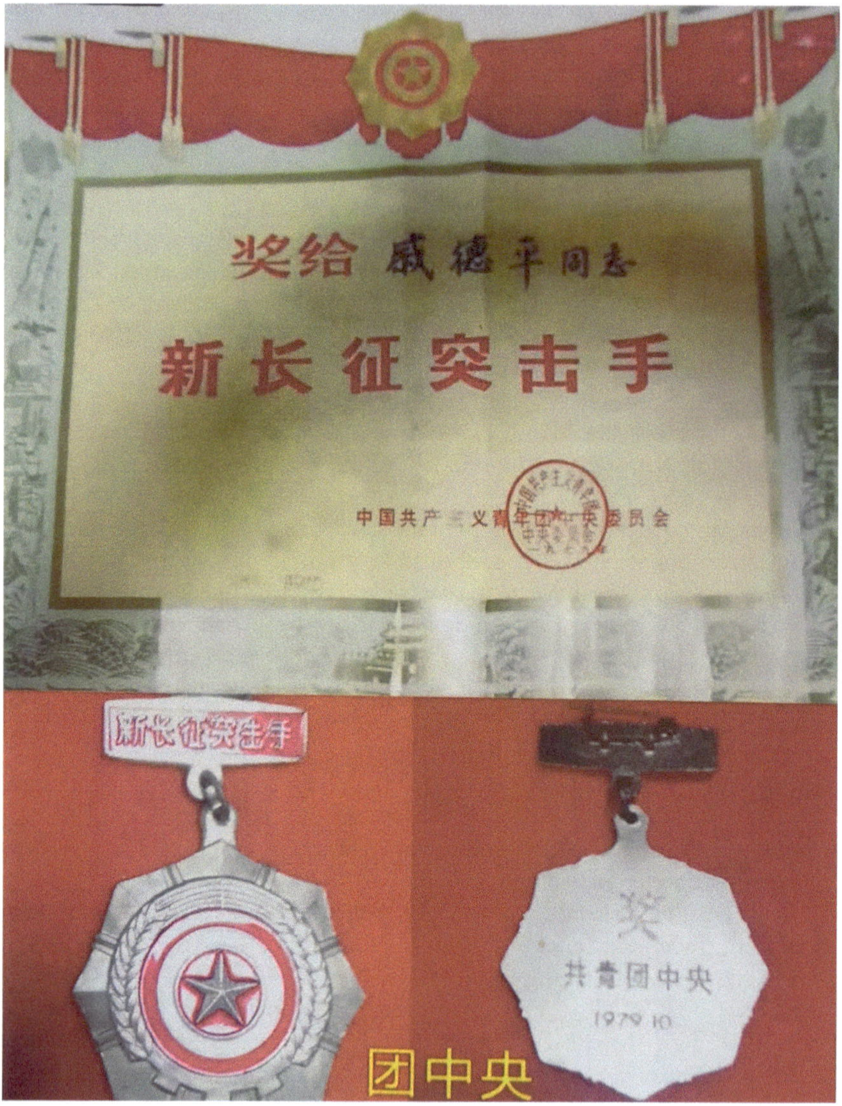

Image 10.1 Shanghai and national awards given for performance ("Shock Troop of the New Long March"), 1978—1979, collection of Qi Deping

where there was no electricity, there's now power, [people who] hadn't seen cars saw cars, and, I think, the effects of Shanghai workers as the vanguard catalyzed the blending of town and country, catalyzed the direct intermingling of workers and peasants, [...] advanced the progress of local society and economy, and gradually advanced the quality of the local cadres and masses.

* * *

桂胜莲 Gui Shenglian, female, Anhui native and worker at a Small Third Front steel mill.

Keywords: critique, finances, frustrations, post-Mao, rural vs. urban, water and irrigation

Later, the Shanghainese left and people from Ma'anshan and Guichi came to take over the factory. Then the factory went bankrupt and shut down. Lots of the metal underground water pipes were dug up and taken away, so the tap water we were drinkin' and using stopped. What a shame! If the Shanghainese had kept at it, I think there wouldn't have been people destroying things and maybe the factory wouldn't have shut down.

When the Shanghainese withdrew, at first when the Ma'anshan people took [the factory] over, it was still pretty good. When the road lamps broke they still fixed 'em up. Then they didn't do it so well, not so much. When the Ma'anshan people first came down here, they also weren't really from the Ma'anshan Steelworks. Lots of them were just various people; lots of them were transferred in from elsewhere. I don't know if they maybe used connections to come over, can't figure it out. Then the cadres in the factory, well, they'd get this person, then that person, but then lots of the things in the factory went missing; you wouldn't see them anymore. I heard some people say that when people were leaving the factory, they loaded up a big truck and went. What all exactly was in those trucks, people like us didn't know. All we knew was that they loaded up a big ol' truck and left. We only knew for sure that the materials in the factory were gotten rid of. Then the county [government] sold off the property, and the money from selling it, all that money? We don't know either.

* * *

洪全旺 Hong Quanwang, male, former branch secretary of a village production brigade near a Small Third Front munitions factory.

Keywords: critique, conflicts, electrification, environment, frustrations, nostalgia, pollution, rural vs. urban, travel and transportation, water and irrigation

I remember, after the Third Front factories moved back to Shanghai, three years later, the former factory head Chen specially drove down here in a car to visit us and brought a lot of Qingdao beers and hosted a meal for us. He drove to the factory to look, to take a look at the old workshops. They were all crying; their tears were coming down, you know. Such a shame; the factory got torn down and the workshops all destroyed.

If they hadn't torn it down, our lives would be better than they are now. A shame! It's also our Dongzhi County government not having much brains for business; they didn't keep up the factory [the Shanghainese] left behind. How do I say it? [...] Like right now, a lot of our people are away working [in towns]; a lot of our land has gone fallow. I didn't even mention the land—you go dig up all that land in the factory to plant crops, but your own good land is all fallow, but you still spend all that time and effort digging up the foundations in that factory for farmland; you're bungling everything. Like us, the New Hong team here, a lot of our good fields and good land haven't been planted; there's no one to plant them. And now our water source is gone too, so we depend on the weather; we count on the sky for feeding ourselves. If it doesn't rain, then we have a bad harvest. It's all gone fallow. When the Third Front factory was still here, they even had a pump station for the water; they drew the water over toward us in their pipes. Now the factory's gone, the station's shut down too, so we count completely on the weather. We can't do the water anymore.

[...] Several factories all shut down. Maybe it's the Dongzhi County government really running out of ideas. So, the Self-Strengthening Factory that used to be part of the Small Third Front set up a few new enterprises, but I heard that from the start the margins weren't very good and the pollution was really bad. They released huge amounts of polluted water into the nearby fields and messed up several of the villages' crops. Then there were fights locally—arguments, physical fights, compensation payments, all of it.

Then the Self-Strengthening Factory got set up—it became the Hua'ertai Company; they got it running. But it hurt the local folks. The pollution was just too bad, so much that the crops wouldn't grow. When the rice plants touched that dirty water, they all died. And when the workers were going to work in there, their noses—these women who worked there for a long time, their cheeks would look like they had red rouge powder on them. You couldn't wash it off, though; it was just bright red. I heard they made nitric acid in there, but I'm not too sure. I didn't really go over there. But I knew that the pollution was way too bad there. So some people moved because you couldn't live there! I heard some of the younger people were infertile because of how bad it was!

* * *

胡善莉 Hu Shanli, female, Anhui native hired into a chemical factory as a concessionary worker.

Keywords: camaraderie, family, nostalgia, sent-down youth, rural vs. urban, water and irrigation

When I got into the factory, the Shanghai people were pretty surprised, saying "this ain't an Anhui girl!" I was pretty lively back then, you know. Back then there weren't many kids who'd had some schooling, and I was a sent-down youth, so I counted as pretty good. [...] That was the last batch of people hired from Dongzhi County by the Shanghai Weilin Factory. [...] In '75. At that time the county radio station was saying that Shengli township needed a radio announcer. When the notification got to my father saying that I was hired into a Small Third Front Shanghai enterprise, my father was so happy! He said, "Hey, Little Li got into a Third Front factory, there's a lot of those, those are factories done by Shanghai people who come down here." At the time I heard, I was so happy too! I went to look at the Third Front factory; truly the Shanghainese factories were different from our local ones. Back then we definitely didn't have tap water locally, but the Third Front factories did, and I saw the buildings in the factories, the electric machinery, and the Shanghai people's pretty strict management. We were all pretty young then, and they treated us new workers especially well.

* * *

季美华 Ji Meihua, female, kindergarten teacher at a Small Third Front steel mill.

Keywords: camaraderie, medical issues, men vs. women, nostalgia, Party members

Yes, you could say female comrades played a lubricating role, helping smooth things over in the male-majority Small Third Front areas. Overall, these experiences of nearly two decades are like they're right before my eyes. We were relatively harmonious. This was a valuable period of riches. Once my husband suddenly got hepatitis and had to be quarantined. I didn't know how to do anything [because] he took care of the housework. It was like the sky fell all of a sudden. This happened in 1980, I think. Wang Zhihong and his wife were really great. They were the first to buy a washing machine. They didn't care that I was dirty, or about the hepatitis; they helped me with my laundry. I haven't forgotten even today. I was too embarrassed to ask them—they offered. Wang Zhihong was a leader back then, but didn't really put up any front or put on any airs. This thing I won't forget for the rest of my life. It was a small thing, but it was a really moving thing back then.

After he became a big official, after he became the Rear Base Bureau Head, I felt like I couldn't really go bothering them anymore, so I stopped visiting them so much. My husband and the Wangs were in the same department. This favor they did us, though, I still hold deep in my heart.

* * *

潘雅珍 Pan Yazhen, female, worked as laboratory technician and in the mechanical department workers' union at a Small Third Front steel mill.

Keywords: critique, environment, finances, frustrations, medical issues, pollution

Self-sufficiency, well, over ten-odd years, the Eight-Five Steelworks did manage that. Sometimes we had extra steel material that we'd go barter for some fruit. Then later on we found out about a problem, one that I had too. When we got in there, we found that people had low white blood cell counts. People looked very sallow. Yes, there were water quality issues too, but this was the minerals. When they had gamma rays down from an airplane to investigate they found that there was radioactive uranium ore here. So the people who lived on the hills were mentally handicapped generation after generation. When we went there, the people who were more sensitive—like I could feel this—had low white blood cell counts, were lethargic, dizzy and headachy, and very sallow in the face. They couldn't figure out what was wrong in Shanghai. But when you stayed for a while in Shanghai, you'd be a little better. Only later did we know it was radiation.

Another time, a few hundred people got sick and were vomiting at the same time. They didn't even fit in the clinics. When Shanghai found out it was a contagious illness, they sealed off the road in to us and wouldn't let us go back to the city. Mm-hmm, we were quarantined. So the water we drank was just the Baiyang River, run once through a filter. Then they found—the health team they sent from Shanghai took everything pretty seriously—they found that animal corpses on the hills would be washed into the river by heavy rain, and that was the cause. We all spent a few months on pins and needles about this, kind of like avian flu these days.

And making our steel, well, that was also a losing deal. The raw materials were all shipped in there from Shanghai, and then we forged it out there. Talking about it now, it's pretty funny. The infrared cameras folks had abroad, they could see even cigarette butts under a tree on those hilltops. How could they possibly not know about such a huge chimney on a steel mill forging steel? But back then it was "prepare for war, prepare for famine, for the people" [TN: a slogan attributed to Mao from the Third Front era], you know. So we did it.

* * *

王金忠 *Wang Jinzhong, male, Anhui native and farmer who worked in a Small Third Front chemical factory.*

Keywords: camaraderie, consumer goods, environment, frustrations, nostalgia, rural vs. urban

Well, the benefits [of having Red Star Factory in Tongding Village], at the time we all said there weren't any for us. But after a few years, the good started coming. At the time, folks here mainly farmed, you know. When they came to build this factory, they took all the land from folks. I remember they took 22 acres from us, and in actuality used 15-odd acres. This meant that they took all this land from folks, and folks complained; they didn't want it, they were worried about what they'd have to eat later on. Then afterward, everyone felt that if you had too many fields, it was hard to plant, and having them taken by the Shanghainese was for the better. After a couple years, the Shanghainese were living here full-time. We developed relationships with them, and they gave us things we didn't have; they provided us everything. Like the house I live in, it used to be the commissary store of the Red Star Factory. The Shanghainese would get some general goods and sell it here, and we all had our eyes opened too. It used to be that folks would have to go to town to buy things, but now they don't have to, they can just buy things here, food and drink too. You could say this factory has been a fountain of happiness for us local folks.

[…] You could say that, before and after the Third Front factory came, we had a total topsy-turvy change here. At first the thinking of us people here was pretty closed off. After Shanghai people came, our thinking was imperceptibly affected by them, then we slowly opened up. We saw Shanghainese lifestyles and living habits and we began to unconsciously imitate them. For example, how we planted in the fields. Back then we would put the seedlings down one by one. The Zhejiang people were smarter and would toss them. When they saw us putting them down one by one they said, why're you doin' it this way, that's so tirin'; just drain the field and throw the seedlings in there like sprinkling confetti, then once they get in there they'll spread out. Then you wait a couple days for them to put down roots, then you go down and move the ones you don't like [the position of]. Isn't that a lot easier? So then we just did it the way they said, and it was easier after all.

* * *

王美玉 Wang Meiyu, female, chair of the Shanghai Rear Base Management Bureau workers' union.

Keywords: conflicts, critique, family, frustrations, living conditions, marriage, nostalgia, politically correct, post-Mao, rural vs. urban, work assignments

Based on the historical conditions of the time, I think building up the Small Third Front was necessary. What if there were a war? We can't use our contemporary standards to look and decide that the Small Third Front was a failure. Our entire Small Third Front was an investment of 700 million. Renminbi at the time was worth something; it was really great. Our arrival also brought new concepts and ideas about living to the locals. Their lives had been very monotonous.

[…] The idea was, then, that if something were to happen, there'd be a way out. The old gentleman [TN: i.e., Mao Zedong] raised the idea of doing the Big Third Front. The Big Third Front started up pretty early and it was tougher there than it was for us. I feel like our Party and our country really mistreated that batch of people. Now the Small Third Front is back, but the Big Third Front is still out there even now. When I talk about it, I get pretty upset. They couldn't be in touch with their families because it was all top secret. Those folks were in the PLA, and just after coming back from liberation, they were sent to the Big Third Front.

Just after destroying the Gang of Four, we went to the All-China Federation of Trade Unions for a conference, and these people were being taken seriously by Party Central. Their flour had ground-up gravel in it, so the buns they steamed would have grit and sand and rocks when they bit into them. After Party Central took notice, they got moved to the cities. Some folks were elderly, so they have a policy that the older folks would get moved to places nearer county seats and could bring a child into those county towns. They were grateful just for that. They never complained. I really respect these old comrades; I feel like they were really remarkable. [...] The Big Third Front gang left in '63 and '64; they settled down in Xinjiang for decades, and when they came back, they had no place to live.

[... When ending the Small Third Front], us Shanghainese moved very slowly. Then they wanted to leave the Small Third Front to Anhui, but they didn't want to take over. On the one hand they thought we Shanghainese were hard to manage; on the other, the [factories] were too scattered and they didn't have the ability to manage us. We thought that leaving all these things to the Anhui people was a shame. The equipment was all basically new. They didn't want us so they brought us back like pieces of luggage and built more factories. I left from the Shanghai No. 7 Radio Factory and I should've been assigned right back there, because in case we went to war, we were supposed to take over their burdens, so when we came back, we should've gone to our original places. The folks who came back were all very pathetic, having to look for new factory buildings themselves.

[...] As the conflicts and contradictions increased, they brought the Small Third Front back. We also did some investigation and study ourselves. A lot of practical problems arose after the Small Third Front went into the mountains. When we all went in, our kids were all small, so we had our parents look after them [in Shanghai]. Then they had to go to school, but our parents were all illiterate and couldn't help with educating the kids. And some people had their siblings all away [outside Shanghai], too, and their parents were ill but had nobody to look after them. All these problems that Shanghainese workers encountered; we'd all have them too. The education in those mountain gullies was definitely not good, definitely couldn't compare to Shanghai. If everyone wanted to sit for exams to get into the magnet schools, that'd be a problem. We did a lot of research and study and got the city to take notice.

At the time, we suggested that the people with difficulties should be allowed to send [one spouse] back to Shanghai, but our superiors didn't take notice, so we had a string of issues on the Rear Base. Youths couldn't find partners and were disaffected in their mindsets, making bad decisions, and things that shouldn't have happened, happened. Then [they] felt that if the Small Third Front problems weren't fixed, [bigger] problems would come. Previously, we thought that educating our kids was a personal problem and didn't think to get Party Central involved. But these issues weren't unique to Shanghai. All the Big and Small Third Fronts around the country had these problems. At first they thought Shanghai had done pretty well, but then with all these other questions, they discovered that Shanghai hadn't necessarily done better than elsewhere.

The All-China Federation of Trade Unions, the National Defense Industries Union that was specifically in charge of the military-industrial network under the Ministry of Defense, they went around the country doing investigations and then had a conference in Beijing. After their meeting, starting in Hunan province—they were also making guns there—their Small Third Front moved to areas closer to the county seat towns. After we saw that, we started to write our own research reports to the city to report on the eight major issues of the Small Third Front.

That was in the 80s. We got that research report to reflect the situation to our superiors. Our Party committee office chairman, Chairman Zhu, was very diligent. They also did an investigation and merged our two reports to send up to the city. But there still wasn't any major response, not until '85, when the Small Third Front was clearly going to return. In '85, the Rear Base Transition Office was looking for locations in Shanghai, in Minhang and Nanxiang, and so forth [in suburban areas]. We thought that rebuilding would be wasteful, but the superiors gave the gist of these people not returning to their original work units but figuring out something themselves.

The real transition was '86; by '87 I'd guess most had gone back. In the process we arranged for a few work units [to receive] the workers. But the workers had a lot to say about this. After they went back to Shanghai, they felt like they were third-class citizens, not real, official Shanghai workers but people who came from the mountains with worse treatment than other people. All the hard, tough jobs got shuffled off on these people. The workers who'd gone back to their old factories would say to us, "We're all third-class citizens now, we don't have any status." Then they gave each person ten-odd square meters [of living space].

We should say that the Small Third Front had a certain purpose and effect at the time. If you separate it out from the history of the time, you'd feel that this was a failure. If you built it up but then abandoned it, wouldn't that be a failure? But if anything had happened, if there really had to be a war fought, without a Small Third Front we'd be hopeless. But selecting such faraway spots [to build the factories] really was a problem. Our biggest failure was picking such dispersed locations. Forget fighting a war; when it was only heavy snow that shut down the mountains, you'd have nowhere to go. You'd get stuck in there; you'd run out of food and starve to death. We had a May Seventh cadre school in our factory, and every work unit planted its own vegetables and fed its own pigs, but most [of our food] got shipped in from Shanghai.

When I think back on those days, it's pretty interesting. From when we were 20-somethings to when we were past 40, all that time we sacrificed in that kind of environment. What kind of contributions did we make? Thinking about it, we didn't contribute squat. It was futile labor. At the time we thought in those mountains, Chairman Mao said that if the Third Front weren't built, he couldn't sleep at night. Now he's sleeping but we can't sleep, because we were in those mountains for more than a decade and all kinds of issues cropped up in our homes. Our kids' educations were a problem. Our elders got sick but didn't have their kids around. My dad was paralyzed and was bedridden so my ma took care of him. Then she broke her hip in a fall and neither of them had anybody around to take care of them. I was too busy with work to go. The work unit's rule was that if elders had no one to take care of them at home, one of a pair of spouses could be sent back to care for them. But neither my husband nor I could leave. Our kids were in elementary school. Not until '82 did my husband go back. But my work was way too busy.

After the smashing of the Gang of Four, we had a lot of work in the [Rear Base] HQ. When I got back to Shanghai, I felt like work was very easy there and you got to leave very early every day. When I was on the Small Third Front, you'd have meetings after work hours, sometimes running until midnight or one in the morning. We didn't really have time for meals or a day off. All our days off were spent at the [grassroots] level [factories]. I basically lived apart from my husband. Originally, we went together to not be separated, but after I went to the HQ, he was in Jixi and I was in Tunxi. It'd take 45 minutes by car, one way, and if you couldn't get a car you couldn't go.

* * *

许汝钟 Xu Ruzhong, male, deputy head and chief engineer of a Small Third Front steelworks.

Keywords: critique, environment, living conditions, medical issues, politically correct, pollution, rural vs. urban, water and irrigation

Then we thought about day-to-day living, so we also boldly used the gas [produced in our No. 8 Workshop] for production to supply the residences. This was a very risky proposition, because this type of gas isn't the same as standard consumer gas. If there were a leak, the enterprise would have to be responsible for gas poisoning among our workers and families. Because we didn't have a very good filtering system, we'd just get rid of the tar and get it over to the workshops that needed it. Often the pipes would be clogged by tar or would have some issue, and it would've been very easy to have a catastrophe on our hands. This was all debated, studied, and approved by the factory Party committee all together.

The gas workshop also caused a water pollution issue, a really serious one. After the gas producers burned the coal, there'd be tar, and tar mixed with polluted water. We had a sedimentation tank, but you couldn't keep it [the water] there all the time. Some of that excess water had to be released, this water polluted with phenol. During heavy rains we'd let it run off, twice a year. The entire Baiyang River would be polluted, and we ourselves were victims too. In name, we used deep well water [for daily use], but really the polluted water had also seeped in there. And there wasn't water treatment infrastructure at the time, either. The water we drank was drawn up from deep wells beside the Baiyang River, pressurized, and delivered to the various factories. We put some thought into managing the pollution and were able to get the crude phenol out, but we couldn't achieve total removal. We ran some tests and got some preliminary results—we'd remove as much as we could in the gas workshop. Crude phenol could be resold again, too. We wanted to keep up this work but that needed big investments, and we couldn't continue because of funding shortages. So, we could only remove the crude phenol.

Local folks knew that half the trees on the hills had been turned black. Sometimes there was too much gas and we couldn't use it all, so we released it into the air; that'd be carbon monoxide with sulfur, and it'd kill trees. The people who've come back, nowadays it's disproportionately common for them to have cancer. Some people were already showing signs there, some had skin allergies, all kinds of very strange symptoms.

* * *

徐小英 *Xu Xiaoying, female, cadre, teacher, and office administrator at a Small Third Front steel mill.*

Keywords: camaraderie, conflicts, critique, education, frustrations, higher education, medical issues, nostalgia, politically correct, post-Mao, rural vs. urban, travel and transportation

I feel like the period of time in the school [was most beneficial] for me even though that time, come to talk of it, was kind of a mess—in [leading the kids'] studies and such. But for myself, I got some deep rewards from it. First in my own knowledge: originally this physics of mine [was bad…] now I can remember Newton's three laws of motion, Archimedes' law, and such. Yup, I can remember pretty well, [my studying left] a pretty deep impression. Later on, in the school now, I had some friends who were all substitute teaching, which was pretty good too. We go out for activities [now] and sometimes—often—meet. Every year we meet up. In the school, including the secondary school principal, the head of the teaching office, Teacher Pu, basically even now we meet up. […] Yu Chanying was principal of the secondary school, and also worked in the education department. Yu Chanying at the time, one year on April 8th, our school had a major event [and she was involved].

'76 April 8th, the time the school organized to go visit tombs, it happened to be Qingming, [the holiday for] tomb visiting. In the people going, their middle school [Party] organization had a homeroom teacher named Huang Zuming. I remember he graduated from Peking University; he was going to sit for the entrance exam for graduate school. When they got together to go, Yu Chanying out of the goodness of her heart said [to him], you should go study, the exam is coming up, so let me help you lead—so she helped him take the students. Then they got here; the car was a car sent by the plant offices, the office of the head of the plant. It was a van for taking workers to and from work. But the seats inside were all straight [against the sides], not horizontal row by row, just made for picking up and dropping off workers. Then when they got there to visit the tombs, in Mt. Jiuhuashan, the van turned over and a bunch of people were injured. One of them became a high paraplegic who never got better. So that was it.

After this happened, the plant central office began to cast blame. "You all went to frolic and goof off—" […but] the school organized [this activity]. Several classes [of students] had gone. One of them had been in the accident. […] Yu Chanying was standing in for somebody else. Then when she came back, she was done with. Yu got fired, and another branch secretary having a meeting at the Rear Base also got a warning and punishment... for this incident, I also got some setbacks. So why I wasn't able to get promoted later on, that was because of this. Because, after people were dealt with, the teachers in our school weren't having it [with the decision from above]. "We organized and sent out the vans through your offices, and the students going to visit tombs doesn't count as goofing off. So the teachers of the school, including myself, all signed a petition; a whole bunch of teachers wrote a letter to our superiors.

A response, yes, [we wrote] a response on this whole thing, to the Rear Base. After our response, our letter was immediately returned, and it got returned to the head of our factory. These days he's dead. Peng Yaochang [the head] at the time, actually—actually he pushed off [blame] to the school so that his factory wouldn't have responsibility, or else it would be a safety accident, and he would be responsible. So he got rid of it and didn't like this. He saw the letter and felt pissed off, definitely pissed off. Yeah, [why did you write] a group petition letter, so on and so on. Actually it was dealt with, but I don't know if it was written into the plant archives. I would know if it had been. According to my internal sources, I should've been able to get in [to a leadership position], but because of this....

[...] Let me think; at the time I said, when Chairman Mao and Chi Heseng were young, they went to tour the wonderful landscape of the Motherland. They called touring the wonderful landscape of the Motherland "reading books not printed on paper," a way to improve one's knowledge. Why did we get dismissed as goofing off and frolicking? Mm-hmm, [visiting tombs] is a very normal thing. [...] He [the plant head] was really pissed off because we had written a joint letter at the time I—yes, it was going above his head to report. So he held this grudge. Then I was like this [talking about Mao] in the letter, so he definitely had some antipathy toward me.

The leaders I met at the main offices were really—you know. The leader in the propaganda department, he was like, because I sometimes have to go visit my husband, he only gave us one visit a year. Only 12 days of family leave every year. I didn't know until later that the family leave worked like this: I had to go first, then he could come. The military didn't care; if you had used it, if you hadn't used it, every year at the end they would still give you a family leave. So, it was weird that our local superiors had regulations on this kind of issue, where I had to go first, and then he could come to me. If he came already, that meant we had already met for the year, and

I wouldn't be able to go. The first time, no one told me this; I didn't know. I hadn't gone to see him that year, so I left.

When I came back, the finance department blocked me and wouldn't let me go. They said your husband seems to have come already. I said he did come. They said this document has a regulation that if he's come over, you can't go. I said you never told me; I didn't know; if you told me ahead of time, then I wouldn't have gone. But telling me after I come back, what am I supposed to do? So then the finance department was okay, but I ran into the boss of the time; he really was unreasonable. How could you not know, he said. You deliberately caused your work to be—caused work to be delayed for the organization. That was so unfair to me then; thinking about it, I was really treated unfairly. I was already suffering at the time, and this leader still didn't care about me, and all this; at the time, I felt I was really wronged. Nowadays this is not possible. For sure it would be more humane, not like this. But back then there were regulations like this, you know.

These years of mine, I stayed some years in that plant, never had a mistake on any document, never lost a single one. Passed [in promotions] by other people, and then when they needed a document, I never lost one. Even though I had a kid. In '76, East China Normal University (ECNU) came to recruit in our plant, because ECNU was going to make a graduate course; there was just one slot for the Rear Base for that course. [...] Because the Eight-Five Steelworks was the largest work unit in the Rear Base bureau, this slot was given to the Eight-Five Steelworks. Eight-Five then called in all the departments, all the workshops, and each of them recommended one person [...] maybe my fate wouldn't be like this today, or maybe it would be the same. The time I was already [working] at the school, so the school recommended me.

Then there was a selection. Then our Party committee secretary said, we won't pick middle and high school [graduates], [...] like me, I spent four years in junior high school; I counted as a four-year vocational middle school grad. So the batch, in the end there were three people left; one of them was already a college [grad], so they removed them; in the end there was me and Wang Wenhua, just the two of us. So then the person who came to recruit from ECNU picked; this entire course had only nine people. So he had a chat with me. I said what I thought—being able to go would be the best. At the time I had an advantage by already being in a school and being the deputy head of teaching affairs. So then the recruiter had my Party committee give their thoughts, who should be taken, and if that person couldn't do it, then there could be a backup.

In the end our Party committee decided that it'd be me as the main person; if my physical exam wasn't good, then Wang Wenhua would substitute for me. Back then I had not a whit of calculation, so I went to do the physical. Wang Wenhua was in the organization department then and hadn't yet come. Another person was also in the organization department and had just transferred in from the Changjiang Hospital; he had told that he was a temporary position in the organization department [...] I can't say his name now, because we all know one another; that wouldn't be good [to give his name away]. At the time, the day of the physical exam, I thought very simple-mindedly, so I went. When I went, I went to the Shanghai Steel Hospital and this person went along too. He wasn't trying to help Wang Wenhua; he wanted to get Wang out of there [in Anhui] so that he could sit more securely in the organization department, you know.

Mm, so then the physical, several indicators, I just checked, all of them were normal, but the indicators for the blood test wouldn't be known until the second day; you didn't find out right there. [...] Zero to five was the normal range for the indicators. So I only knew until after the notifications came down. It turned out that Wang Wenhua got chosen to go to ECNU. So then our Party committee secretary Lin went to ask, why didn't Xu Xiaoying get it this time, didn't we already agree, and didn't you already go talk to her, why [not let her go], just because she had a little problem in her physical. So my driver [her husband] was upset; after we had them get that physical report, the Shanghai Steel Hospital took it and asked me, Little Xu, yours doesn't pass; if you're sick, go run another one, do another physical. If that turned out normal, that would mean that there was a problem on their end, something not right; if the [exam] isn't normal, then you go, get treatment. So I went for another test; it was normal, you know. In the normal range.

So then the plant main office heard about this; the Party committee secretary Feng Xiuzhi at this time, she told me, Little Xu, they didn't take you this time; if there's another quota next time you'll have the first spot. But then that chance went away. Wang Wenhua then stayed on at ECNU; all the people in that course stayed, then she—it was basically cadre training. She later on was the assistant dean of foreign languages in there. It's to say, I did kind of get the short end of the stick quite a lot. Thank the Heavens for finally letting us come back, come back to Shanghai. At the time I'd think about it all and feel a bit [helpless]. But we were all simple back then; we didn't know to go to the "back door"; we didn't know much, that was that (Image 10.2).

Image 10.2 New Light Factory workers lighting firecrackers to celebrate news of their imminent return to Shanghai, mid-1980s, collection of Liu Jinguo

[…] Then in the last couple years we also went a couple times to the Eight-Five Steelworks; me and some colleagues from school went once to see the Eight-Five Steelworks. Now it's quick [to get there]; it used to take us 40-some hours. The factory got a boat, 41 hours. Now it's a train, six or seven hours and you're there. We just went to Guichi; four of us took a cab to Guichi, 100 yuan for a taxi. The driver was real good, took us to each place we stayed before, the workshops and such, let us go take a look. Well, he was a cabbie; our Eight-Five Steelworks used to be really famous in Guichi. After we went [we] brought the locals a lot, a lot of good things. This cabbie used to be living in this kind of […] after we left […] he'd worked in here before. He was really kind to us, so he'd wait for us at every spot. Then we were embarrassed and gave him 20 more yuan, gave him 120 yuan.

Mm, because the housing we were renting was all taken down by them. Now I feel like I have so many friends; this was a treasure from having gone to the Small Third Front; really this treasure is more important than money. Mm, I feel like no matter how much money you have now, money is like our age: I don't take it that seriously. Just this sentiment, we were 24 hours [a day] in the Small Third Front, this feeling I feel like [...] because nowadays many older people feel themselves aging and beginning to think of their families, think of their friends. You can't buy that with money. Mm, yes. Now there are many friends at my side, all of them from the Eight-Five Steelworks. Some people envy me, including people at the No. 5 Shanghai Steelworks. They would say, how were you all so kumbaya at the Eight-Five Steelworks?

* * *

章亚光 Zhang Yaguang, male, Anhui native of a village neighboring a Small Third Front factory, later a local historian and lawyer.

Keywords: conflicts, critique, electrification, finances, frustrations, living conditions, pollution, post-Mao, rural vs. urban, weapons

[TN: The following translation comes from a written recollection penned by Zhang in August and September 2012.]

I've never understood why Party Central would want "flowers to bloom all over" and make such a production of the Small Third Front in the mountainous areas of so many places. The military-industrial goods they made on the Small Third Front could be made just the same in a big or middle-sized city. Why suffer moving all that out to a mountain gully? Once, doing research for a case, I went to a helicopter factory in Jingdezhen, Jiangxi, that used to be out in Heilongjiang. To defend against the "Soviet revisionists" starting a war, they moved it down to Jingdezhen. The factory was at the outskirts of town, not a mountainous area. There was a public security substation just outside the factory and the police officers took us into the factory. Inside it was military troops on guard. The area of the factory was very large and there were guards everywhere; if we didn't have this police officer guiding us, it would've been really difficult for our work. It's precisely because of this experience that I think the Small Third Front Shanghai staged in the mountains of southern Anhui was clearly erroneous at the highest levels of decision-making.

For example, first [the Small Third Front] destroyed the ecological environment of the mountains. Second, there was no way to keep them secret. You didn't need high-altitude spy planes or satellites; just take the nighttime test rounds fired off by the Radiance Factory practically every other day; how could that possibly stay secret? Third, workers coming to these mountain gullies from the big city couldn't possibly settle down and stay satisfied. Even the minority of the workers who came in couples couldn't settle down. This was no different from the "sent-down youth" or cadres sent to the May Seventh cadre schools for manual labor. These were all failures in our nation's history. To put it bluntly, they were Mao Zedong's failures. Fourth, the four factories in the mountain valleys on the north bank of the Dengyuan River—Brightness, Radiance, Plains-Burning, Ten-Thousand-Miles—they were all making anti-aircraft missiles early on, mostly to support Vietnam and resist America. I've heard that American jets fly very high, and these missiles weren't very accurate (I'm not in the know on this—I don't know if the low accuracy was the fault of the missiles or of the guns). Fifth, once the military-industrial work stopped and they started making civilian goods, because of the impact of many objective and subjective factors, the quality of the first-military, then-civilian products wasn't ideal. Sixth, shipping raw materials in and shipping finished products out meant high transportation overhead costs, so these enterprises were widely running losses. By 1985, without any other way out, they just pulled them all back. How could this be anything other than a policy error? How could this be anything other than burdening the people and wasting resources?

But, exactly how many "people" were "burdened" and how many "resources" were "wasted," that I couldn't tell you exactly. Just from Jixi County, per the 1998 edition of the county gazetteer [TN: Zhang compiled this edition], there were 23 enterprises and operations for the Shanghai Small Third Front in Jixi County [...] of which ten were industrial and one was a power management unit. They occupied a total of 919,400 square meters [...] they began to make clocks and watches, electric fans, integrated circuits, packaging and printed materials, and machinery. In 1985 their workers totaled 9115 people and they had 6420 machines, with fixed assets totaling 63.85 million yuan and liquid assets allotted by the government totaling 19.1 million yuan. Their output was worth 44 million yuan annually, with tax contributions of 3.19 million yuan. [...] Then again, all those buildings, all those machines getting transferred for free to Jixi County in 1985, if you tally it up, that was a real windfall for Jixi.

[...] [If the factories moved inland from Shanghai] hadn't been "dispersed," but "small-scale concentrated," and located near county seat towns—moved to the county seats of Jixi, Jingde, Ningguo, Guichi, Jing, and She counties—then they'd have been properly done back then and would've had huge positive effects on the development of local urbanization later on.

Let's just take Jixi. The county seat is ringed by mountains and the Yangzhi River loops around the town. If ten Small Third Front factories were all built near the city, they'd be near both hills and water. These days, only the Red Star Factory is in the boundaries of the new city; Serving the People Factory and Guarding the Seas Factory have some hope of being included as the urban boundaries expand in the future. But the seven other factories [in Jixi county] aren't in the city bounds or in local towns. Only the factory buildings and machinery for Seapeak Factory are being fully used. None of the others are being as productive as they could be. The Brightness Factory had a punching machine. I hear that back then the entire nation had just three punching machines like this. Later it got sold off at a bargain price. Of course, the equipment and machinery that got sold off cheaply was far from limited to this one machine or this one factory! These state-of-the-art machines were mostly picked up by Zhejiang entrepreneurs as great deals. After being handed over to Jixi, the Brightness Factory was briefly successful, but then due to systematic issues (from being state-owned) and secondarily due to technological issues, soon it collapsed.

[...] In fact, the county's other state-owned enterprises [TN: often abbreviated as SOE], all of them medium and smaller enterprises, didn't even benefit that much from changing their statuses. Workers all said that the collapses of one SOE after another mostly meant "the temple got poorer but the abbots got richer." And this isn't just Jixi County's problem. All over the nation, the same pattern. Why this succession of corrupt officials and cadres? Another old saw: a problem in the system. The key is that supervisory organs aren't doing their job. Even though the Party has disciplinary committees, and the state has an inspectorate, and the law enforcement agencies have an anti-corruption bureau, the effectiveness of their work has left the people a lot to be desired. But that's another subject.

[...] If these ten factories and the Ruijin Hospital were all built near the county seat towns, not only would the area of the towns have greatly expanded, these factory and hospital buildings and the equipment could have been fully used and large quantities of state-of-the-art equipment wouldn't have been sold off for pennies and large numbers of buildings wouldn't have been left in shambles.

[...] The biggest contribution of the Shanghai Small Third Front to Jixi was linking up the high-voltage electricity. In 1951, Jixi township began building the Huoli Electric Plant and it began operation in April of the following year, producing 7600 kilowatt-hours of electricity a year; in 1955, they added to their equipment and began generating 18,900 kilowatt-hours of electricity a year. In 1958, they were amalgamated into the county silk-reeling factory, generating 79,000 kilowatt-hours a year. [...] What does an annual production of 7600 kwh look like? That's how much me, my son, and my daughter use up in one year in our three households. [...] But at the time, not a single family had household electrical appliances like a TV, a laundry machine, an electric fan, a refrigerator, an electric range, air conditioning, and so forth. We didn't have the money and they didn't have the supplies. [...] What I mean is that the Jixi township's ability to generate power was pathetic. After Liberation, a few places in the Jixi countryside built "little hydropower" plants and farmers got electric lights. But the vast majority of places didn't have any power at all and were still using vegetable oil and kerosene lamps. For weddings or funerals, they usually burned pinewood briquettes in iron braziers, which you could add to whenever you liked as it burned. A few people used pressurized kerosene lamps. They burned kerosene but you had to inject air into it first, and as you were using it, too. When I was a kid apprenticed to a shop, lighting the pressurized kerosene lamp was my nightly business.

The 703 electricity station of the Shanghai Rear Base was originally in Ningguo [County] but moved to East Huayang Street in the Jixi county seat in July 1972. [...] Nineteen Third Front work units, work units and offices were along the Wuhu-Tunxi and Jixi-Hujiaxiang roads, 41 factories, eight work units for the Anhui-Jiangxi Railroad, and 127 administrative villages. [...] In 1963, I was transferred from Wuhu back to my hometown for work. That night I first arrived, there were only lights here and there in the county town, because the silk-reeling factory needed to provide for their production needs first, so the electricity sent to offices, work units, and residents was severely inadequate. Lightbulbs wouldn't be at full brightness, and often you'd have outages. Streetlights especially were widely spaced, with low-wattage bulbs that the folks called "ghost fire" jokingly. When the silk-reeling factory stopped work for the day, the power plant also stopped, and the town was even more deeply plunged into darkness. After high-voltage electricity began running in June 1970, you could say it was a total, topsy-turvy change. The town shone brilliantly. Folks smiled and their backup candles went basically unused.

County-owned enterprises especially benefited in productivity from the reliable power supply.

[...] Speaking of some negative impacts, I don't know about elsewhere, so I'll stick to talking about the Brightness Factory. First, it reduced the amount of arable land on which farmers in Yingzhou Village depended for survival. [...] The Brightness Factory occupied [over] 35 acres of land and had over 72,000 square feet of buildings. [...] of the ten Small Third Front factories that moved into Jixi from Shanghai, the land taken up by the Brightness Factory was only second to the Radiance Factory, and the former had the most staff. As far as I know, that over 35 acres of land were mostly wet paddy fields and a small portion was dry land. Leaving out roads, paths, and other non-farmed land, there were over 30 acres of arable land. The majority belonged to the Yingzhou Brigade and a small portion to the Maojing Brigade. [...] In 1965, Yingzhou Village had 1370 people and about 247 acres of arable land, or 0.18 acres per person. [...] The land taken by the Brightness Factory was equivalent to 180 people losing their farmland. Though they did hire workers from among those whose lands were taken, I estimate that the total number hired from the Yingzhou and Maojing Brigades wasn't over 30 in all.

In the land the Brightness Factory occupied, a substantial portion was from my hometown's Forever Red Production Team, which had a worker hiring quota of just five people. They only hired four in actuality because one person couldn't pass the physical exam. But this quota was also taken up by powerful people in the county. I can't say for sure how many workers the Brightness Factory hired in Yingzhou Commune, but I know one thing for sure: cadres at the county and village levels used the quotas to get their own kids into the factories. These kids were often sent-down youths who first transferred themselves into the production teams with hiring quotas in Yingzhou, then officially and proudly became workers at the Brightness Factory.

Second, the ecosystem was harmed. [...] The Brightness Factory was in Oil Gulch in Yingzhou, a deep gully between two steep ridges. The environment had been in a virgin state, with lush hillsides, pure waters, and lovely scenery. After the factory moved in, it changed completely. Of course, with development comes destruction, that's the rule. The issue, though, was high-level errors in decision-making, which caused parts of the original ecosystem that need not have been ruined to be destroyed. This responsibility lies not with the factory but with higher-level decision-makers. Third, severe pollution of the environment. One was pollution from residential sources. Nearly 1600 workers plus their families meant about 2000 people. Their eating, drinking, and refuse created huge amounts of lifestyle wastes that tainted the environment. Another was pollution from production. This was a problem of utmost severity. I'm not an insider, but I figure that the factory's electroplating process used toxic chemicals (possibly cyanide) that were expelled into the stream. In Jixi, we call streams "gulches," and that stream was called "Oil Gulch" from ancient times. That was also the village name. We called it Oil Gulch because a layer of mineral oils floated on the surface. Master Yun, the ancestor of people surnamed Zhang in the Yingzhou area, had fled here from Changhua's Lan Village [in Zhejiang] with his grandmother and mother in 1120 from Fang La's rebellion [TN: an uprising against the ruling Song dynasty, concentrated in the Zhejiang and Jiangsu areas]. [...] Polluting the source of the water, and so completely, caused the wells in the lower half of Yingzhou Village to be affected. The factory installed water taps in the lower village, with taps next to each water well for villagers to use.

Back then, country folks' ecological consciousness was basically nil, plus the Brightness Factory was a military industry, so nobody dared raise questions. This affair was really touch-and-go, because once there was enough cyanide in the water, that would kill people. When I think about it nowadays I still get so frightened that I break into a cold sweat. These days the village has its own water plant and villagers mostly all use tap water; the wells are mostly sealed up.

* * *

张燕芳 Zhang Yanfang, female, teacher turned production statistics and logistics cadre at a steel mill.

Keywords: camaraderie, children, conflicts, finances, frustrations, intellectuals, living conditions, men vs. women, nostalgia, pay and benefits, work assignments

Of course, I did have to regularly go [meet with the team captains below me]. We also had so-called production work. How much stuff came in this month, what did we need to ship, what special assignments did we have. For example, when the temperatures were high, we'd made cold beverages. There weren't these [premade] cold beverages back then, only powdered mixes, but it was really tasty. You'd have this tart plum powder, cocoa powder, all the powders you'd stock up on, and arrange it. Every week you had to meet [with the team captains]. Yes, going over every week's production tasks, if there was anything, if there were any problems, what should you all do down there [at the grassroots]. When our number one was there, he'd lead [the meetings]. His word was our command. If he were out on business, there was another older comrade, not in very good health. Basically, they weren't there much. Later on, they were a little better for a while. [Interviewer: Did you ever feel like then, because your number one boss was always out on business trips and the other comrade wasn't in good health, that you had a lot of things on just your back weighing you down?] Well, I was used to it. The whole machinery was like being a gear-wheel, used to turning. Back then I was real careful. In the end back then I was young and female comrades couldn't be weighted down.

Sure, sure, how could there not be [people who doubted my work ability and such]? But I didn't care. Why? Because my temperament's like a male comrade's. I didn't care. Let me give you an example. The group captain in our cafeteria didn't get along so well with others, [yes,] a man, an older gentleman. Actually he was really great, just a bit cranky tempered. [...] Yes, yes, [as long as I acted based on my own principles, that was fine]. So I feel like this old comrade [Chi, my number one boss,] really taught us that. And another one who oversaw logistics in the Shanghai office, named Shen, was also like that. He'd go into debt to take people out [to eat in order to source food and other supplies]. Why? For the factory. There wasn't any other way then. If you wanted this, there was none. If you wanted that, there was none. What to do? Over 6000 people need food and clothes and things. You really paid for it out of your own pocket.

Even now I really, I'm really impressed with and admire these two people. So sometimes if old Chi weren't around or something, I'd be alone here, and some vegetable distributor or seafood distributor person came; if I said "I'll leave this alone, old Chi isn't here, I can't receive you," that was impossible. So I had no choice but to receive them. I'd go into the cafeteria, I'd say, oh, get me a table. I'm also not a drinker, or a smoker, right. No way around it. I'd pay. The two people in the cafeteria were really good. We had nowhere else, just the cafeteria to receive [visitors]. The cafeteria was really good. "Oh, Zhang Yanfang, you go be like that old man, the old man's family doesn't take care of it, you have to take care of it." I'd say no matter, the old man's money is money, my money is money, if there's money coming, if it's for factory business, I have to show up and receive them. At this point ten bucks for a table [of food] was very good. Eight bucks, eight bucks, eight bucks, [the cafeteria people would say], all right, a discount for you. That was that.

[Among ourselves, people were] really good. In all honesty, it was really you thinking on my behalf and me thinking on yours. So if old Chi were there, he'd say, "I told you, don't worry about it. Don't pull out your wallet, it has nothing to do with you, eh." Touching, wasn't it? So many times, now I talk and think about it, the human relationships [then], I don't know how, [they were] really, really great, really, really good. Especially our old Chi and such. I don't feel like there was any not being suited [to a work assignment, in an office or on the floor]. Anyway, whatever they had me do, I'd do it.

I was real comfortable in the workshop. The workshop, right? Apart from three really tough months, ordinarily if there were something, we'd help them down below [on the floor]—because production statistics was just this little bit of work, from the raw materials to the finished products, and shipping out, right, just these things. [If there weren't] other things to do, then you go down, go on the hammer and help them do some small things. When they're running water samples—because when your material's ready, you have to press out a set of samples to the product testing room to test them. After you press out the samples, you'd be helping others with their tasks, right, sometimes swappin' ideas with the workers, male and female colleagues lookin' after each other, right. What else is there? The workshop is comfortable. Logistics was tough. Lots of things to do. Look, the pork's here, the meat's here, you go like this to haul it, everyone gritted their way through it. A truck of these cutlassfish arrives, you go do this [hauling], 40 pounds a slab, really.

[...] Because our two leaders, three leaders—no, three people—I'm not a leader, really, I'm a minor character. Our number one was an old revolutionary, a retired cadre. He's passed on now. He was really, really great. From Shandong, fought his way down [during the civil war], came to Shanghai. This old gentleman...his family is really living well these days. He had a son and a daughter, they live in the Nanyang Apartments, do you know those? Behind the Portman [Ritz-Carlton Shanghai Hotel, on Nanjing West Road]. What a great neighborhood. Mayor Chen Yi gave him that housing himself [...] Yes, this old gentleman, he showed me their commission, signed personally by Chen Yi. He was in the first group of department heads after Liberation in Shanghai. Nowadays, a department head is nothing! At the time, the Mayor had to approve a department head. Chen Yi approved him. Chen Yi's commission letter. This old comrade made 92 bucks for his salary. A lot, eh? Forty-five for housing. on hundred and thirty-five bucks. How many people could have that kind of salary back then? [Interviewer: Most people only had 30-some bucks.] Right? He didn't bring a cent of it home. He had three kids; not a cent went home.

[In Shanghai, managing both work and household] was a lot of effort, really a lot of effort. So then I didn't go to the No. 5 Steelworks, you know, I got transferred out. I was treated as a special hardship [case], because I was an only child, and only children got special hardship treatment at that time. That is, all of them were prioritized before the dissolution [of the Small Third Front]; my dossier had already arrived at the Office of National Defense Workers, and they were preparing to move me back to Shanghai. With just that [being an only child], I could be transferred. All only children with parents without other children in Shanghai could be transferred back to Shanghai. Because at that time I'd been at the Eight-Five's outpost office working, I was pretty familiar [with things]. They told me to stay at the Shanghai No. 5 Steelworks; I said it wasn't that I didn't like the No. 5, I do like the No. 5, but I said I really couldn't handle it, with an old man and a little guy [at home], every day me coming and going, I really couldn't take it. I said I didn't want to go to the No. 5, I could be put anywhere, closer to Shanghai, closer to home. So then they put me in the Design Institute, the Bund Design Institute, [address] No. 1 The Bund; now it's closed down.

Yeah, a horizontal transfer. [...] My formal transfer was probably after the Rectification, '87, I guess; in '87 I was moved to the Design Institute, then worked there until I retired. It was easier, but intellectuals are hard to work with, harder than workers. Oh yes, intellectuals are very pretentious, but workers are pretty down to earth. I really liked the Eight-Five Steelworks' atmosphere, but the Eight-Five Steelworks, well, to be truthful, there were also many, many conflicts, many difficulties that arose. The losses to the state were very large, too.

At the Design Institute it was all right; conflicts happen anywhere, but the conflicts at the Design Institute, well, they weren't easy to clear up, oh no, intellectuals, really. At that time some older intellectuals were really scary. If they got unhappy with you, they'd write "people's letters" to the Bureau, saying that the Party committee secretary was using an outsider, because I went [to the Institute] later on, right.

No, [I didn't become committee secretary there]; I was in the [Party] organization, the disciplinary committee secretary. When I first went, I wasn't that either; I began by doing my own work. Yes yes, [even after being promoted, they'd still talk about me being from the outside]. Nothing to do about that. So everyone—the really beat-around-the-bush things about these intellectuals is that you can't handle their methods. People like me, [direct] like cannons, after going from place to place, are best suited to the Eight-Five Steelworks. Yes, even though I'd count as a little tiny intellectual myself, right—but I'm just too itty bitty, this intellectual here.

* * *

Further Reading

On Environment and Ecology in the Mao era

Judith Shapiro, *Mao's War against Nature: Politics and the Environment in Revolutionary China*. Cambridge: Cambridge University Press, 2001.

On Post-Mao Social, Political, and Economic Transformations

Richard Baum, *Burying Mao: Chinese Politics in the Age of Deng Xiaoping*. Princeton: Princeton University Press, 1994.

Geremie Barmé and John Minford eds., *Seeds of Fire: Chinese Voices of Conscience*. New York: Bloodaxe Books, 1988.

Geremie Barmé and Linda Jaivin eds., *New Ghosts, Old Dreams: Chinese Rebel Voices*. New York: Times Books, 1992.

Merle Goldman, *Sowing the Seeds of Democracy in China: Political Reform in the Deng Xiaoping Era*. Cambridge, MA.: Harvard University Press, 1994.

Merle Goldman and Elizabeth Perry eds., *Changing Meanings of Citizenship in Modern China*. Cambridge, MA: Harvard University Press, 2002.

Mel Gurtov, "Swords into Market Shares: China's Conversion of Military Industry to Civilian Production." *China Quarterly* 134 (1993), 213–241.

Joe Leung, "Dismantling the 'Iron Rice Bowl': Welfare Reforms in the People's Republic of China." *Journal of Social Policy* 23:3 (1994), 341–361.

Elizabeth Perry and Christine Wong, *The Political Economy of Reform in Post-Mao China*. Cambridge, MA: Harvard University Press, 1985.

Ezra F. Vogel, *Deng Xiaoping and the Transformation of China*. Cambridge, MA: Harvard University Press, 2011.

On Remembering the Mao Era

Ann Anagnost, *National Past-Times: Narrative, Representation, and Power in Modern China*. Durham, NC: Duke University Press, 1997.

Gail Hershatter, *The Gender of Memory: Rural Women and China's Collective Past.* Berkeley: University of California Press, 2013.

Hanchao Lu, "Nostalgia for the Future: The Resurgence of an Alienated Culture in China." *Pacific Affairs* 75:2 (2002), 169–186.

Klaus Mühlhahn, "'Remembering a Bitter Past': The Trauma of China's Labor Camps, 1949-1978." *History and Memory* 16:2 (2004), 108-139.

Ching Kwan Lee and Guobin Yang eds., *Re-Envisioning the Chinese Revolution: The Politics and Poetics of Collective Memories in Reform China*. Stanford: Stanford University Press, 1997.

Rofel, Lisa, *Other Modernities: Gendered Yearnings in China After Socialism.* Berkeley: University of California Press, 1999.

Sebastian Veg ed., *Popular Memories of the Mao Era: From Critical Debate to Reassessing History.* Hong Kong: Hong Kong University Press, 2019.

Informant Biographies

毕文中 Bi Wenzhong, b. 1957, male. Interviewed May 2012 by Hu Jing. Studied 1966–1977 at Xiangyu Secondary School. From 1982 to 1996, village secretary and village Party Branch Secretary in Xincha Village, Xiangyu Township, Dongzhi County (the former site of the Self-Strengthening Chemical Plant).

卞建华 Bian Jianhua, b. circa 1950, female. Interviewed March 2011 by Xu Youwei and Wu Jing. Former driver with the Rear Base Management Bureau Militia Headquarters, 1970–1980.

卜晓明 Bu Xiaoming, b. circa 1950, female. Interviewed April 2010 by Wu Jing and Lu Haoxuan. Internist and attending physician at the Shanghai Rear Base Rujin Hospital from 1975 to 1984.

陈金洋 Chen Jinyang, b. circa 1950, male. Interviewed in January 2019 by Chen Yingying. Doctor and obstetrician in the Rear Base Health and Hygiene team starting in 1975, with additional responsibilities in the Rear Base Public Health Office.

陈克智 Chen Kezhi, b. 1943, male. Interviewed May 2012 by Hu Jing. Accountant, village head, and village Party Branch Secretary in Meijie Village, Meijie Township, Guichi County from 1963 to 1985.

陈兰志 Chen Lanzhi, b. 1939, male. Native of Bengbu, Anhui, Chen studied abroad in the USSR and taught at the Hefei University of Technology, then served as the head of the Anhui Third Front Office and

Y. Xu, Y. Y. Wang, *Everyday Lives in China's Cold War Military-Industrial Complex*, Palgrave Studies in Oral History,
https://doi.org/10.1007/978-3-030-99688-8

the deputy head of the Anhui Economic Committee during the transfer of the Small Third Front to local control.

储瑛娣 Chu Yingdi, b. 1947, female. Interviewed June 2010 by Wu Jing and Zhu Jiawen. Joined the CCP in 1971 and rose to deputy Party Secretary for the Steep Cliff Factory from 1975 to 1988; served as the Party Branch Secretary for the Shanghai Electricity and Electric Apparatus Plant after her return to Shanghai in 1988.

丁秀玉 Ding Xiuyu, b. 1947, female. Interviewed March 2013 by Wu Xiaomin. Physics laboratory technician at the Eight-Five Steelworks from 1970 to 1972; Organization Department staff from 1972 to 1973; deputy head of the Propaganda department, 1973 to 1979; deputy Party Branch Secretary at the July 21st Workers' University, 1979 to 1980; Party Branch Secretary of the two factory elementary schools and kindergarten, 1980–1984; Birth Planning Office manager, 1984–1987.

傅锡林 Fu Xilin, b. 1942, female. Interviewed April 2013 by Wu Xiaomin. Graduate of the Tianjin Normal University (class of 1968), secondary school teacher of mathematics and history at the Eight-Five Steelworks from 1972 to 1984.

伏如山 Fu Rushan, b. 1947, male. Worker in the Jiangxi-based 9334 Factory that specialized in making fuse explosives (later the National Guangming Machinery Factory) set up by the Shanghai Electric Tool Factory. Five hundred and forty-four of the letters that Fu sent to and received from his family members have been the subject of a book chapter (Xu Youwei, "Geming hongliu zhong de pingfan shenghuo—yi Jiangxi xiao sanxian jianshe gongren Fu Rushan 544 feng jiashu wei zhongxin de chutan" (Ordinary Life in the Revolutionary Torrent: A Discussion Based on Jiangxi Small Third Front Worker Fu Rushan's 544 Letters), in Jin Guangyao and Dai Jianbing, eds., *Geren shenghuo shi (1949–1978)* Individual Life Histories 1949–1978, Shanghai: Shanghai University Press, 2015. 78–92.

葛鼎学 Ge Dingxue, b. 1955, male. Interviewed December 2011 by Xu Youwei, Wu Jing, and Li Ting. Worker at the Eight-Five Steelworks starting in 1974.

顾国籁 Gu Guolai, b. 1948, male. Interviewed October 2012 by Xu Youwei and Hu Jing. Worker 1970–1976, then technician, engineer, administrator (deputy department head and Guichi Construction Bureau deputy bureau chief), and Guichi county head 1984–1987; later deputy mayor of Anqing.

桂胜莲 Gui Shenglian, b. 1946, female. Interviewed May 2012 by Hu Jing. Native of Meijie Village, Meijie Township, Guichi County; family's land was requisitioned for the Small Third Front, thus began working at the Eight-Five Steelworks in 1972 until 1988; continued work at the Guichi Steelworks until 1995, when she retired.

洪明来 Hong Minglai, b. 1934, male. Interviewed May 2012 by Hu Jing. Anhui native, farmer, former branch secretary and village head of Dragon's Hill village, Dongzhi County, Xiangyu Township, adjacent to the Satellite Chemical Factory.

洪全旺 Hong Quanwang, b. 1945, male. Interviewed May 2012 by Hu Jing. Anhui native, farmer, former branch secretary and village head of Dragon's Hill village, Dongzhi County, Xiangyu Township, adjacent to the Satellite Chemical Factory.

胡进 Hu Jin b. 1949, female. Interviewed March 2013 by Wu Xiaomin. In 1977, worked at the Wuqi Farm as propaganda worker and chalkboard newsletter creator; moved in 1982 to serve as union officer and accountant at the Transport Department.

胡善莉 Hu Shanli b. 1954, female. Interviewed August 2012 by Hu Jing. Native of Dongzhi County, Anhui; hired into the Satellite Chemical Factory in Dongzhi as concessionary worker 1975–1986.

季美华 Ji Meihua, b. 1949, female. Interviewed March 2013 by Wu Xiaomin. Eight-Five Steelworks kindergarten teacher, 1970–1986.

刘存龙 Liu Cunlong, b. 1914, male. Interviewed June 2018 by Wang Qike, Cheng Yingying, and Yi Haixia. Head of the Planning Team for the Eight-Five Steelworks; later, worker and cadre at the Steelworks, then staff at the Small Third Front Shanghai offices.

刘玉香 Liu Yuxiang, female. Interviewed April 2012 by Hu Jing and Li Yun. Peasant farmer neighboring the former Satellite Chemical Factory, current resident of Dabei Village, Yaodu Township, Dongzhi County.

吕建昌Lü Jianchang, b. 1954, male. Worked at the Ruijin Hospital on the Shanghai Small Third Front as a pharmacist from 1972 to 1980. Entered the History Department of Fudan University upon returning to Shanghai; currently a professor in Shanghai University's history department.

潘雅珍 Pan Yazhen, b. 1944, female. Interviewed April 2013 by Wu Xiaomin. Worked as laboratory technician and in the mechanical department workers' union at the Eight-Five Steelworks.

庞金来 Pang Jinlai, male. Interviewed April 2012 by Hu Jing and Li Yun. Peasant farmer neighboring the former Satellite Chemical Factory, captain of the Laopang production team in Dabei Village, Yaodu Township, Dongzhi County.

邱云德 Qiu Yunde, b. 1931, male. Interviewed July 2012 by Xu Youwei and Li Ting. Graduate of Shanghai's Southeastern Higher Pharmacy Professional School and assigned to a pharmacist position at the Guangci Hospital affiliated with Shanghai No. 2 Hospital. Joined the CCP in 1956 and sent to the Shanghai Small Third Front in June 1970 as a member of the Rear Base Health and Hygiene Work Team and First Deputy Team Leader. Transferred back to Shanghai in 1979.

瞿惠相 Qu Huixiang, b. 1948, male. Worked at the rocket test site, the political work team, the propaganda department, the education department, and the workers' children's school of the Cooperation Machinery Factory.

沈嘉麒 Shen Jiaqi, b. 1940, male. Interviewed by Xu Youwei and Wu Jing in August 2010. Graduate of a technical college and entered the CCP in 1962. Worker at the Hudong shipyard in Shanghai from 1956 to 1959, served in the People's Navy East Sea Fleet Communications Unit, rising to the rank of Platoon Leader from 1959 to 1965. Cadre in the Shanghai Merchant Marine Propaganda Department from 1965 to 1972, then served in the Shanghai Rear Base Management Bureau Party Committee Secretariat, the Propaganda Department, and the Theory and Education Office from 1972 to 1986.

史志定 Shi Zhiding, b. 1948, male. Interviewed by Xu Youwei, Wu Jing, and Li Ting in February 2011. Graduated vocational secondary school in 1968 and assigned to the Eight-Five Steelworks, during which time he served as the Youth League Branch Secretary of the 01 Workshop, the factory Youth League deputy secretary, and the Party Branch Secretary of the 04 Workshop after joining the Party in 1979, winning kudos from the Rear Base such as the "New Long March Shock Trooper" award and for excellence as a Youth League cadre.

孙继雯 Sun Jiwen, b. 1948, female. Graduated from the Shanghai No. 2 School of Science and Technology. Served at the Victory Machine Factory, the Victory Cement Factory, and the Jinggangshan Machine Factory. Returned to Shanghai in 1986 to work at the Technical Information Service Computer Center of the Shanghai Municipal Committee for Science.

汪福琪 Wang Fuqi, b. 1944, male. Interviewed March 2012 by Hu Jing. Received undergraduate degree in 1966, worked in enterprise management and cultural departments of the Jixi County government in Anhui. Began work in Jixi County executive offices in 1981, holding posts including deputy and full director of the Jixi County Planning Committee; Small Third Front Transfer Office deputy director.

王根富 Wang Genfu, b. 1940, male. Interviewed May 2011 by Wu Jing. Joined the People's Liberation Army in March 1958 and entered the CCP in August 1960. Graduated from the Nanjing Army Ordnance Engineering School in 1963 and became a military representative on the Shanghai Small Third Front in June 1969. Transferred to the Shanghai Municipal Defense Industry Office in August 1971 and became deputy general manager of the Shanghai National Defense Technological Development General Company in 1993.

王金忠 Wang Jinzhong b. 1957, male. Interviewed July 2012. Entered the Red Star Chemical Factory in November 1975; stayed after the handover until 1987, transferred to the Changjiang Bike Parts Factory, then transferred back to Red Star as head of the resource management group in 1989; worked at the Jinxing Factory 1993–1998, transferred to the Huatai Chemical Factory in 1998, bought himself out with 15,000 RMB from the Huatai Chemical Corporation in 2003 and has since farmed at home.

王美玉 Wang Meiyu, b. circa 1942, female. Interviewed January 2013 by Wu Jing and Li Ting. Former worker at the Shanghai Instrumentation and Electronics Company's Small Third Front factory; later became the chair of the Shanghai Rear Base Management Bureau's workers' union.

王妙才 Wang Miaocai, b. circa 1950, male. Interviewed June 2018 by Zhou Shengqi and Yi Haixia along with 张福信 Zhang Fuxin, male. Wang initially served in the Security Department of the Sun-Facing Factory, then rose to serve as factory head. Zhang succeeded him as department head of the Sun-Facing Factory's Security Department.

王世益 Wang Shiyi, b. circa 1950, male. Interviewed April 2012 by Hu Jing and Li Yun. Anhui native and retired elementary school teacher in Dongzhi County, villager near the Yangtze River Machine Repair Factory.

王文青 Wang Wenqing, b. circa 1945, female. Interviewed by Wu Xiaomin in March 2013. Worked at the Shanghai No. 5 Steelworks until transferred to the Eight-Five Steelworks in 1971, where she was on the Revolutionary Committee, the Propaganda Team, the Youth League Committee, and was made deputy chair of the factory union.

王燕珍 Wang Yanzhen, b. circa 1940, female. Interviewed with her husband Zhu Yuelin (below) in September 2013 by Wu Xiaomin. Joined the CCP in 1956. Began work at the No. 5 Shanghai Steelworks, transferred to the Eight-Five Steelworks 1969 as political cadre. In 1973 began work at the Shanghai Rear Base Management Bureau; in 1984 began work at the Small Third Front Coordination Office. Transferred back to the No. 2 Shanghai Steelworks in 1988 and retired in 1993.

汪援胜 Wang Yuansheng. b. 1963, male. Interviewed March 2012 by Hu Jing. Former Jingde County Small Third Front Rear Base communications station staff. As of 2012, Jingde County Xinyuan Textile Factory assistant general manager.

伍先权 Wu Xianquan, b. 1949, male. Interviewed May 2012 by Hu Jing. Native of Dongzhi County, Anhui. Served as enlisted soldier in Sichuan, 1970–1975; hired by the Self-Strengthening Chemical Factory in 1975, then transferred to the Longjiang Water Plant, then returned to Self-Strengthening in 1978. Began driving cargo trucks at Self-Strengthening in 1989, following the handover of the factory to local administration, until retiring in 2009.

许春华 Xu Chunhua, b. 1947, male. Interviewed April 2017. Anhui native and worker in the No. 4 Workshop at the Small Third Front's Eight-Five Steelworks.

许汝钟 Xu Ruzhong, b. 1938, male. Graduate of the Beijing Steel Institute in 1957, Xu served as a technician and technical cadre at the Shanghai No. 7 Steelworks and other Shanghai-based steel mills before being sent to the Small Third Front in 1970, where he was deputy factory head as well as chief engineer at the Eight-Five Steelworks.

徐小英 Xu Xiaoying, b. 1945, female. Interviewed March 2013 by Wu Xiaomin. Eight-Five Steelworks Basic Infrastructure Department Communist Youth League Branch Secretary, Eight-Five Steelworks Propaganda Department staff, secondary school physics teacher and academic affairs deputy director; rose to Party Branch Secretary, factory office typist and confidential secretary; factory head office recorder and clerk.

徐新东 Xu Xindong, male. Interviewed alongside Zhang Weide (below) in August 2012 by Hu Jing. Assistant to Zhang Weide during the period of the Small Third Front's transfer from Shanghai to Guichi. Currently the deputy head of the Guichi Urban District Committee.

杨爱玉 Yang Aiyu, b. 1963, female. Interviewed July 2012 by Hu Jing alongside her husband, 张要华 Zhang Yaohua, b. 1960. Both are Anhui natives and villagers near the Small Third Front Longjiang Water Plant in Xiangyu Township, Dongzhi County.

杨秀珍 Yang Xiuzhen, b. 1951, female. Interviewed March 2013 by Wu Xiaomin. Former staff member and Party Branch Secretary of the Eight-Five Steelworks Pier from 1972 to 1979, cadre in the Eight-Five Steelworks Organization Department from 1979.

应长荣 Ying Changrong, b. 1950, male. Originally from Ningbo, Zhejiang. Began working at the Shanghai Number Nine Radio Factory in 1968 and went to the Spark Factory on Shanghai's Small Third Front in 1970, working as a driver and as the transport department deputy director. After returning to Shanghai in 1986, worked in the administration and the Institute of History at the Shanghai Academy of Social Sciences.

余顺生 Yu Shunsheng, male. Until 2013, deputy head of Niutou Township political consultative office in Guichi district, Chizhou City, Anhui; as of 2016, head of the Qiupu sub-district People's Congress work committee, Guichi District, Chizhou City, Anhui.

袁彩霞 Yuan Caixia, b. 1953, female. Interviewed August 2011 by Xu Youwei, Wu Jing, and Li Ting. Born in Guoyang County in northern Anhui, she worked as an English teacher in her home county before marrying into a position at the Anhui Steep Cliff Factory.

张福信 Zhang Fuxin, male. Interviewed June 2018 by Zhou Shengqi and Yi Haixia along with 王妙才Wang Miaocai, b, circa 1950, male. Wang initially served in the security department and rose to serve as factory head of the Sun-Facing Factory. Zhang succeeded him as department head of the Sun-Facing Factory's Security Department.

张渭德 Zhang Weide, b. 1941, male. Interviewed alongside Xu Xindong (above) in August 2012 by Hu Jing. Native of Dongzhi County, Anhui. Worker and People's Commune Secretary from 1958 to 1981. County Propaganda bureau chief and deputy County Head from 1981 to 1986; Mayor of Guichi during the completion of the Small Third Front transfer 1987–1989 (Guichi County became the city of Guichi in 1987). Retired in 2004.

张薇薇 Zhang Weiwei, b. 1949, female. Interviewed April 2013 by Wu Xiaomin. Worked in propaganda, education, and technology inspection at the Eight-Five Steelworks between 1970 and 1987; continued working in the education department of the Shanghai No. 5 Steelworks after returning to the city.

章亚光 Zhang Yaguang, b. 1936, male. Anhui native, joined the Party in 1971. Local historian and lawyer in Jixi County; lived in a village near the Shanghai Small Third Front's Brightness Factory.

张燕芳 Zhang Yanfang b. 1944, female. Interviewed March 2013 by Wu Xiaomin. Former secondary school teacher in Shanghai (Russian language, politics), circa 1964–1966. Former Eight-Five Steelworks workshop production statistics staff, 1971–1973; logistics department cadre, circa 1973–1982.

章炎盛 Zhang Yansheng b. 1934, male. Interviewed April 2012 by Hu Jing. Former Party secretary of Xiangyu township, Dongzhi County, 1968–1976; served various roles on the Dongzhi Revolutionary Committee, the Dongzhi County Committee, and the Dongzhi Politics and Legal Affairs Committee. One of the overseers of the Small Third Front transfer to local control in Dongzhi.

赵连洪 Zhao Lianhong, b. 1946, male. Interviewed July 2018 by Xuan Haixia. Cadre in the security department of the Shanghai Instrumentation and Electronics Company on the Small Third Front.

赵惠瑛 Zhao Huiying, female. Interviewed March 2013 by Wu Xiaomin. Worker on the Small Third Front, 1970–1976; head of the Eight-Five Steelworks Kindergarten, 1976–1986; continued working at a kindergarten in Shanghai after 1986.

朱岳林 Zhu Yuelin, b. 1937, male. Interviewed with his wife Wang Yanzhen (above) in September 2013 by Wu Xiaomin. Graduated from the Shanghai No. 2 Normal School in 1958, made Communist Youth League Branch Secretary at the Yuxin Secondary School and joined the CCP in April 1960. Deputy Party Secretary of Xinyu Secondary School, 1963–1964; 1964–1970, staff in the Shanghai Municipal Committee External Affairs Group Office; 1970–1973, Shanghai Eight-Five Steelworks office supervisor; 1973, Shanghai Rear Base Management Bureau Party Committee Office deputy chief and Small Third Front Adjustment Office deputy chief.

Glossary[1]

All-China Federation of Trade Unions [中华全国总工会, 全国总工会, 全总] The sole national-level trade union in the PRC, an affiliate of the Chinese Communist Party and represented at the Chinese People's Political Consultative Conference, the main advisory body to the central Party and state administration.

Attack with Words, Defend with Force [文攻武卫] A slogan of the Cultural Revolution, first used in the aftermath of the July 1967 Wuhan Incident, where factional violence led to the detention and public "struggling" of a Central Cultural Revolution Group member. Groups calling themselves "Attack with Words, Defend with Force HQs" appeared across the nation, contributing in their turn to the violence of the era.

Beating-smashing-looting elements [打砸抢分子] A term for people, typically aligned with "rebel" factions, seen as disturbing social order during the Cultural Revolution. They were often targets for purges and punishment after Mao's death.

Big-character posters [大字报] Hand-written posters usually used to publicly denounce or criticize people or policies.

[1] Some terms used and translated colloquially in the text are included here along with the original Chinese for reference (many of them are also noted and glossed in the text).

Y. Xu, Y. Y. Wang, *Everyday Lives in China's Cold War Military-Industrial Complex*, Palgrave Studies in Oral History,
https://doi.org/10.1007/978-3-030-99688-8

Chinese Communist Party (Party) [中国共产党; 党] Ruling political party of the People's Republic of China. Often known as simply "the Party" (*dang*) in colloquial speech. Often abbreviated as CCP or CPC (Communist Party of China) in English.

Cleansing the class ranks [清理阶级队伍] A 1968 campaign supposedly focusing on "traitors, spies, capitalist roaders, counterrevolutionaries, and members of the Five Black Categories" [an older designation for political undesirables, including landlords, wealthy farmers, counter-revolutionaries, Rightists, and bad elements] that often targeted a range of popular upstarts from the early, violent phases of the Cultural Revolution.

Communist Youth League (Youth League, League, CYL) [中国共产主义青年团; 共青团] Party organization for older teenagers and people into their late twenties, often colloquially abbreviated as *Gong qing tuan* or simply *tuan*, like *dang* ("the Party"). "Youth League" or "League" is used throughout this book to convey the shortened forms.

"Cow demons and snake spirits" [牛鬼蛇神] Epithet for various enemies and villains during the Cultural Revolution.

Cowshed [牛棚] Nickname for the often improvised holding cells where cadres, intellectuals, and other political targets were kept during the Cultural Revolution.

Criticizing Lin Biao and Confucius Movement (Criticizing Lin, Criticizing Confucius) [批判林彪批判孔子运动; 批林批孔] A campaign formally begun three years after Lin Biao's death in September 1971 that, linked Lin to the ancient philosopher Confucius for systematic political attack.

CultRev [文革] The Great Proletarian Cultural Revolution, or *Wuchan jieji wenhua dageming* [无产阶级文化大革命], is often abbreviated colloquially as "Cultural Revolution" *Wenhua dageming* [文化大革命] or *Wen'ge*; "CultRev" is used throughout this book to convey the shortest form.

Dai Liqing [戴立清] A leading Shanghai "rebel worker" during the Cultural Revolution who fell from grace for being associated with the "Gang of Four" in October 1976. Dai was accused of "counterrevolutionary" activities and sentenced to fifteen years of imprisonment in 1982.

"Dig tunnels deep, store grain everywhere, never seek hegemony" [深挖洞, 广积粮, 不称霸] A slogan attributed to Mao from the Third Front era.

Eating bitterness [吃苦] A common expression for enduring hardship or difficult conditions, especially material deprivation or physically strenuous tasks.

Exchanging revolutionary experiences [全国大串联] Travel throughout the country by Red Guards and youth in the early Cultural Revolution, including free rides on boats, trains, and buses.

Five-Good Families [五好家庭] A campaign with origins in the 1950s that promulgated "honoring elders and caring for the young," "equality between men and women," "harmony between husbands and wives," "frugality in housekeeping," and "solidarity among neighbors."

Four Cleanups Movement [四清运动] A 1963–1965 campaign, often seen as the prelude to the Cultural Revolution, mainly targeting rural villages to "purify politics, purify economics, purify the organization, and purify thought" against "revisionism" in the disastrous aftermath of the PRC's falling-out with the Soviet Union and the Great Leap Forward.

Four Facings Toward [四个面向] Campaign that began in 1969 to send urban cadres, intellectuals, and students "facing toward the borders," "facing toward the workers and peasants," "facing toward the grassroots." Many were sent far away from their original schools, workplaces, and homes for years. Refer also to "sent-down youth" and "Supporting the Interior."

Gang of Four [四人帮] Retrospective epithet for the clique of four Party members who held great power during the Cultural Revolution, with Mao Zedong's fourth and final wife Jiang Qing [江青] as their leader. The other members were writer and commentator Zhang Chunqiao [张春桥], literary critic Yao Wenyuan [姚文元], and worker turned Red Guard Wang Hongwen [王洪文]. The four were sentenced as "counterrevolutionaries" following the death of Mao Zedong in the fall of 1976. Jiang and Wang received sentences of life imprisonment while Yao received a 20-year sentence and Zhang's original life sentence was reduced to 18 years. Jiang killed herself in 1991. Wang died of illness in 1992, followed by Zhang and Yao in 2005.

"Grand Alliance" [大联合] Drawn from a directive from Party Central in 1968 urging the cessation of armed factional conflicts during the Cultural Revolution.

June 1 (Children's Day) [六一儿童节; 六一] National holiday celebrating minor children, usually accompanied by performances, release from class, and other festivities.

June 26 Directive [六二六指示] Instructions from Mao Zedong in 1965 to prioritize healthcare and medicine for rural residents throughout the country. As a result, clinics and hospitals sent their staff on medical tours of rural areas, and rural cooperative healthcare situated in the communes was also expanded.

July 21st Industrial University [七二一大学] Cultural Revolution-era part time engineering and technical study programs set up by factories based on a July 1968 comment by Mao Zedong in favor of short-course, vocationally geared educations for current industrial workers.

Liberation [解放] Typically referring to the founding of the People's Republic of China in October 1949 and/or to the victory of the Red Army over the Nationalist troops in a certain locality, which might have preceded or followed the PRC founding.

Loyalty dance [忠字舞] A Cultural Revolution choreographic fixture, regularly performed by both professionals and ordinary citizens around the country.

March Eighth (International Women's Day) [三八妇女节; 三八] Major holiday in March, on the basis of a similar holiday celebrated since at least the early twentieth century by socialist and labor-rights movements around the world.

May Seventh Cadre School [五七干校] Where cadres around the country were "sent down" for rural, manual labor during the Cultural Revolution, based on Mao's "May Seventh Directive" of 1966.

National Day [国庆节] Major holiday on October 1, marking the founding of the PRC.

Old three cohort [老三届] Junior and senior high school students in the three graduating classes of 1966, 1967, and 1968 who were unable to graduate on time due to the Cultural Revolution's disruption of instruction. Most who finally departed school in 1968 were "sent down" to rural regions.

One Strike-Three Anti [一打三反] Campaign that set out to "strike" counterrevolutionaries and oppose graft, theft, and embezzlement; anti-profiteering, extravagance, and waste; and bureaucratism. Launched in January 1970.

Organization [组织] The customary shorthand for referring to the Party or Youth League organization, the complex, powerful, and often secretive network which oversees the staffing and human resources for the Party at central and local levels. "Party" [党] is often used in more abstract ways than "organization."

People's Communes [人民公社] Administrative and economic units for collectivized agriculture that were implemented throughout the rural PRC after 1958, lasting until 1983. Equivalent to a twenty-first-century township, communes were subdivided into work brigades and work teams.

People's Liberation Army (PLA) [人民解放军; 解放军] The military of the PRC, the successor to the Red Army that fought against Japanese and other Chinese forces from the 1930s through the 1940s.

"Prepare for war, prepare for famine, for the people" [备战, 备荒, 为人民] A slogan attributed to Mao from the Third Front era.

Progressive, pioneering, advanced [先进] Politically correct or activist by the standards of the time. Antonym of "backward" [落后], referring to those who were seen as unenthusiastic or actively defiant toward the Party line.

Recalling Bitterness, Thinking of Sweetness meal [忆苦思甜饭] Politically ritualized meal of low-value items like rough taro and corn buns or wild vegetables consumed to highlight material progress under the CCP.

Reform and Opening [改革开放] Refers to the marketization, opening to international investment and trade, and privatization policies undertaken under Deng Xiaoping's leadership beginning in 1978. The period since 1978 is often known as the "reform era."

Resist US Aggression, Aid Korea [抗美援朝] The campaign to support North Korean troops against US-led United Nations forces during the Korean War.

Sent-down youth Known as the "going up to the mountains and down to the countryside" [上山下乡] movement, the dispatching of young people from cities to, typically, rural communities beginning in the 1950s through the 1970s. Especially during the Cultural Revolution, youth who had been "sent down" [下放] were often students who had been prevented from continuing their educations or finding work, and were known as "intellectual youth". Also known as "rustication," sending down overlapped with other initiatives like "Supporting the Interior" [支援内部; 支内], the May Seventh cadre schools, and the "Four Facings Toward" [四个面向].

Stinking number nine [臭老九] Cultural Revolution epithet for an intellectual or highly educated student. The number nine refers to people in the nine "black categories": landlords, rich peasants, counterrevolutionaries, bad elements, rightists, traitors, spies, capitalist roaders, and capitalist intellectuals.

Strike Hard campaign [严厉打击刑事犯罪活动; 严打] A 1983–1986 campaign against criminal activity under Deng Xiaoping's leadership that gave heavy penalties including public executions and reform-through-labor sentences to many thousands, including those guilty of such "offenses" as unconventional sexual liaisons.

Three Disciplines and Eight Attentions [三大纪律八项注意] A list of disciplinary items for the PLA based on a directive to the Red Army in wartime, including being courteous, being respectful toward women, and paying for damages to civilian goods.

Three-Good Student [三好学生] An honor for students in primary and secondary school for "good grades, good athletics, and good character."

Three Supports and Two Militaries [三支两军] An initiative by the CCP leadership in early 1967 to send PLA troops to schools and other work units nationwide to stabilize the factional warfare and political tumult of the Cultural Revolution. The Three Supports were "Support the Interior" [支援内部; 支内], "Support the Left" [支援左派群众; 支左], and "Support Industry" [支援工业; 支工]; the Two Militaries were Military Management [军事管制] and Military Training [军事训练].

Three years of natural disaster [三年自然灾害] The official designation for the years of famine and economic shortage accompanying the Great Leap Forward campaigns, from 1958 to 1961. Also known as the Great Famine [大饥荒], usually in sources outside the PRC.

Wang Hongwen [王洪文] A leading figure during the Cultural Revolution in Shanghai and a member of the "Gang of Four."

Work brigade/work team [生产大队; 大队; 生产队] Sub-units of People's Communes. Work brigades corresponded roughly with villages in the number of people they included. Production teams were the lowest unit of rural political and economic administration, at about ten to 20 households and about 100 people.

Worker-peasant-soldier students [工农兵学员] People who attended universities in the late Cultural Revolution, who had been admitted on the basis of their class backgrounds.

Young Pioneers [中国少年先锋队; 少先队] The youth organization of the CCP, for children of elementary-school age, modeled after similar organizations for children in the Soviet Union.

Index

Y. Xu, Y. Y. Wang, *Everyday Lives in China's Cold War Military-Industrial Complex*, Palgrave Studies in Oral History, https://doi.org/10.1007/978-3-030-99688-8

Kolibri 360 GmbH
Ferdinand-Jühlke-Straße 7
99095 Erfurt, Deutschland
produktsicherheit@kolibri360.de